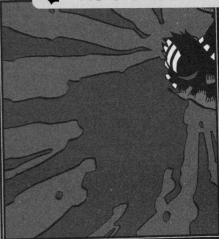

YAGA CASTLE (PART 8)

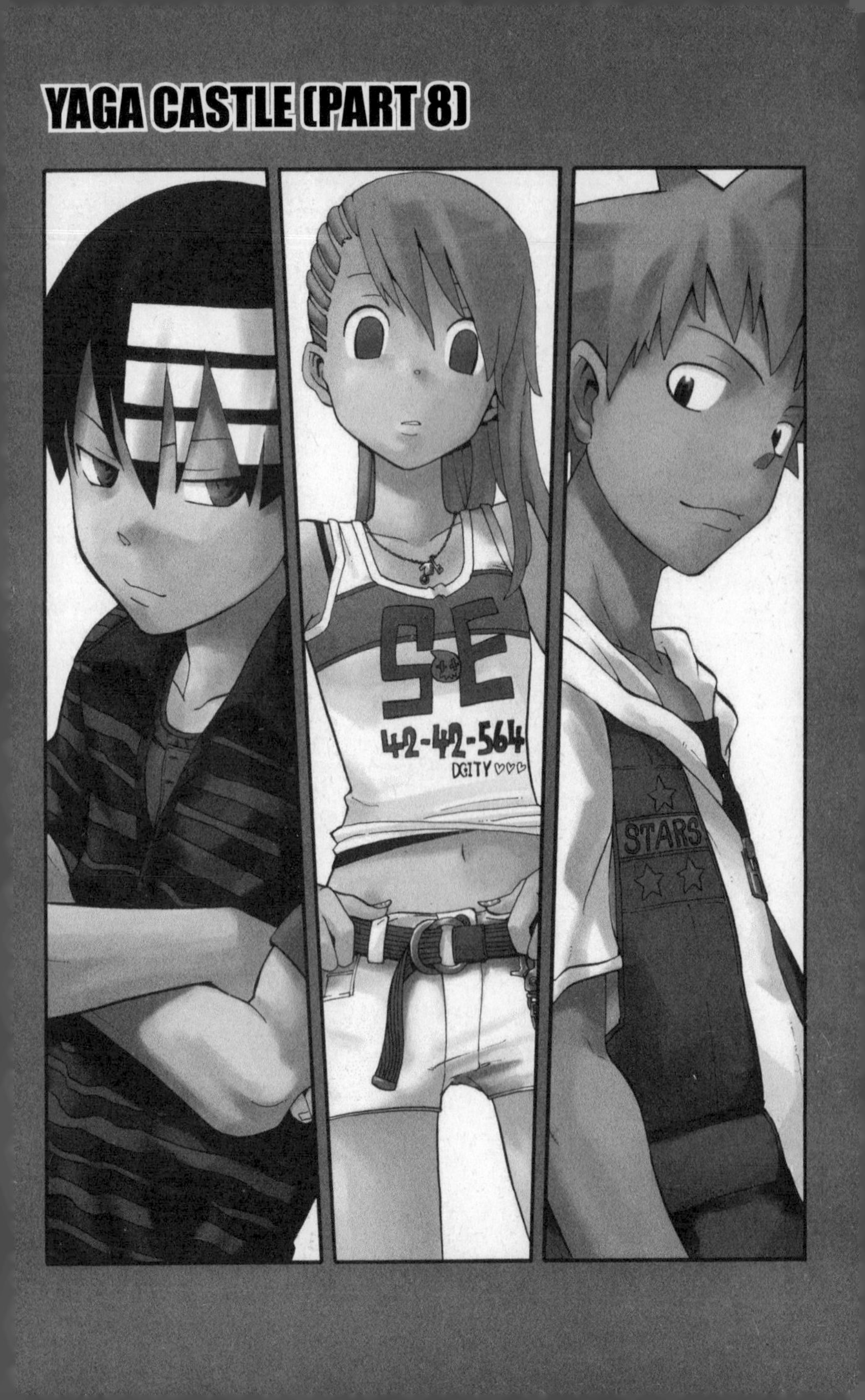
STARS
SE
42-42-564
DCITY

CHAPTER 53: OPERATION CAPTURE BABA

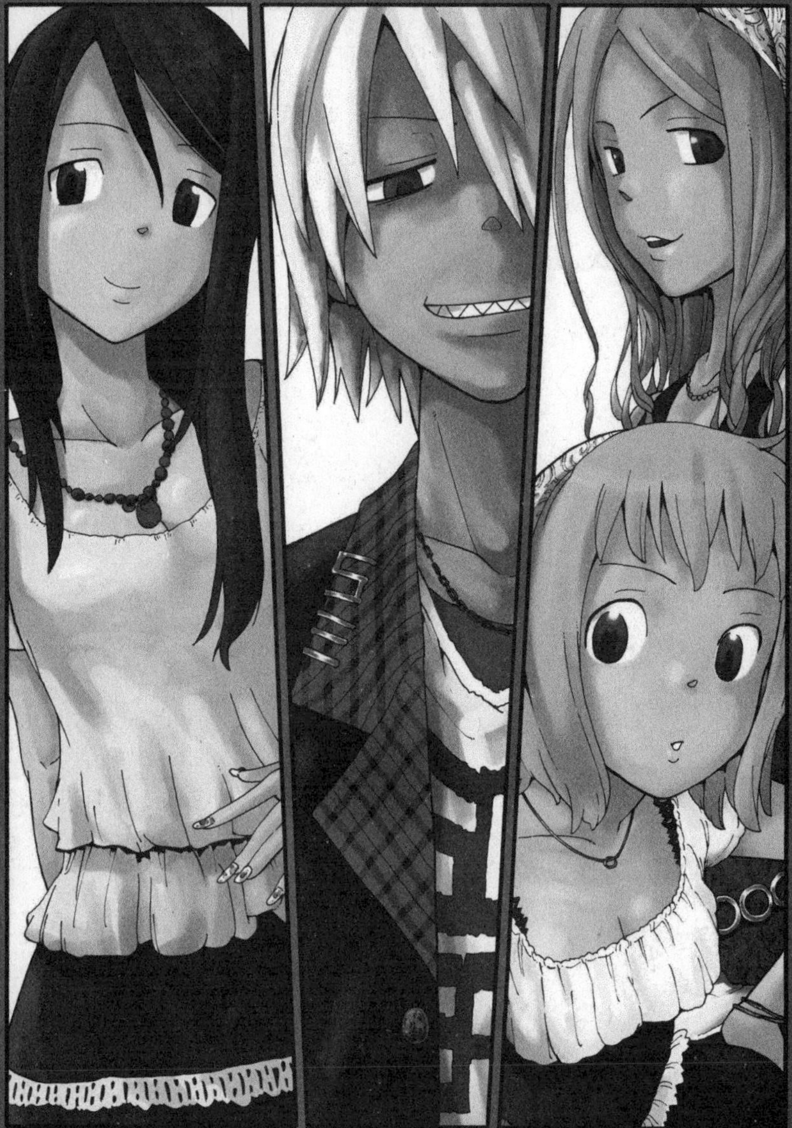

SOUL EATER

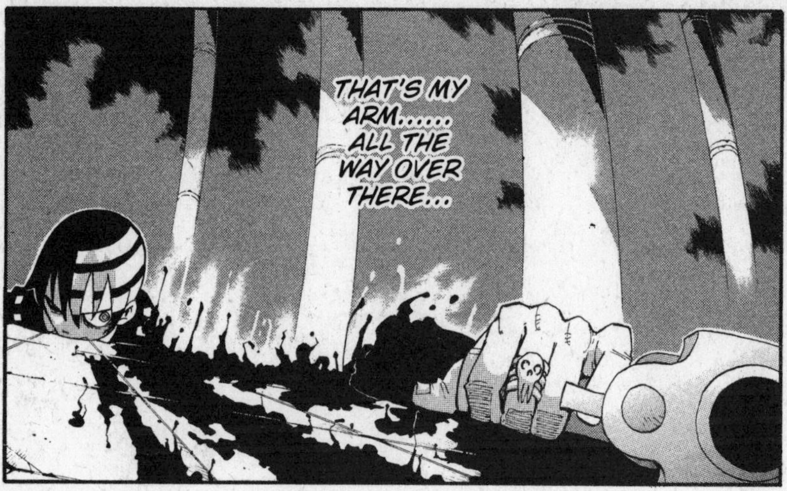
THAT'S MY ARM...... ALL THE WAY OVER THERE...

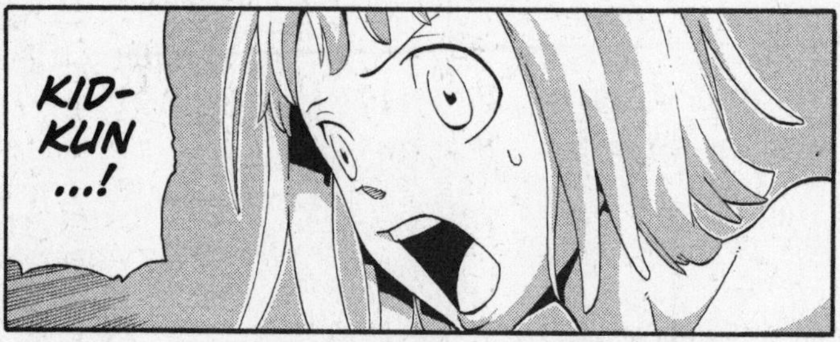
KID-KUN ...!

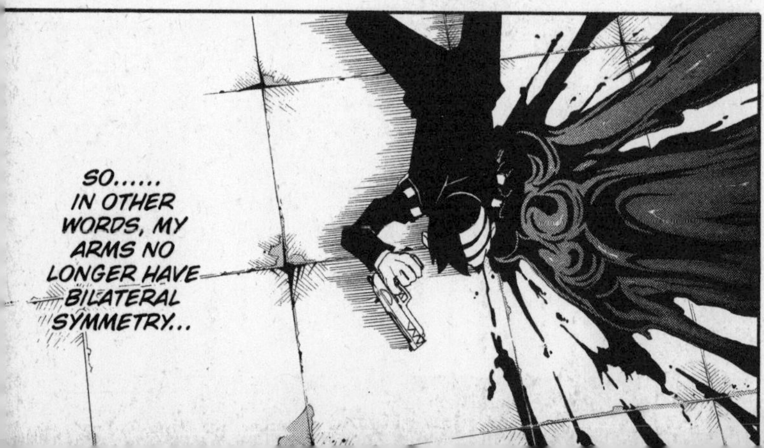
SO...... IN OTHER WORDS, MY ARMS NO LONGER HAVE BILATERAL SYMMETRY...

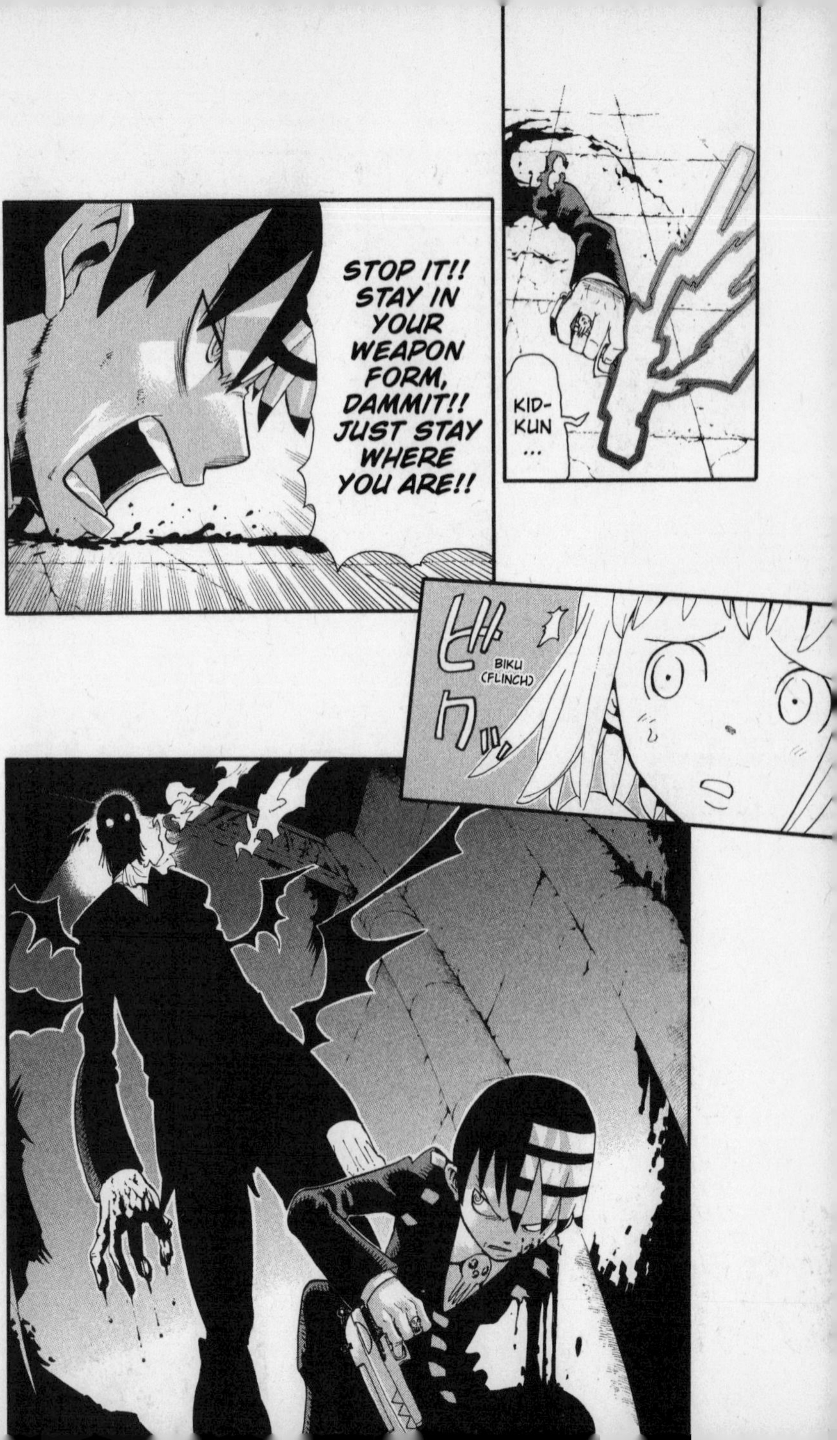
KID-KUN ...
STOP IT!! STAY IN YOUR WEAPON FORM, DAMMIT!! JUST STAY WHERE YOU ARE!!
BIKU (FLINCH)

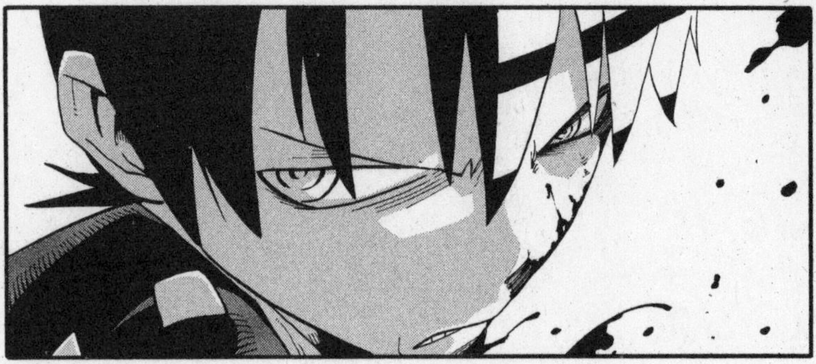

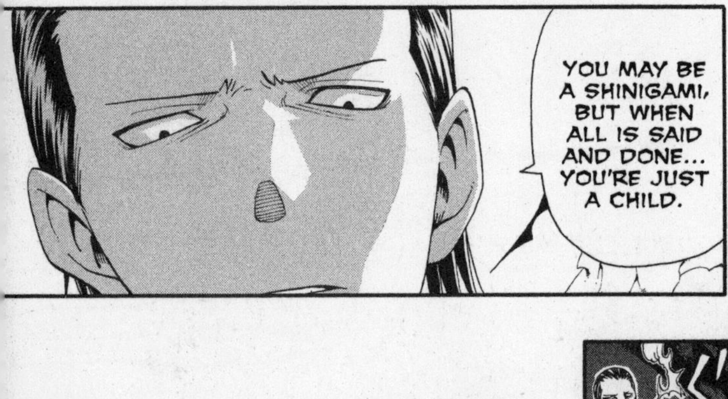
YOU MAY BE A SHINIGAMI, BUT WHEN ALL IS SAID AND DONE... YOU'RE JUST A CHILD.

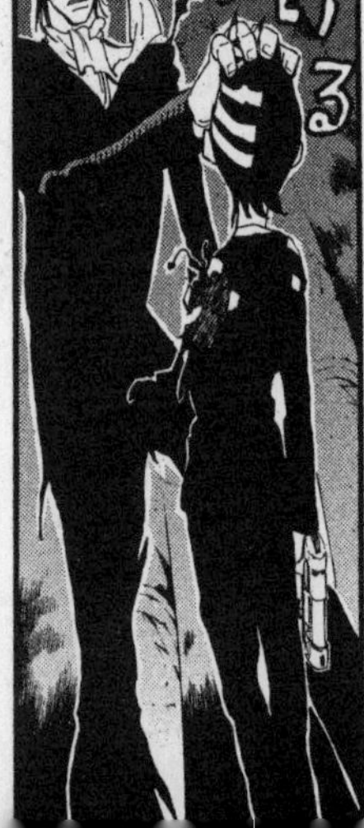
GUIRU (GRAB)

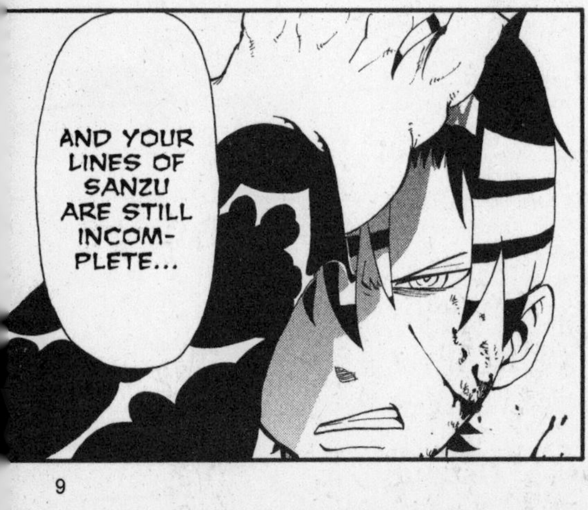
AND YOUR LINES OF SANZU ARE STILL INCOM-PLETE...

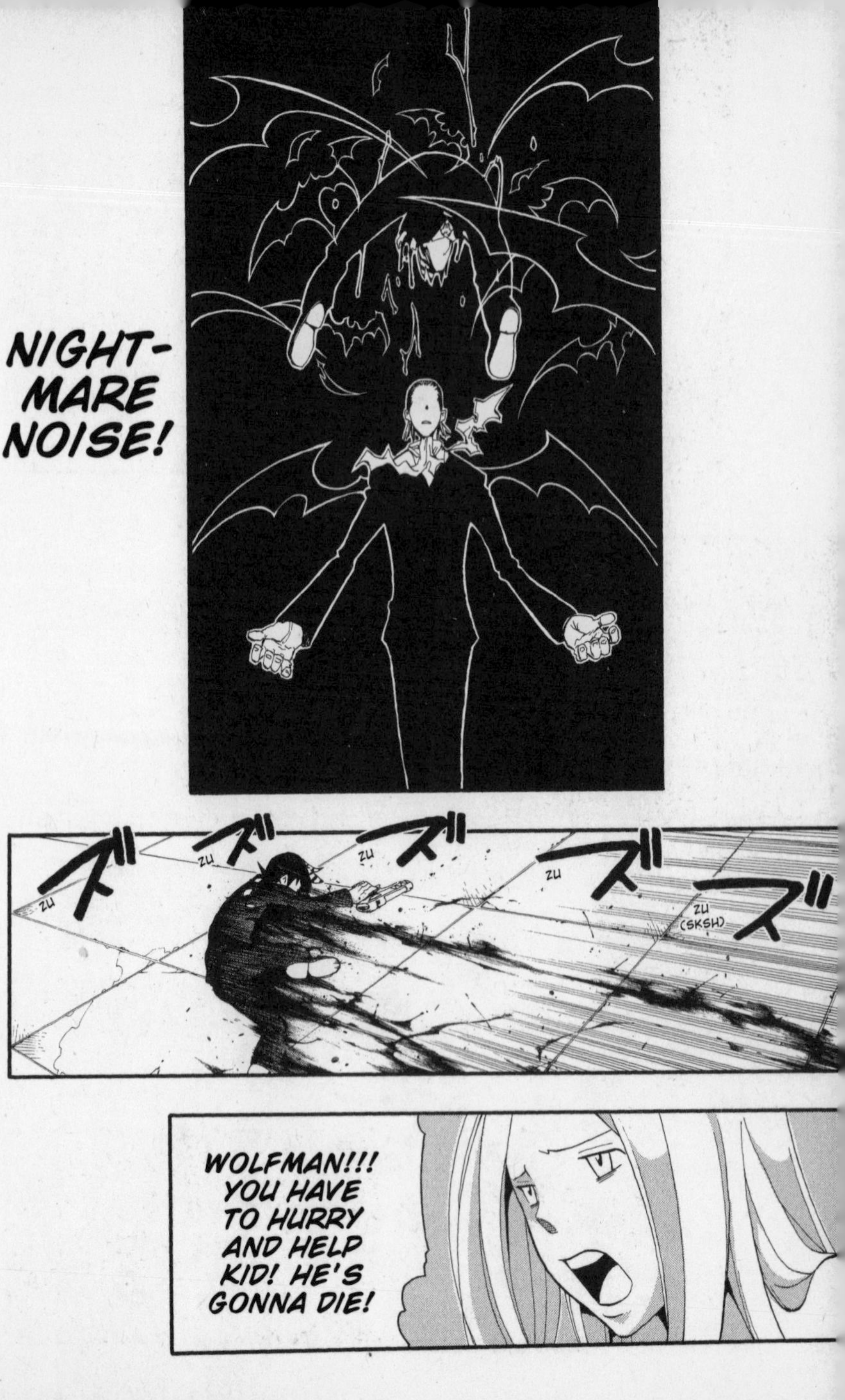
NIGHT-MARE NOISE!
ズ
ZU (SKSH)
ズ
ZU
ズ
ZU
ズ
ZU
ズ
ZU
WOLFMAN!!! YOU HAVE TO HURRY AND HELP KID! HE'S GONNA DIE!

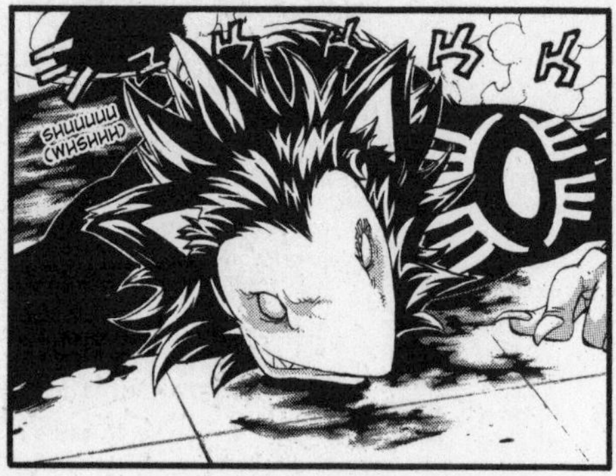
SHUUUUU (WHSHHH)
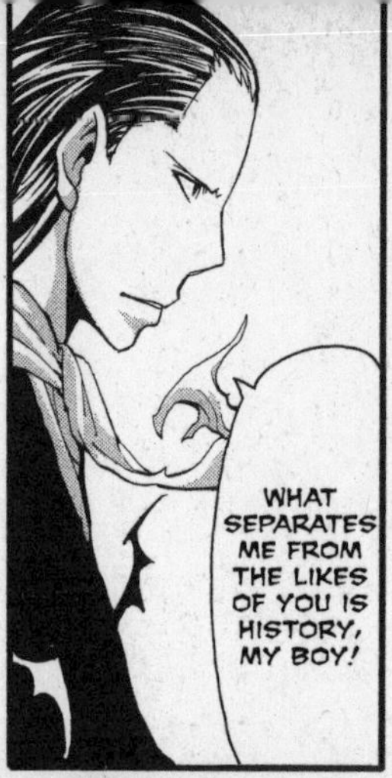
WHAT SEPARATES ME FROM THE LIKES OF YOU IS HISTORY, MY BOY!
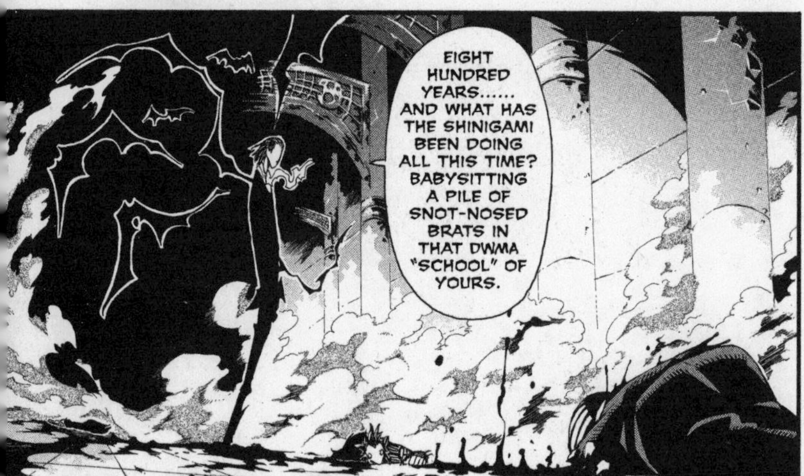
EIGHT HUNDRED YEARS...... AND WHAT HAS THE SHINIGAMI BEEN DOING ALL THIS TIME? BABYSITTING A PILE OF SNOT-NOSED BRATS IN THAT DWMA "SCHOOL" OF YOURS.
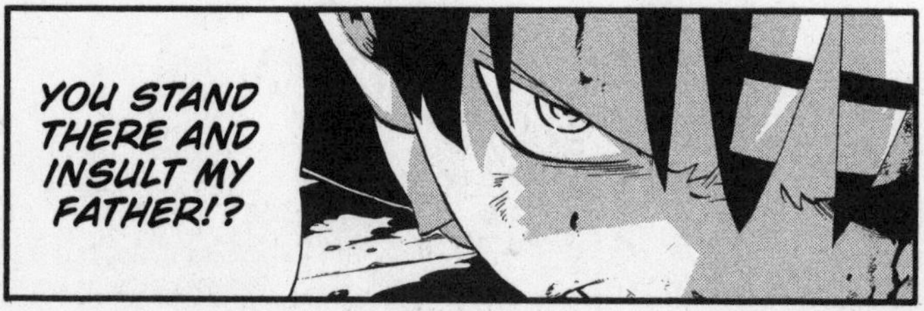
YOU STAND THERE AND INSULT MY FATHER!?

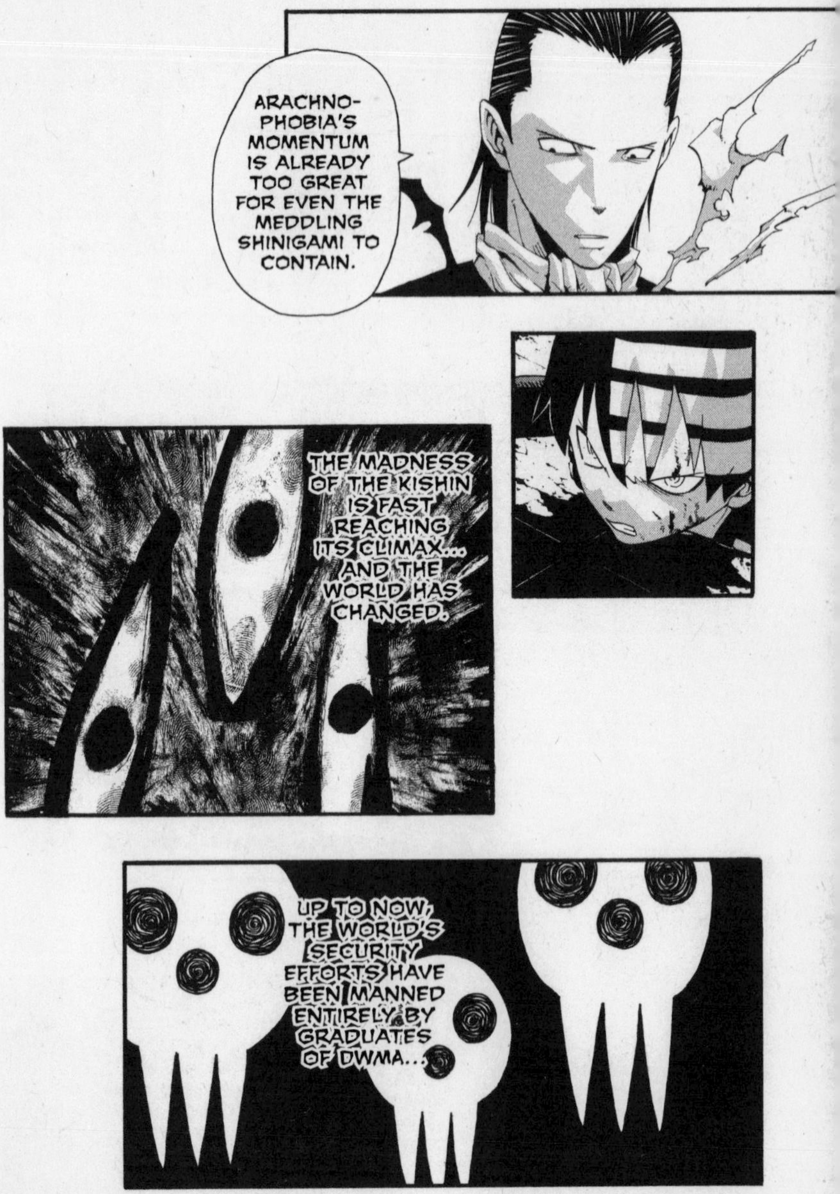
ARACHNOPHOBIA'S MOMENTUM IS ALREADY TOO GREAT FOR EVEN THE MEDDLING SHINIGAMI TO CONTAIN.
THE MADNESS OF THE KISHIN IS FAST REACHING ITS CLIMAX... AND THE WORLD HAS CHANGED.
UP TO NOW, THE WORLD'S SECURITY EFFORTS HAVE BEEN MANNED ENTIRELY BY GRADUATES OF DWMA...

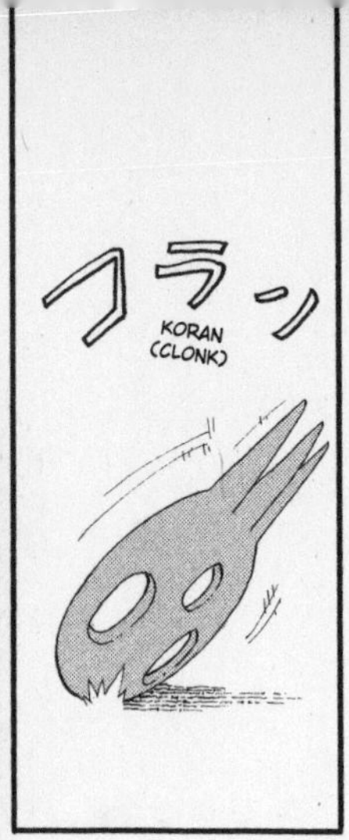
KORAN
(CLONK)

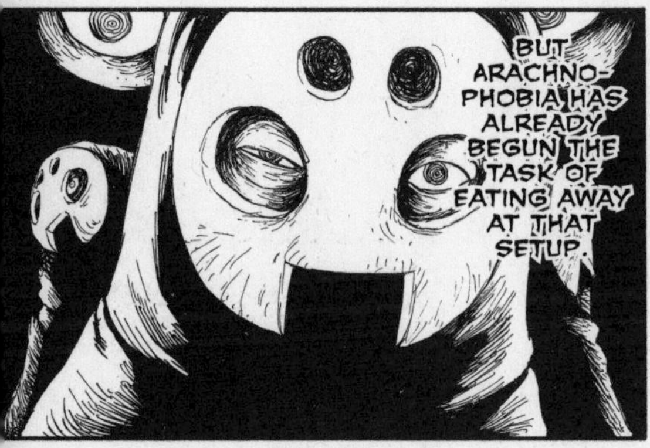
BUT ARACHNOPHOBIA HAS ALREADY BEGUN THE TASK OF EATING AWAY AT THAT SETUP.

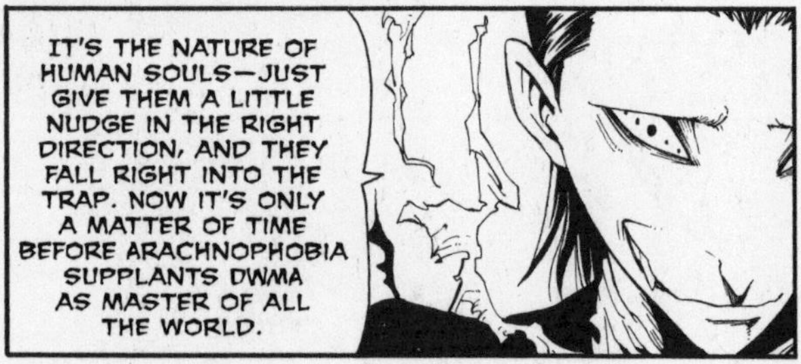
IT'S THE NATURE OF HUMAN SOULS—JUST GIVE THEM A LITTLE NUDGE IN THE RIGHT DIRECTION, AND THEY FALL RIGHT INTO THE TRAP. NOW IT'S ONLY A MATTER OF TIME BEFORE ARACHNOPHOBIA SUPPLANTS DWMA AS MASTER OF ALL THE WORLD.

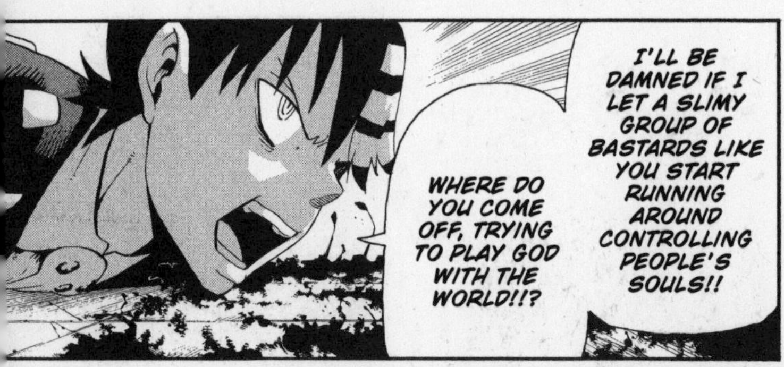
I'LL BE DAMNED IF I LET A SLIMY GROUP OF BASTARDS LIKE YOU START RUNNING AROUND CONTROLLING PEOPLE'S SOULS!!
WHERE DO YOU COME OFF, TRYING TO PLAY GOD WITH THE WORLD!!?

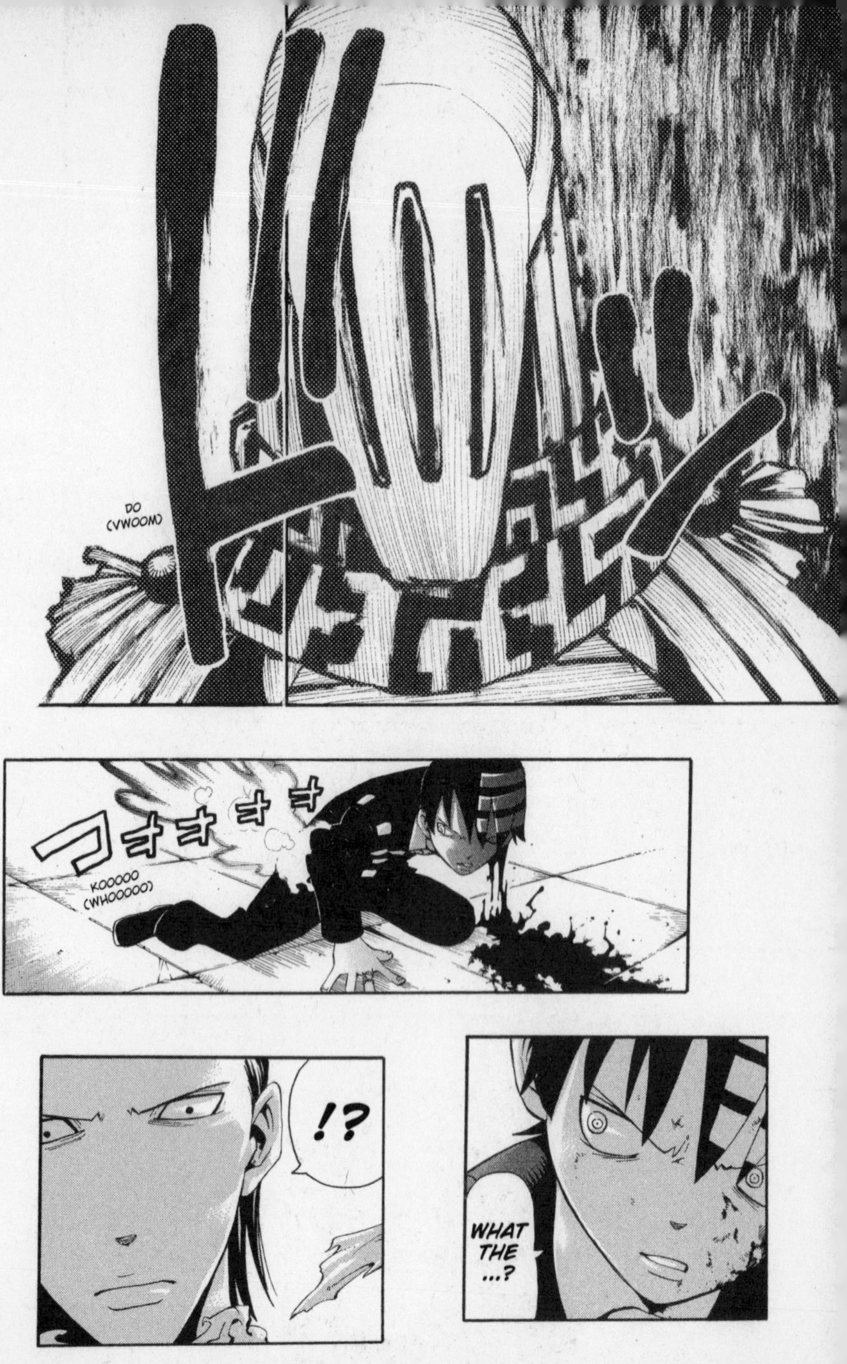
DO
(VWOOM)
フォオオオ
KOOOOO
(WHOOOOO)
WHAT THE ...?
!?

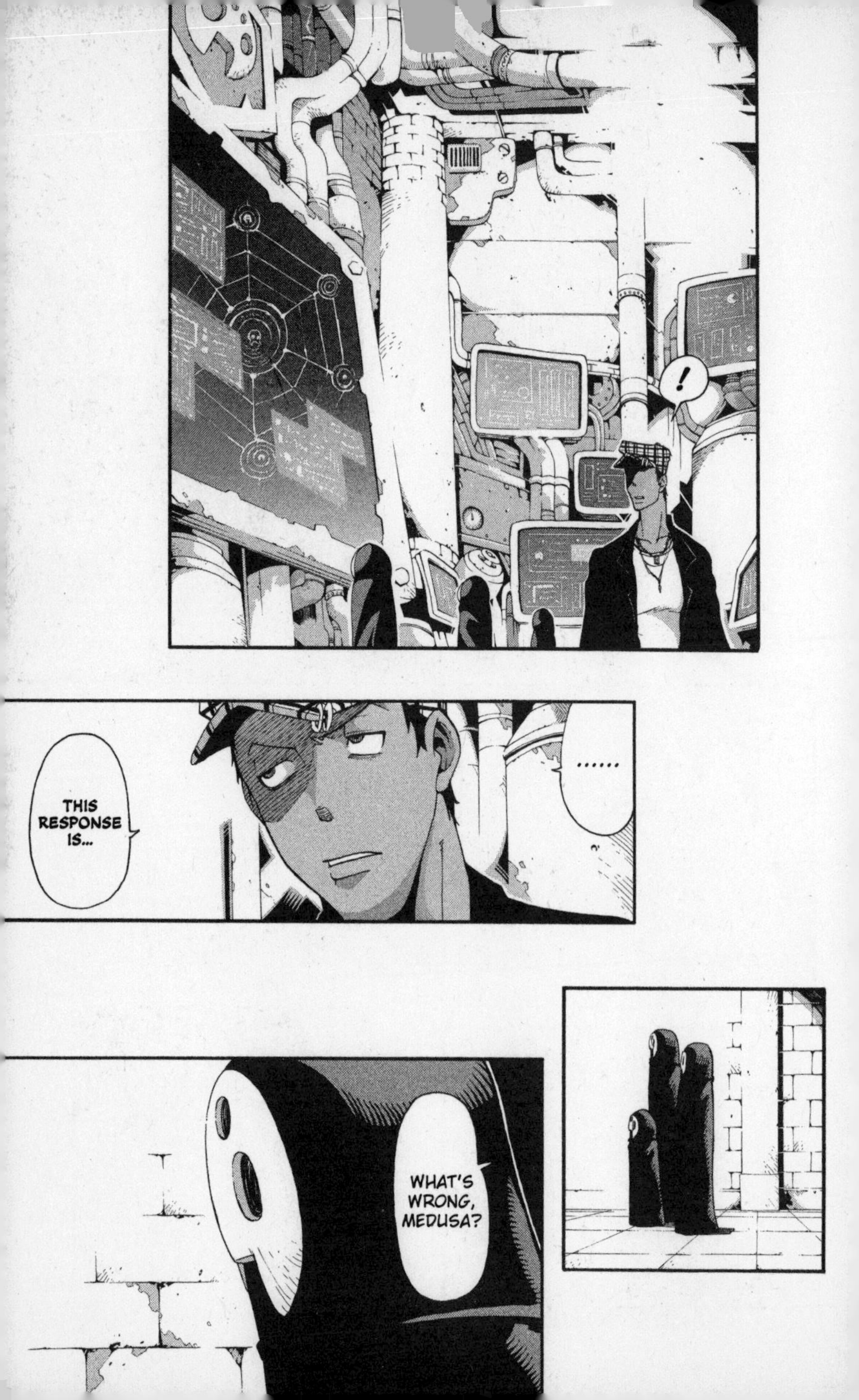
!
......
THIS RESPONSE IS...
WHAT'S WRONG, MEDUSA?

WHAT'S HAP-
PENING TO
ME...?

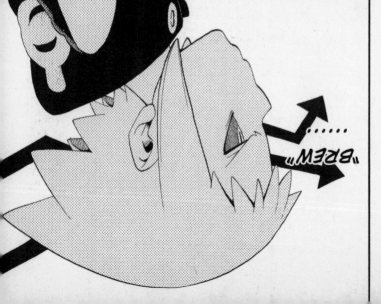

"BREW"......

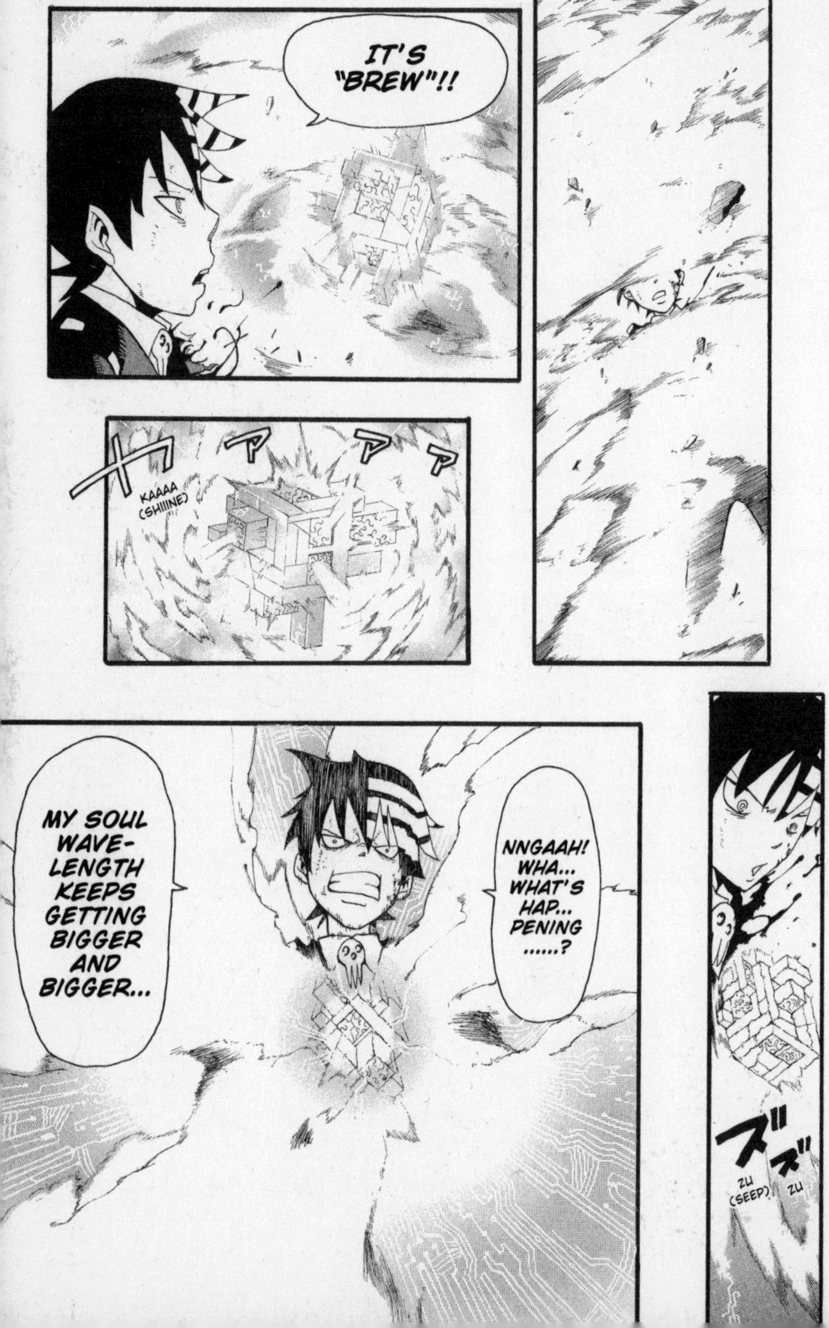
IT'S "BREW"!!
KAAAA (SHIIINE)
ZU (SEEP) ZU
NNGAAH! WHA... WHAT'S HAP... PENING ......?
MY SOUL WAVE-LENGTH KEEPS GETTING BIGGER AND BIGGER...

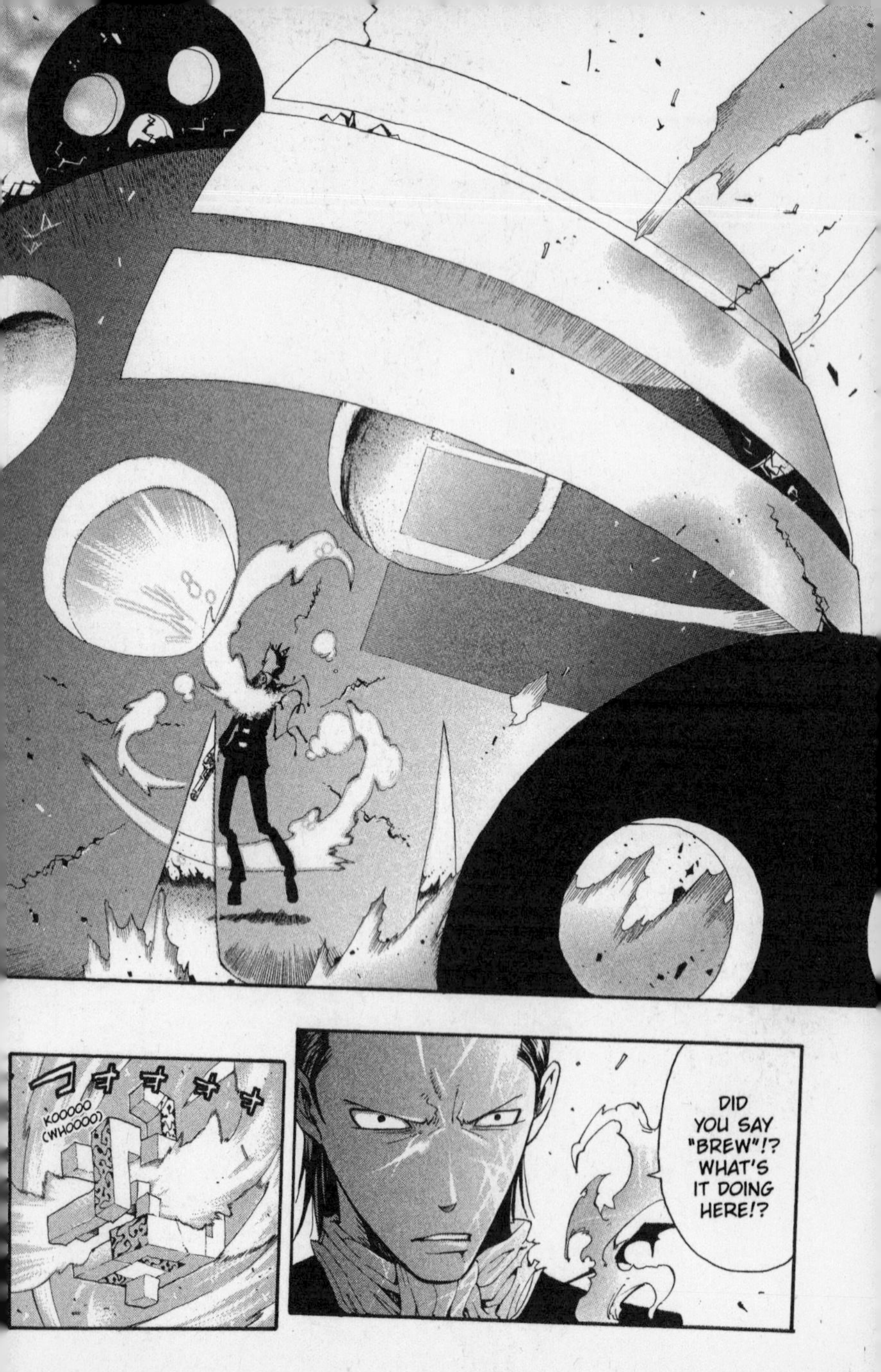
DID YOU SAY "BREW"!? WHAT'S IT DOING HERE!?
KOOOOO (WHOOOO)

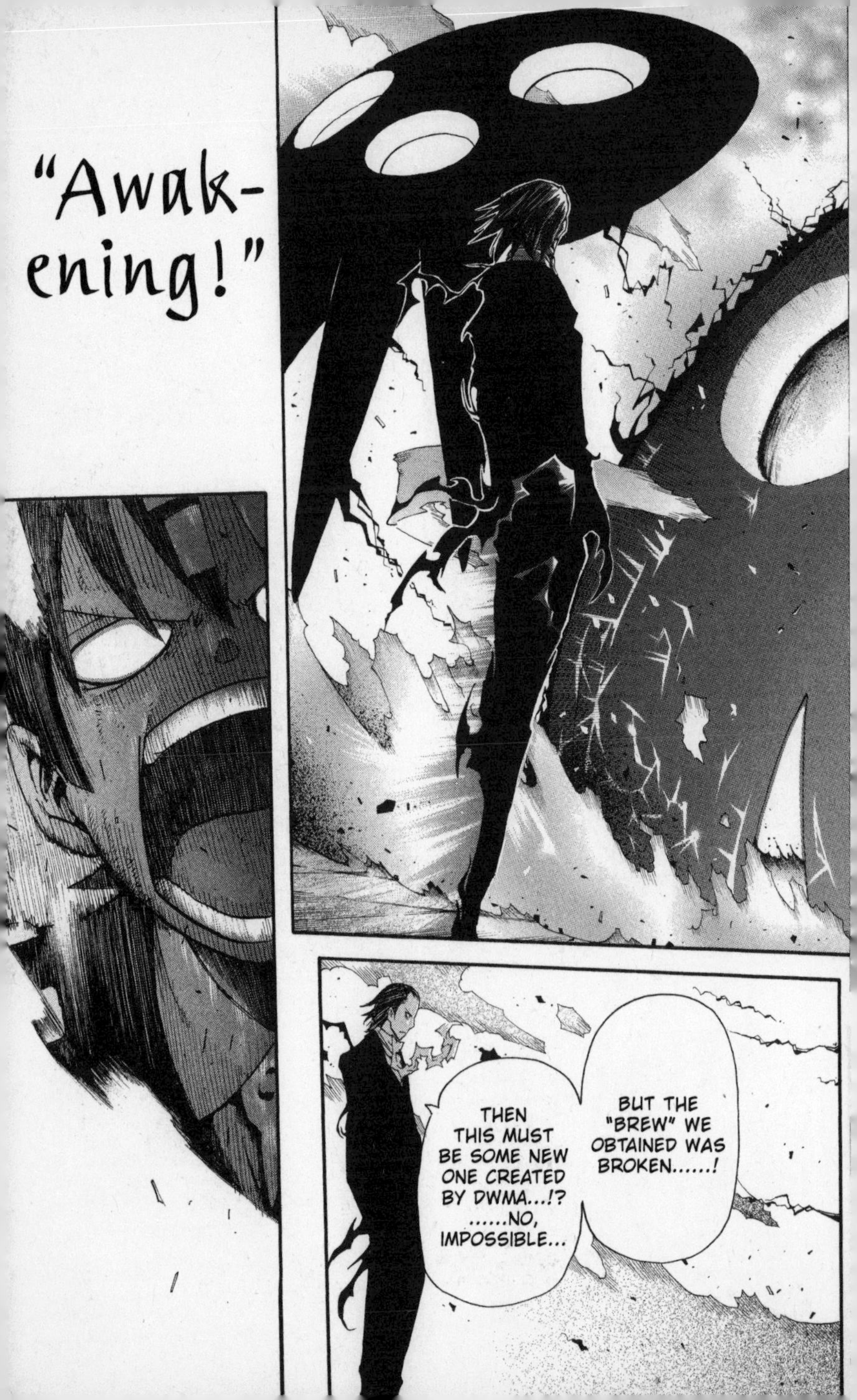
BUT THE "BREW" WE OBTAINED WAS BROKEN......!
THEN THIS MUST BE SOME NEW ONE CREATED BY DWMA...!? ......NO, IMPOSSIBLE...
"Awak-ening!"

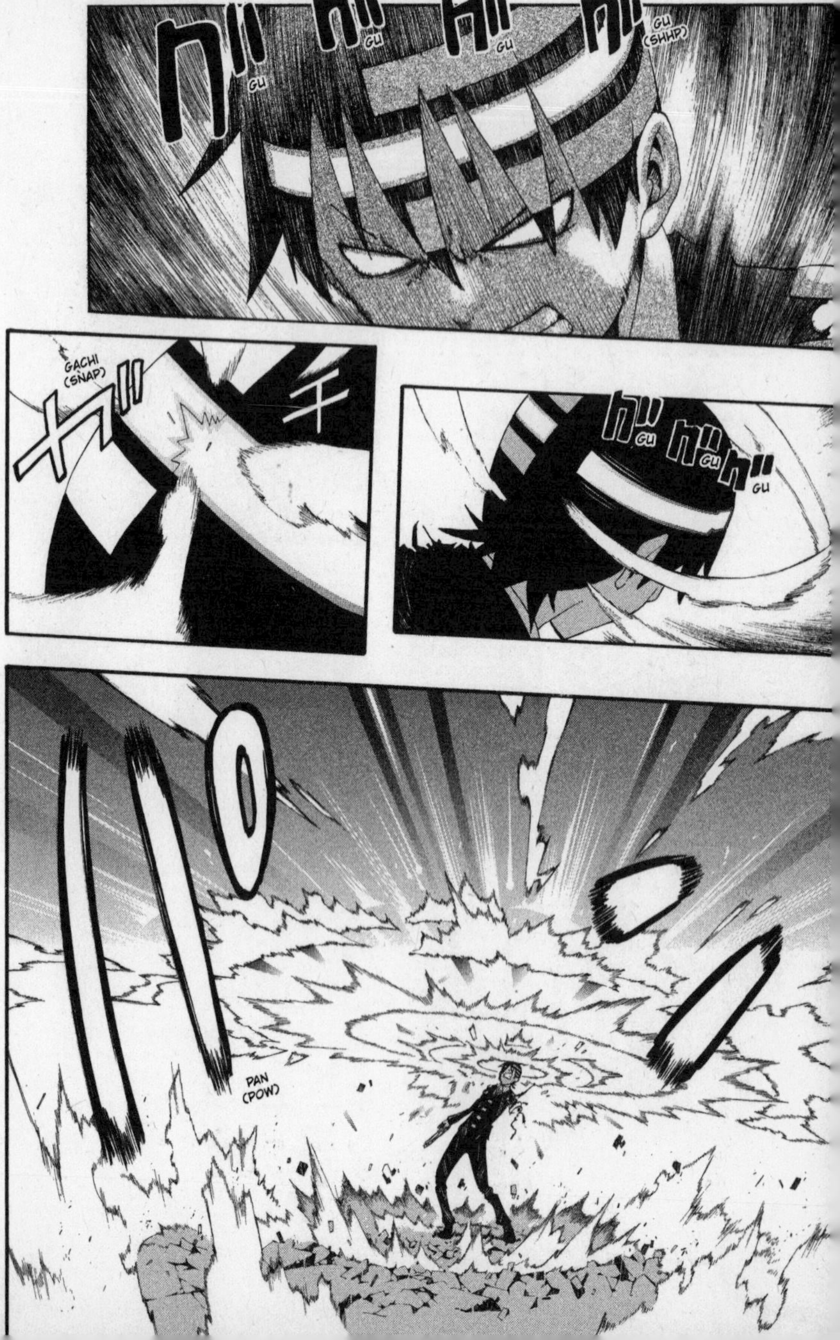
GU GU GU GU (SHHP)
GU GU GU
GACHI (SNAP)
PAN (POW)

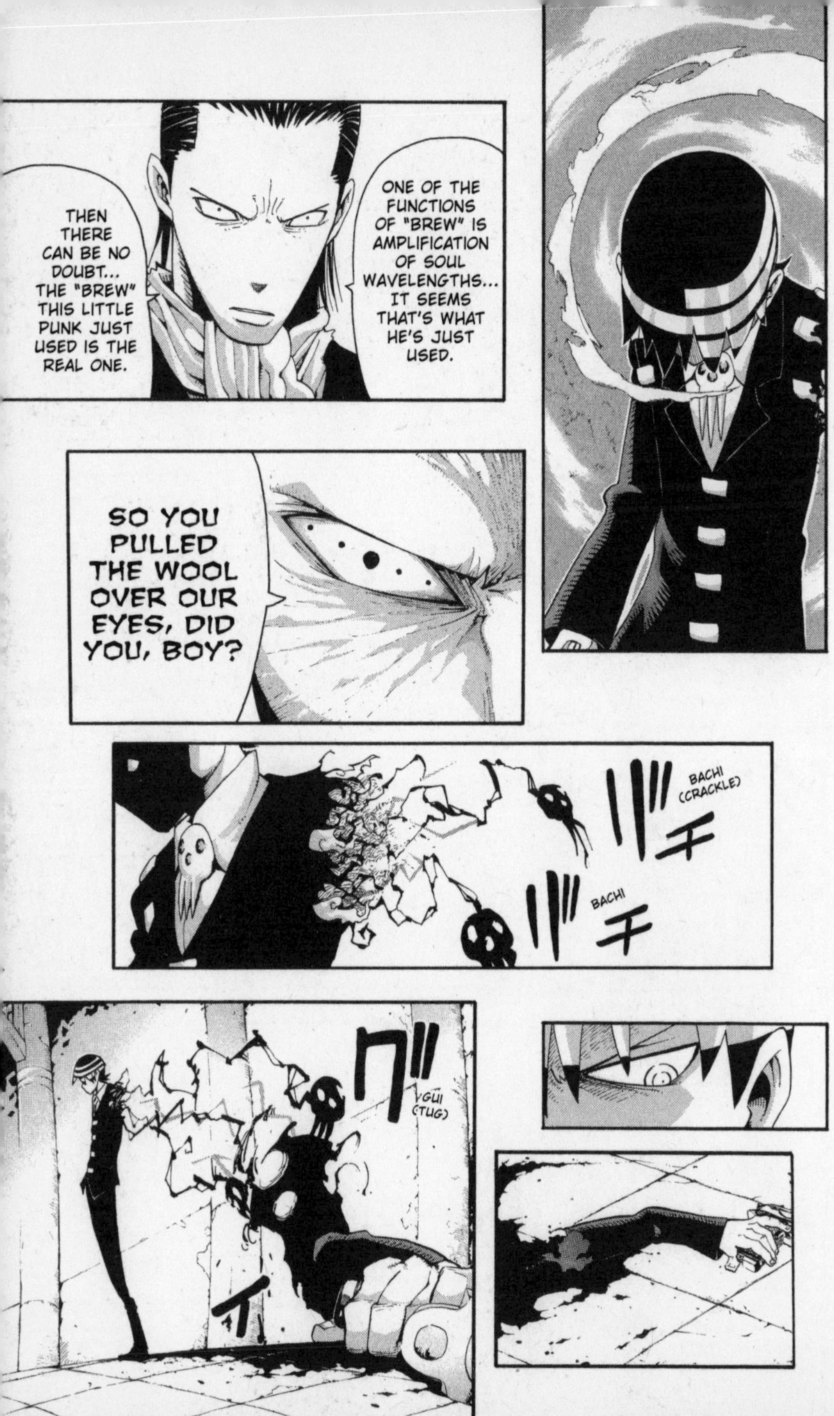
ONE OF THE FUNCTIONS OF "BREW" IS AMPLIFICATION OF SOUL WAVELENGTHS... IT SEEMS THAT'S WHAT HE'S JUST USED.
THEN THERE CAN BE NO DOUBT... THE "BREW" THIS LITTLE PUNK JUST USED IS THE REAL ONE.
SO YOU PULLED THE WOOL OVER OUR EYES, DID YOU, BOY?
BACHI (CRACKLE)
BACHI
GUI (TUG)

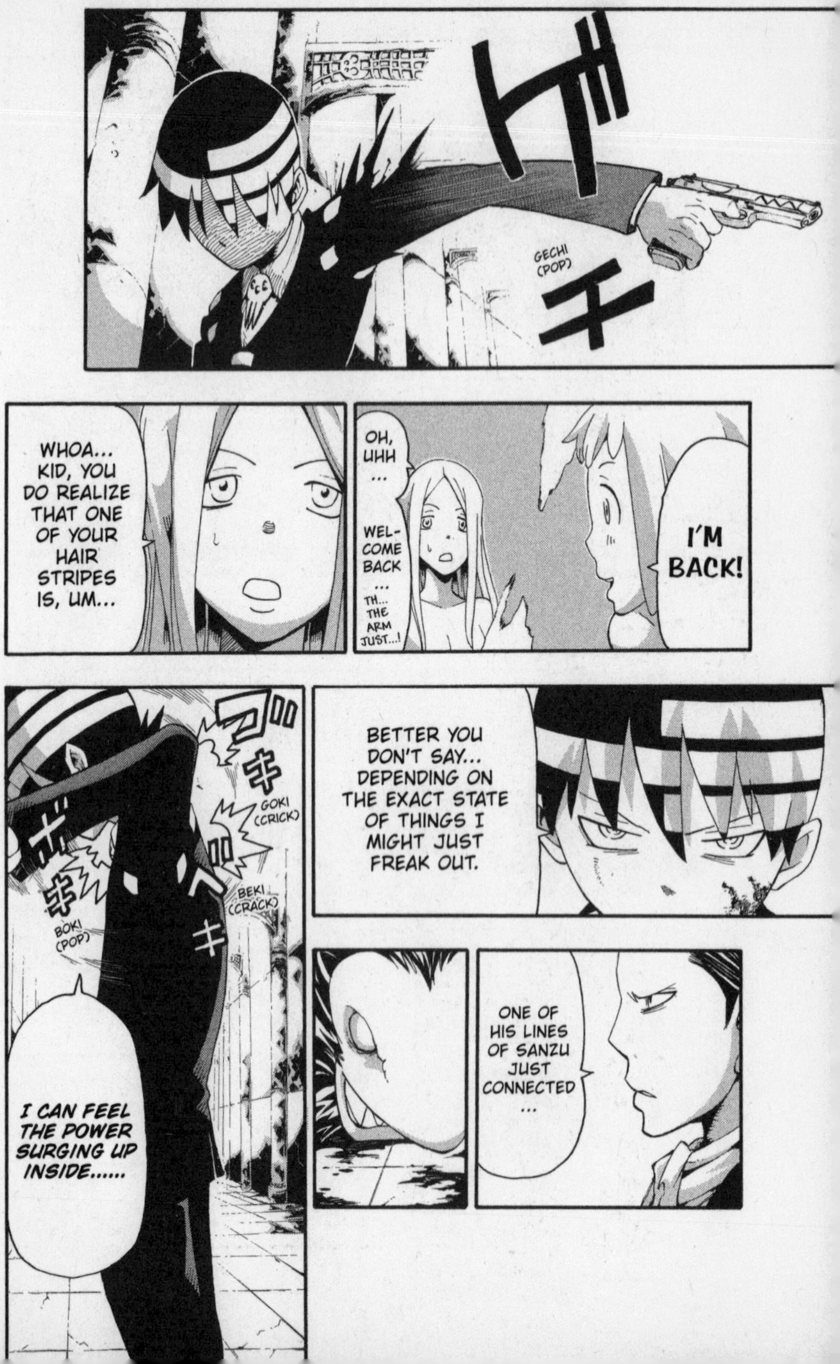
GECHI (POP)
I'M BACK!
OH, UHH ...
WEL-COME BACK ...
TH... THE ARM JUST...!
WHOA... KID, YOU DO REALIZE THAT ONE OF YOUR HAIR STRIPES IS, UM...
BETTER YOU DON'T SAY... DEPENDING ON THE EXACT STATE OF THINGS I MIGHT JUST FREAK OUT.
ONE OF HIS LINES OF SANZU JUST CONNECTED ...
GOKI (CRICK)
BEKI (CRACK)
BOKI (POP)
I CAN FEEL THE POWER SURGING UP INSIDE......

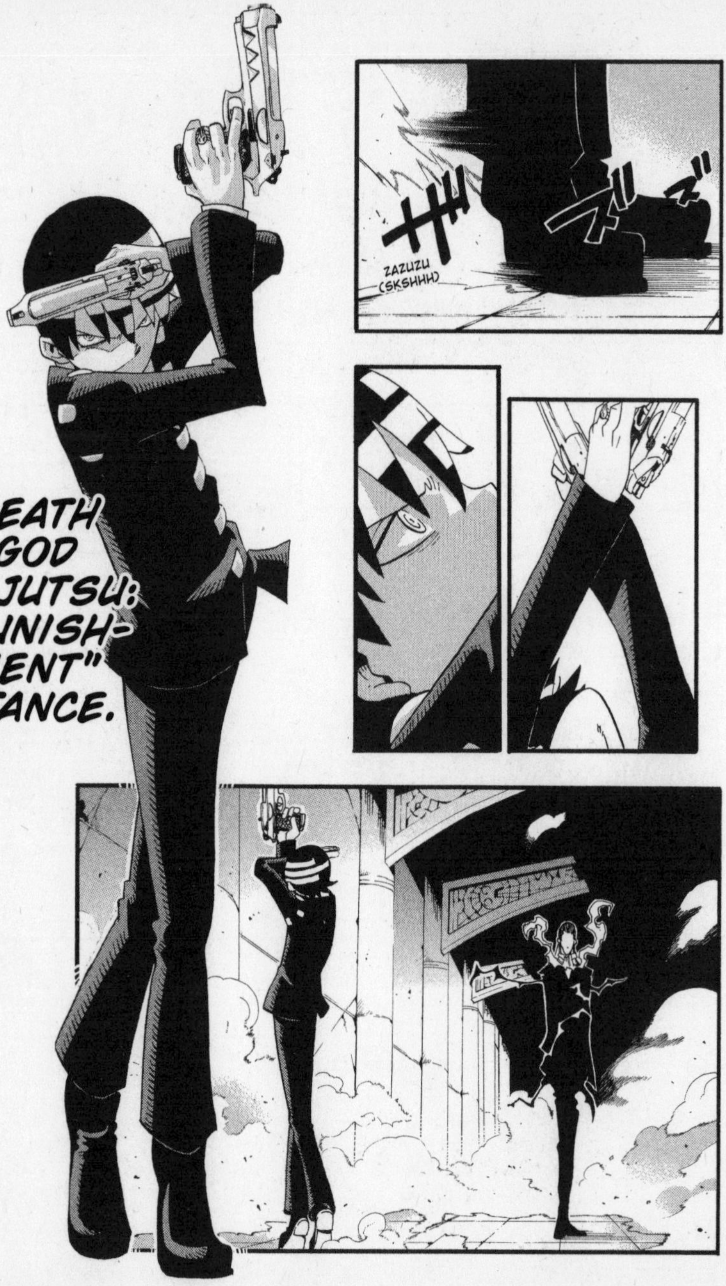
ZAZUZU (SKSHHH)
DEATH GOD TAIJUTSU: "PUNISHMENT" STANCE.

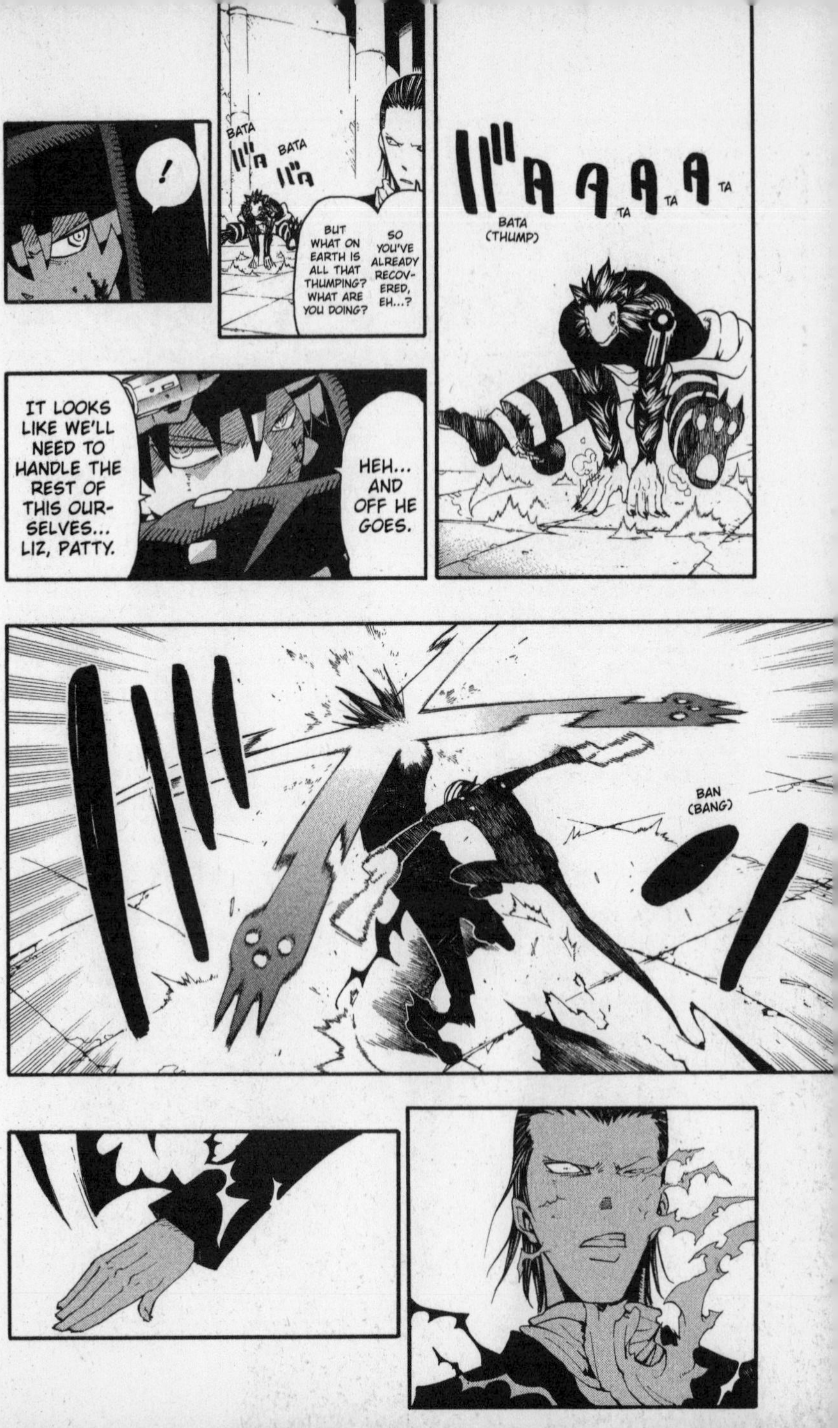
BATA
TA TA TA
BATA
(THUMP)
BATA
BATA
SO YOU'VE ALREADY RECOV-ERED, EH...?
BUT WHAT ON EARTH IS ALL THAT THUMPING? WHAT ARE YOU DOING?
!
HEH... AND OFF HE GOES.
IT LOOKS LIKE WE'LL NEED TO HANDLE THE REST OF THIS OUR-SELVES... LIZ, PATTY.
BAN
(BANG)

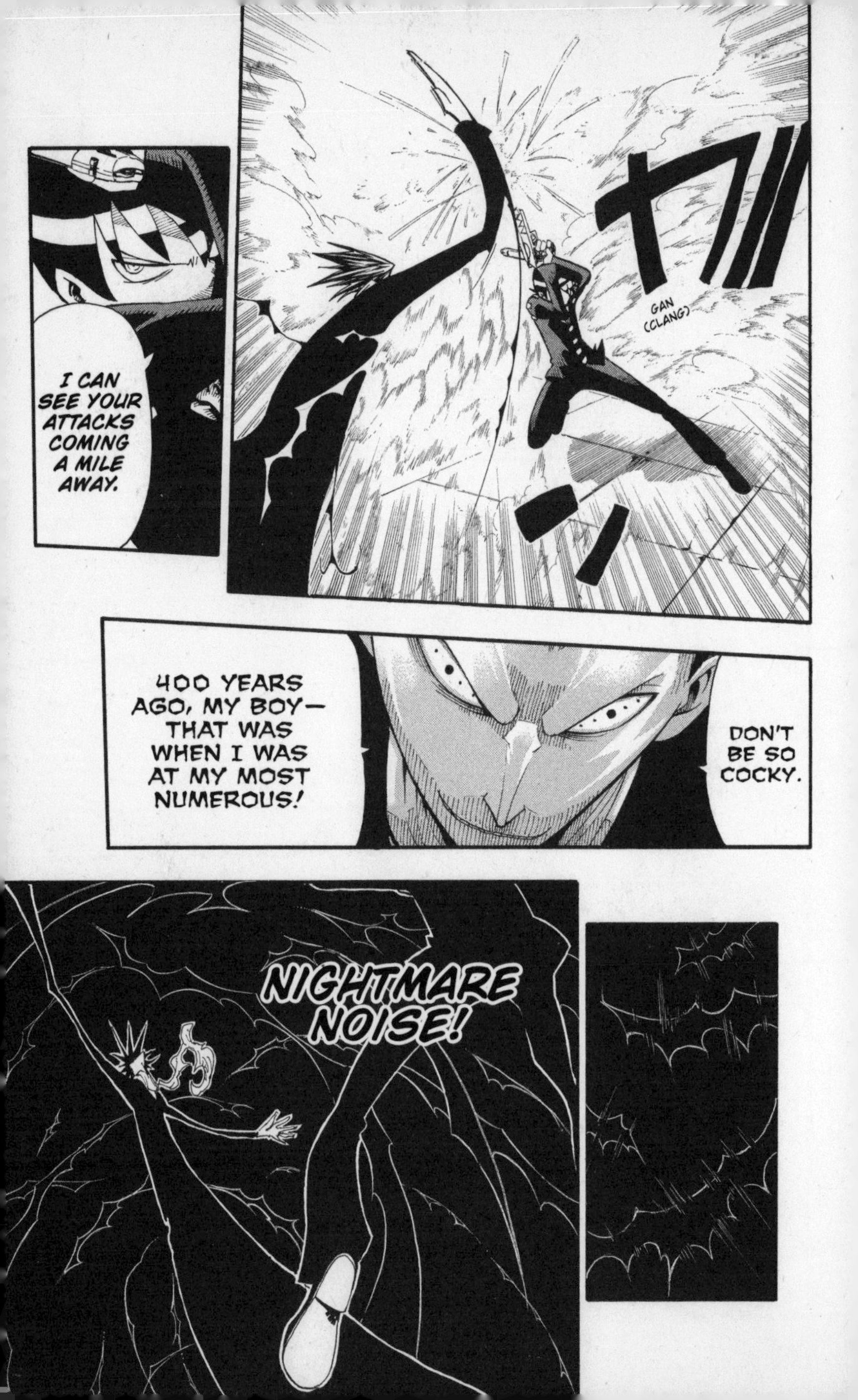
GAN
(CLANG)
I CAN SEE YOUR ATTACKS COMING A MILE AWAY.
DON'T BE SO COCKY.
400 YEARS AGO, MY BOY—THAT WAS WHEN I WAS AT MY MOST NUMEROUS!
NIGHTMARE NOISE!

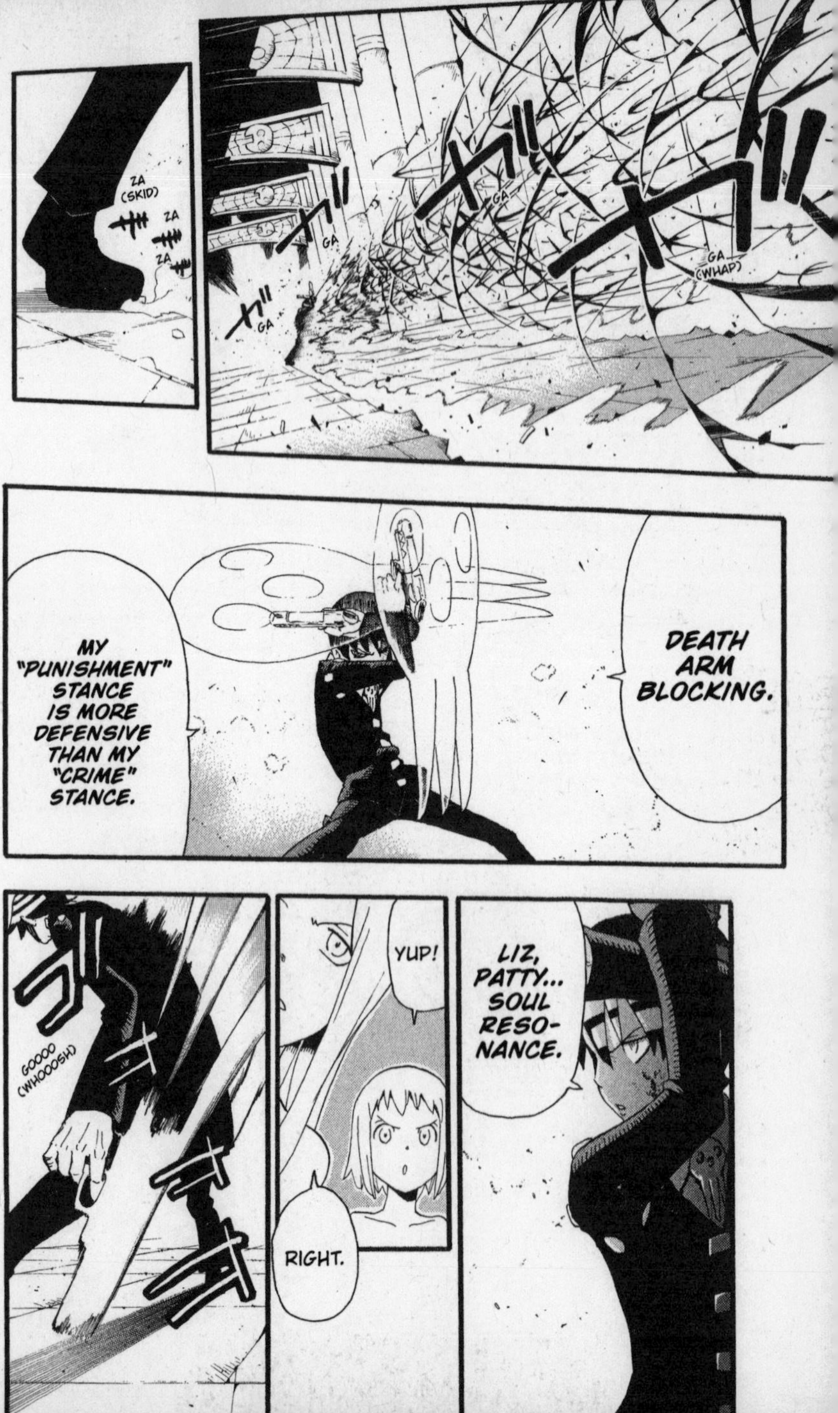
GA (WHAP)
GA
GA
GA
ZA (SKID)
ZA
ZA
DEATH ARM BLOCKING.
MY "PUNISHMENT" STANCE IS MORE DEFENSIVE THAN MY "CRIME" STANCE.
LIZ, PATTY... SOUL RESO-NANCE.
YUP!
RIGHT.
GOOOO (WHOOOSH)

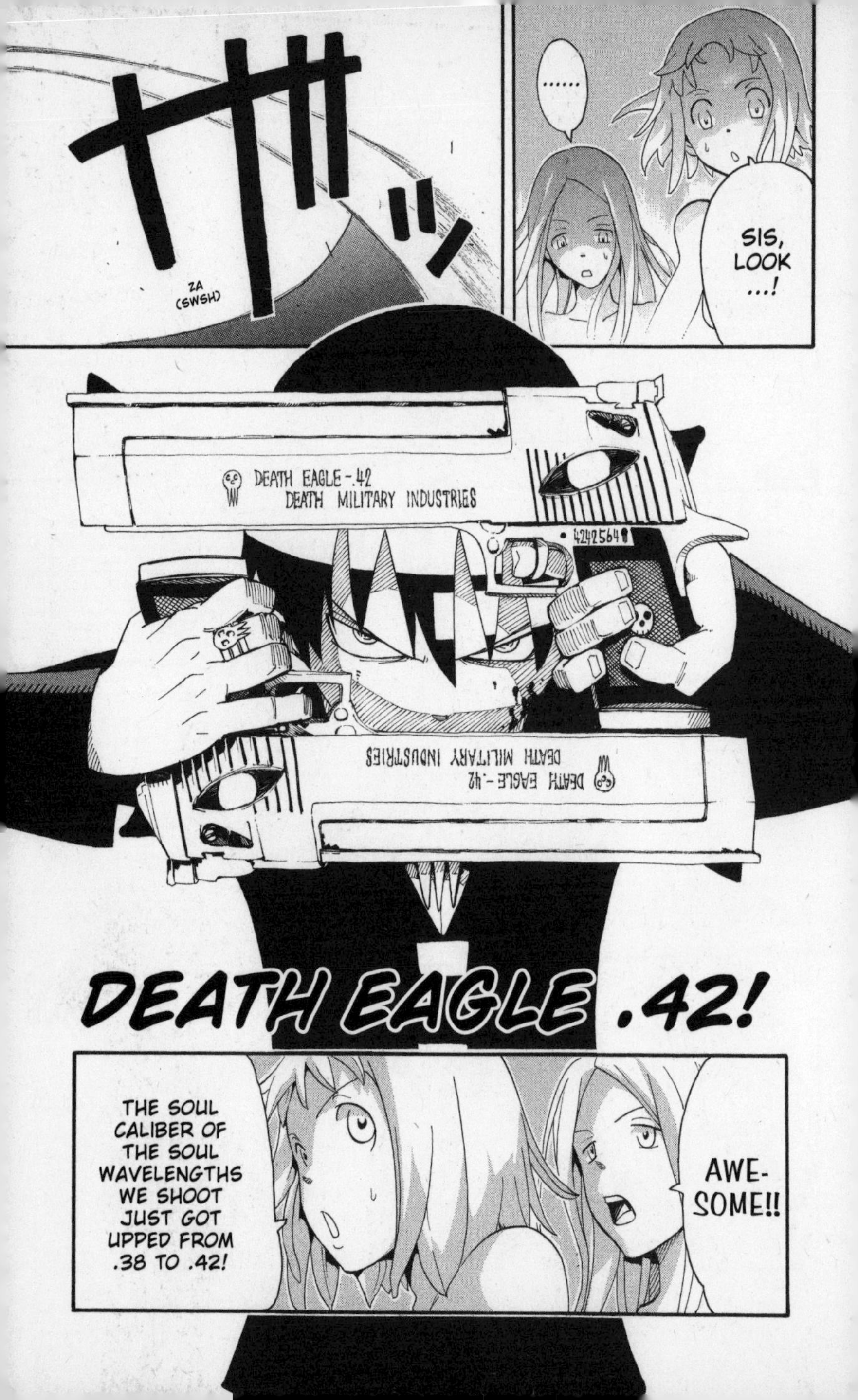
SIS, LOOK ...!
......
ZA (SWSH)
DEATH EAGLE-.42
DEATH MILITARY INDUSTRIES
4242564
DEATH EAGLE-.42
DEATH MILITARY INDUSTRIES
DEATH EAGLE .42!
AWE-SOME!!
THE SOUL CALIBER OF THE SOUL WAVELENGTHS WE SHOOT JUST GOT UPPED FROM .38 TO .42!

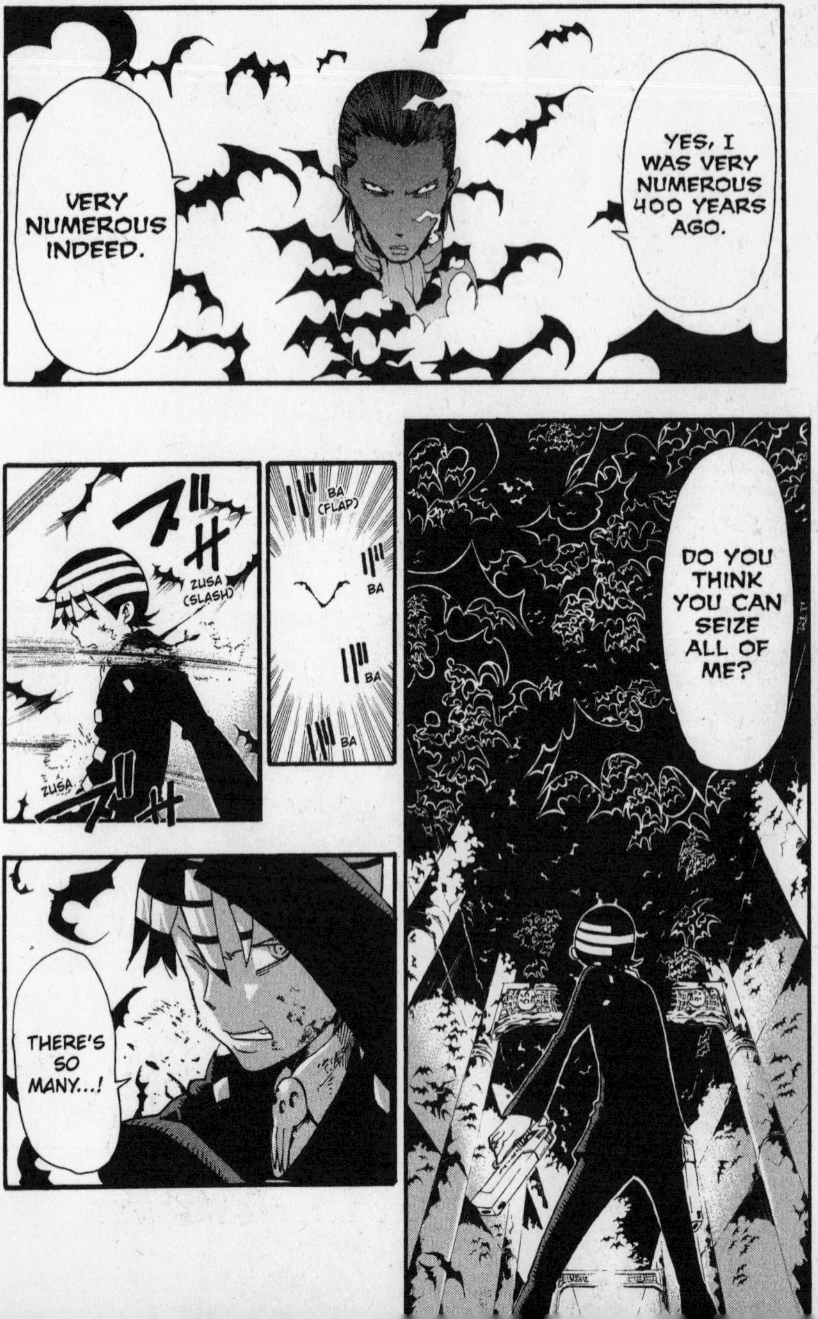
YES, I WAS VERY NUMEROUS 400 YEARS AGO.
VERY NUMEROUS INDEED.
DO YOU THINK YOU CAN SEIZE ALL OF ME?
BA (FLAP)
BA
BA
BA
ZUSA (SLASH)
ZUSA
THERE'S SO MANY...!

WHAT THE HELL IS THIS?

DARK-NESS DISCORD.

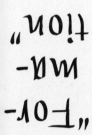

"For-ma-tion"

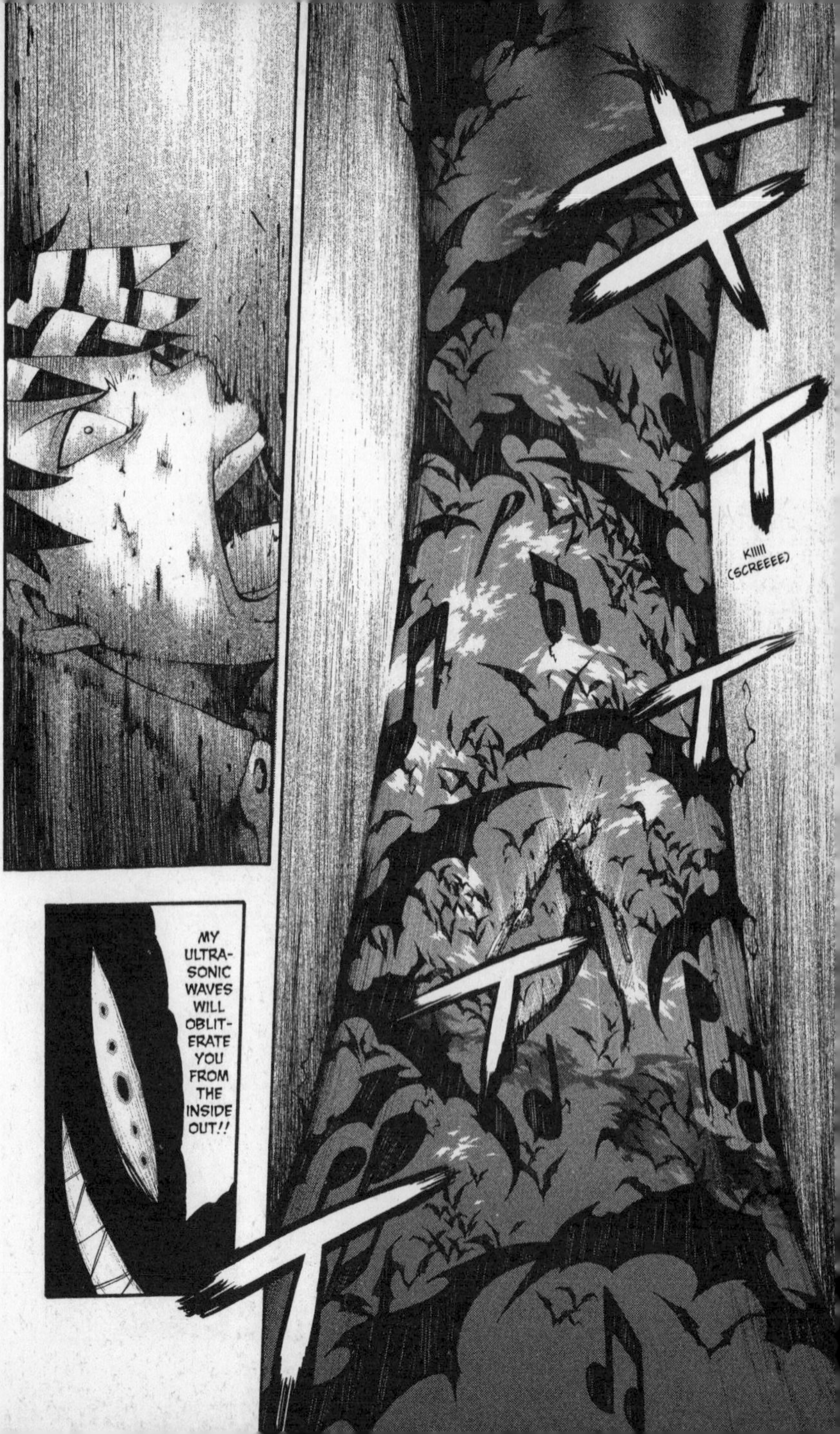
KIIIII (SCREEEE)
MY ULTRA-SONIC WAVES WILL OBLIT-ERATE YOU FROM THE INSIDE OUT!!

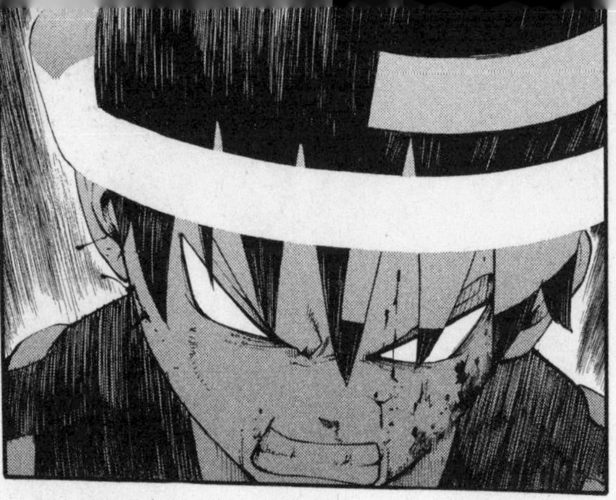

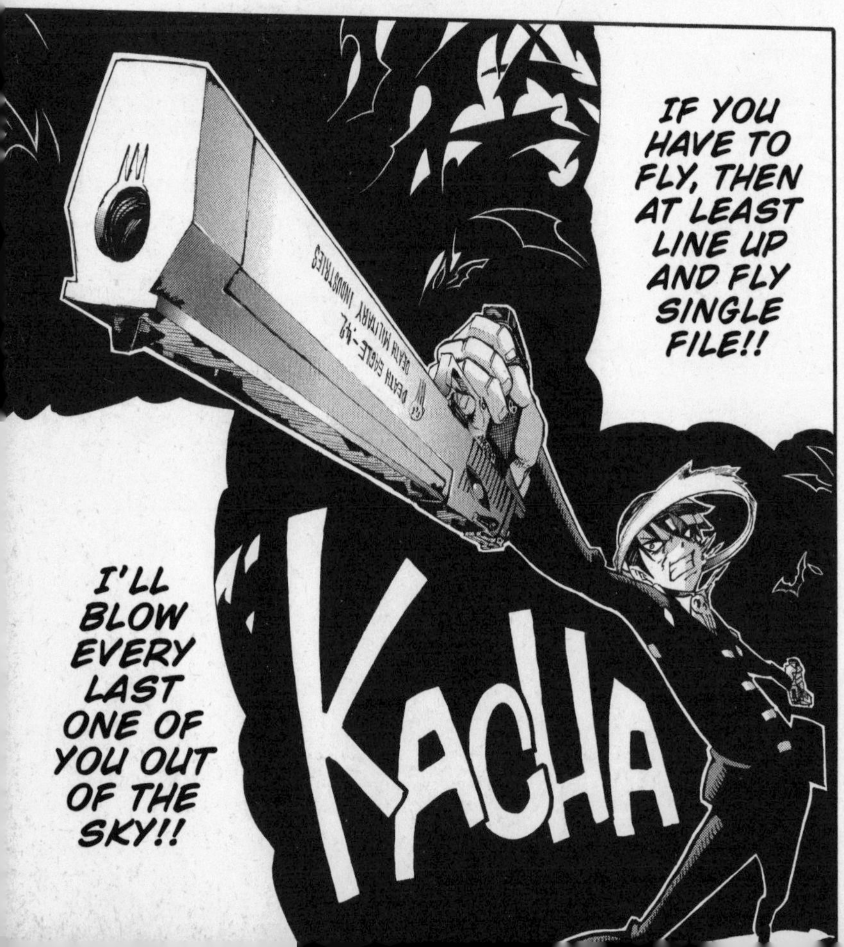
IF YOU HAVE TO FLY, THEN AT LEAST LINE UP AND FLY SINGLE FILE!!
DEATH EAGLE-.42
DEATH MILITARY INDUSTRIES
KACHA
I'LL BLOW EVERY LAST ONE OF YOU OUT OF THE SKY!!

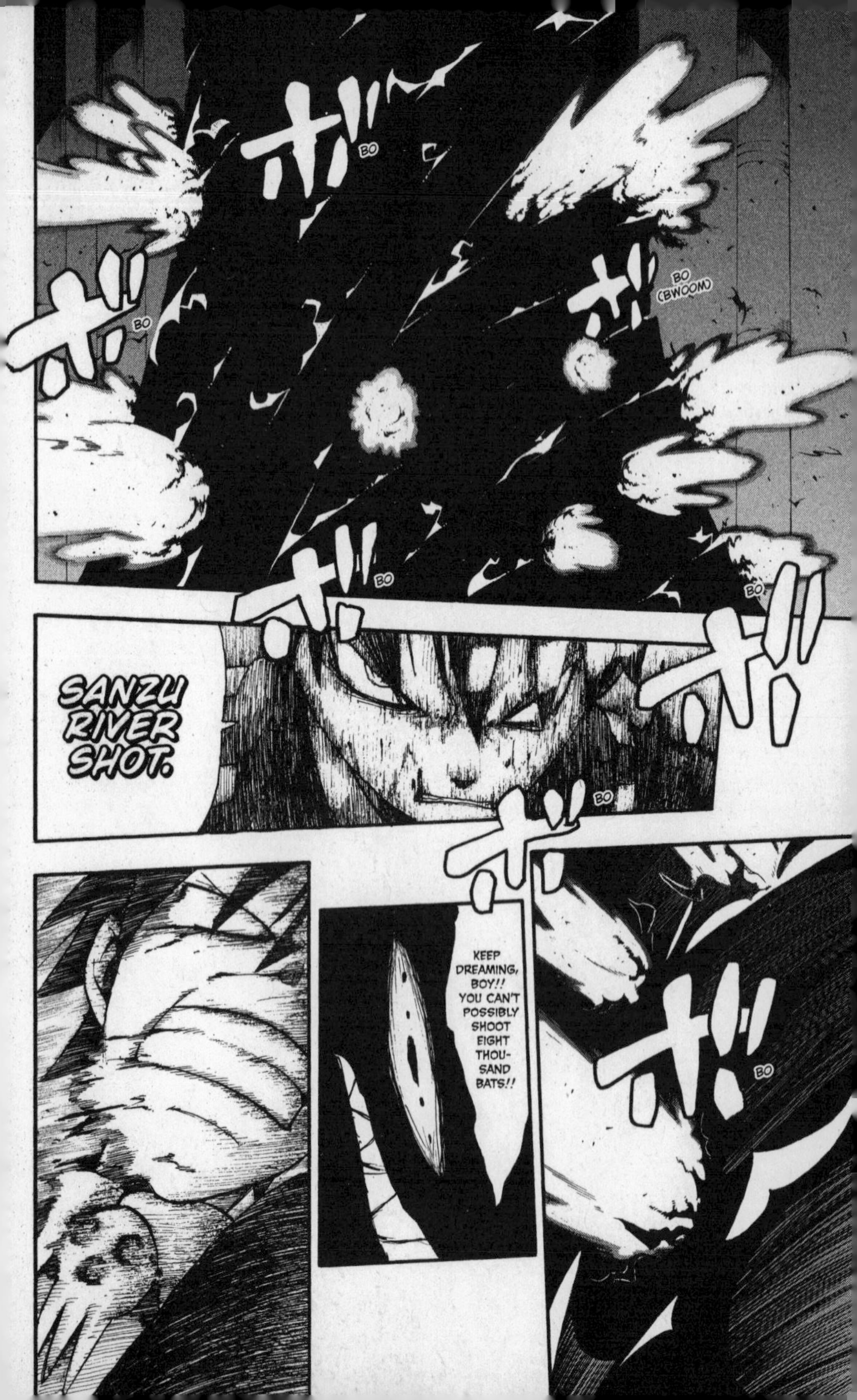
BO
BO (BWOOM)
BO
BO
BO
BO
SANZU RIVER SHOT.
BO
BO
KEEP DREAMING, BOY!! YOU CAN'T POSSIBLY SHOOT EIGHT THOU-SAND BATS!!

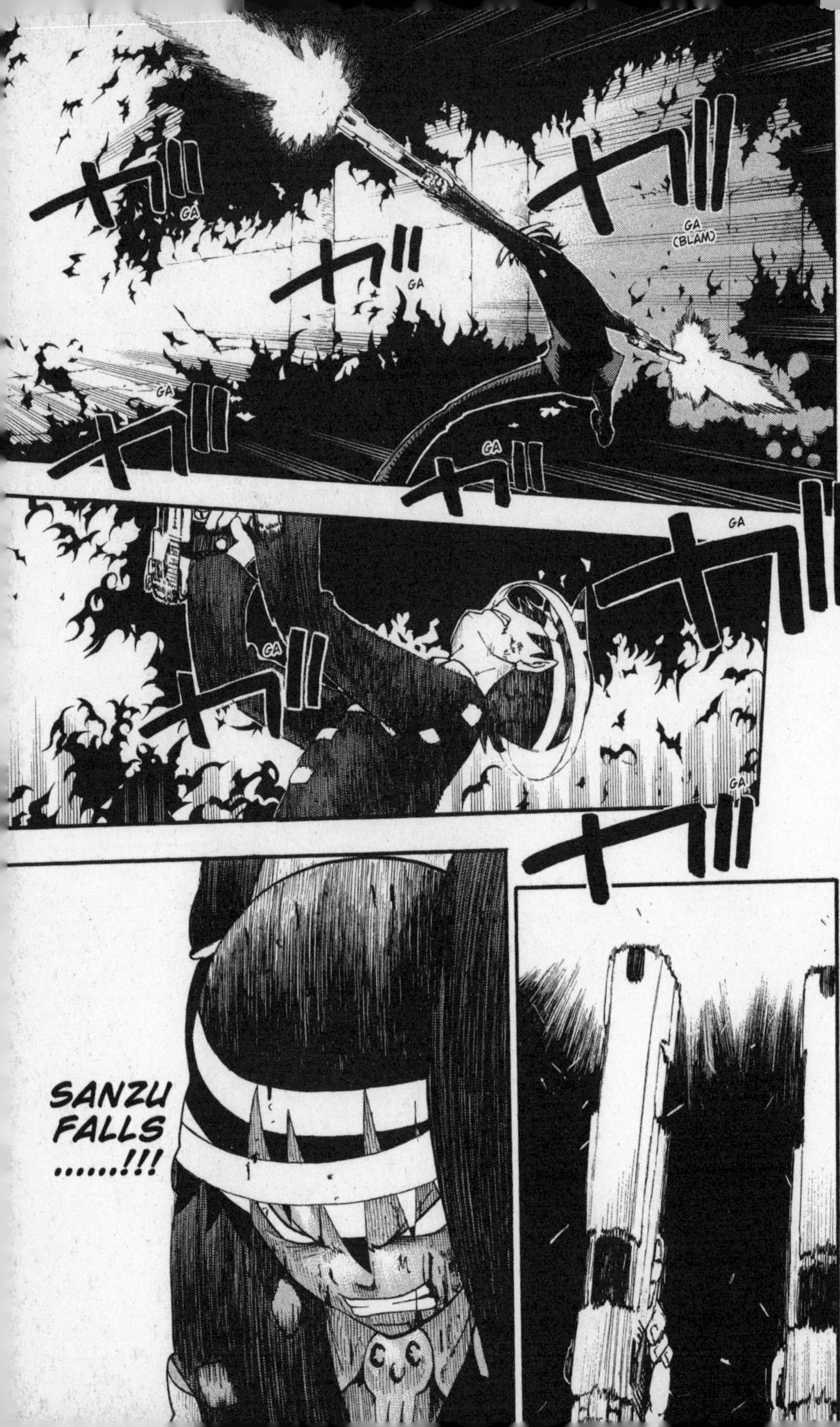
GA
(BLAM)
GA
GA
GA
GA
GA
GA
GA
SANZU
FALLS
......!!!

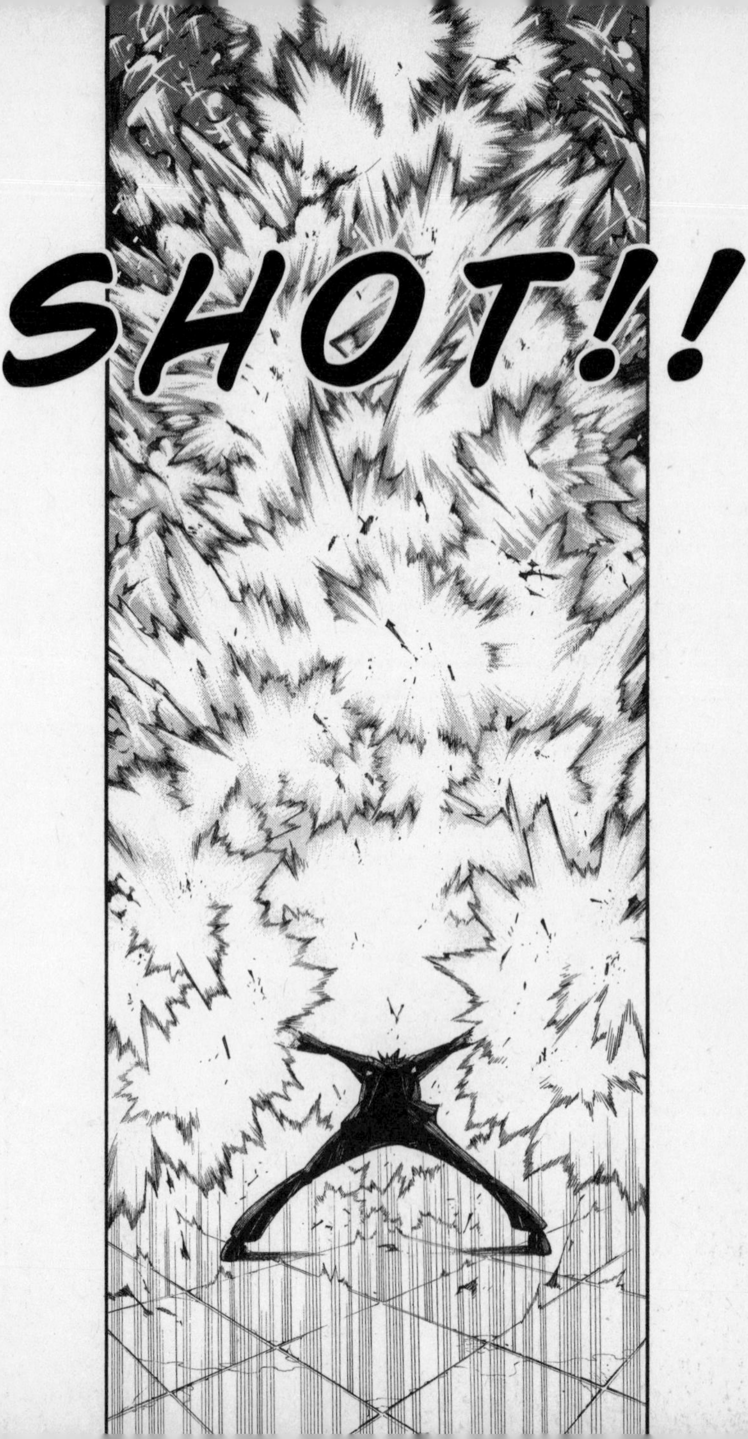
SHOT!!

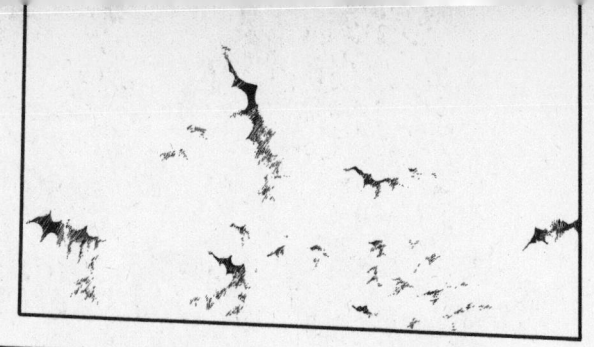

"BREW"...

GAKU
(SLUMP)

KUH...

YOU...
SHINI-
GAMI...!

BUT MY ATTACK
HAS LEFT YOU
WITH MASSIVE
INTERNAL DAMAGE,
BOY...INDEED,
IT SEEMS WE'VE
BOTH PAID A PRICE
FOR THIS LITTLE
CONFRONTATION.

GON
(CLONK)

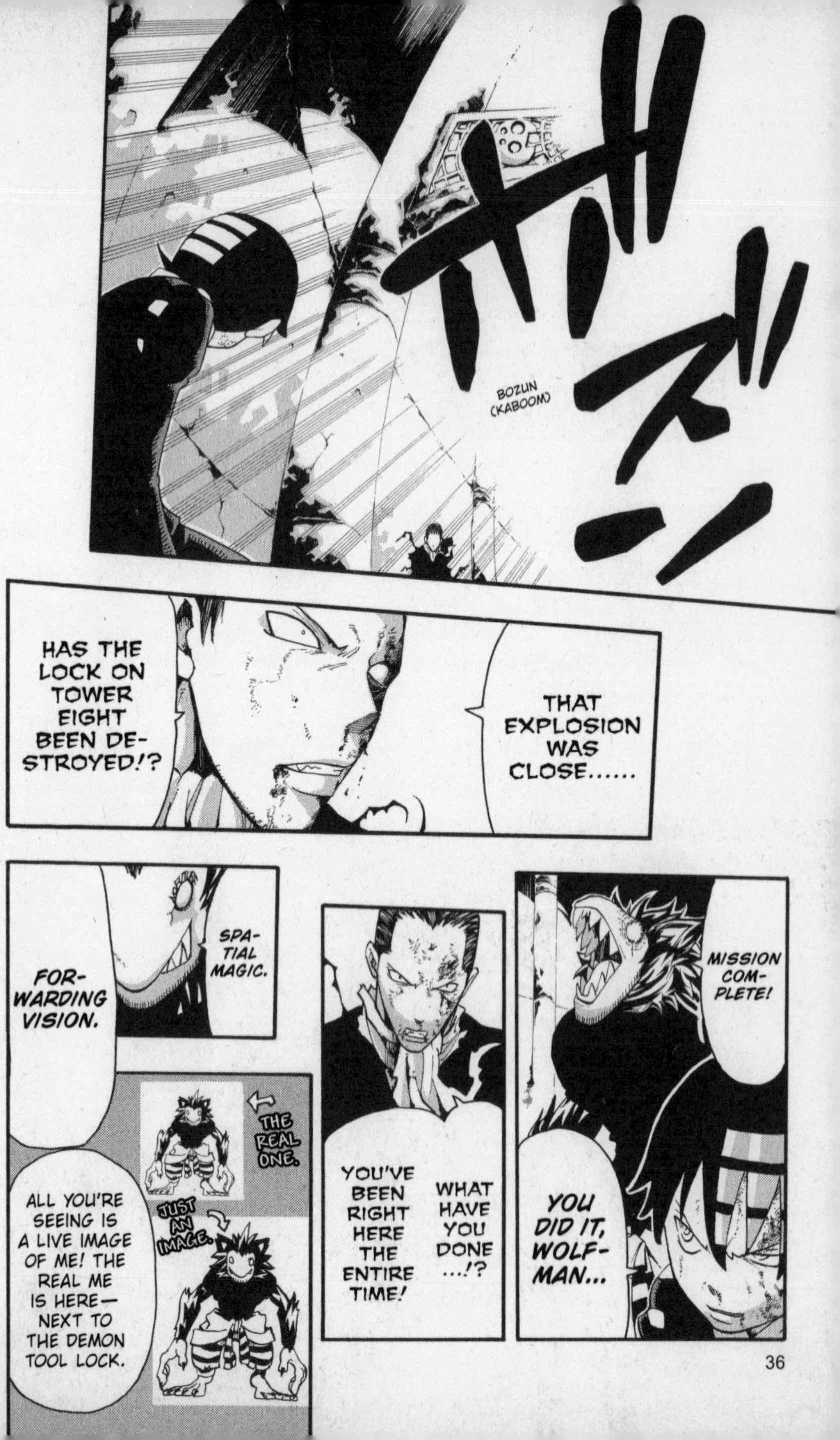

BOZUN (KABOOM)
HAS THE LOCK ON TOWER EIGHT BEEN DE-STROYED!?
THAT EXPLOSION WAS CLOSE......
MISSION COM-PLETE!
YOU DID IT, WOLF-MAN...
WHAT HAVE YOU DONE ...!?
YOU'VE BEEN RIGHT HERE THE ENTIRE TIME!
SPA-TIAL MAGIC.
FOR-WARDING VISION.
THE REAL ONE.
JUST AN IMAGE.
ALL YOU'RE SEEING IS A LIVE IMAGE OF ME! THE REAL ME IS HERE—NEXT TO THE DEMON TOOL LOCK.

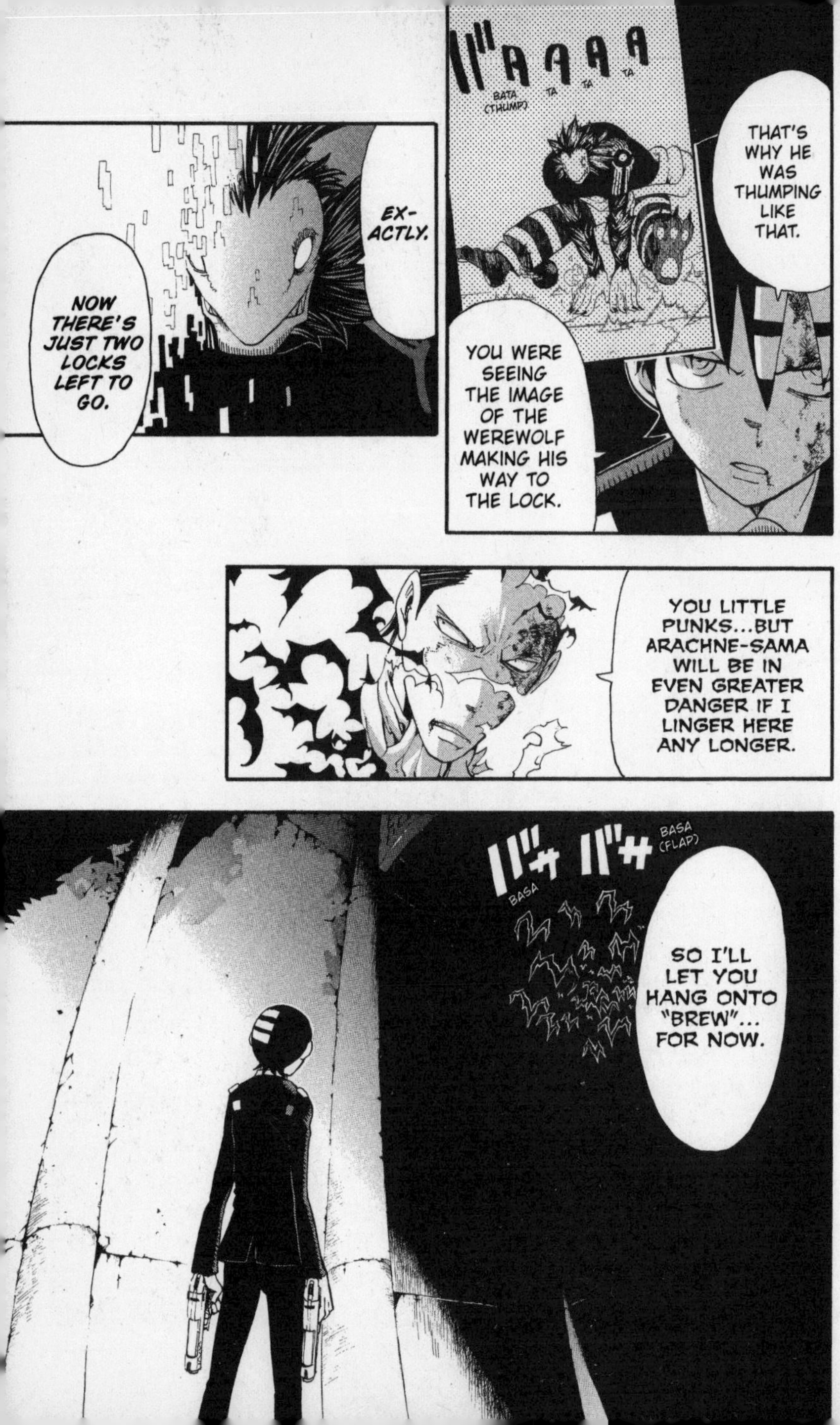
BATA (THUMP) TA TA TA
THAT'S WHY HE WAS THUMPING LIKE THAT.
YOU WERE SEEING THE IMAGE OF THE WEREWOLF MAKING HIS WAY TO THE LOCK.
EX-ACTLY.
NOW THERE'S JUST TWO LOCKS LEFT TO GO.
YOU LITTLE PUNKS...BUT ARACHNE-SAMA WILL BE IN EVEN GREATER DANGER IF I LINGER HERE ANY LONGER.
BASA (FLAP) BASA
SO I'LL LET YOU HANG ONTO "BREW"... FOR NOW.

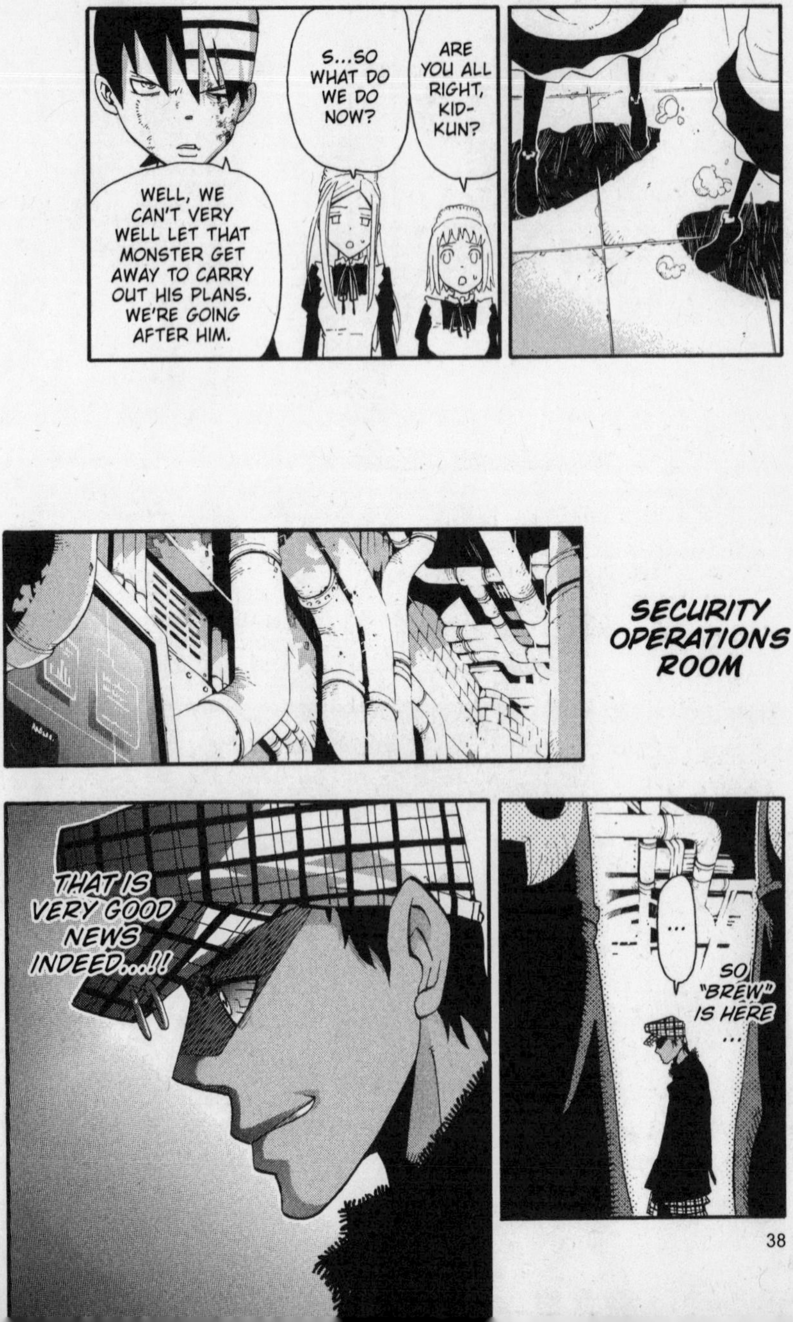
ARE YOU ALL RIGHT, KID-KUN?
S...SO WHAT DO WE DO NOW?
WELL, WE CAN'T VERY WELL LET THAT MONSTER GET AWAY TO CARRY OUT HIS PLANS. WE'RE GOING AFTER HIM.
SECURITY OPERATIONS ROOM
...
SO "BREW" IS HERE ...
THAT IS VERY GOOD NEWS INDEED...!!

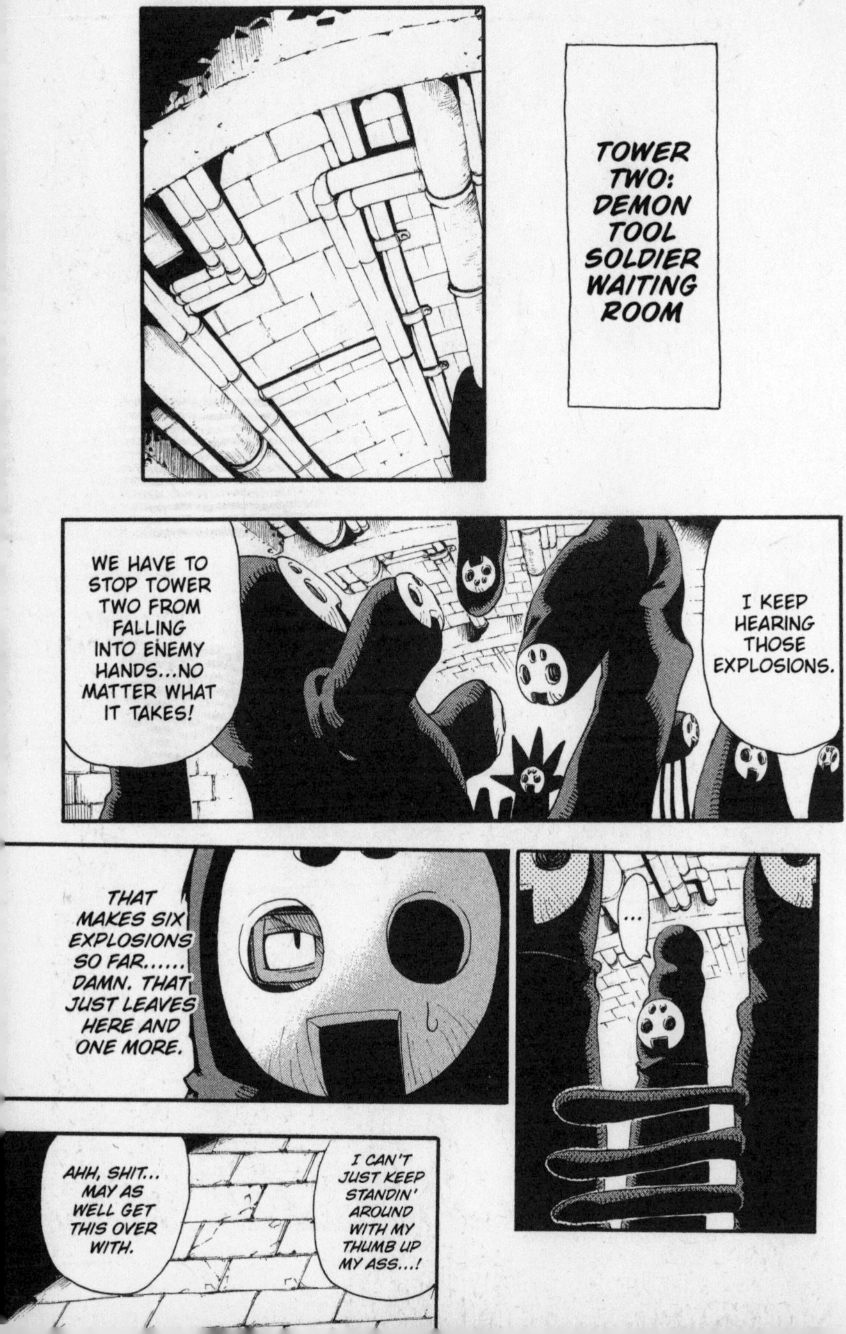
TOWER TWO: DEMON TOOL SOLDIER WAITING ROOM
I KEEP HEARING THOSE EXPLOSIONS.
WE HAVE TO STOP TOWER TWO FROM FALLING INTO ENEMY HANDS...NO MATTER WHAT IT TAKES!
...
THAT MAKES SIX EXPLOSIONS SO FAR...... DAMN. THAT JUST LEAVES HERE AND ONE MORE.
I CAN'T JUST KEEP STANDIN' AROUND WITH MY THUMB UP MY ASS...!
AHH, SHIT... MAY AS WELL GET THIS OVER WITH.

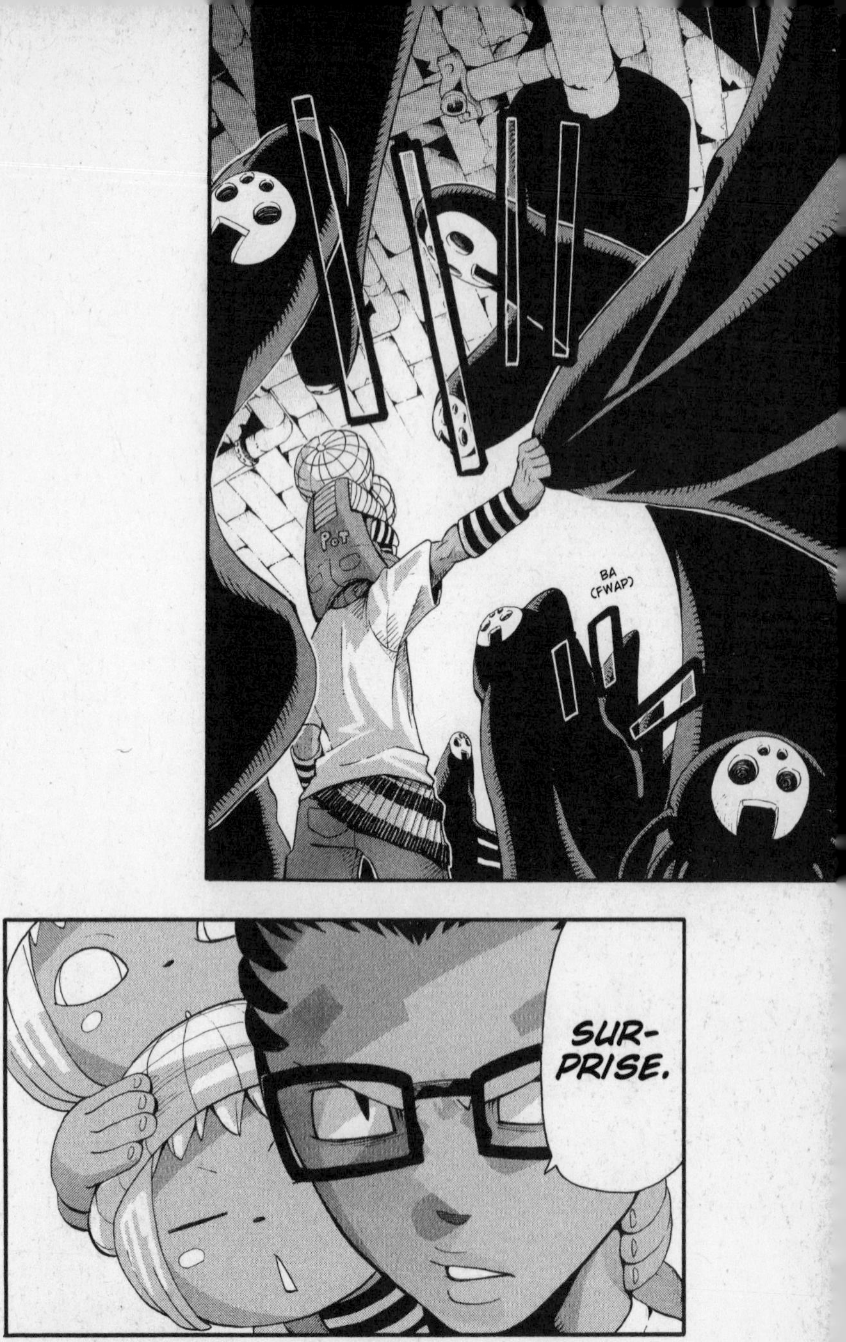
BA (FWAP)
SUR-PRISE.

SOUL EATER

CHAPTER 54: OPERATION CAPTURE BABA YAGA CASTLE (PART 9)

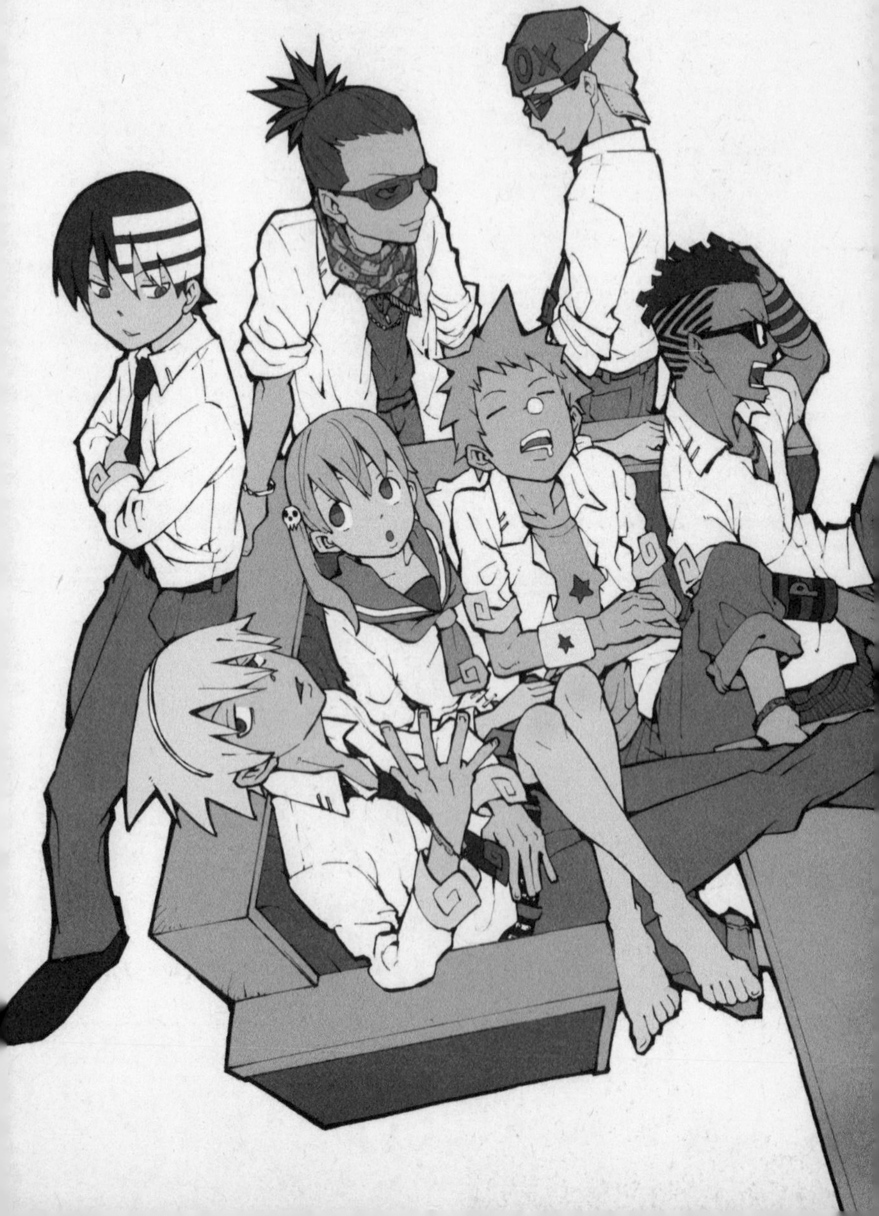
OX

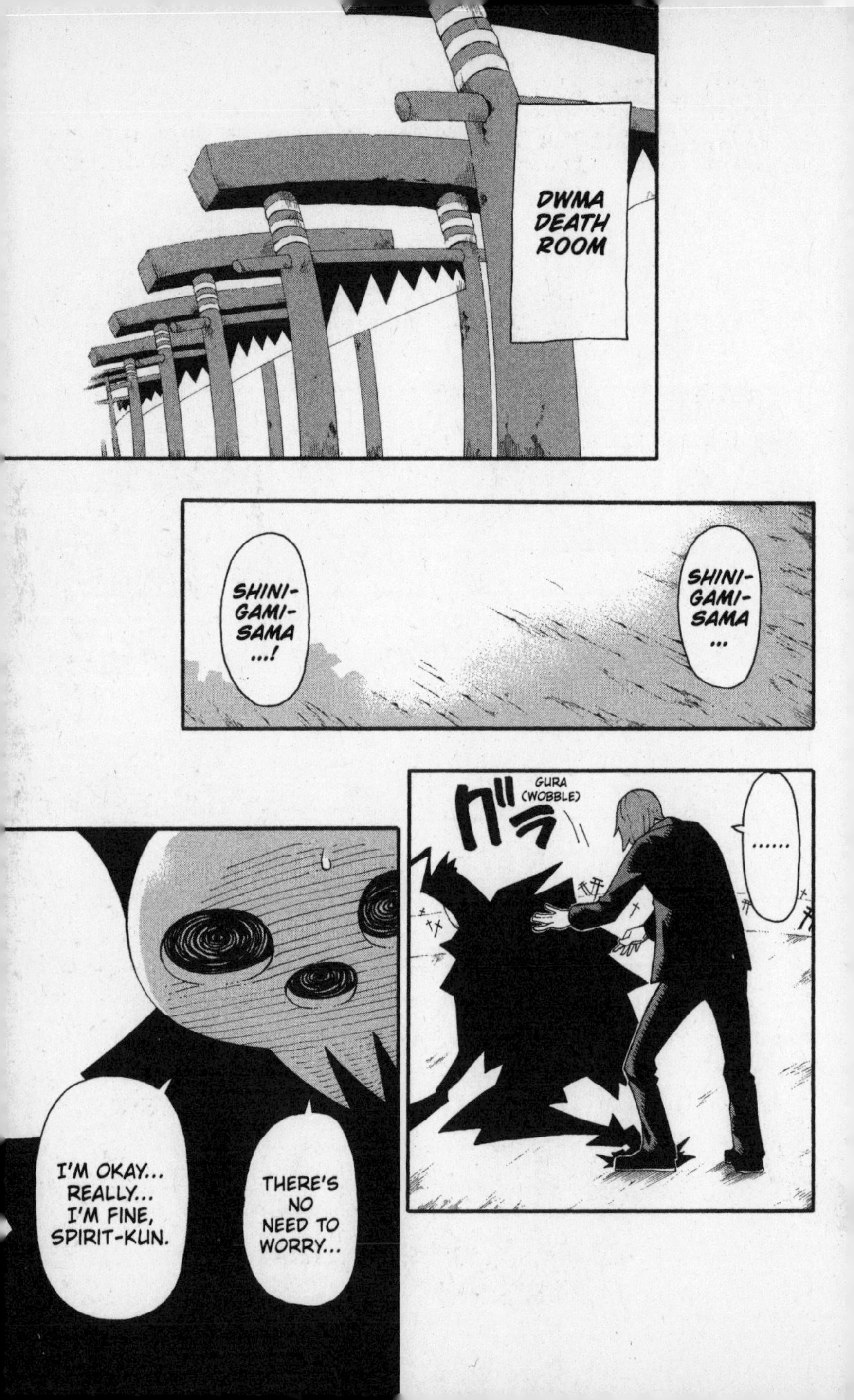
DWMA DEATH ROOM
SHINI-GAMI-SAMA ...
SHINI-GAMI-SAMA ...!
......
GURA (WOBBLE)
I'M OKAY... REALLY... I'M FINE, SPIRIT-KUN.
THERE'S NO NEED TO WORRY...

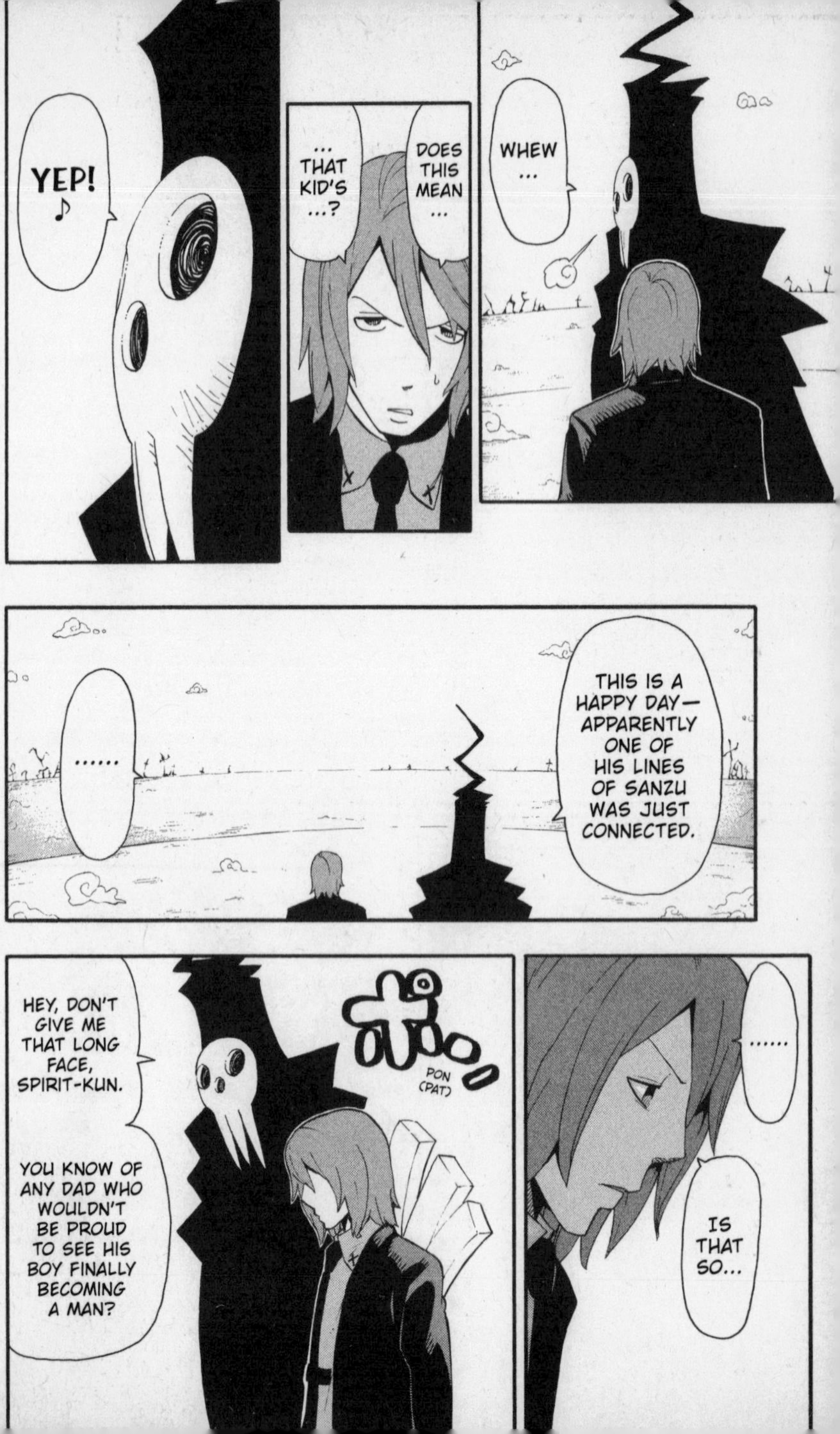
WHEW ...
DOES THIS MEAN ...
... THAT KID'S ...?
YEP! ♪
THIS IS A HAPPY DAY— APPARENTLY ONE OF HIS LINES OF SANZU WAS JUST CONNECTED.
......
......
IS THAT SO...
PON (PAT)
HEY, DON'T GIVE ME THAT LONG FACE, SPIRIT-KUN.
YOU KNOW OF ANY DAD WHO WOULDN'T BE PROUD TO SEE HIS BOY FINALLY BECOMING A MAN?

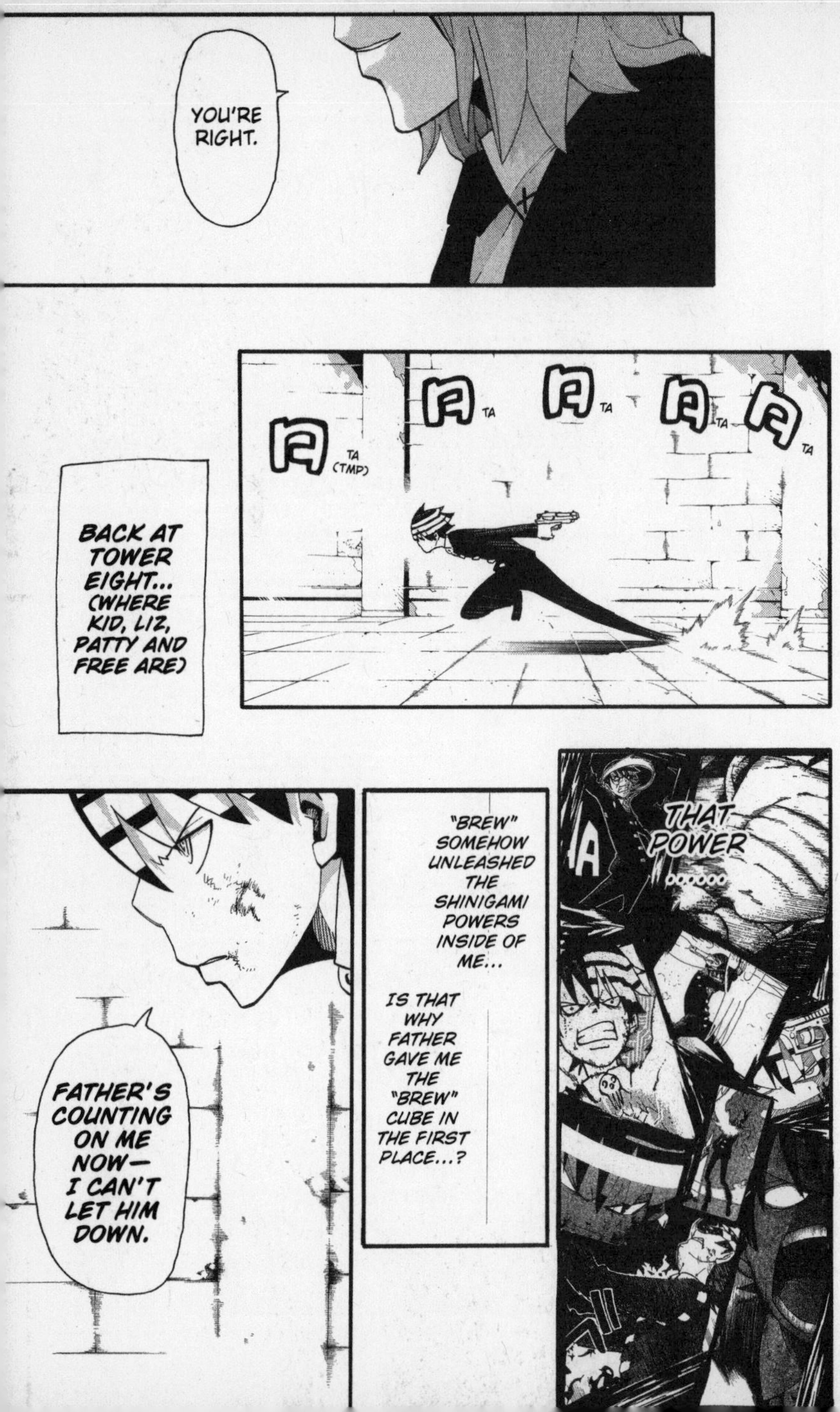
YOU'RE RIGHT.
TA TA TA TA TA (TMP)
BACK AT TOWER EIGHT... (WHERE KID, LIZ, PATTY AND FREE ARE)
THAT POWER ......
"BREW" SOMEHOW UNLEASHED THE SHINIGAMI POWERS INSIDE OF ME...
IS THAT WHY FATHER GAVE ME THE "BREW" CUBE IN THE FIRST PLACE...?
FATHER'S COUNTING ON ME NOW— I CAN'T LET HIM DOWN.

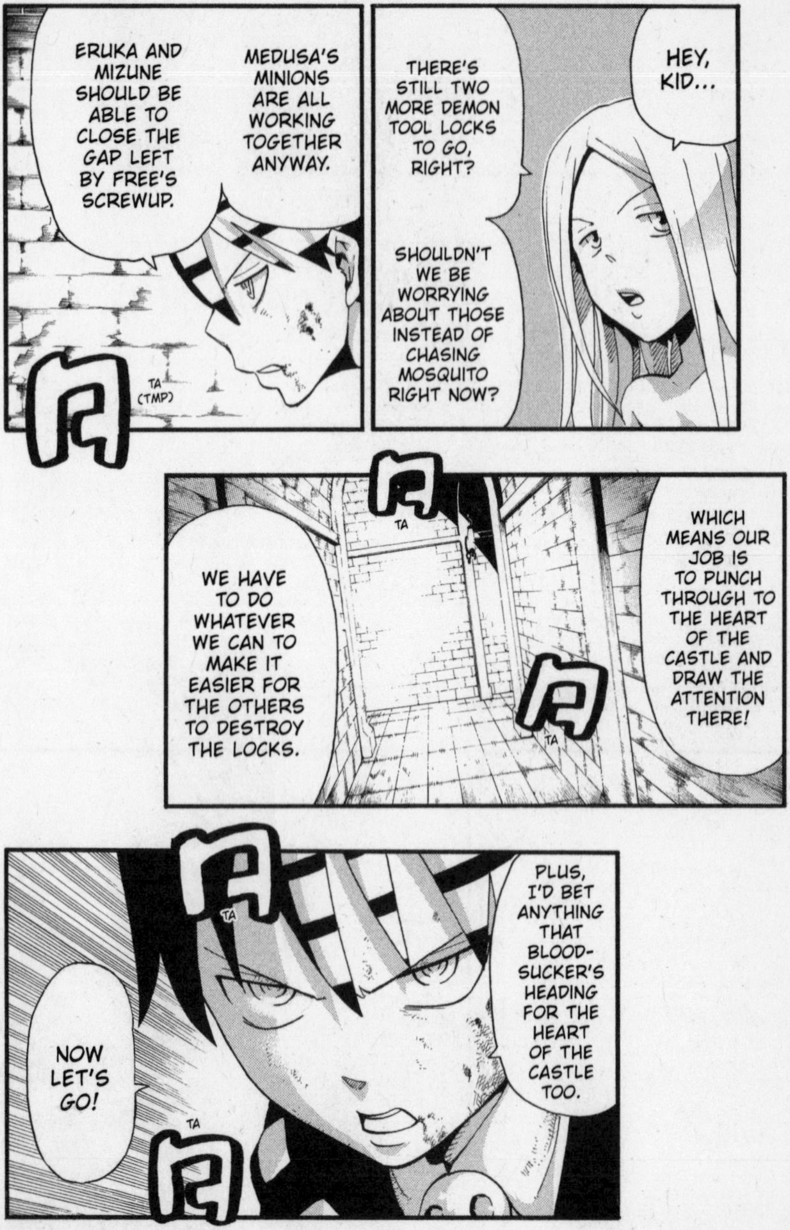
HEY, KID...
THERE'S STILL TWO MORE DEMON TOOL LOCKS TO GO, RIGHT?
SHOULDN'T WE BE WORRYING ABOUT THOSE INSTEAD OF CHASING MOSQUITO RIGHT NOW?
MEDUSA'S MINIONS ARE ALL WORKING TOGETHER ANYWAY.
ERUKA AND MIZUNE SHOULD BE ABLE TO CLOSE THE GAP LEFT BY FREE'S SCREWUP.
TA (TMP)
TA
WHICH MEANS OUR JOB IS TO PUNCH THROUGH TO THE HEART OF THE CASTLE AND DRAW THE ATTENTION THERE!
TA
WE HAVE TO DO WHATEVER WE CAN TO MAKE IT EASIER FOR THE OTHERS TO DESTROY THE LOCKS.
PLUS, I'D BET ANYTHING THAT BLOOD-SUCKER'S HEADING FOR THE HEART OF THE CASTLE TOO.
TA
NOW LET'S GO!
TA

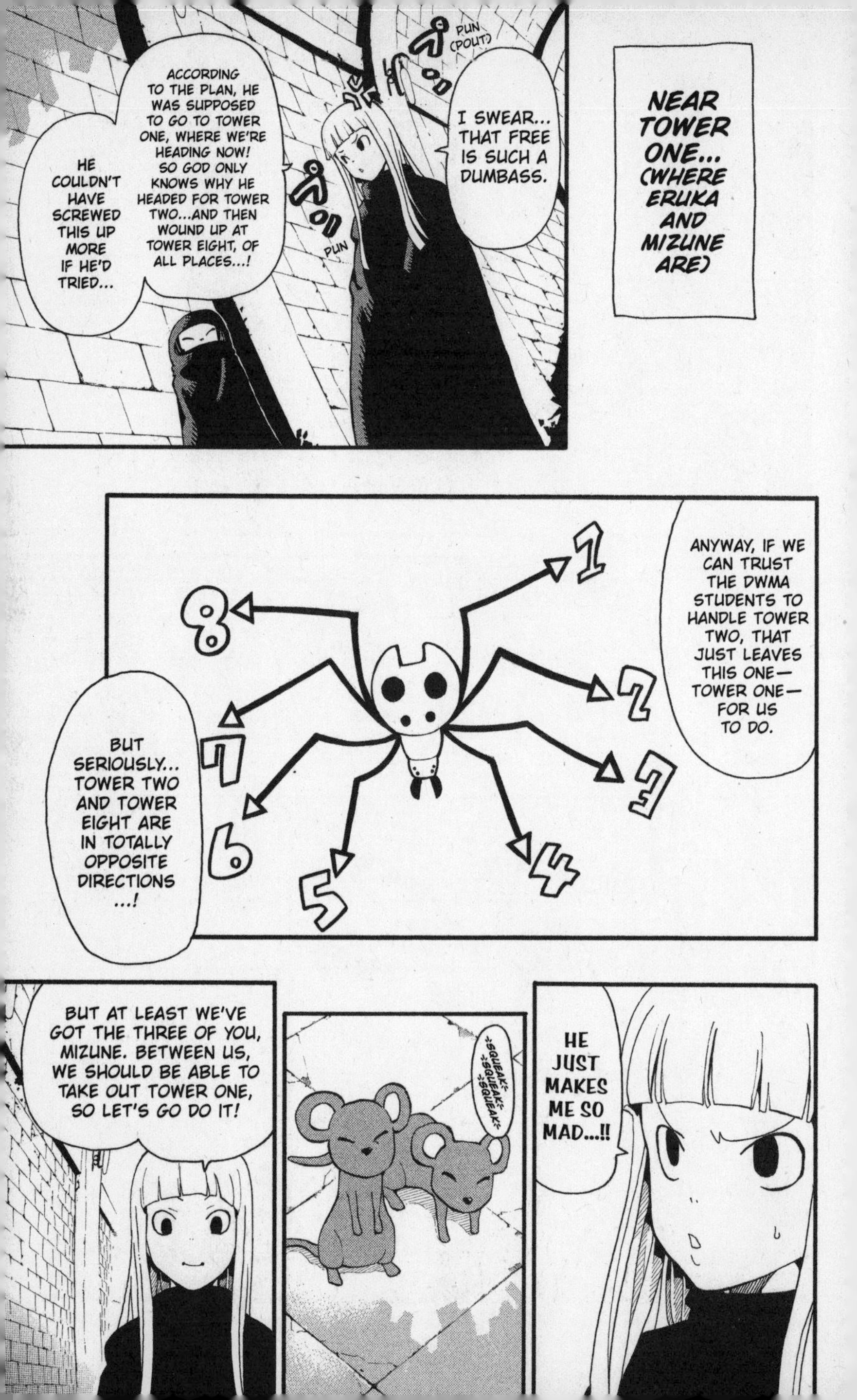
NEAR TOWER ONE... (WHERE ERUKA AND MIZUNE ARE)
PUN (POUT)
I SWEAR... THAT FREE IS SUCH A DUMBASS.
PUN
ACCORDING TO THE PLAN, HE WAS SUPPOSED TO GO TO TOWER ONE, WHERE WE'RE HEADING NOW! SO GOD ONLY KNOWS WHY HE HEADED FOR TOWER TWO...AND THEN WOUND UP AT TOWER EIGHT, OF ALL PLACES...!
HE COULDN'T HAVE SCREWED THIS UP MORE IF HE'D TRIED...
ANYWAY, IF WE CAN TRUST THE DWMA STUDENTS TO HANDLE TOWER TWO, THAT JUST LEAVES THIS ONE—TOWER ONE—FOR US TO DO.
BUT SERIOUSLY... TOWER TWO AND TOWER EIGHT ARE IN TOTALLY OPPOSITE DIRECTIONS ...!
HE JUST MAKES ME SO MAD...!!
~SQUEAK~ ~SQUEAK~ ~SQUEAK~
BUT AT LEAST WE'VE GOT THE THREE OF YOU, MIZUNE. BETWEEN US, WE SHOULD BE ABLE TO TAKE OUT TOWER ONE, SO LET'S GO DO IT!

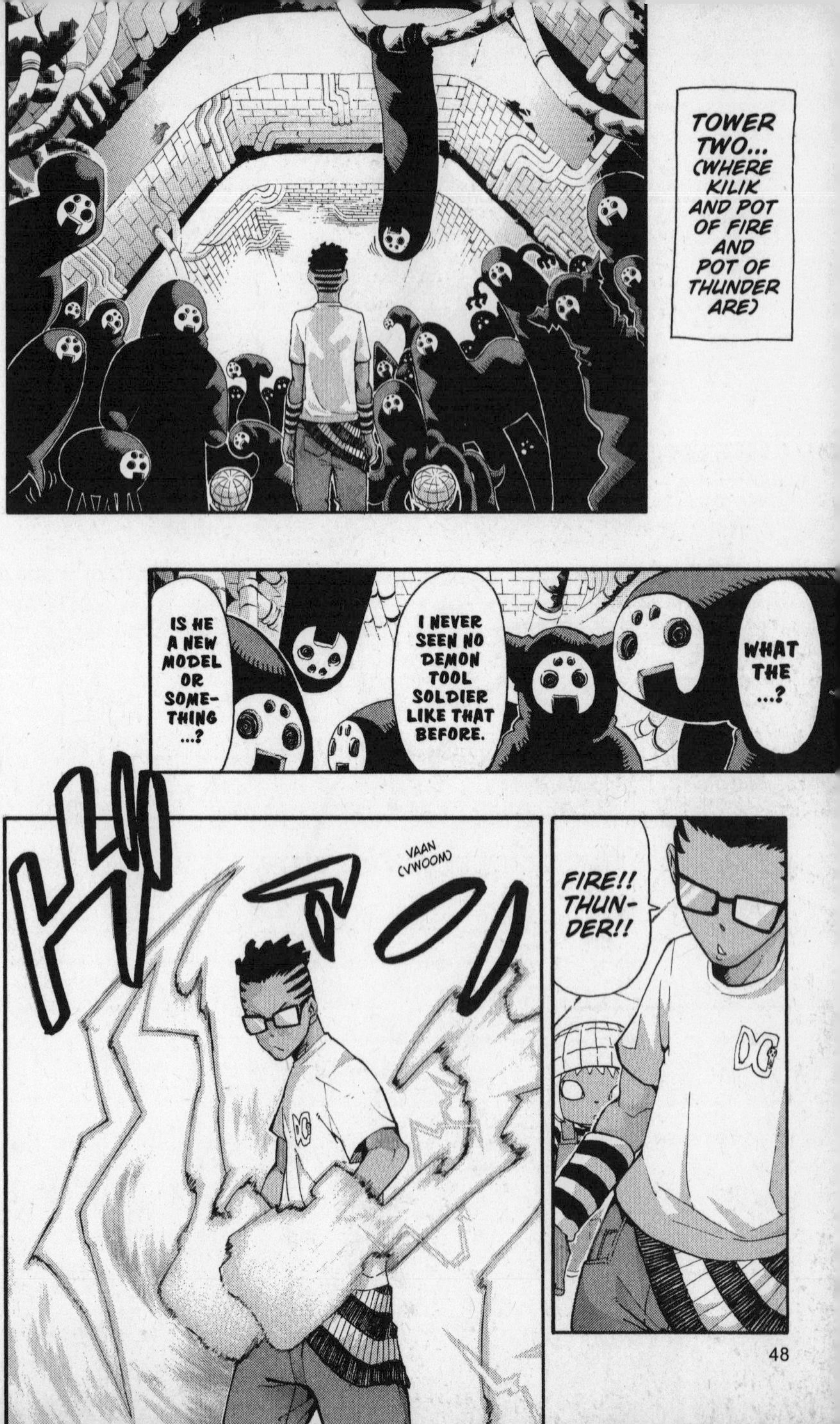
TOWER TWO... (WHERE KILIK AND POT OF FIRE AND POT OF THUNDER ARE)
WHAT THE ...?
I NEVER SEEN NO DEMON TOOL SOLDIER LIKE THAT BEFORE.
IS HE A NEW MODEL OR SOME-THING ...?
FIRE!! THUN-DER!!
VAAN (VWOOM)

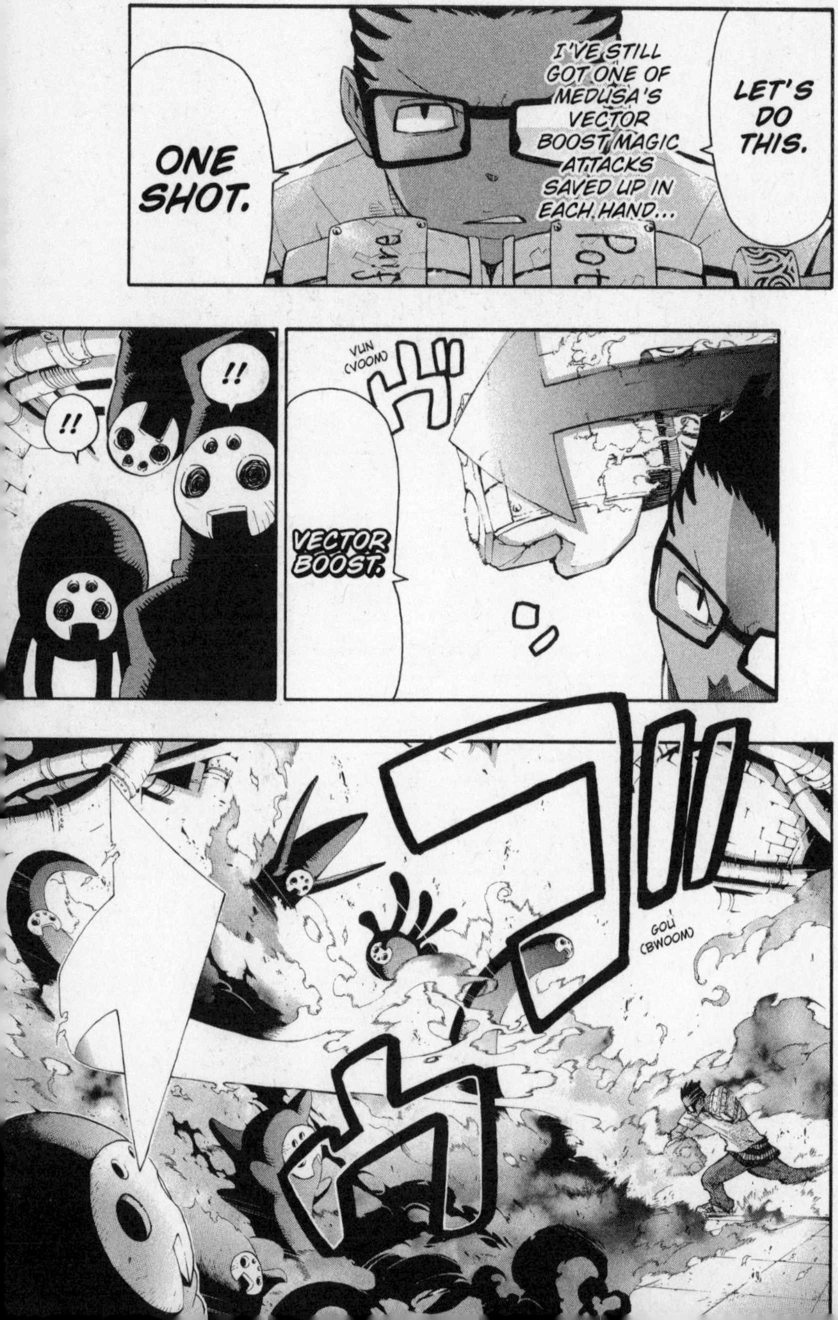
LET'S DO THIS.
I'VE STILL GOT ONE OF MEDUSA'S VECTOR BOOST MAGIC ATTACKS SAVED UP IN EACH HAND...
ONE SHOT.
VUN (VOOM)
VECTOR BOOST.
!!
!!
GOU (BWOOM)

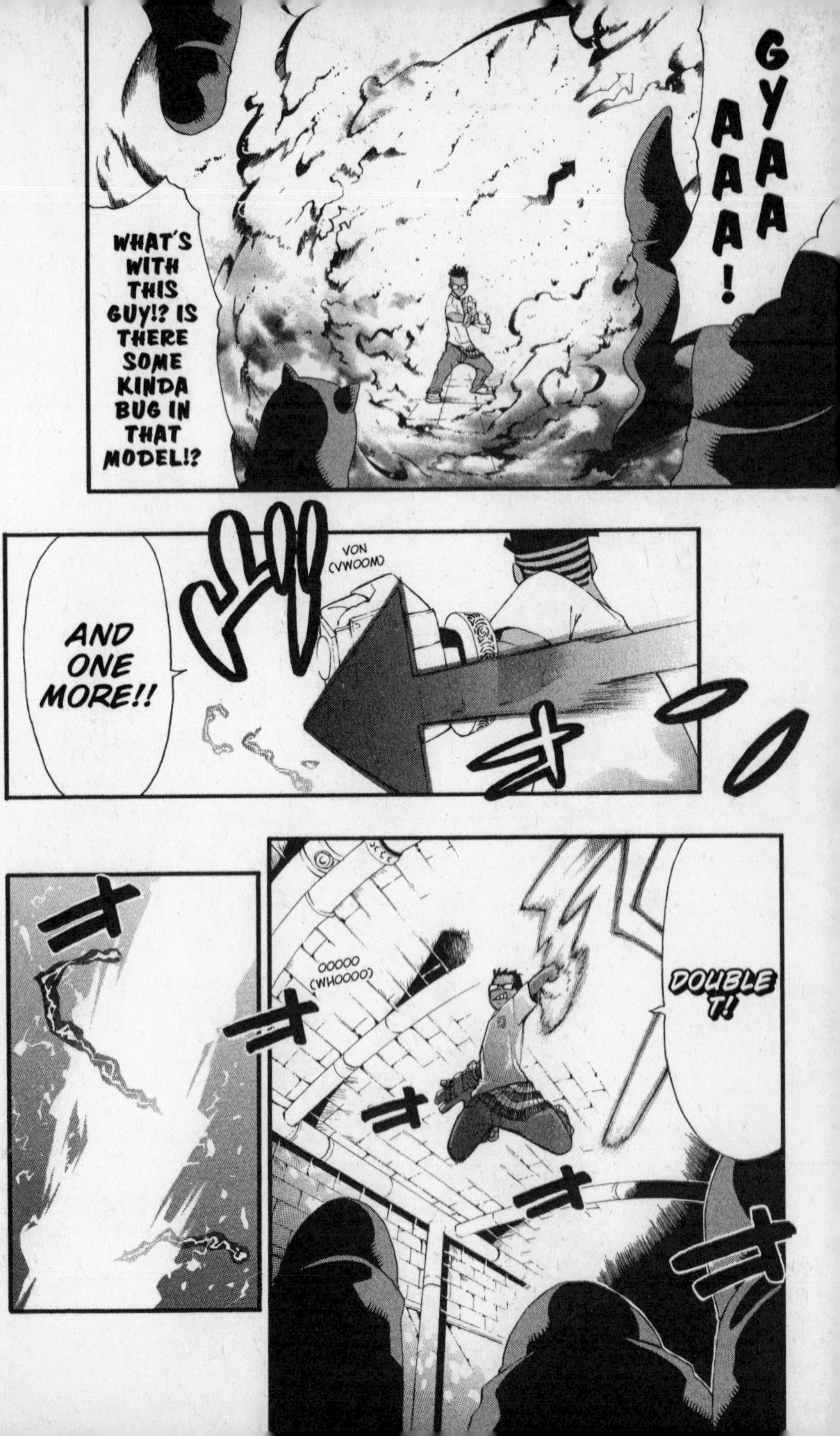
GYAAAAA!
WHAT'S WITH THIS GUY!? IS THERE SOME KINDA BUG IN THAT MODEL!?
VON (VWOOM)
AND ONE MORE!!
DOUBLE T!
OOOOO (WHOOOO)

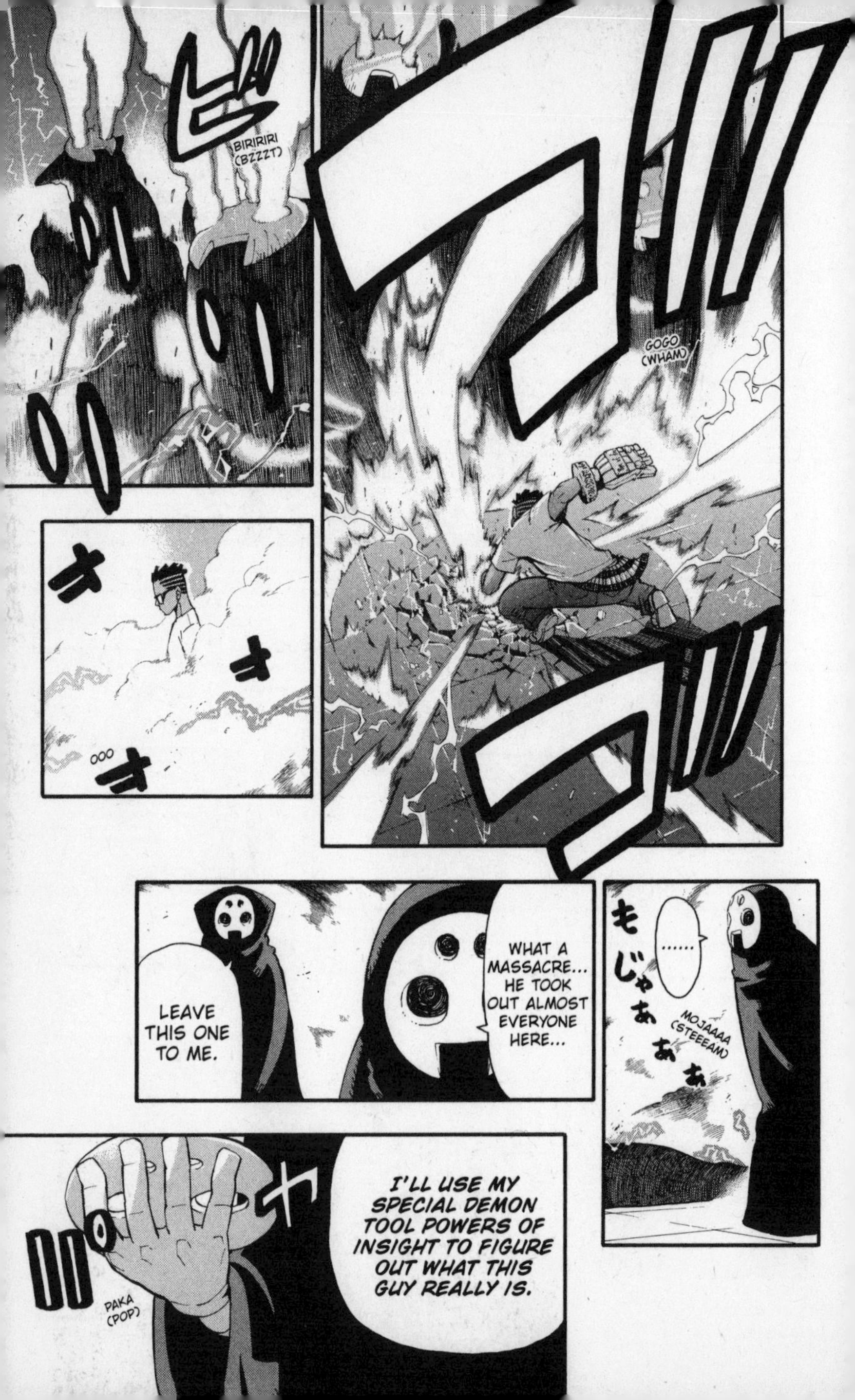
GOGO (WHAM)
BIRIRIRI (BZZZT)
OOO
もじゃあああ
MOJAAAA (STEEEAM)
......
WHAT A MASSACRE... HE TOOK OUT ALMOST EVERYONE HERE...
LEAVE THIS ONE TO ME.
I'LL USE MY SPECIAL DEMON TOOL POWERS OF INSIGHT TO FIGURE OUT WHAT THIS GUY REALLY IS.
PAKA (POP)

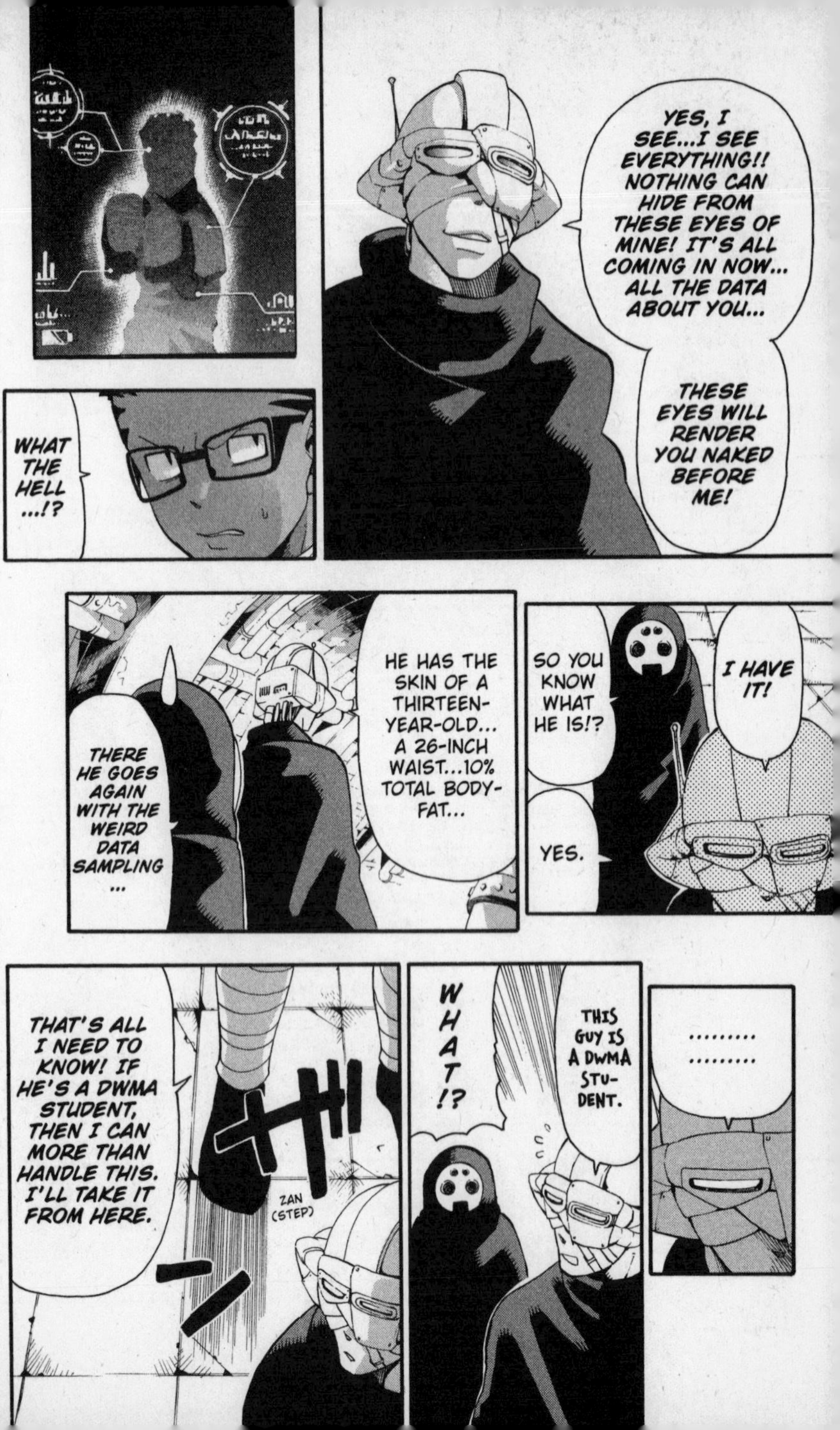
YES, I SEE...I SEE EVERYTHING!! NOTHING CAN HIDE FROM THESE EYES OF MINE! IT'S ALL COMING IN NOW... ALL THE DATA ABOUT YOU...
THESE EYES WILL RENDER YOU NAKED BEFORE ME!
WHAT THE HELL ...!?
I HAVE IT!
SO YOU KNOW WHAT HE IS!?
YES.
HE HAS THE SKIN OF A THIRTEEN-YEAR-OLD... A 26-INCH WAIST...10% TOTAL BODY-FAT...
THERE HE GOES AGAIN WITH THE WEIRD DATA SAMPLING ...
....
....
THIS GUY IS A DWMA STU-DENT.
WHAT !?
THAT'S ALL I NEED TO KNOW! IF HE'S A DWMA STUDENT, THEN I CAN MORE THAN HANDLE THIS. I'LL TAKE IT FROM HERE.
ZAN (STEP)

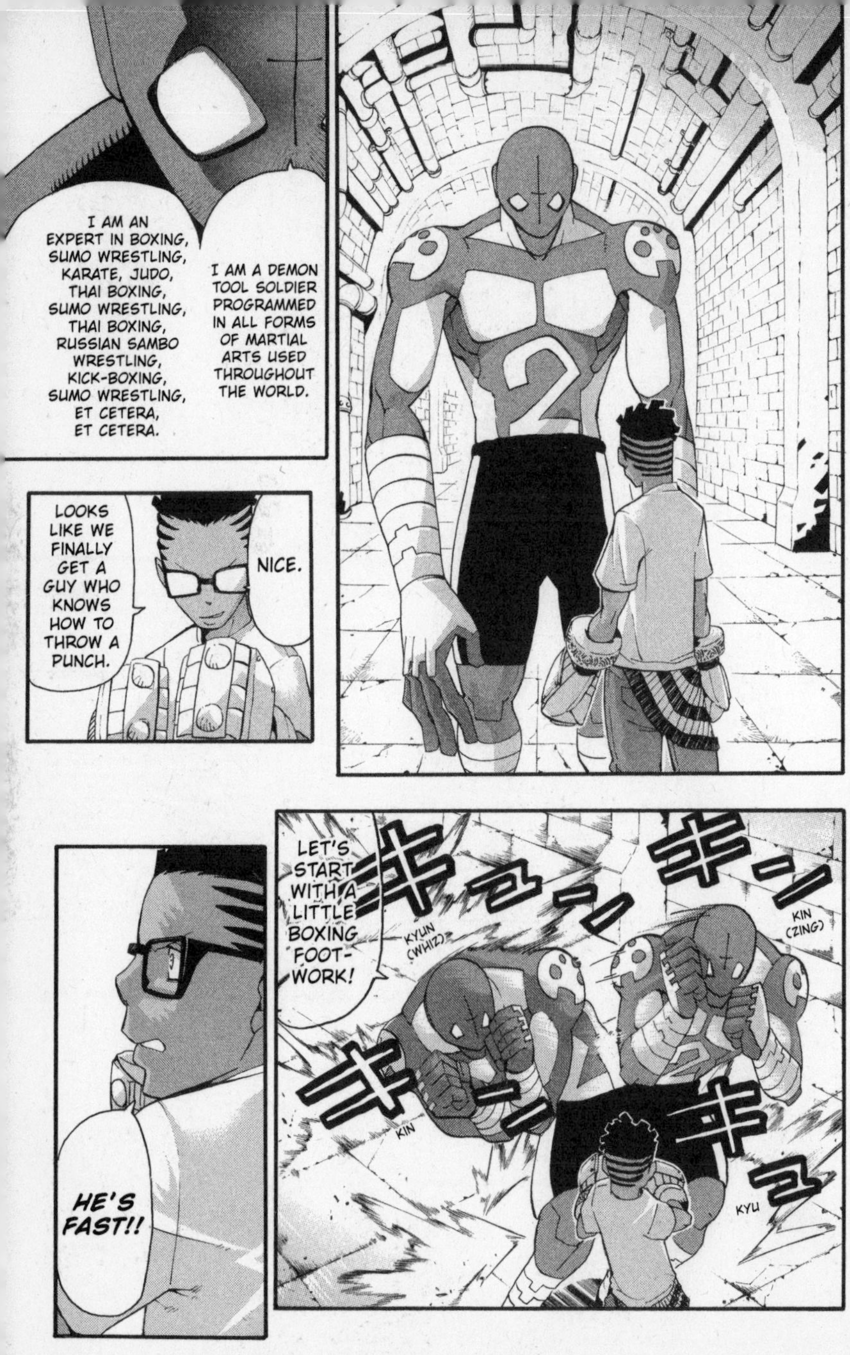
I AM AN EXPERT IN BOXING, SUMO WRESTLING, KARATE, JUDO, THAI BOXING, SUMO WRESTLING, THAI BOXING, RUSSIAN SAMBO WRESTLING, KICK-BOXING, SUMO WRESTLING, ET CETERA, ET CETERA.
I AM A DEMON TOOL SOLDIER PROGRAMMED IN ALL FORMS OF MARTIAL ARTS USED THROUGHOUT THE WORLD.
NICE.
LOOKS LIKE WE FINALLY GET A GUY WHO KNOWS HOW TO THROW A PUNCH.
LET'S START WITH A LITTLE BOXING FOOT-WORK!
KIN (ZING)
KYUN (WHIZ)
KIN
KYU
HE'S FAST!!

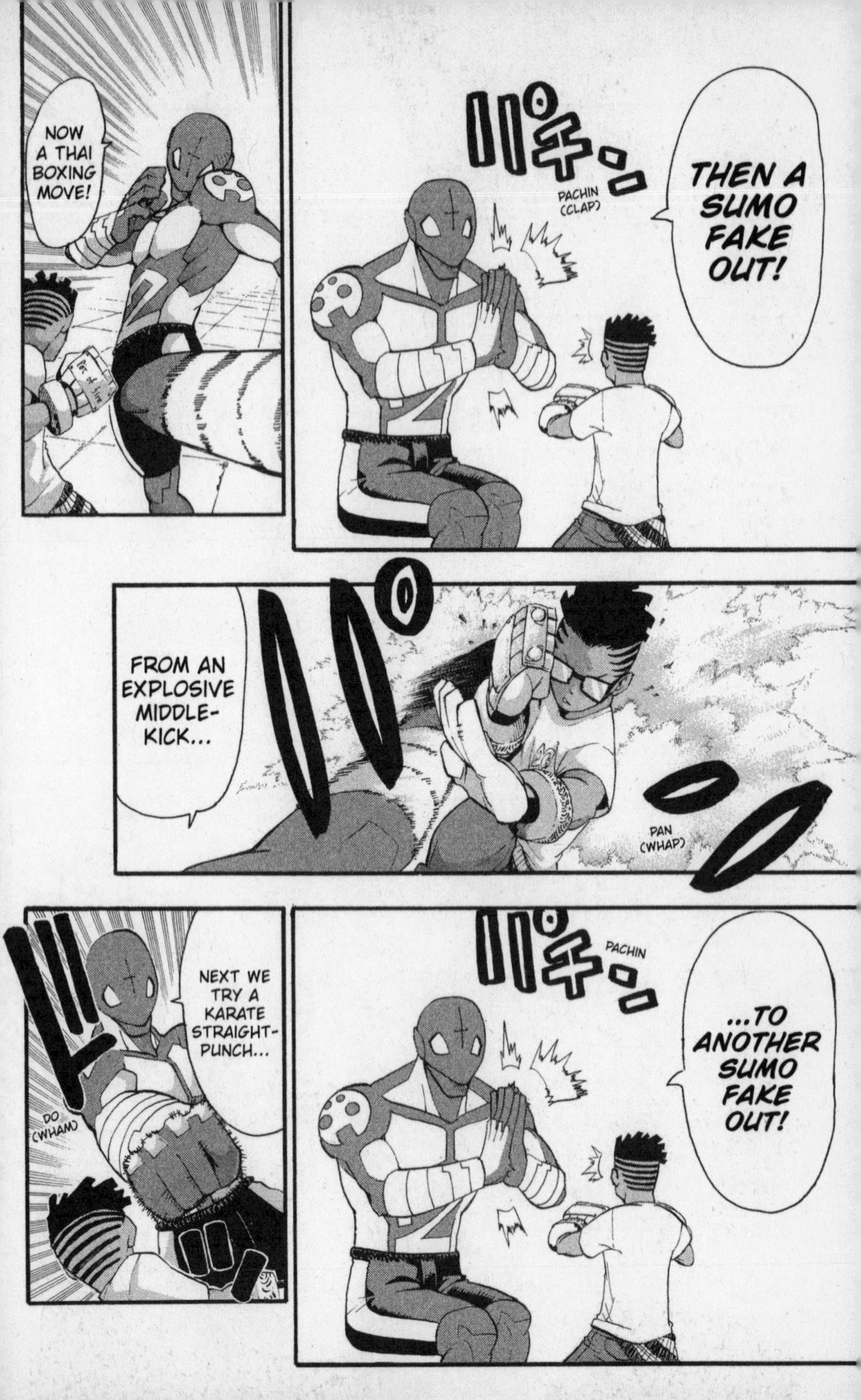
PACHIN
THEN A SUMO FAKE OUT!
PACHIN (CLAP)
NOW A THAI BOXING MOVE!
FROM AN EXPLOSIVE MIDDLE-KICK...
PAN (WHAP)
PACHIN
...TO ANOTHER SUMO FAKE OUT!
NEXT WE TRY A KARATE STRAIGHT-PUNCH...
DO (WHAM)

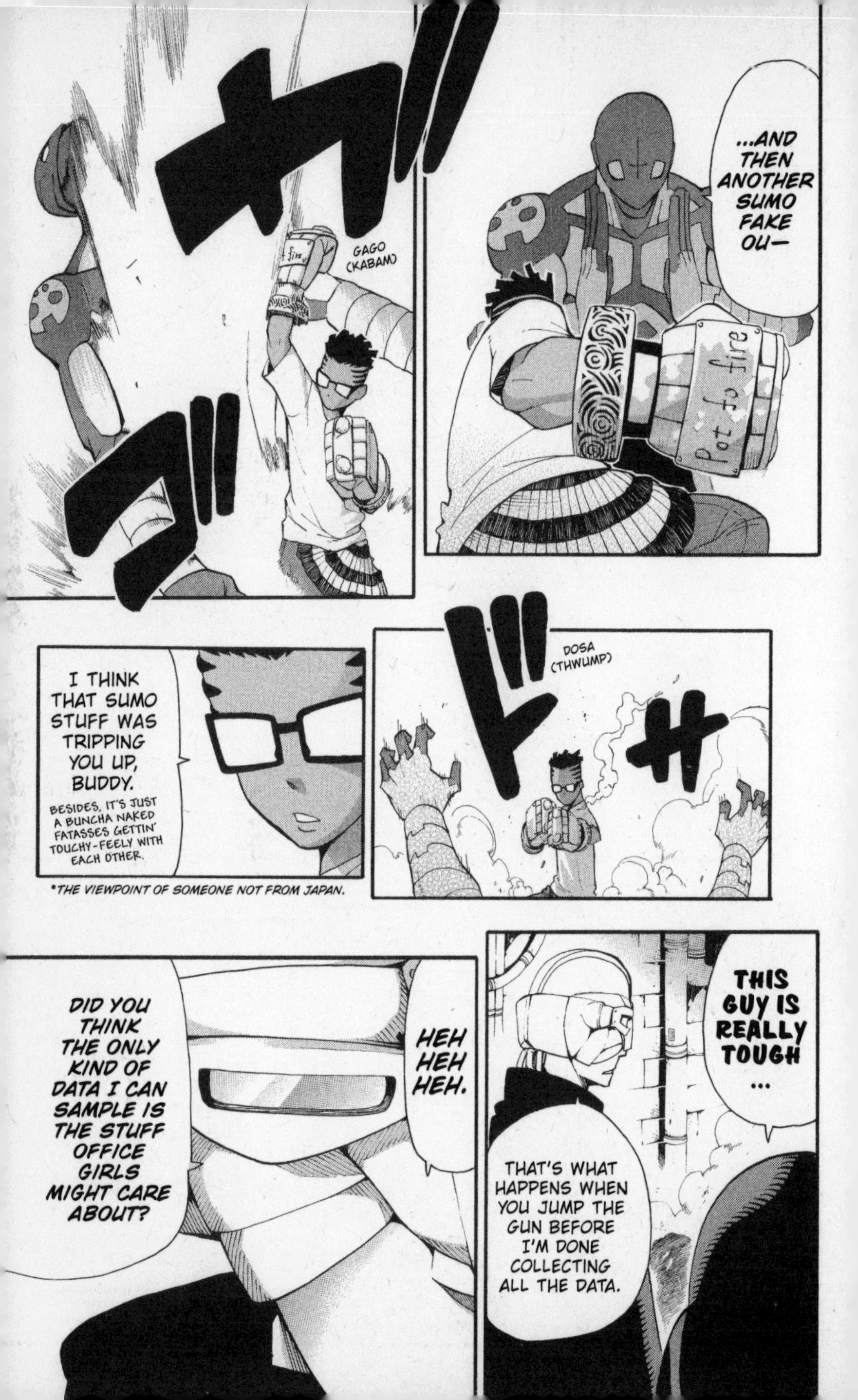

...AND THEN ANOTHER SUMO FAKE OU—
GAGO (KABAM)
DOSA (THWUMP)
I THINK THAT SUMO STUFF WAS TRIPPING YOU UP, BUDDY.
BESIDES, IT'S JUST A BUNCHA NAKED FATASSES GETTIN' TOUCHY-FEELY WITH EACH OTHER.
*THE VIEWPOINT OF SOMEONE NOT FROM JAPAN.
THIS GUY IS REALLY TOUGH...
THAT'S WHAT HAPPENS WHEN YOU JUMP THE GUN BEFORE I'M DONE COLLECTING ALL THE DATA.
HEH HEH HEH.
DID YOU THINK THE ONLY KIND OF DATA I CAN SAMPLE IS THE STUFF OFFICE GIRLS MIGHT CARE ABOUT?

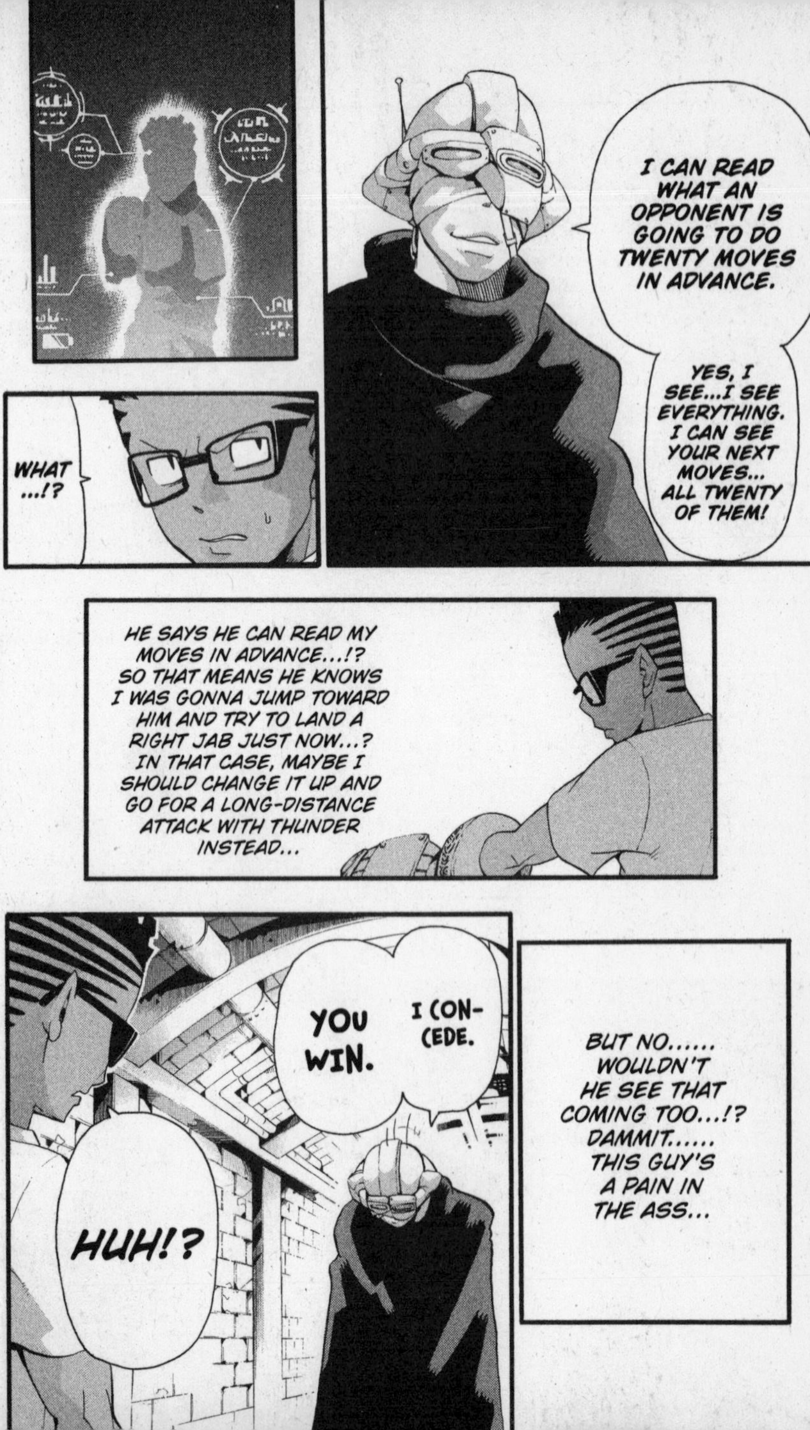
I CAN READ WHAT AN OPPONENT IS GOING TO DO TWENTY MOVES IN ADVANCE.
YES, I SEE...I SEE EVERYTHING. I CAN SEE YOUR NEXT MOVES... ALL TWENTY OF THEM!
WHAT ...!?
HE SAYS HE CAN READ MY MOVES IN ADVANCE...!? SO THAT MEANS HE KNOWS I WAS GONNA JUMP TOWARD HIM AND TRY TO LAND A RIGHT JAB JUST NOW...? IN THAT CASE, MAYBE I SHOULD CHANGE IT UP AND GO FOR A LONG-DISTANCE ATTACK WITH THUNDER INSTEAD...
BUT NO...... WOULDN'T HE SEE THAT COMING TOO...!? DAMMIT...... THIS GUY'S A PAIN IN THE ASS...
I CON-CEDE.
YOU WIN.
HUH!?

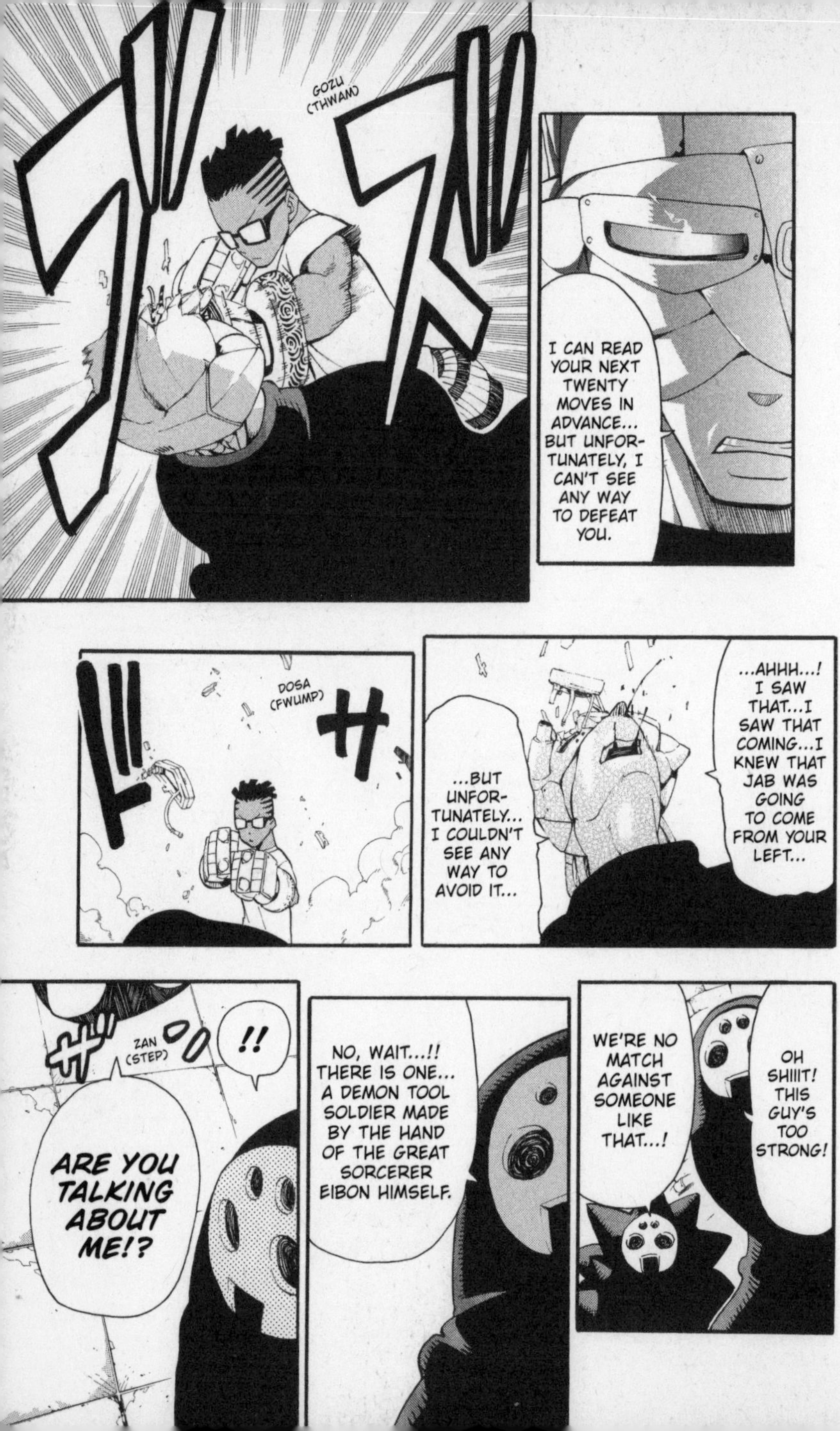
I CAN READ YOUR NEXT TWENTY MOVES IN ADVANCE... BUT UNFORTUNATELY, I CAN'T SEE ANY WAY TO DEFEAT YOU.
GOZU (THWAM)
...AHHH...! I SAW THAT...I SAW THAT COMING...I KNEW THAT JAB WAS GOING TO COME FROM YOUR LEFT...
...BUT UNFORTUNATELY... I COULDN'T SEE ANY WAY TO AVOID IT...
DOSA (FWUMP)
OH SHIIIT! THIS GUY'S TOO STRONG!
WE'RE NO MATCH AGAINST SOMEONE LIKE THAT...!
NO, WAIT...!! THERE IS ONE... A DEMON TOOL SOLDIER MADE BY THE HAND OF THE GREAT SORCERER EIBON HIMSELF.
!!
ZAN (STEP)
ARE YOU TALKING ABOUT ME!?

DEMON TOOL SOLDIER MORUBI
......
YEP. I'M THE TOY DEMON TOOL SOLDIER MORUBI.
YOU... YOU'RE THE...!?
POCHI (CLICK)
PAN (BANG)
PON (BONG)
ZUDON (STOMP)
GASHAN (CLAN)
BABAAAN (DADUUUM)
....
....
HEY!!
WAAH!
WHEE!

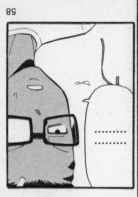

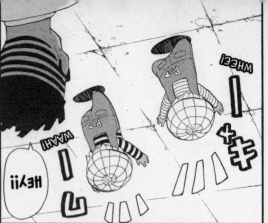

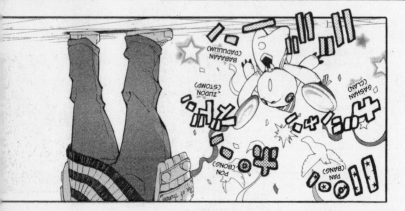

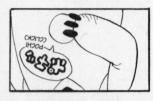

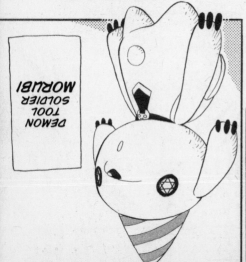

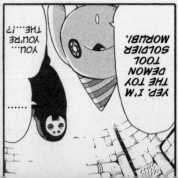

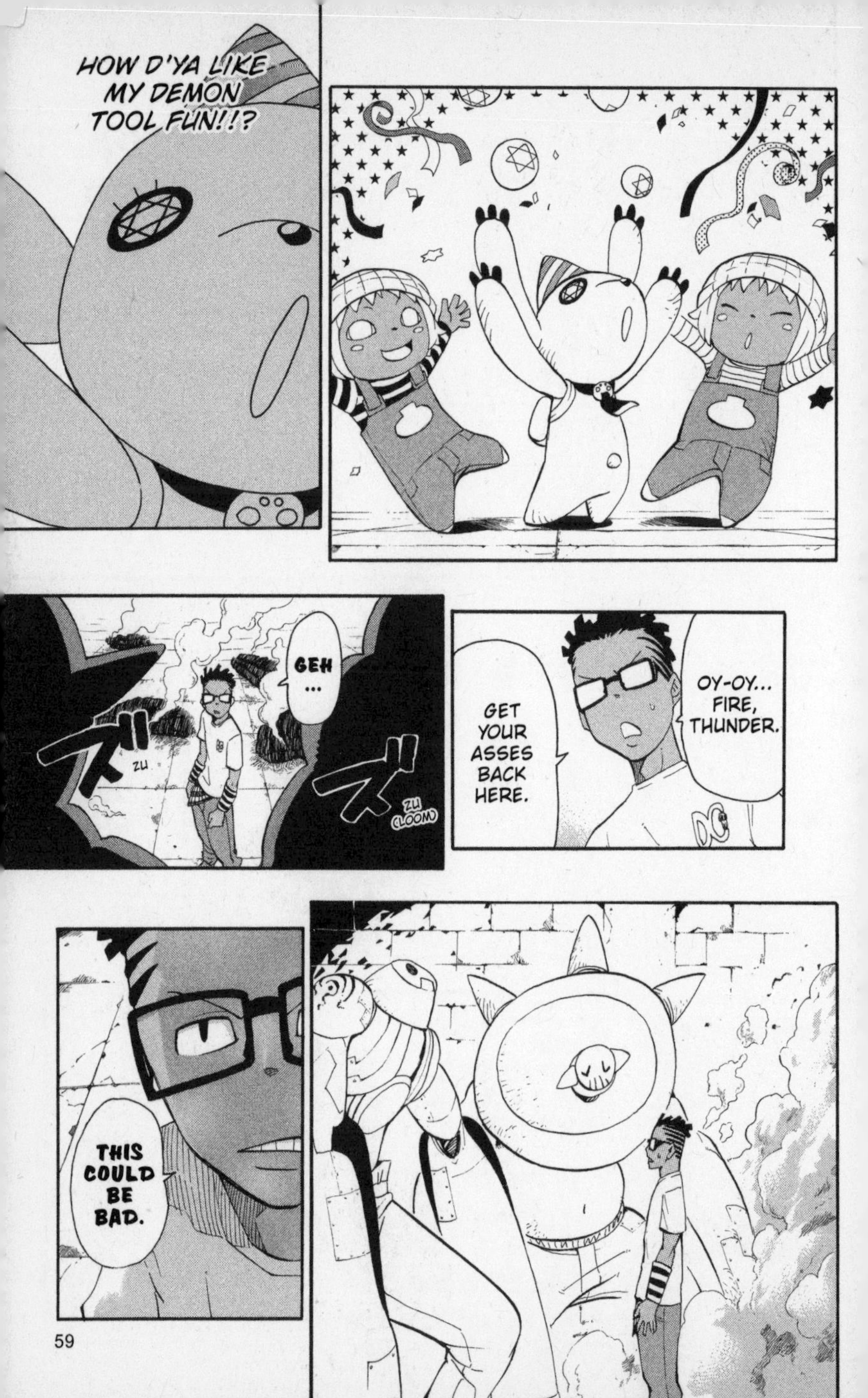
HOW D'YA LIKE MY DEMON TOOL FUN!!?
OY-OY... FIRE, THUNDER.
GET YOUR ASSES BACK HERE.
GEH ...
ZU
ZU (LOOM)
THIS COULD BE BAD.

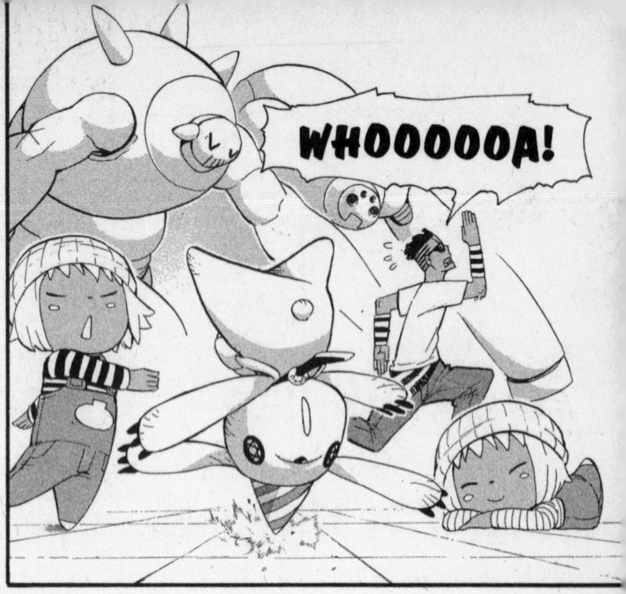
WHOOOOOA!

TOWER ONE

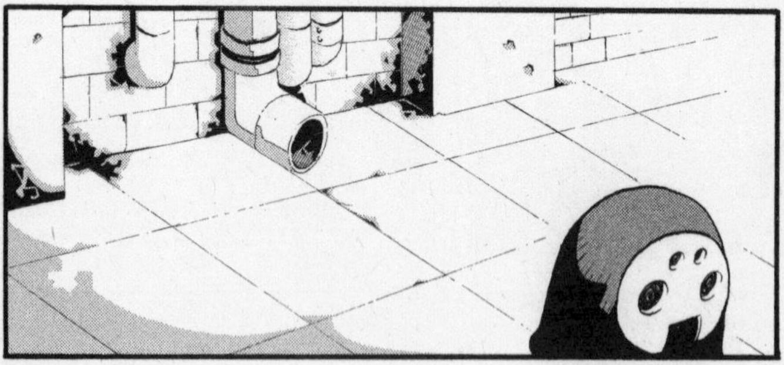

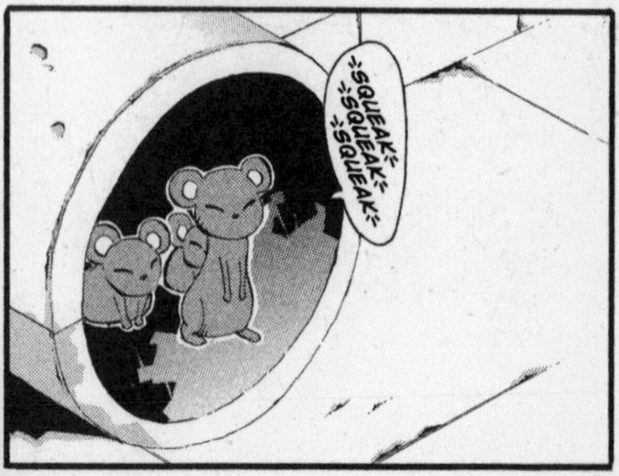
SQUEAK SQUEAK SQUEAK

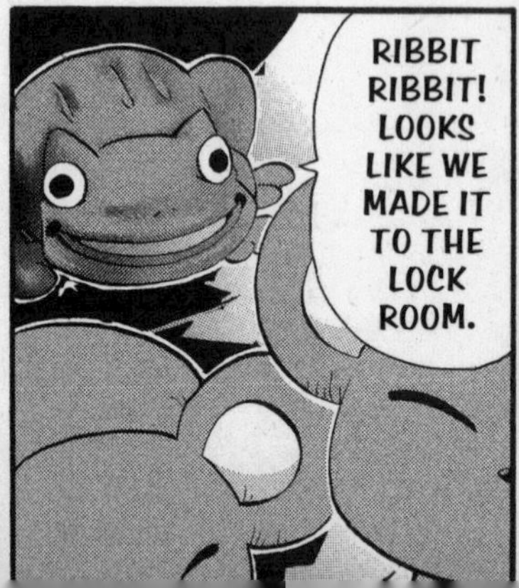
RIBBIT RIBBIT! LOOKS LIKE WE MADE IT TO THE LOCK ROOM.

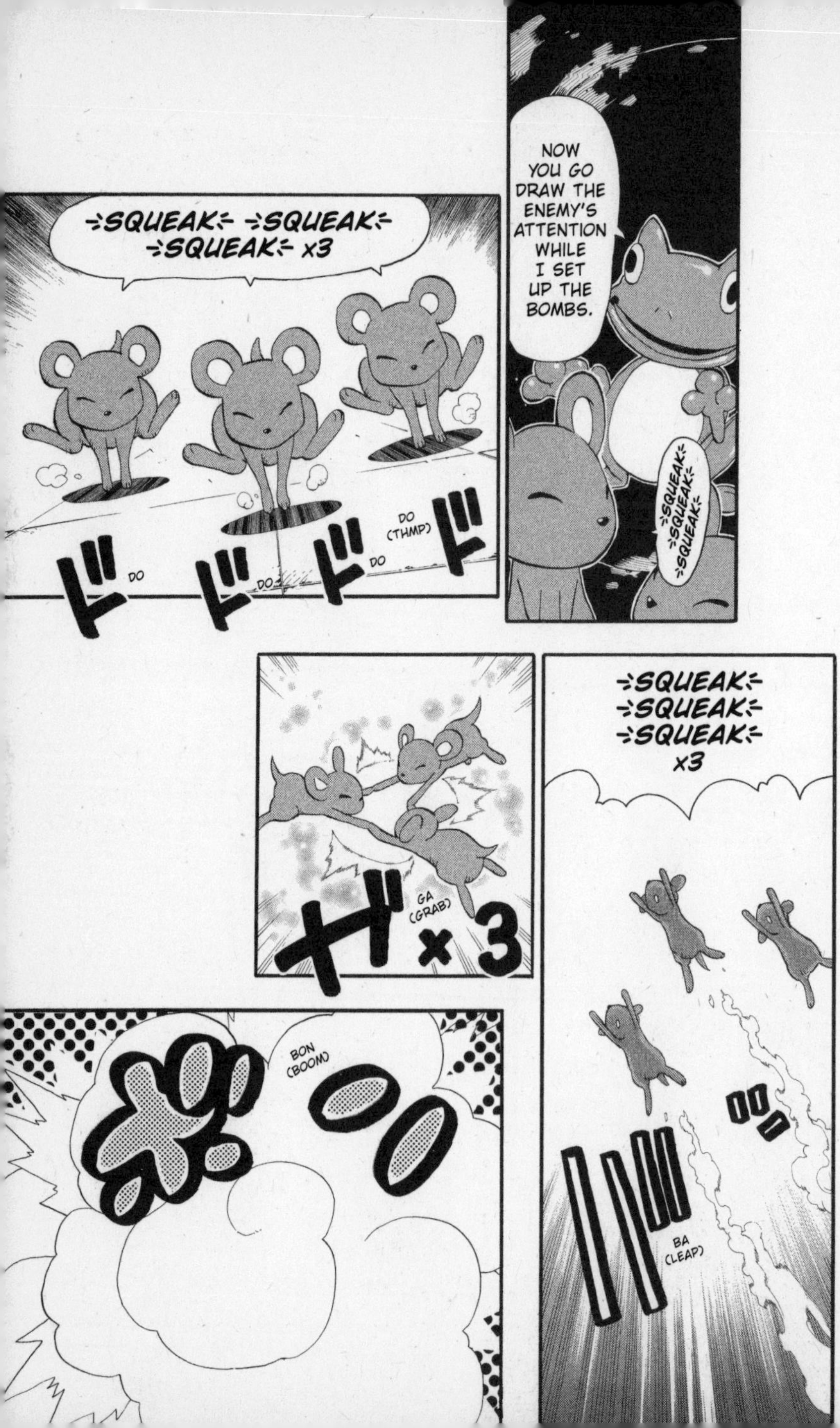
NOW YOU GO DRAW THE ENEMY'S ATTENTION WHILE I SET UP THE BOMBS.
SQUEAK SQUEAK SQUEAK
SQUEAK SQUEAK SQUEAK x3
DO (THMP)
DO
DO
DO
SQUEAK SQUEAK SQUEAK x3
BA (LEAP)
GA (GRAB)
x3
BON (BOOM)

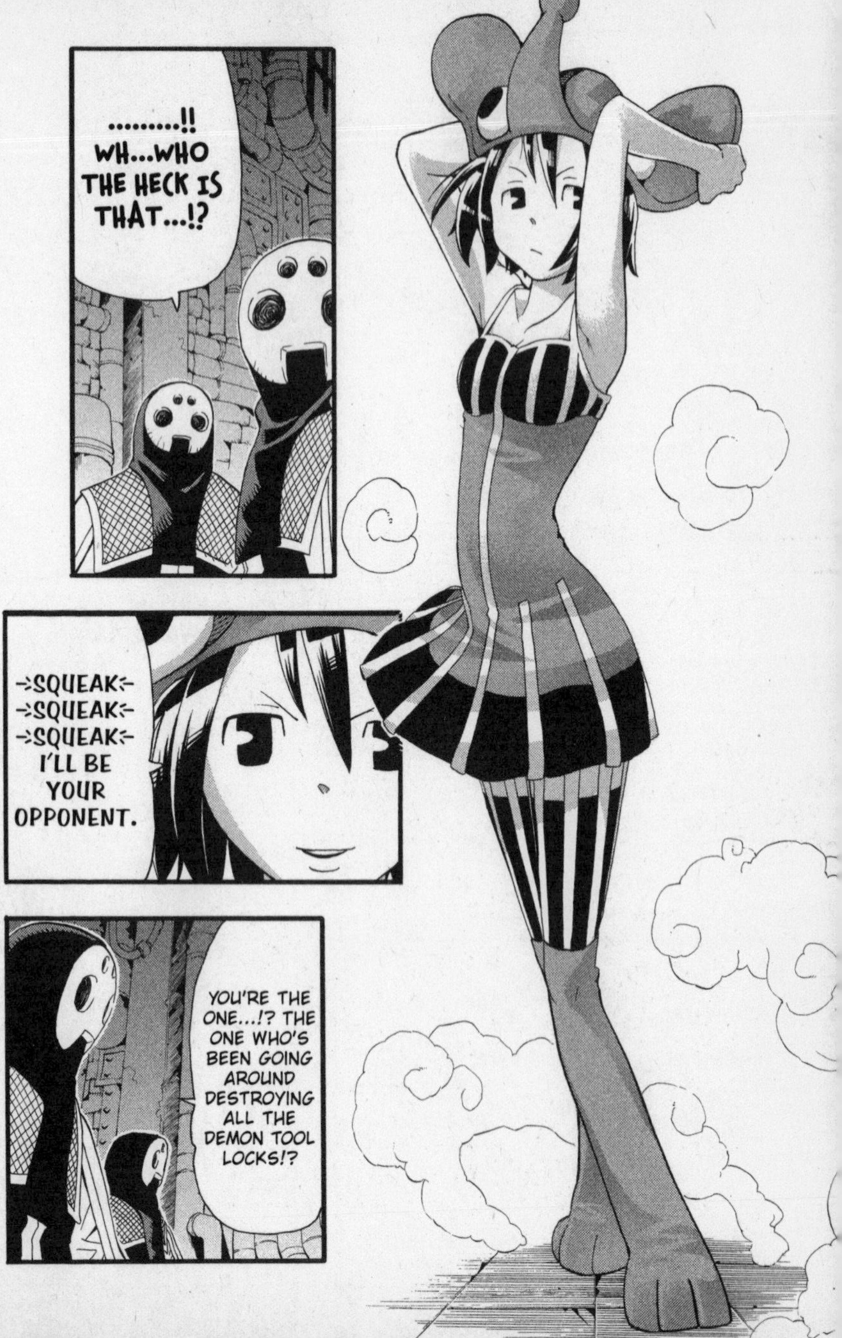
..........!! WH...WHO THE HECK IS THAT...!?
-SQUEAK- -SQUEAK- -SQUEAK- I'LL BE YOUR OPPONENT.
YOU'RE THE ONE...!? THE ONE WHO'S BEEN GOING AROUND DESTROYING ALL THE DEMON TOOL LOCKS!?

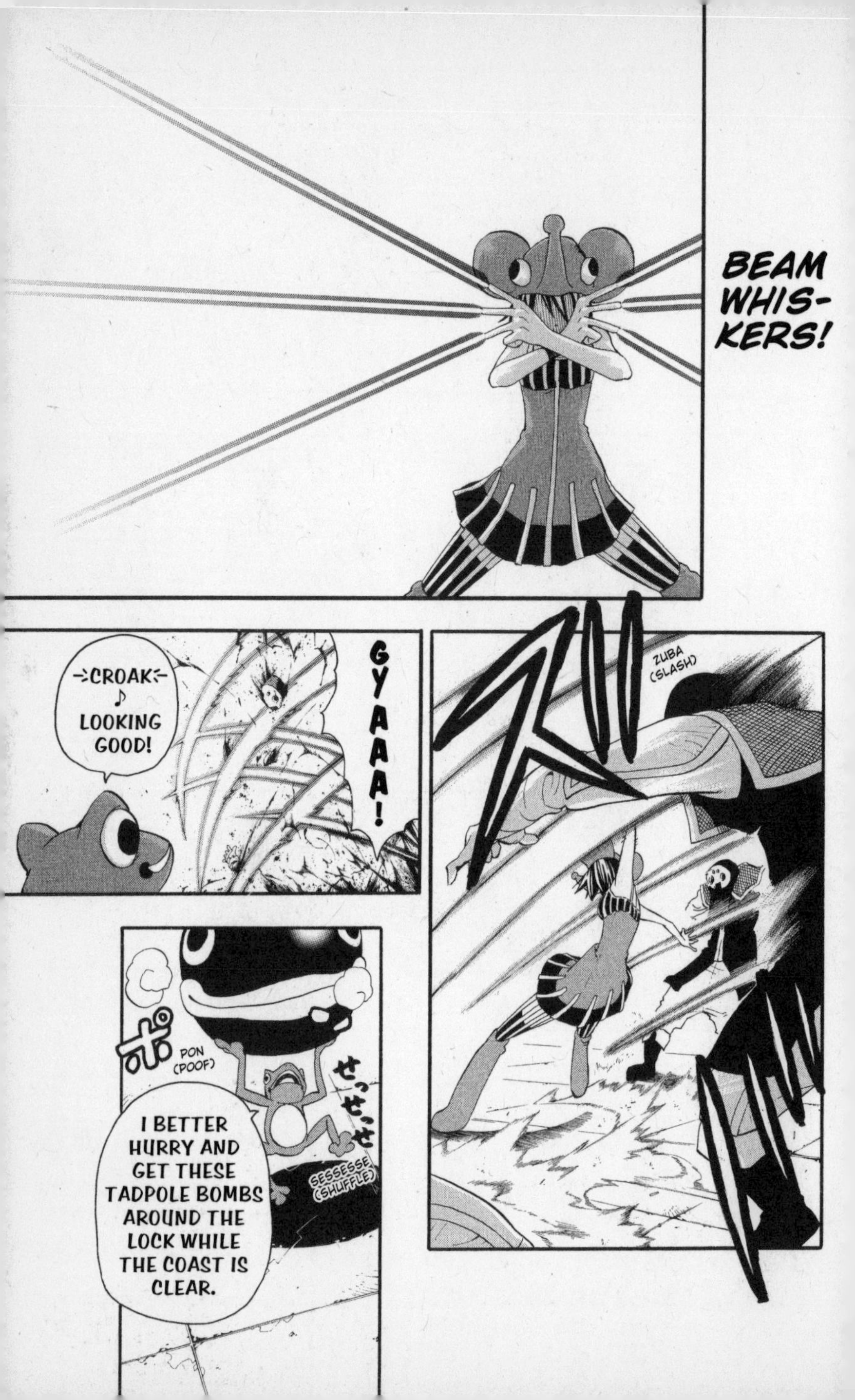
BEAM WHISKERS!
ZUBA (SLASH)
GYAAAA!
~CROAK~ ♪ LOOKING GOOD!
ポ
PON (POOF)
せっせっせ
SESSESSE (SHUFFLE)
I BETTER HURRY AND GET THESE TADPOLE BOMBS AROUND THE LOCK WHILE THE COAST IS CLEAR.

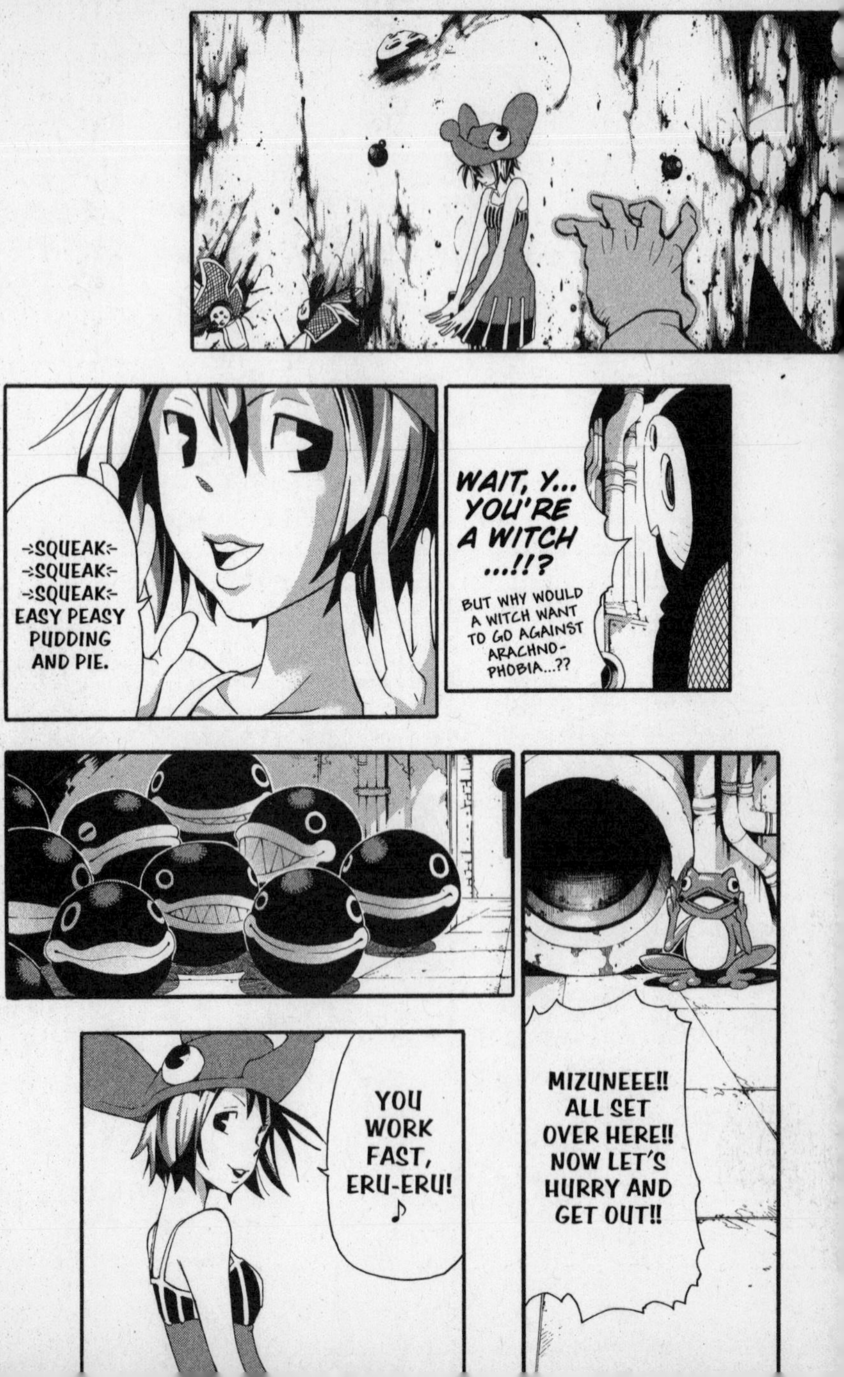
WAIT, Y... YOU'RE A WITCH ...!!?
BUT WHY WOULD A WITCH WANT TO GO AGAINST ARACHNOPHOBIA...??
-SQUEAK- -SQUEAK- -SQUEAK- EASY PEASY PUDDING AND PIE.
MIZUNEEE!! ALL SET OVER HERE!! NOW LET'S HURRY AND GET OUT!!
YOU WORK FAST, ERU-ERU! ♪

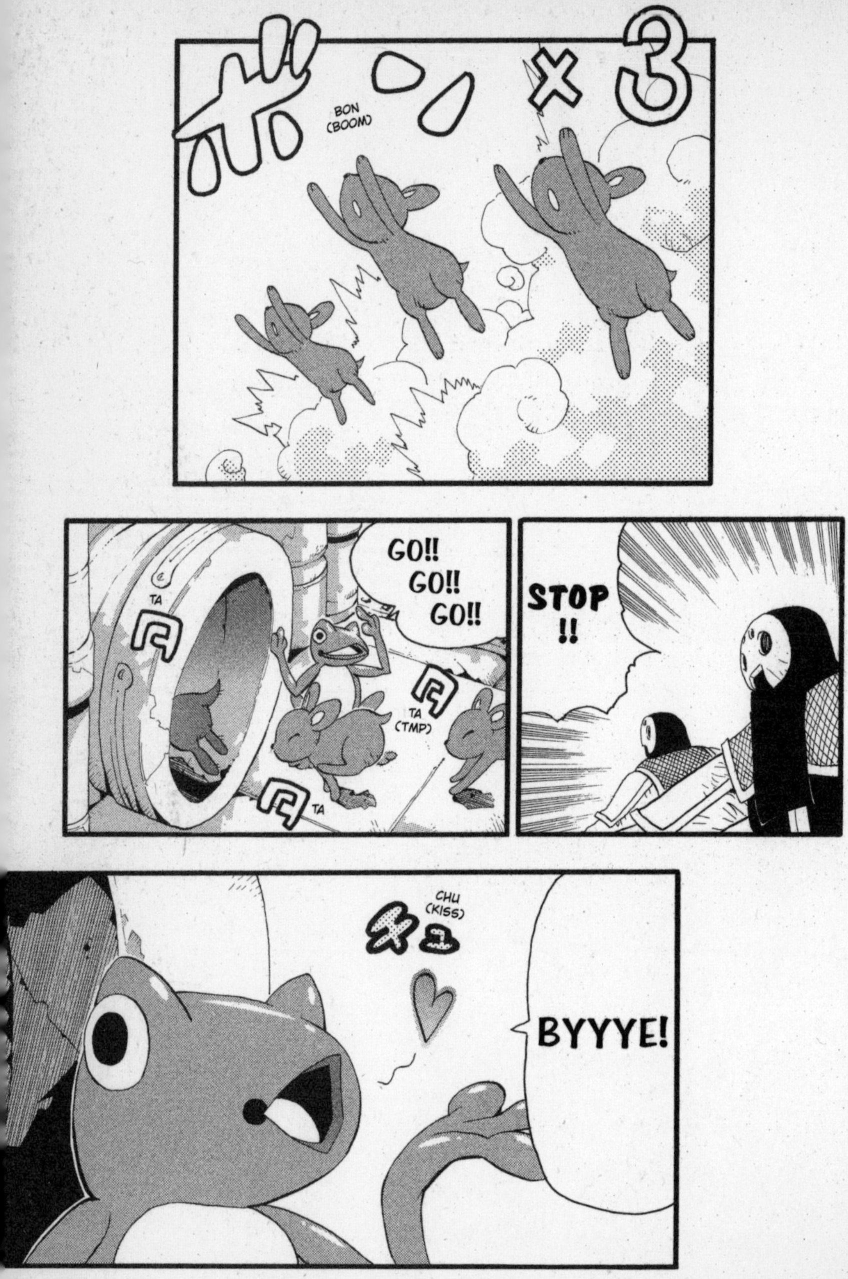
ボン x 3
BON (BOOM)
STOP !!
GO!! GO!! GO!!
TA
TA (TMP)
TA
チュ
CHU (KISS)
BYYYE!

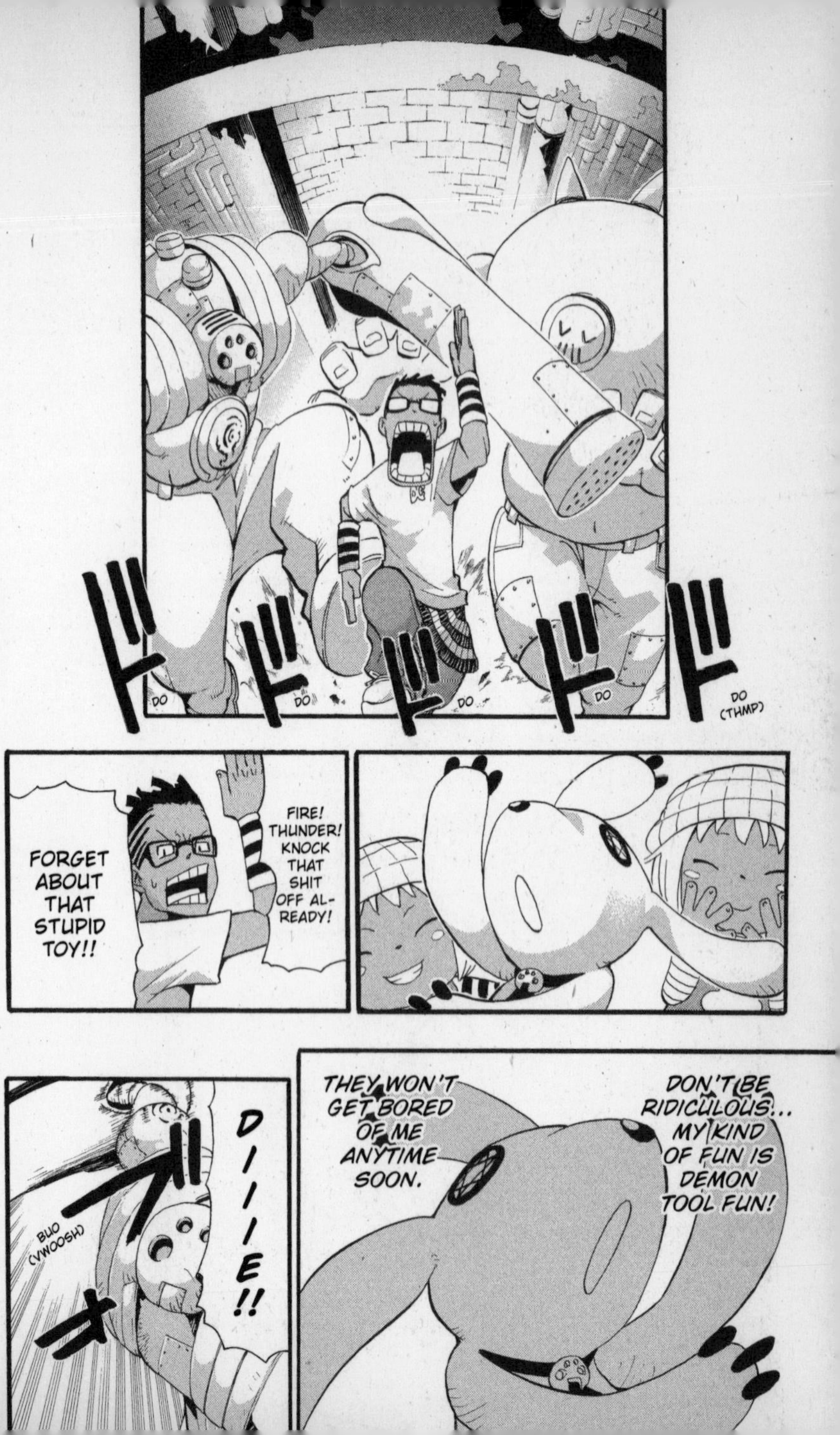
DO
(THMP)
DO
DO
DO
DO
FIRE! THUNDER! KNOCK THAT SHIT OFF AL-READY!
FORGET ABOUT THAT STUPID TOY!!
DON'T BE RIDICULOUS... MY KIND OF FUN IS DEMON TOOL FUN!
THEY WON'T GET BORED OF ME ANYTIME SOON.
DIIIE!!
BUO
(VWOOSH)

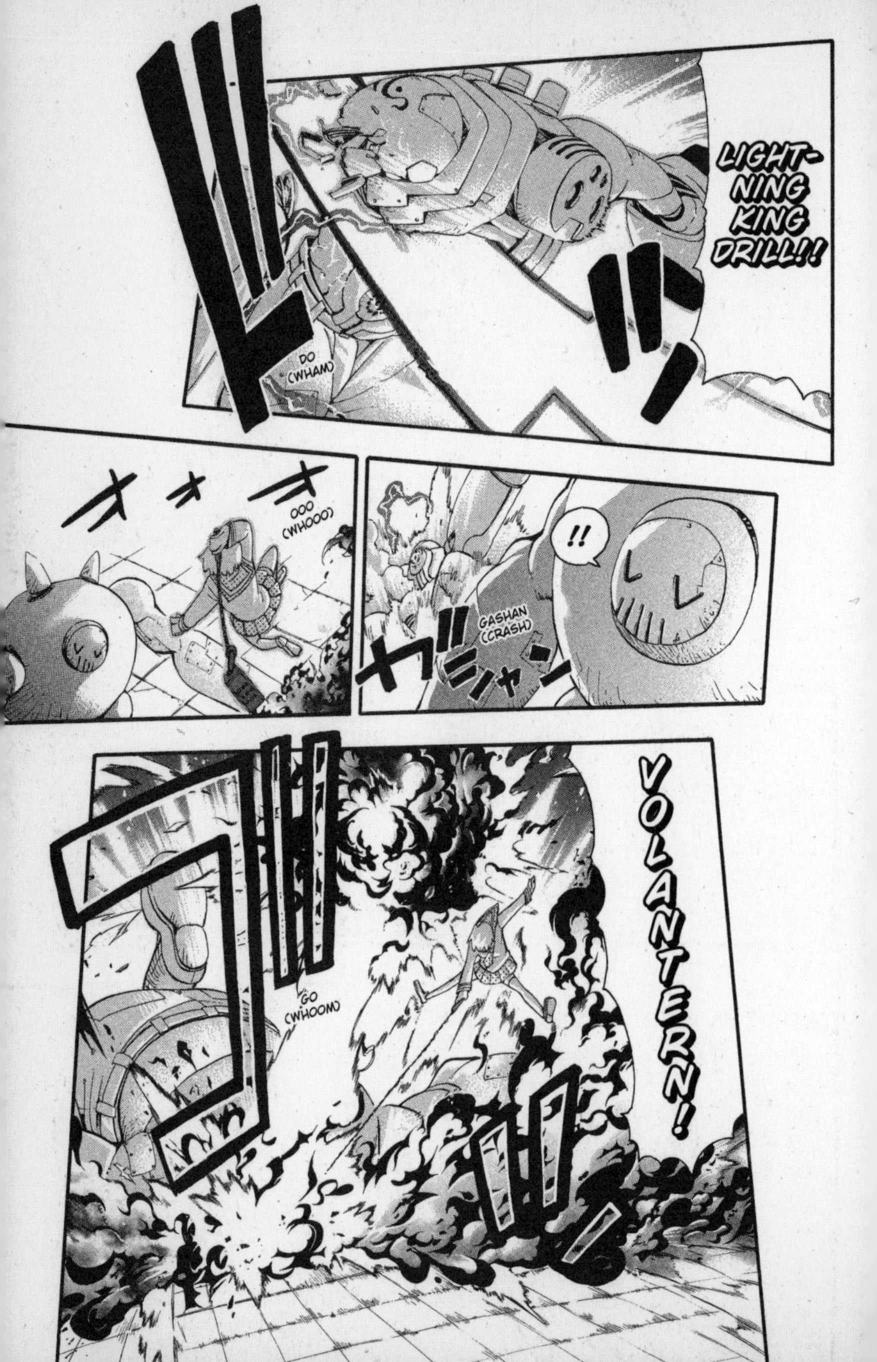
LIGHTNING KING DRILL!!
DO (WHAM)
!!
GASHAN (CRASH)
OOO (WHOOO)
VOLANTERN!
GO (WHOOM)

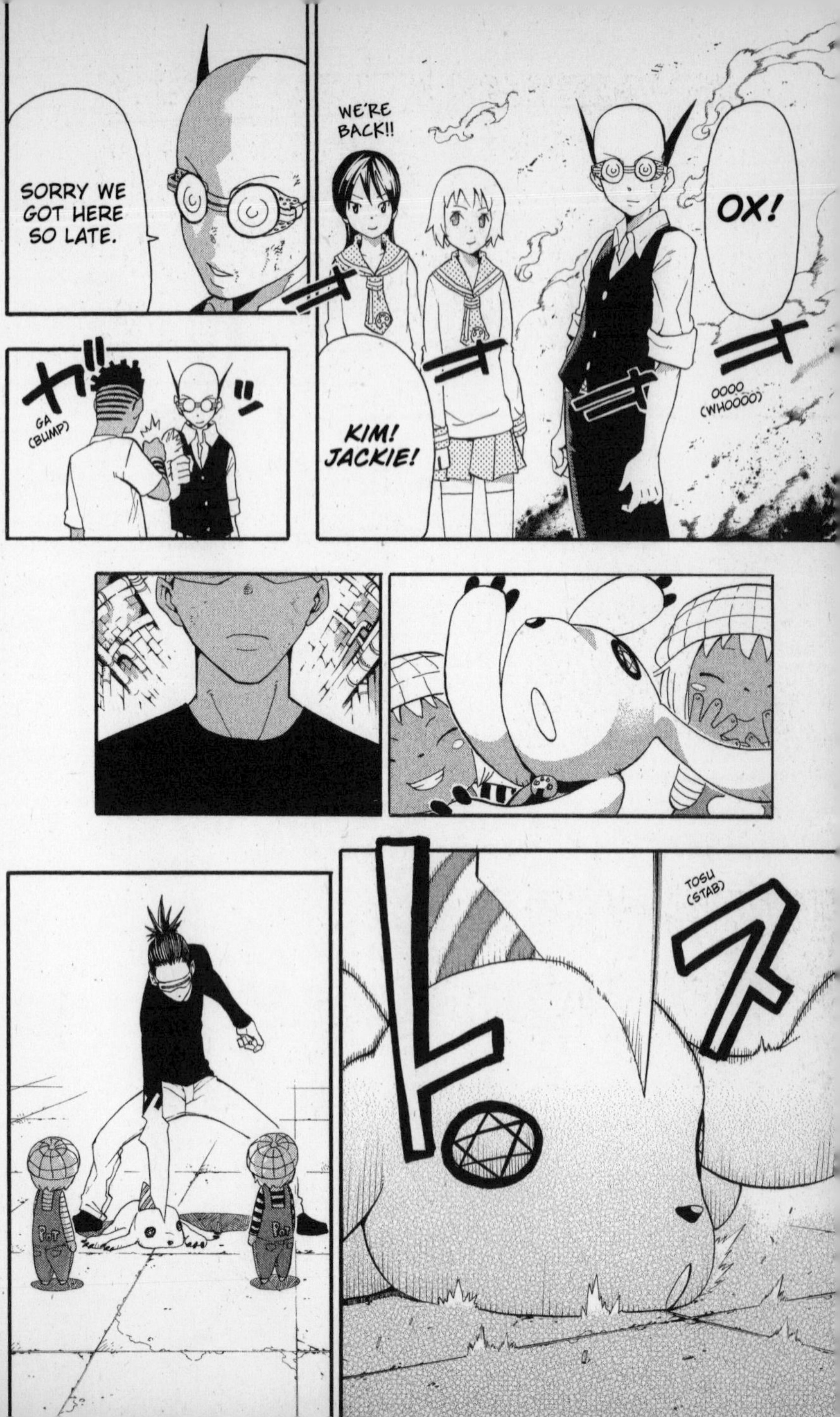
OX!
OOOO
(WHOOOO)
WE'RE
BACK!!
KIM!
JACKIE!
SORRY WE
GOT HERE
SO LATE.
GA
(BUMP)
TOSU
(STAB)

I THINK THAT'S ALL OF THEM.

R...

......

......

RIGHT...

NOW LET'S HURRY AND GO FIND THAT DEMON TOOL.

......

PURU
(TREMBLE)

PURU

PURU

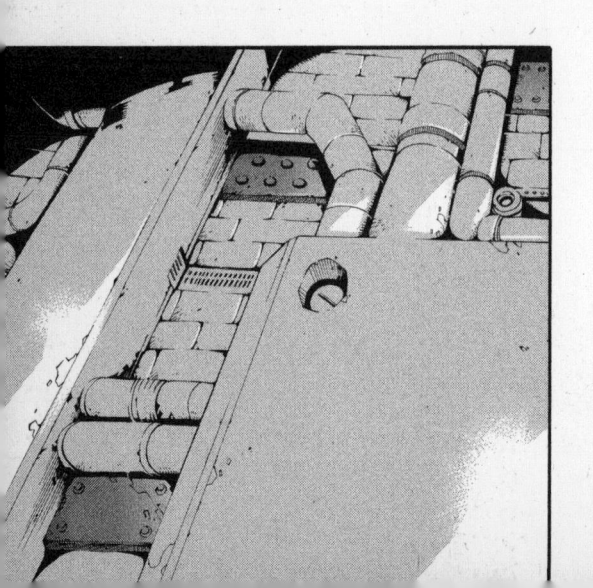

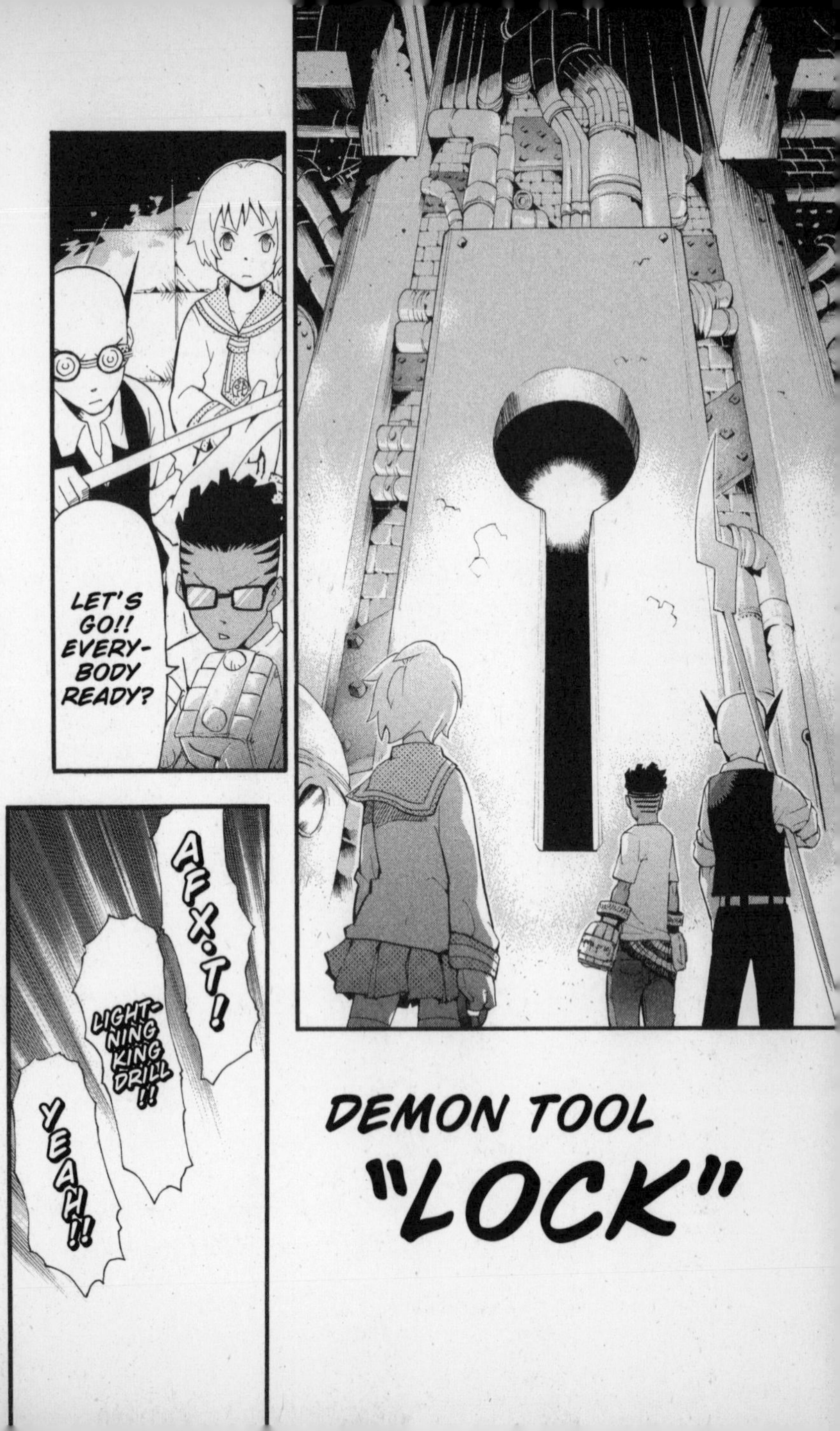
DEMON TOOL "LOCK"
LET'S GO!! EVERY-BODY READY?
AFX.T!
LIGHT-NING KING DRILL!!
YEAH!!

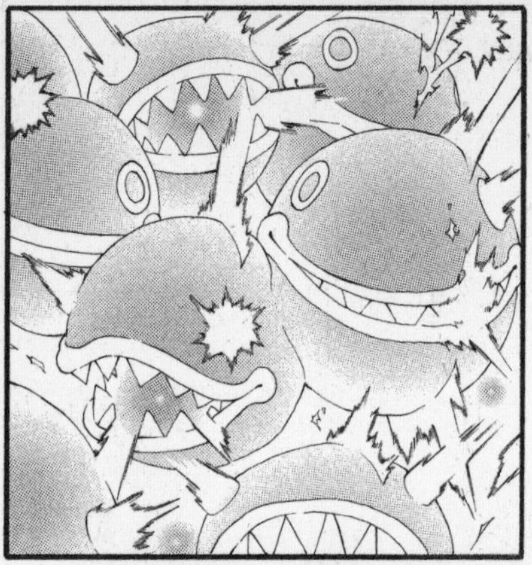
DEMON TOOL LOCKS ONE THROUGH EIGHT......
...ALL TARGETS OF DEMO-LITION ......

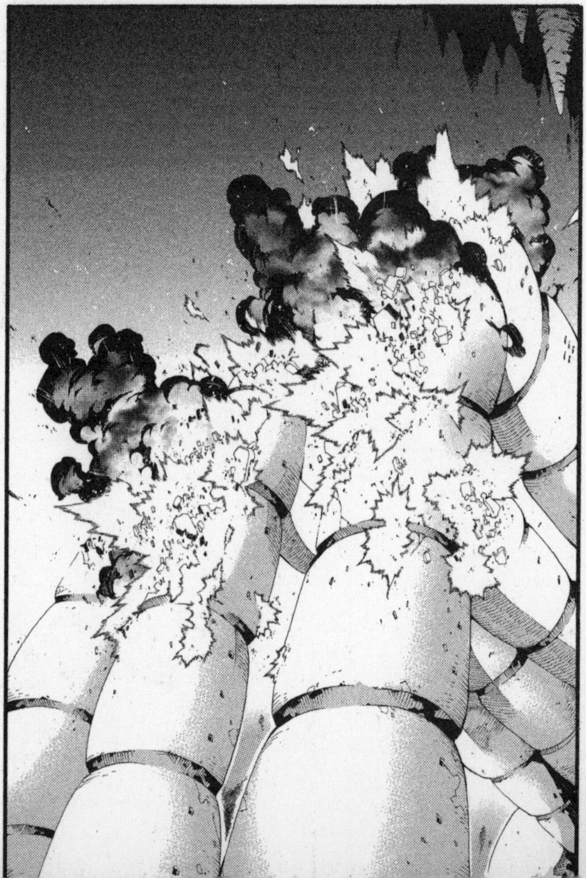
...DESTROYED!

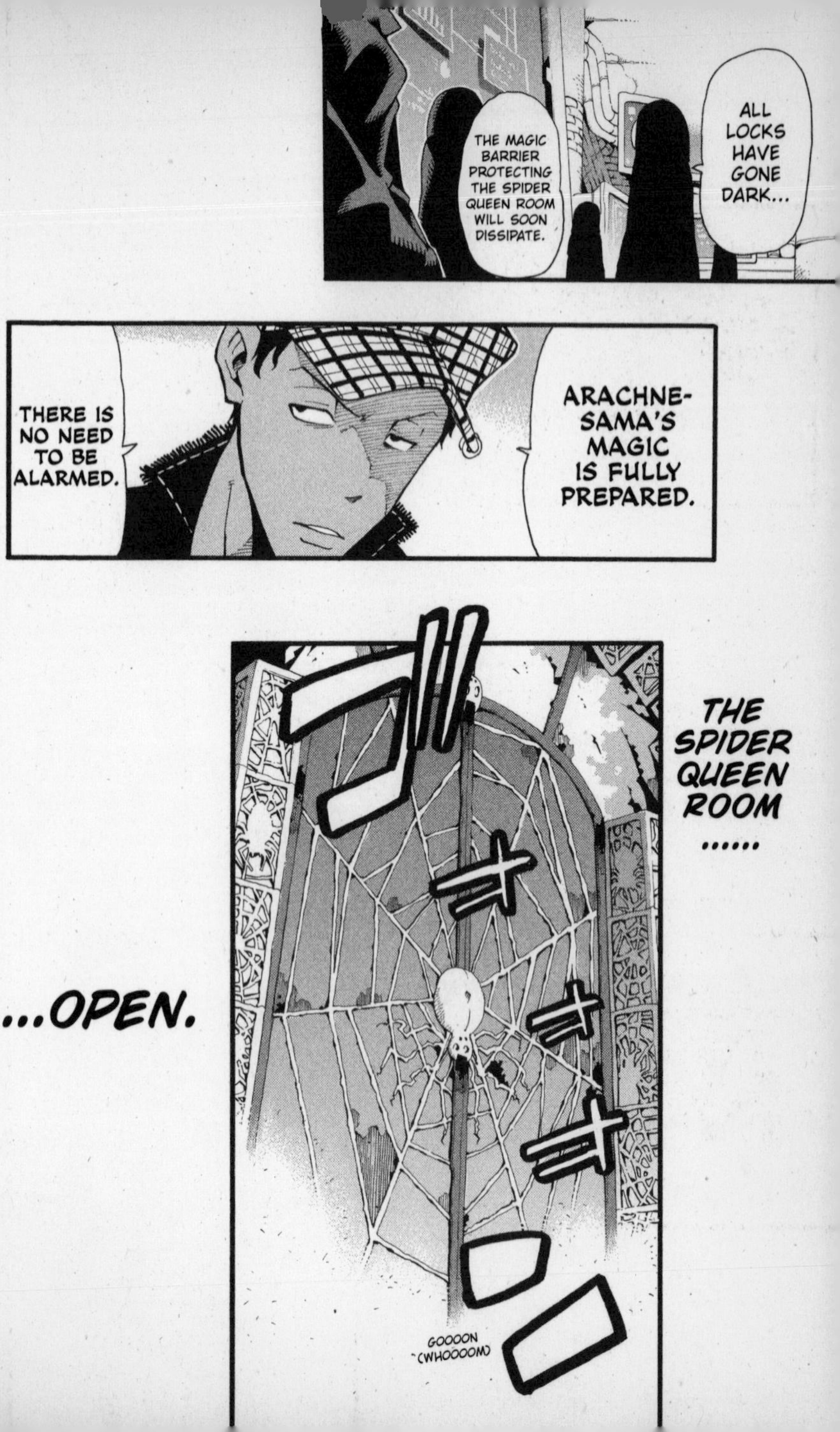
ALL LOCKS HAVE GONE DARK...
THE MAGIC BARRIER PROTECTING THE SPIDER QUEEN ROOM WILL SOON DISSIPATE.
ARACHNE-SAMA'S MAGIC IS FULLY PREPARED.
THERE IS NO NEED TO BE ALARMED.
THE SPIDER QUEEN ROOM ......
...OPEN.
GOOOON (WHOOOOM)

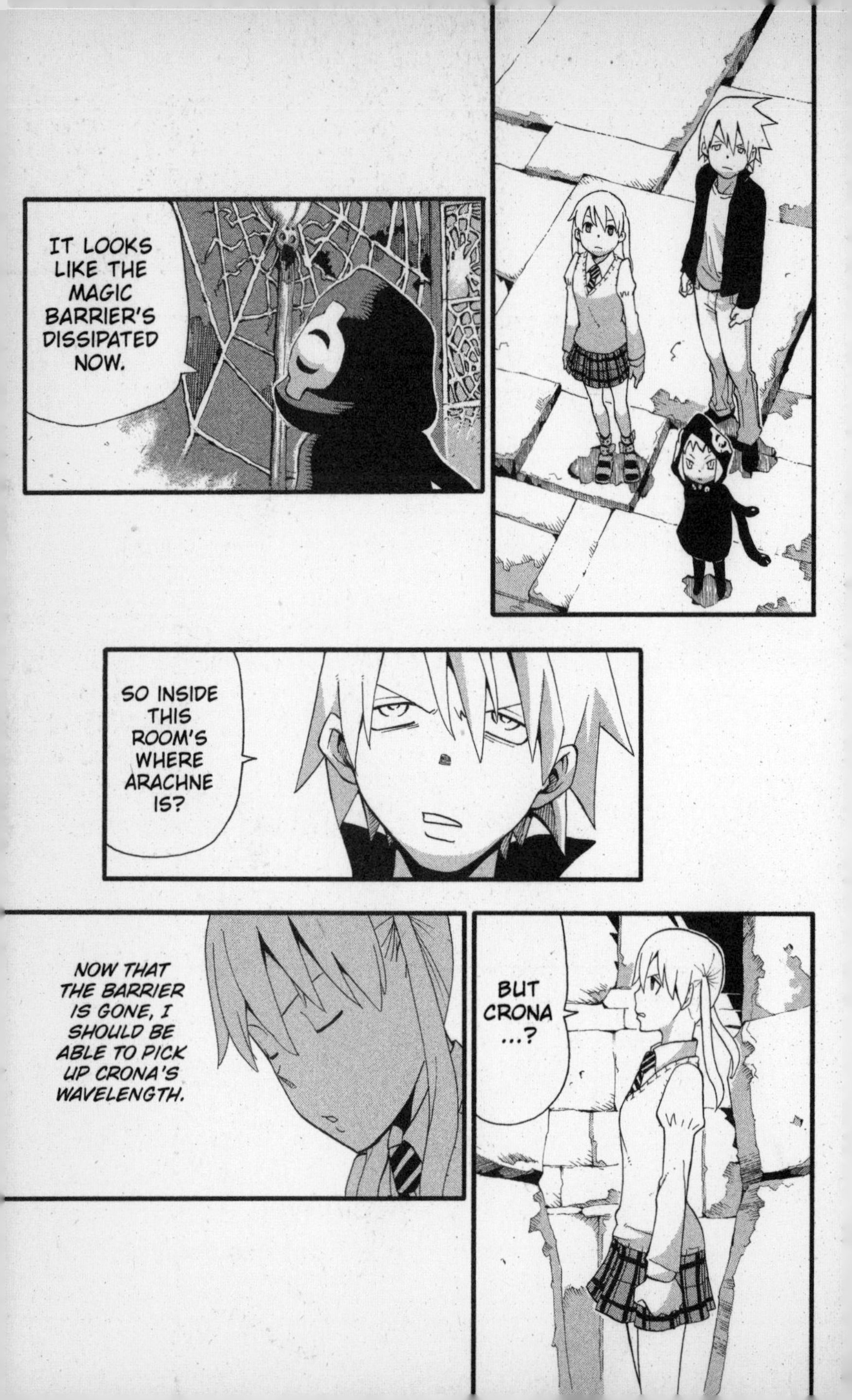
IT LOOKS LIKE THE MAGIC BARRIER'S DISSIPATED NOW.
SO INSIDE THIS ROOM'S WHERE ARACHNE IS?
BUT CRONA ...?
NOW THAT THE BARRIER IS GONE, I SHOULD BE ABLE TO PICK UP CRONA'S WAVELENGTH.

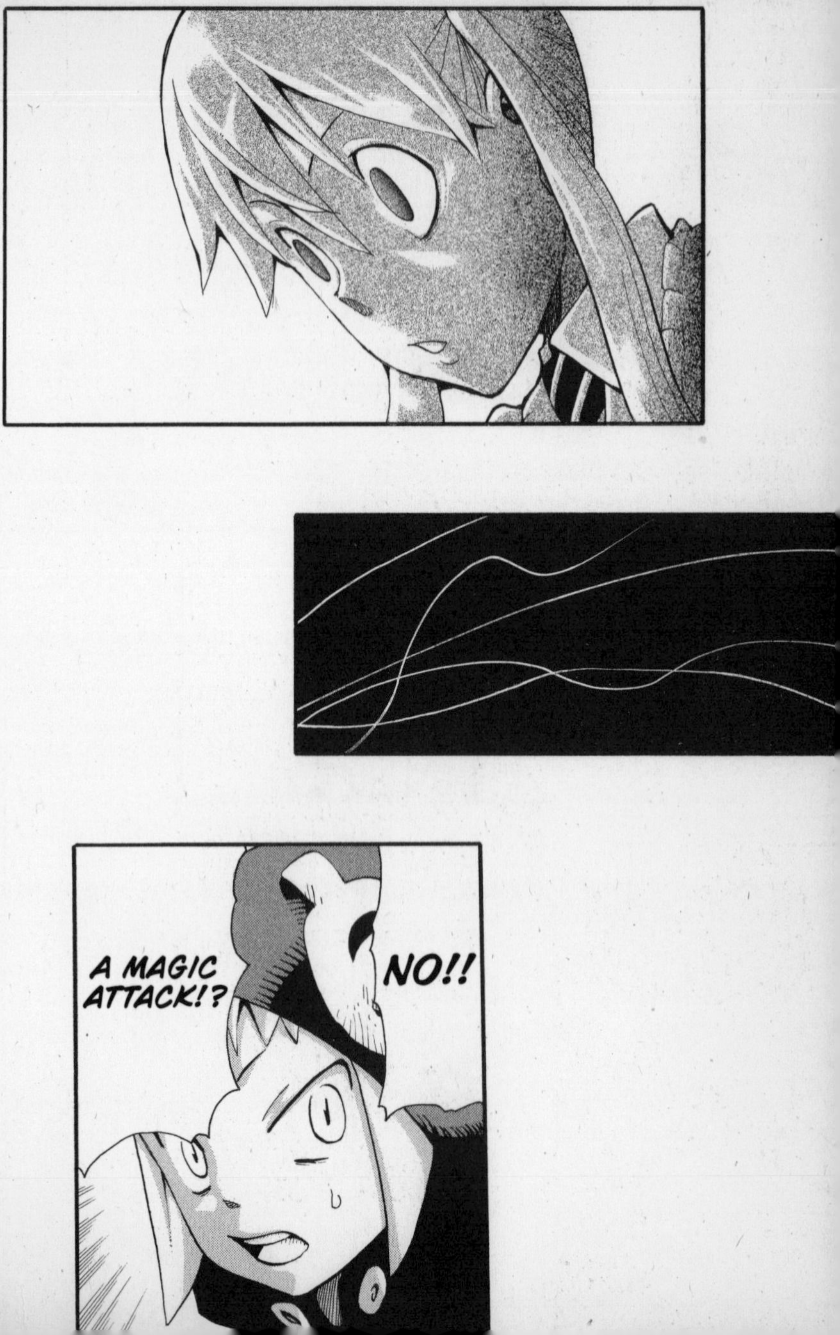
NO!!
A MAGIC ATTACK!?

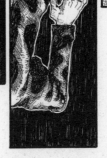

¿!

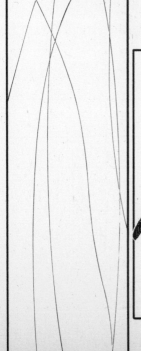

KIIRON (CLONK)

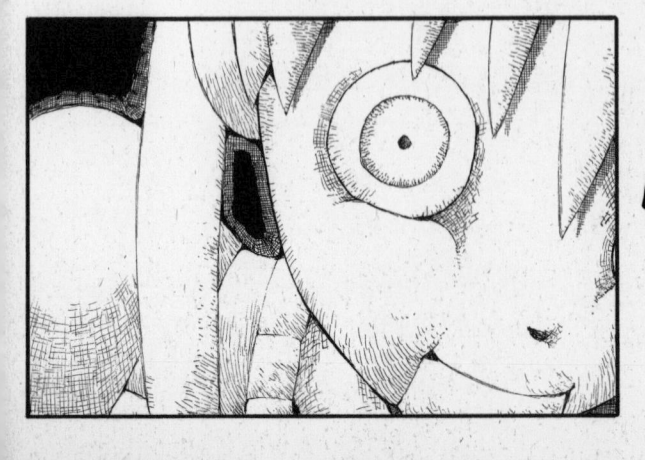

WHAT'S THIS!?

SOUL EATER

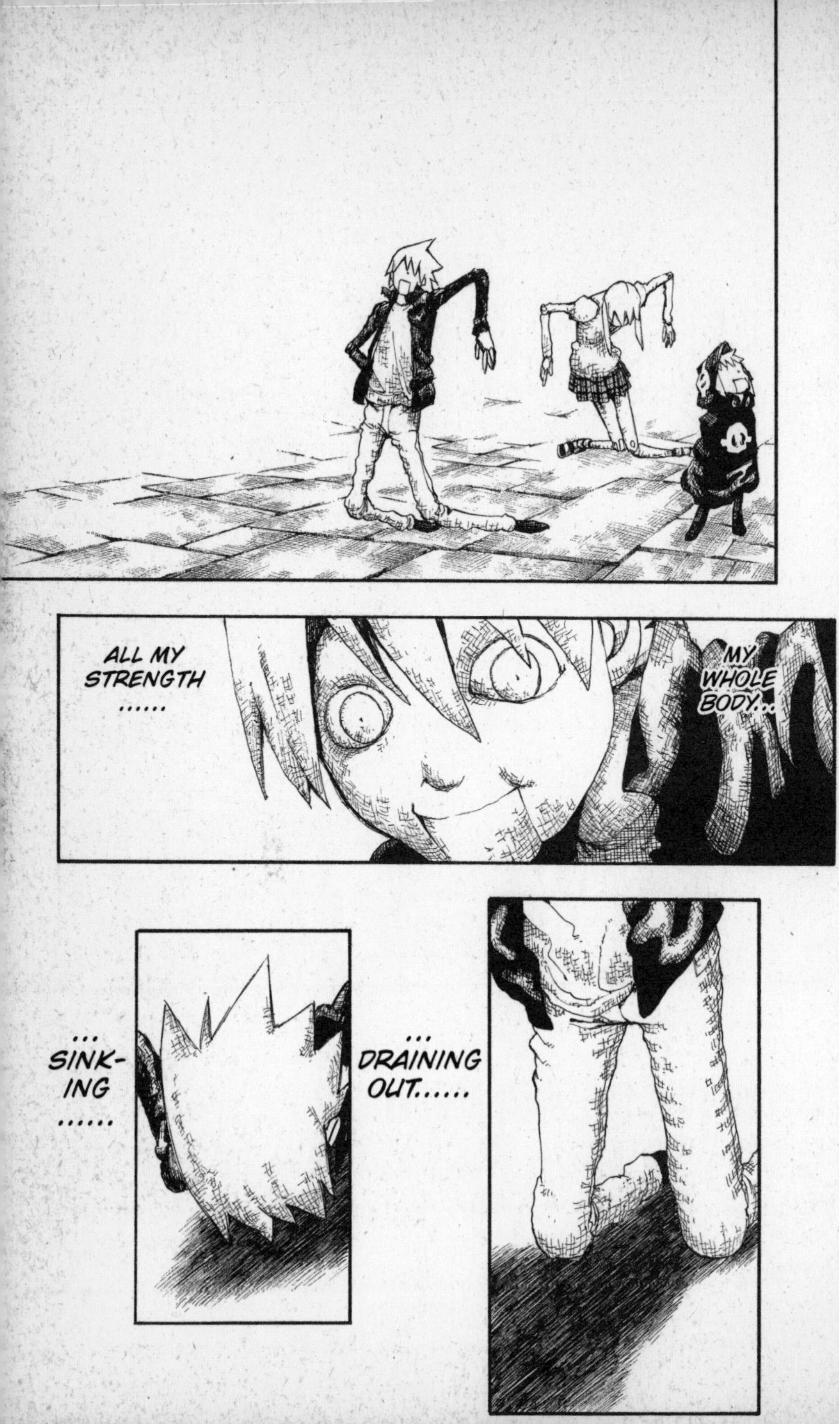
MY WHOLE BODY...
ALL MY STRENGTH ......
...DRAINING OUT......
...SINK-ING ......

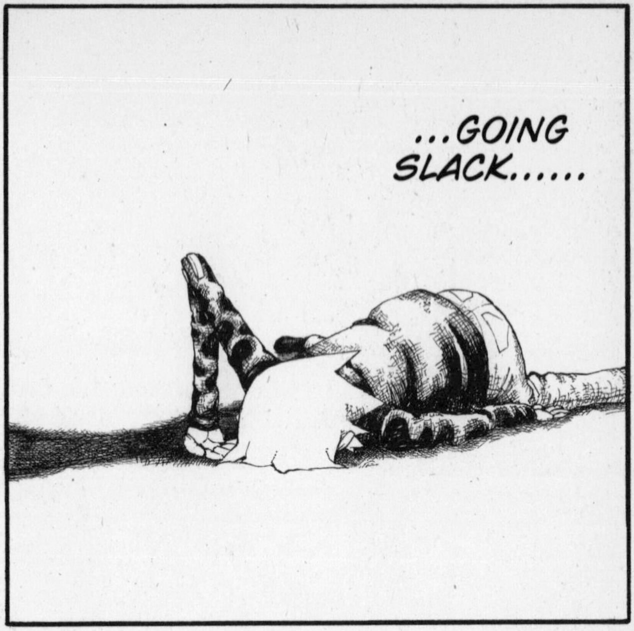
...GOING SLACK......

SOUL EATER

CHAPTER 55: OPERATION CAPTURE BABA YAGA CASTLE (PART 10)

... OGRE

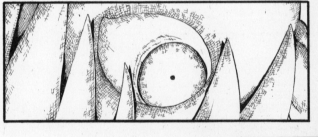

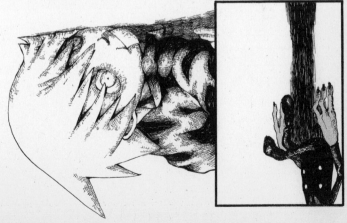

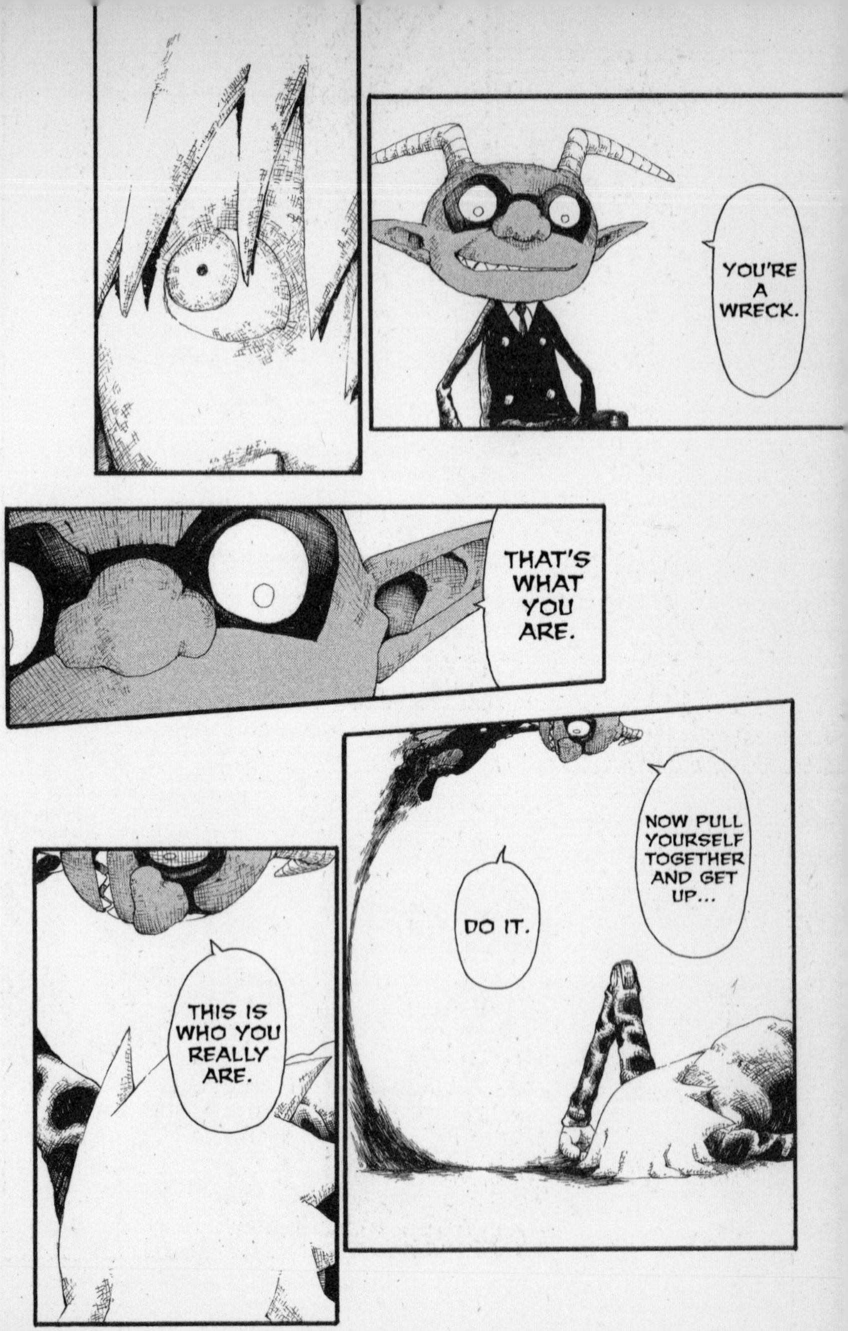
YOU'RE A WRECK.
THAT'S WHAT YOU ARE.
NOW PULL YOURSELF TOGETHER AND GET UP...
DO IT.
THIS IS WHO YOU REALLY ARE.

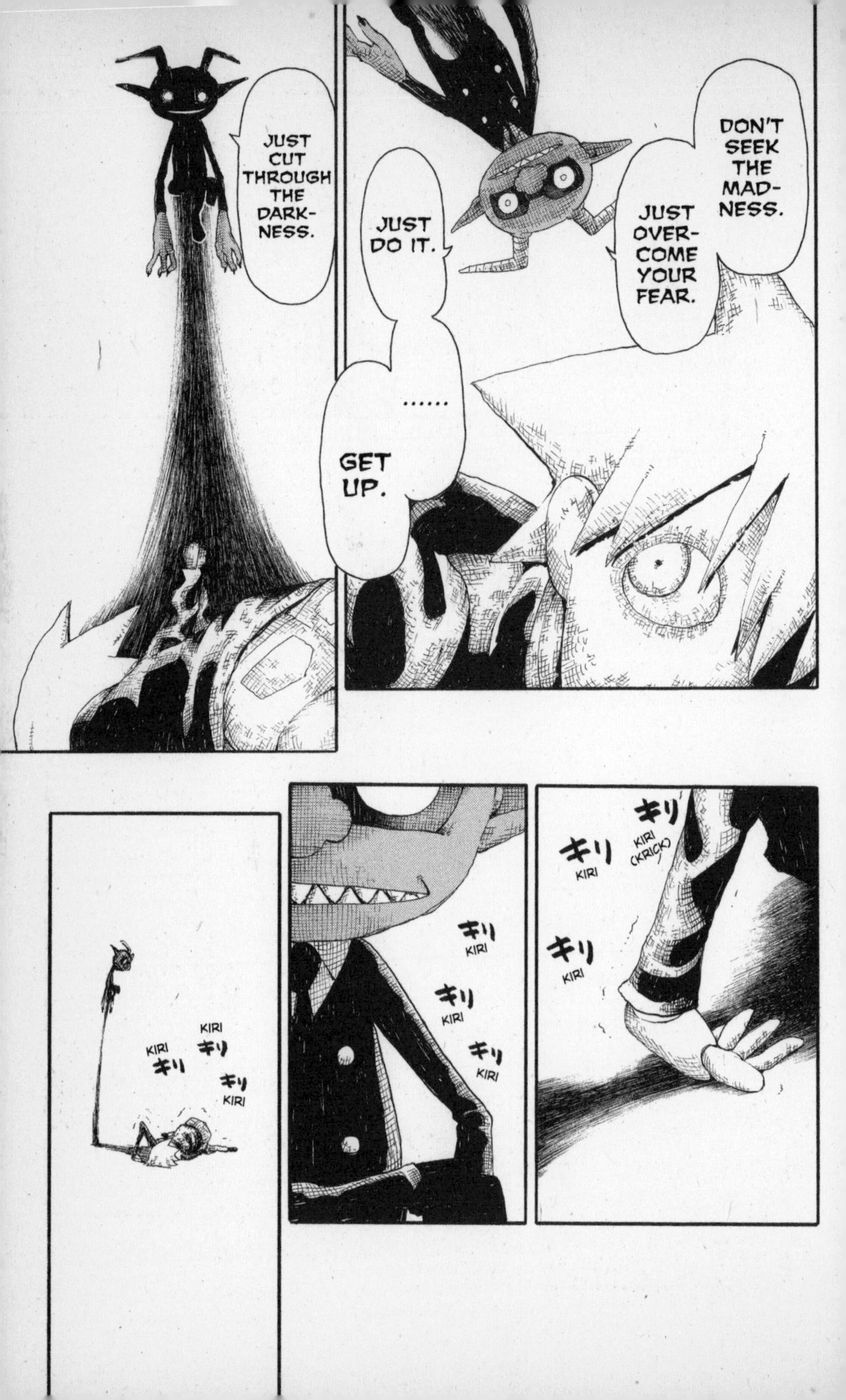
DON'T SEEK THE MAD-NESS.
JUST OVER-COME YOUR FEAR.
JUST DO IT.
......
GET UP.
JUST CUT THROUGH THE DARK-NESS.
キリ KIRI (KRICK)
キリ KIRI
キリ KIRI
キリ KIRI
キリ KIRI
キリ KIRI
キリ KIRI
キリ KIRI
キリ KIRI

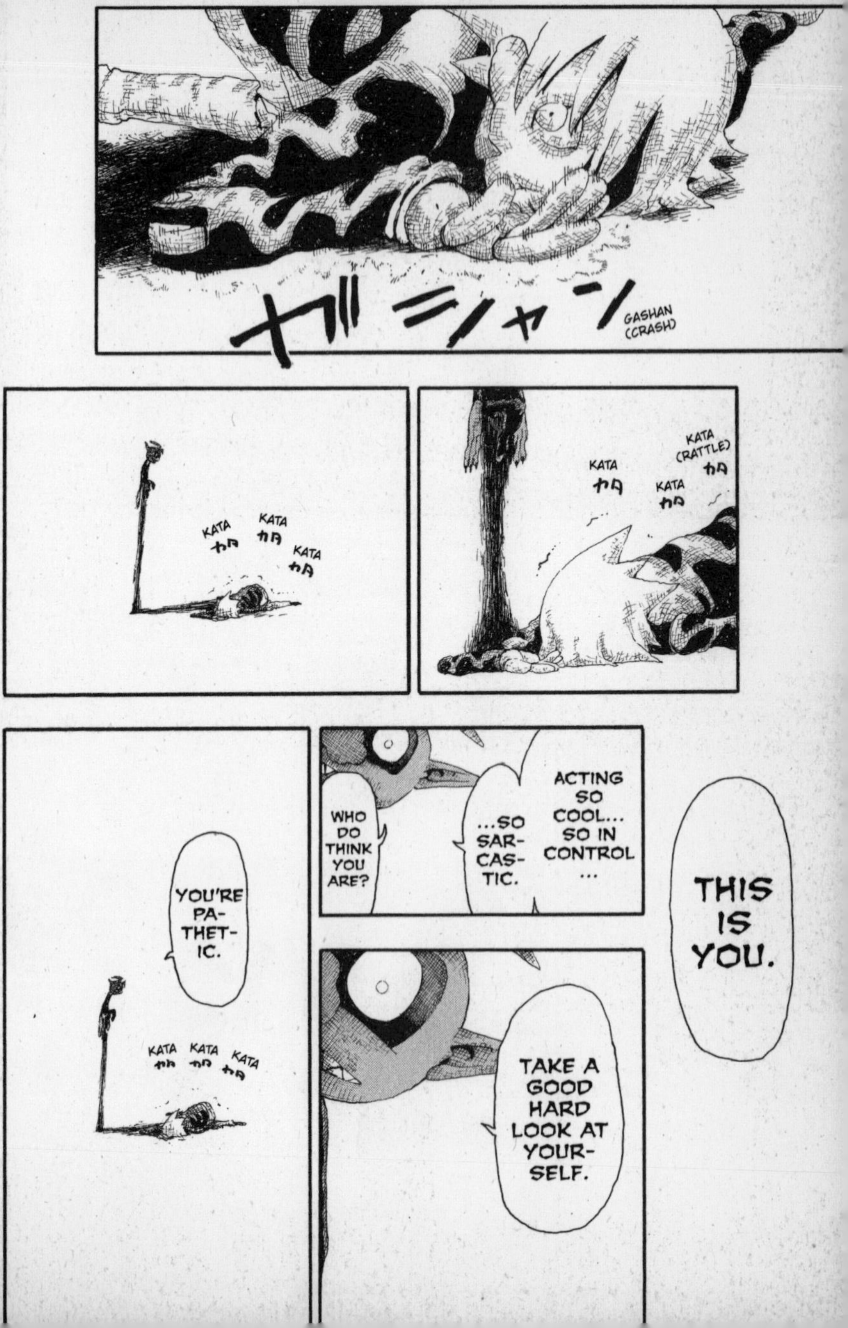
ガシャン
GASHAN (CRASH)
KATA (RATTLE) カタ
KATA カタ
KATA カタ
KATA カタ
KATA カタ
KATA カタ
WHO DO THINK YOU ARE?
...SO SARCASTIC.
ACTING SO COOL... SO IN CONTROL...
TAKE A GOOD HARD LOOK AT YOURSELF.
THIS IS YOU.
YOU'RE PATHETIC.
KATA カタ
KATA カタ
KATA カタ

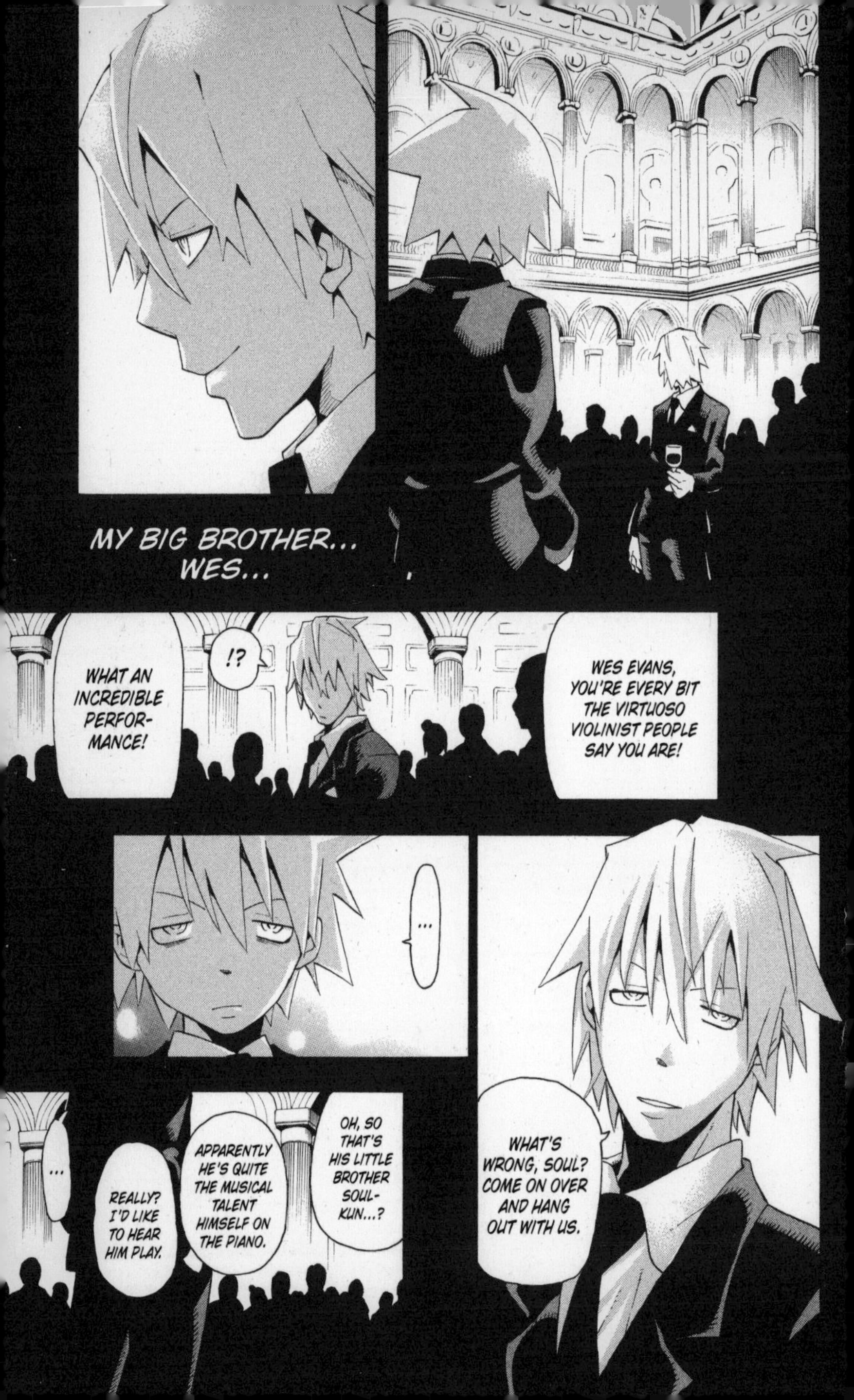
MY BIG BROTHER... WES...
WES EVANS, YOU'RE EVERY BIT THE VIRTUOSO VIOLINIST PEOPLE SAY YOU ARE!
!?
WHAT AN INCREDIBLE PERFOR-MANCE!
WHAT'S WRONG, SOUL? COME ON OVER AND HANG OUT WITH US.
...
OH, SO THAT'S HIS LITTLE BROTHER SOUL-KUN...?
APPARENTLY HE'S QUITE THE MUSICAL TALENT HIMSELF ON THE PIANO.
REALLY? I'D LIKE TO HEAR HIM PLAY.
...

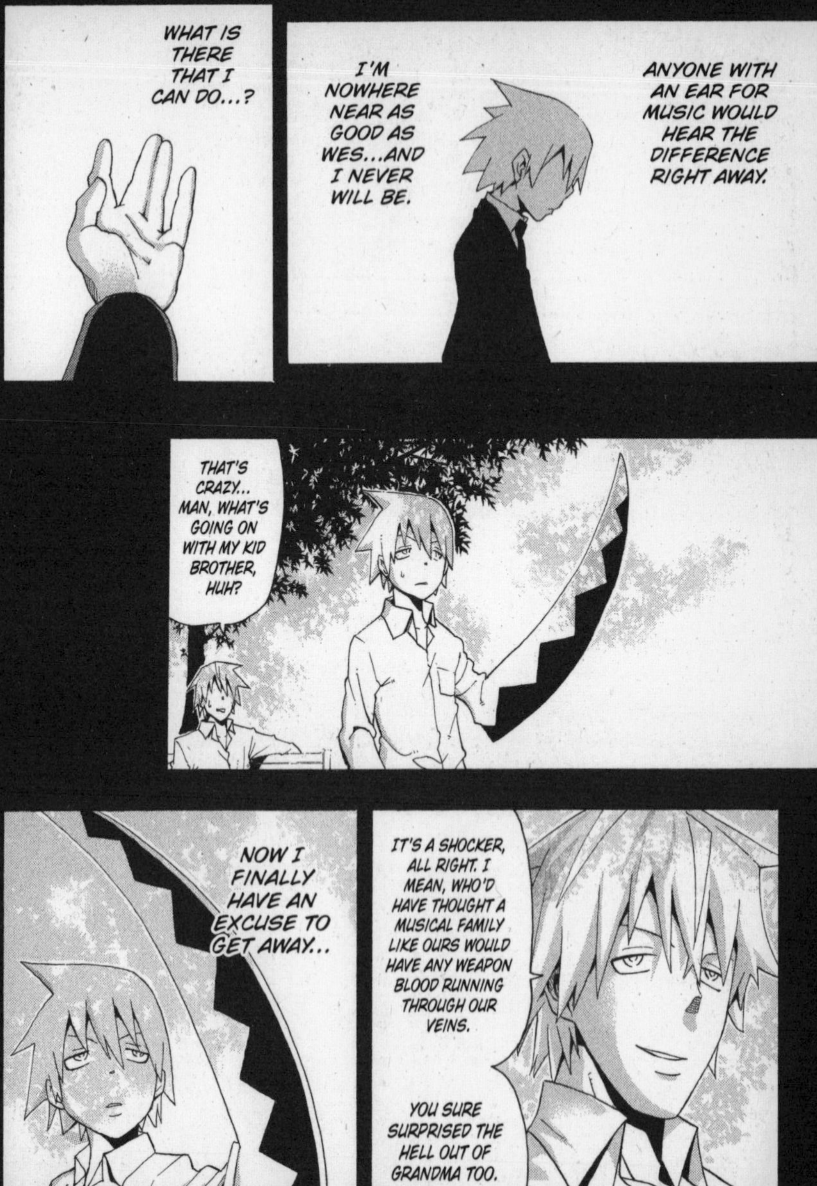
ANYONE WITH AN EAR FOR MUSIC WOULD HEAR THE DIFFERENCE RIGHT AWAY.
I'M NOWHERE NEAR AS GOOD AS WES...AND I NEVER WILL BE.
WHAT IS THERE THAT I CAN DO...?
THAT'S CRAZY... MAN, WHAT'S GOING ON WITH MY KID BROTHER, HUH?
IT'S A SHOCKER, ALL RIGHT. I MEAN, WHO'D HAVE THOUGHT A MUSICAL FAMILY LIKE OURS WOULD HAVE ANY WEAPON BLOOD RUNNING THROUGH OUR VEINS.
YOU SURE SURPRISED THE HELL OUT OF GRANDMA TOO.
NOW I FINALLY HAVE AN EXCUSE TO GET AWAY...

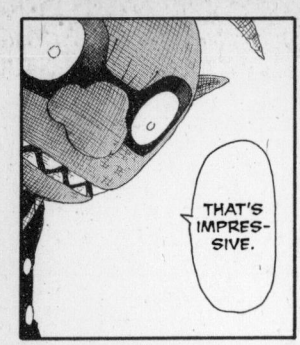

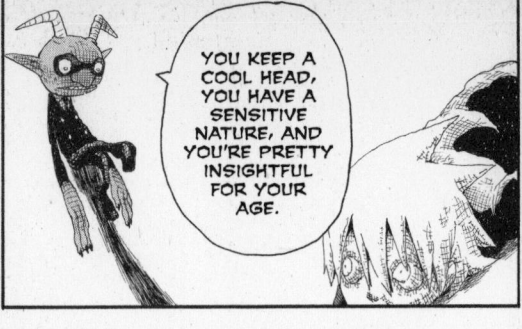

YOU KEEP A COOL HEAD, YOU HAVE A SENSITIVE NATURE, AND YOU'RE PRETTY INSIGHTFUL FOR YOUR AGE.
THAT'S IMPRES-SIVE.
AND YOU HAVE YOUR MOMENTS... MOMENTS OF MAKING WISE CHOICES AND STICKING TO THE PATH YOU'VE CHOSEN.
ALSO IMPRES-SIVE.
BUT HOW DID YOU FIND THAT PATH? WITH CYNICISM, THAT'S HOW.
YOU FOUND IT BY REJECTING ALL THE OTHER PATHS AS "STUPID" OR "NO GOOD"... CYNICALLY DISMISSING EVERYTHING UNTIL YOU WOUND UP ON THIS ONE.
WHAT DO YOU WANT TO DO? WHAT DO YOU WANT TO BE? WHAT DO YOU BELIEVE IN?
WHAT DIRECTION DO YOU WANT YOUR LIFE TO GO IN? TELL ME.
WELL?

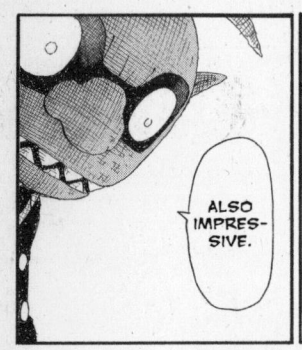

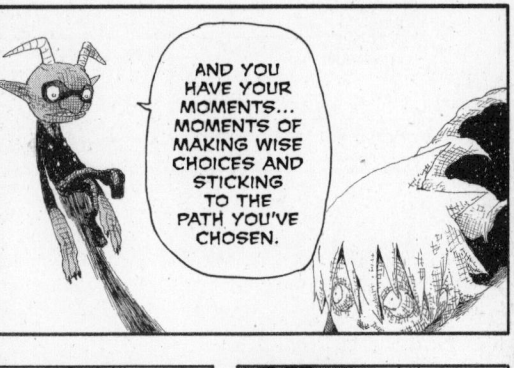

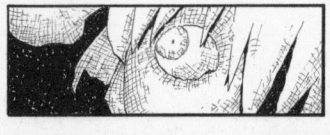

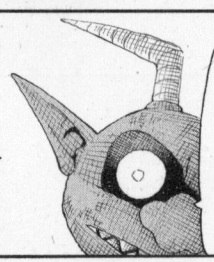

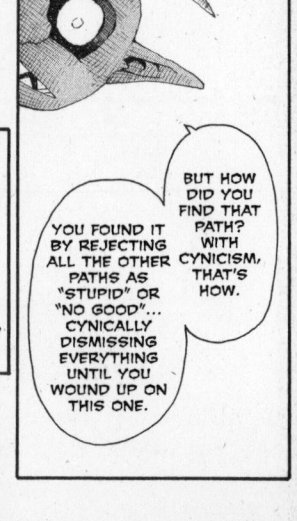

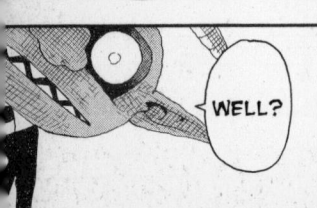

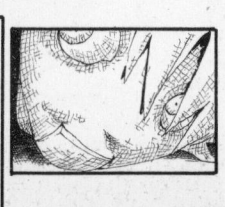

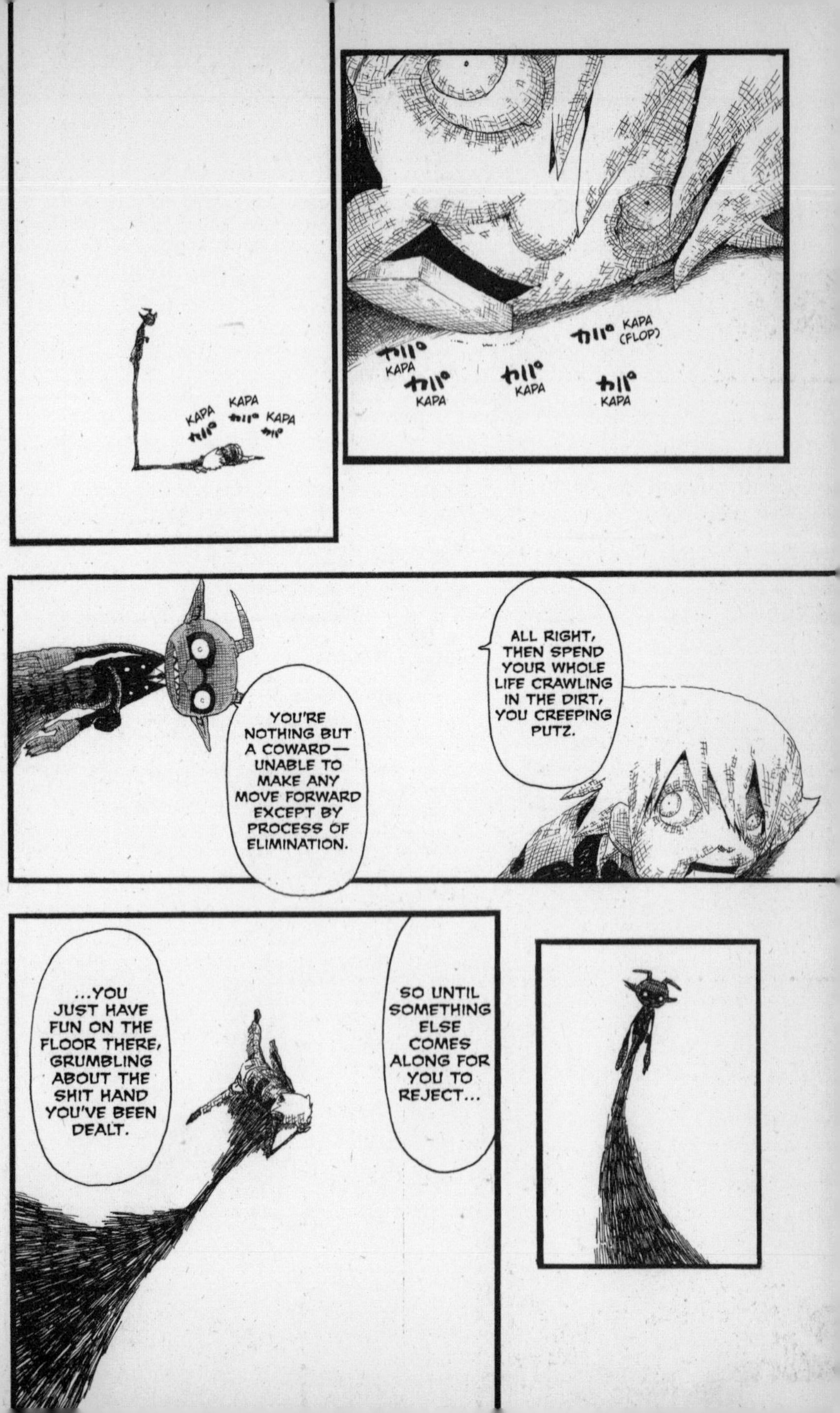
カパ KAPA (FLOP)
カパ KAPA
カパ KAPA
カパ KAPA
カパ KAPA
KAPA カパ
KAPA カパ
KAPA カパ
ALL RIGHT, THEN SPEND YOUR WHOLE LIFE CRAWLING IN THE DIRT, YOU CREEPING PUTZ.
YOU'RE NOTHING BUT A COWARD—UNABLE TO MAKE ANY MOVE FORWARD EXCEPT BY PROCESS OF ELIMINATION.
SO UNTIL SOMETHING ELSE COMES ALONG FOR YOU TO REJECT...
...YOU JUST HAVE FUN ON THE FLOOR THERE, GRUMBLING ABOUT THE SHIT HAND YOU'VE BEEN DEALT.

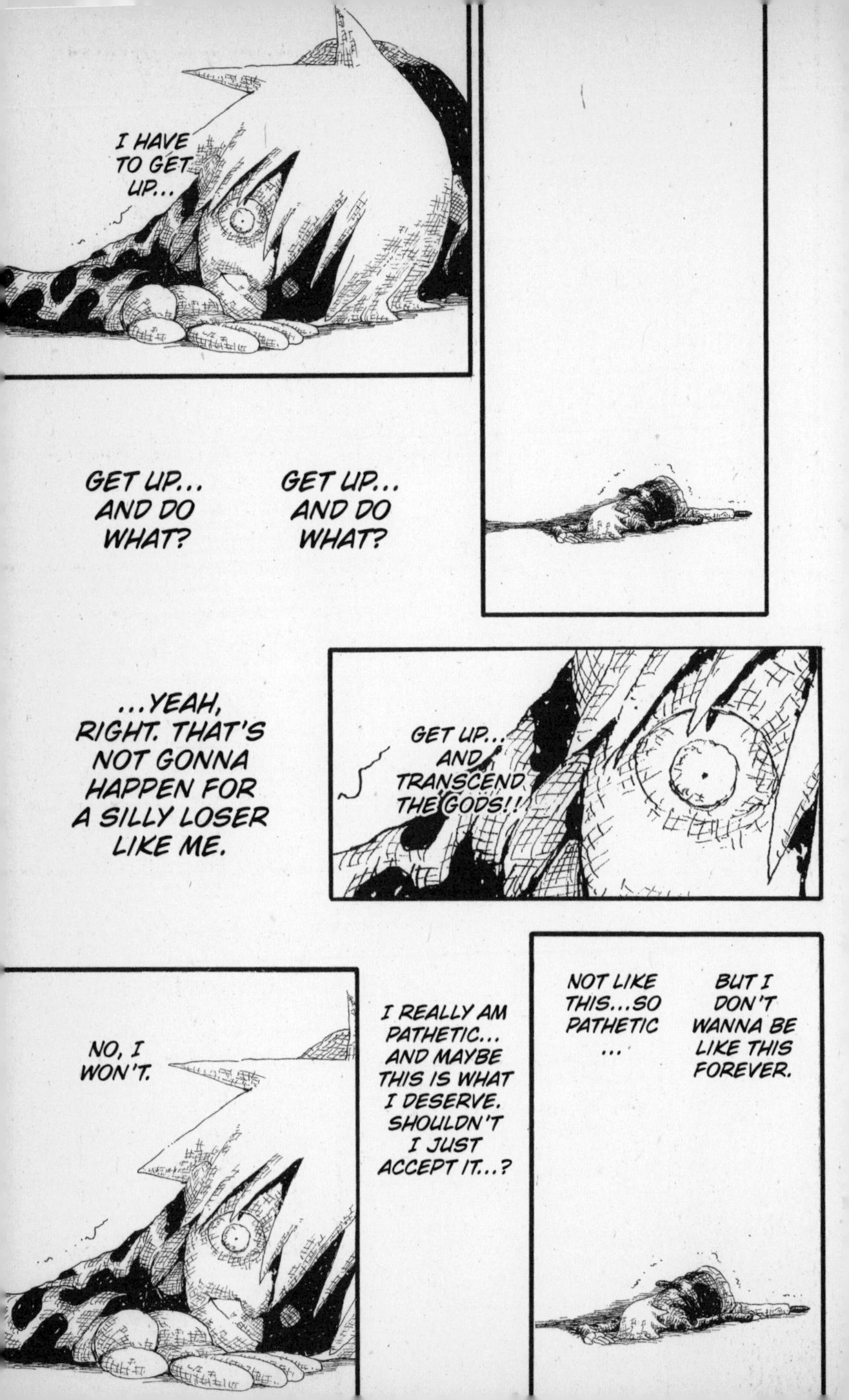
I HAVE TO GET UP...
GET UP... AND DO WHAT?
GET UP... AND DO WHAT?
GET UP... AND TRANSCEND THE GODS!!
...YEAH, RIGHT. THAT'S NOT GONNA HAPPEN FOR A SILLY LOSER LIKE ME.
BUT I DON'T WANNA BE LIKE THIS FOREVER.
NOT LIKE THIS...SO PATHETIC ...
I REALLY AM PATHETIC... AND MAYBE THIS IS WHAT I DESERVE. SHOULDN'T I JUST ACCEPT IT...?
NO, I WON'T.

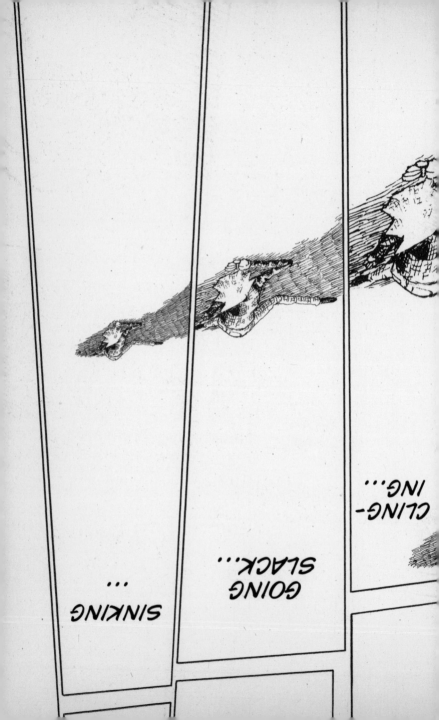

SINKING
...

GOING
SLACK...

CLING-
ING...

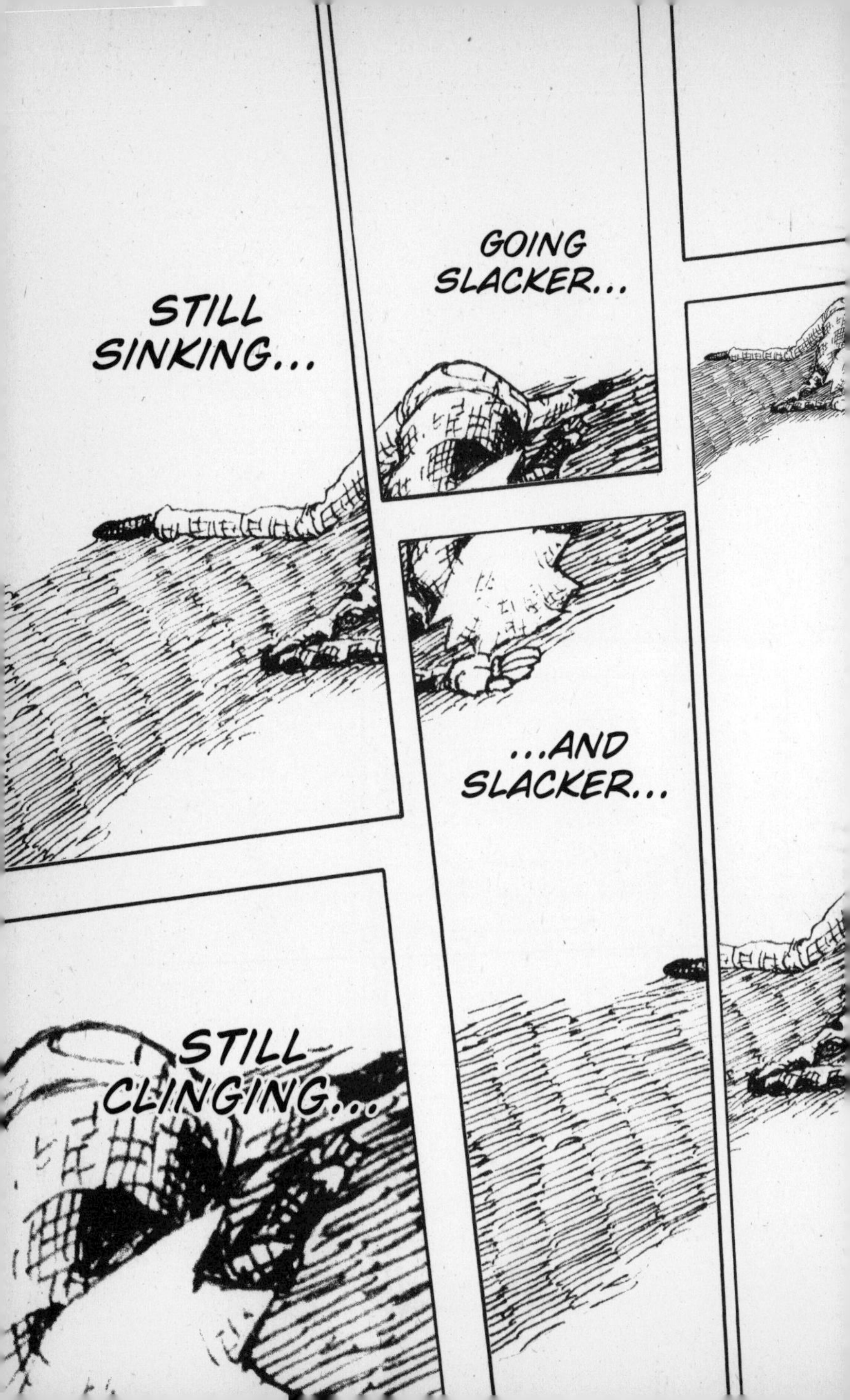
GOING SLACKER...
...AND SLACKER...
STILL SINKING...
STILL CLINGING...

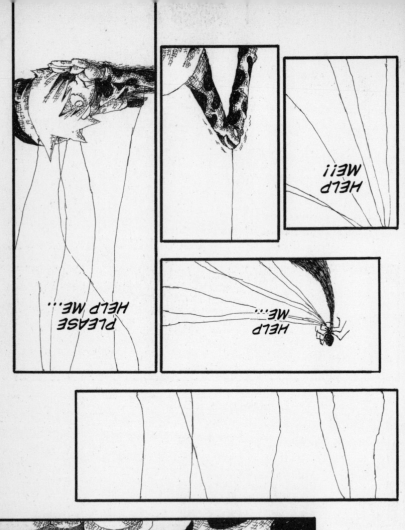

HELP ME!!

HELP ME...

PLEASE HELP ME...

HELP ME...

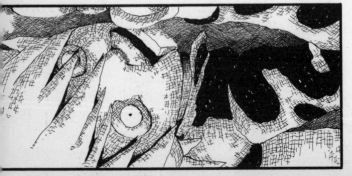

...ON

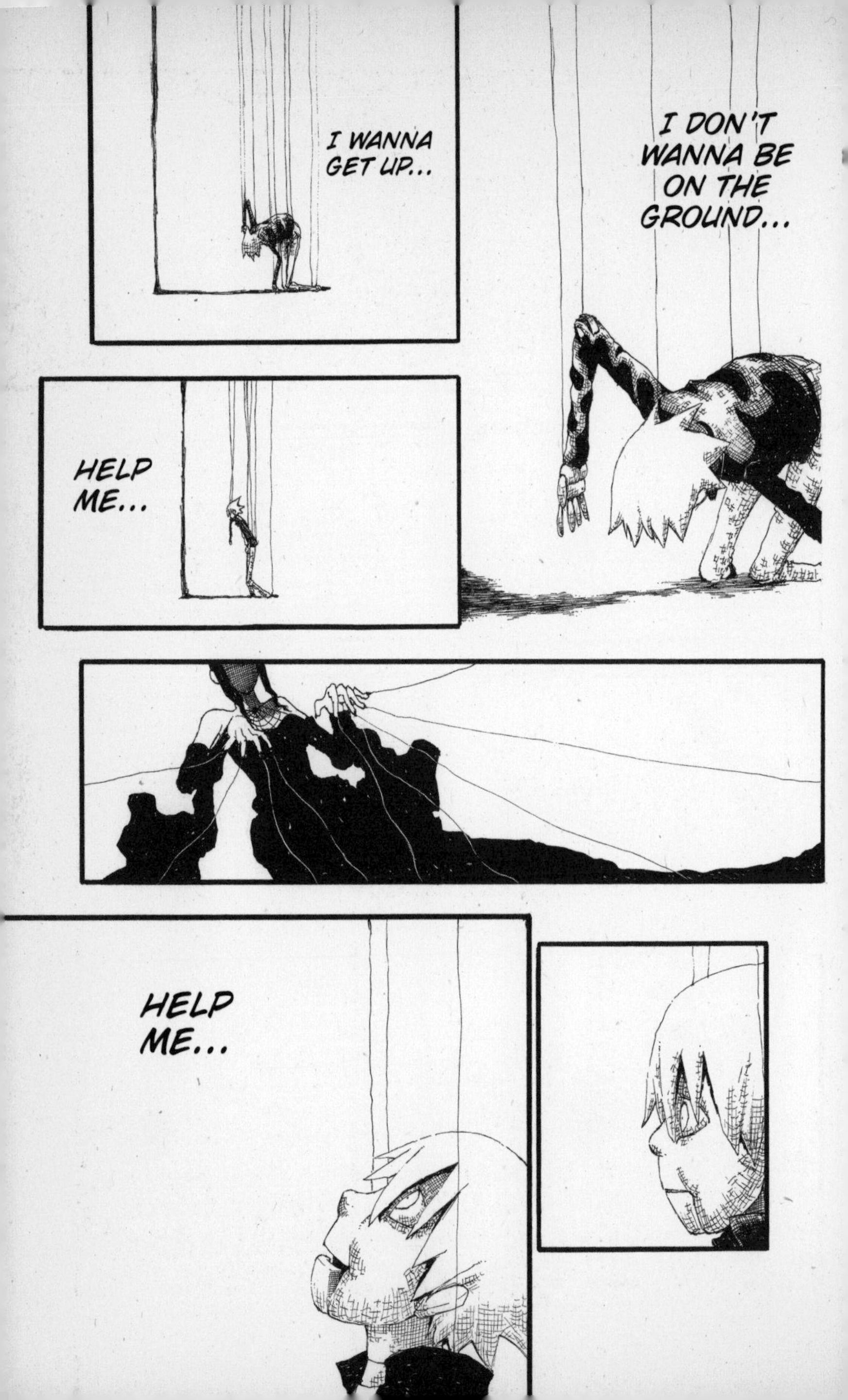
I DON'T WANNA BE ON THE GROUND...
I WANNA GET UP...
HELP ME...
HELP ME...

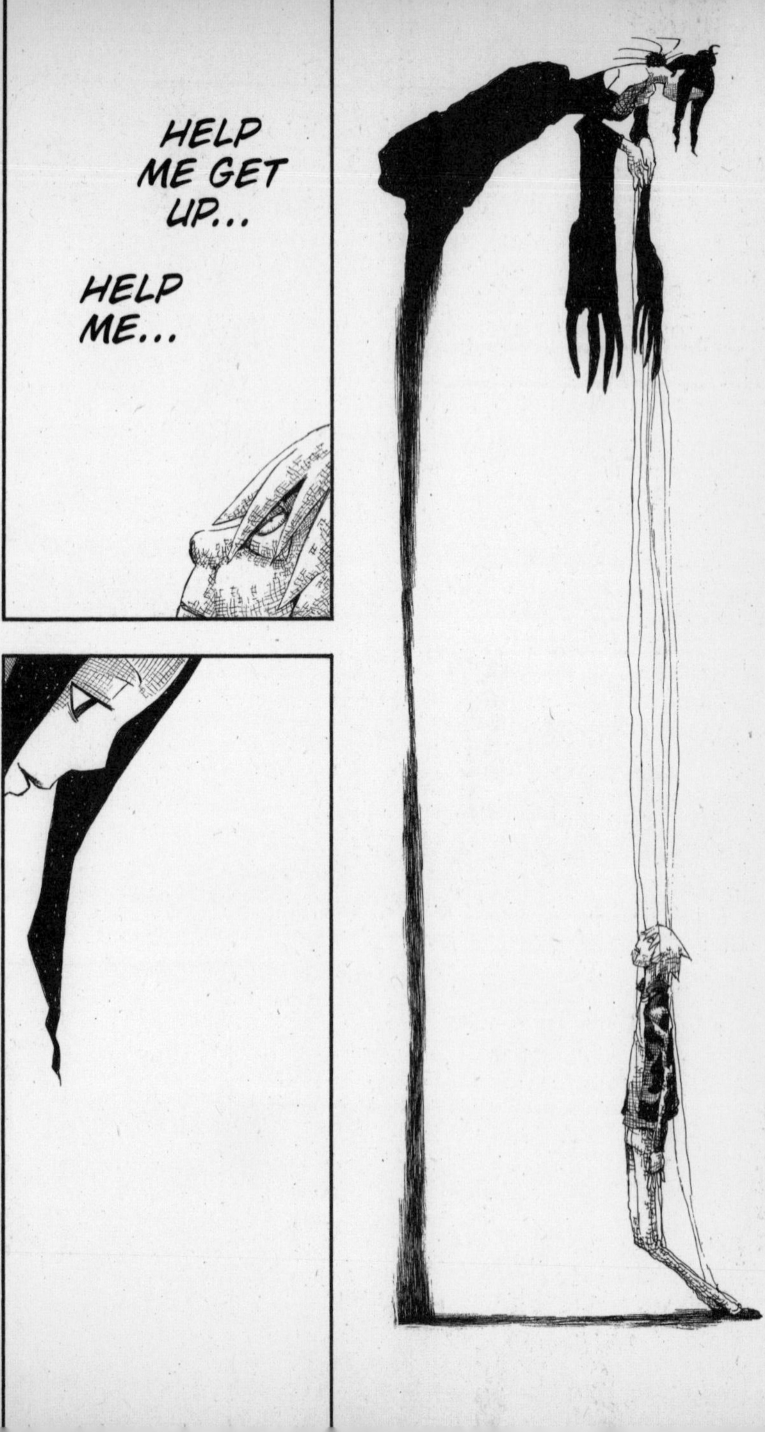
HELP ME GET UP...
HELP ME...

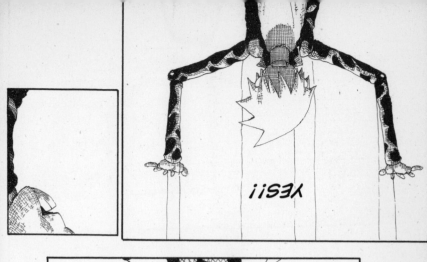

YES!!

I WILL.

HELP ME...

HELP ME...

I WILL GUIDE YOU AND SHOW YOU THE WAY.

YOU DON'T HAVE TO WORRY ANY-MORE ABOUT WHAT PATH YOU SHOULD FOLLOW. SOUL, I HAVE IT ALL TAKEN CARE OF.

THIS DARKNESS BINDS US TOGETHER, SOUL. YOU MUSTN'T TRY TO CUT FREE OF IT.

I'M SAVED!!!
MAKAAAA...
!!

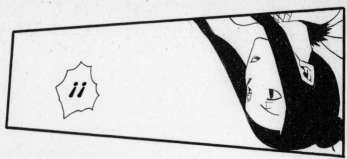

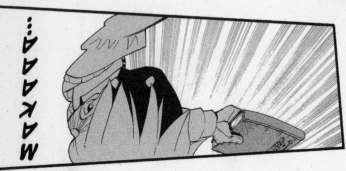

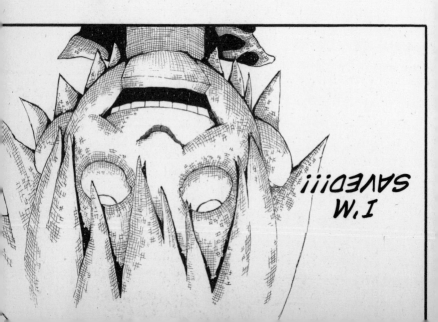

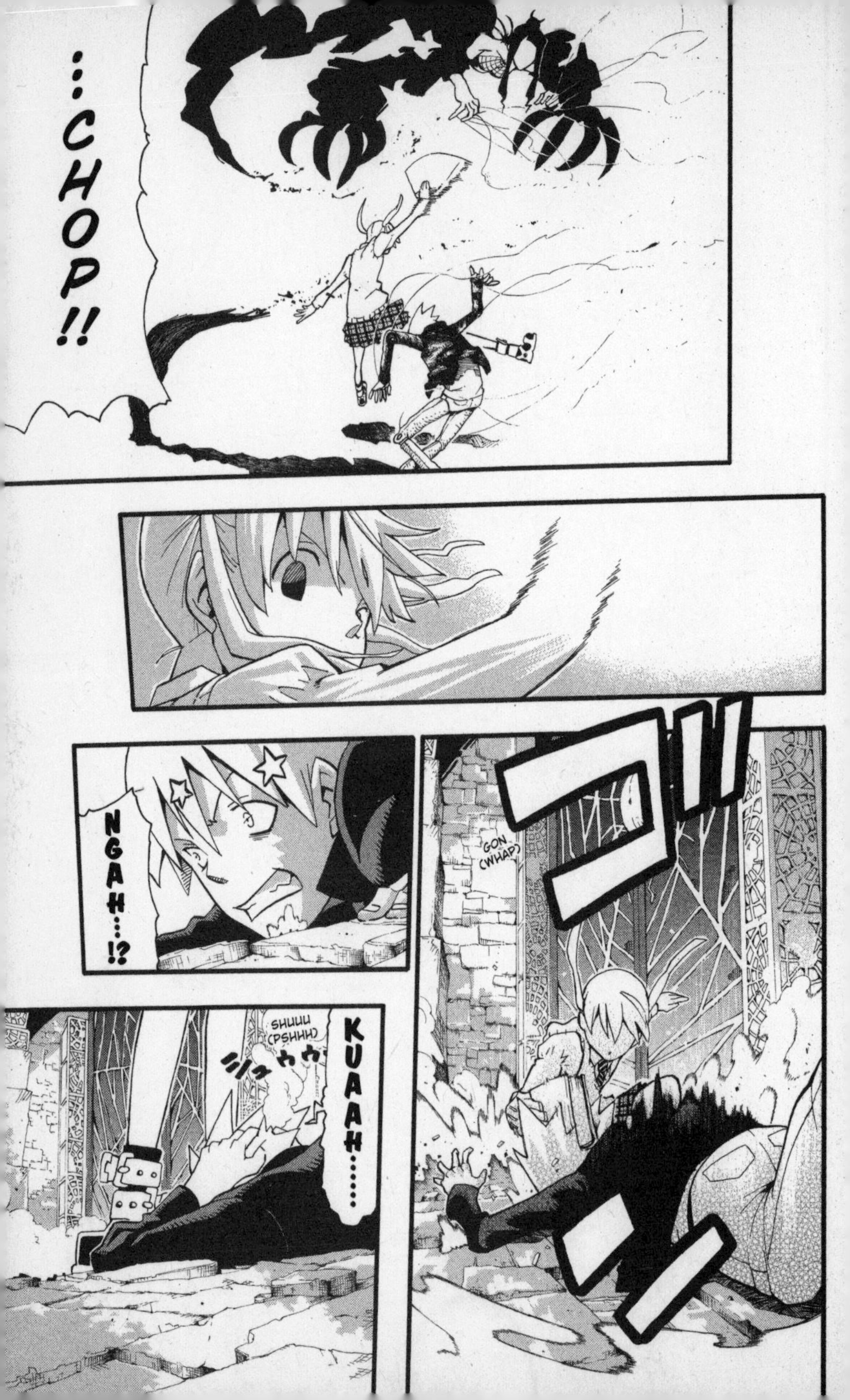
...CHOP!!
GON (WHAP)
NGAH...!?
SHUUU (PSHHH)
KUAAH......

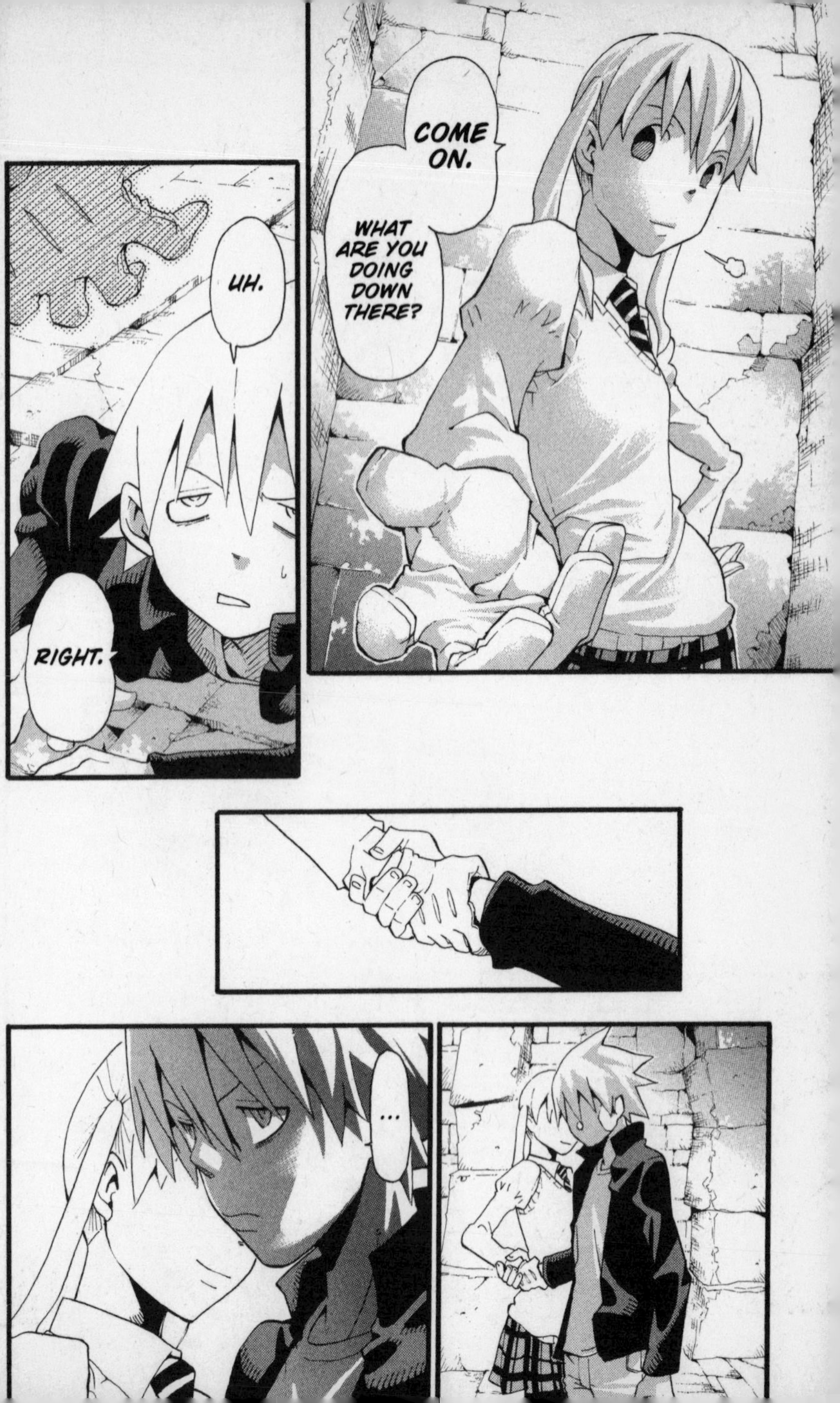
COME ON.
WHAT ARE YOU DOING DOWN THERE?
UH.
RIGHT.
...

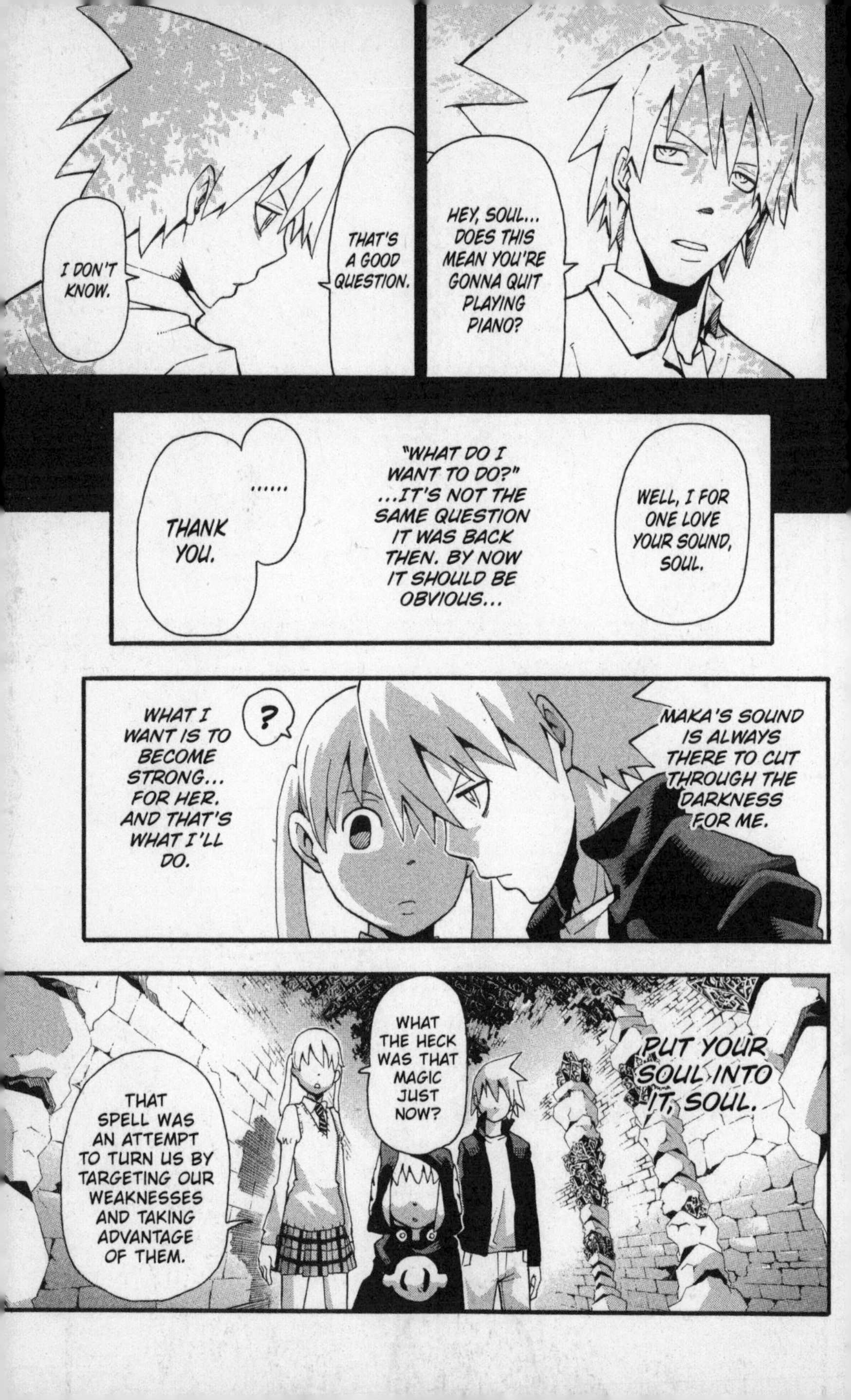
HEY, SOUL... DOES THIS MEAN YOU'RE GONNA QUIT PLAYING PIANO?
THAT'S A GOOD QUESTION.
I DON'T KNOW.
WELL, I FOR ONE LOVE YOUR SOUND, SOUL.
"WHAT DO I WANT TO DO?" ...IT'S NOT THE SAME QUESTION IT WAS BACK THEN. BY NOW IT SHOULD BE OBVIOUS...
......
THANK YOU.
MAKA'S SOUND IS ALWAYS THERE TO CUT THROUGH THE DARKNESS FOR ME.
?
WHAT I WANT IS TO BECOME STRONG... FOR HER. AND THAT'S WHAT I'LL DO.
PUT YOUR SOUL INTO IT, SOUL.
WHAT THE HECK WAS THAT MAGIC JUST NOW?
THAT SPELL WAS AN ATTEMPT TO TURN US BY TARGETING OUR WEAKNESSES AND TAKING ADVANTAGE OF THEM.

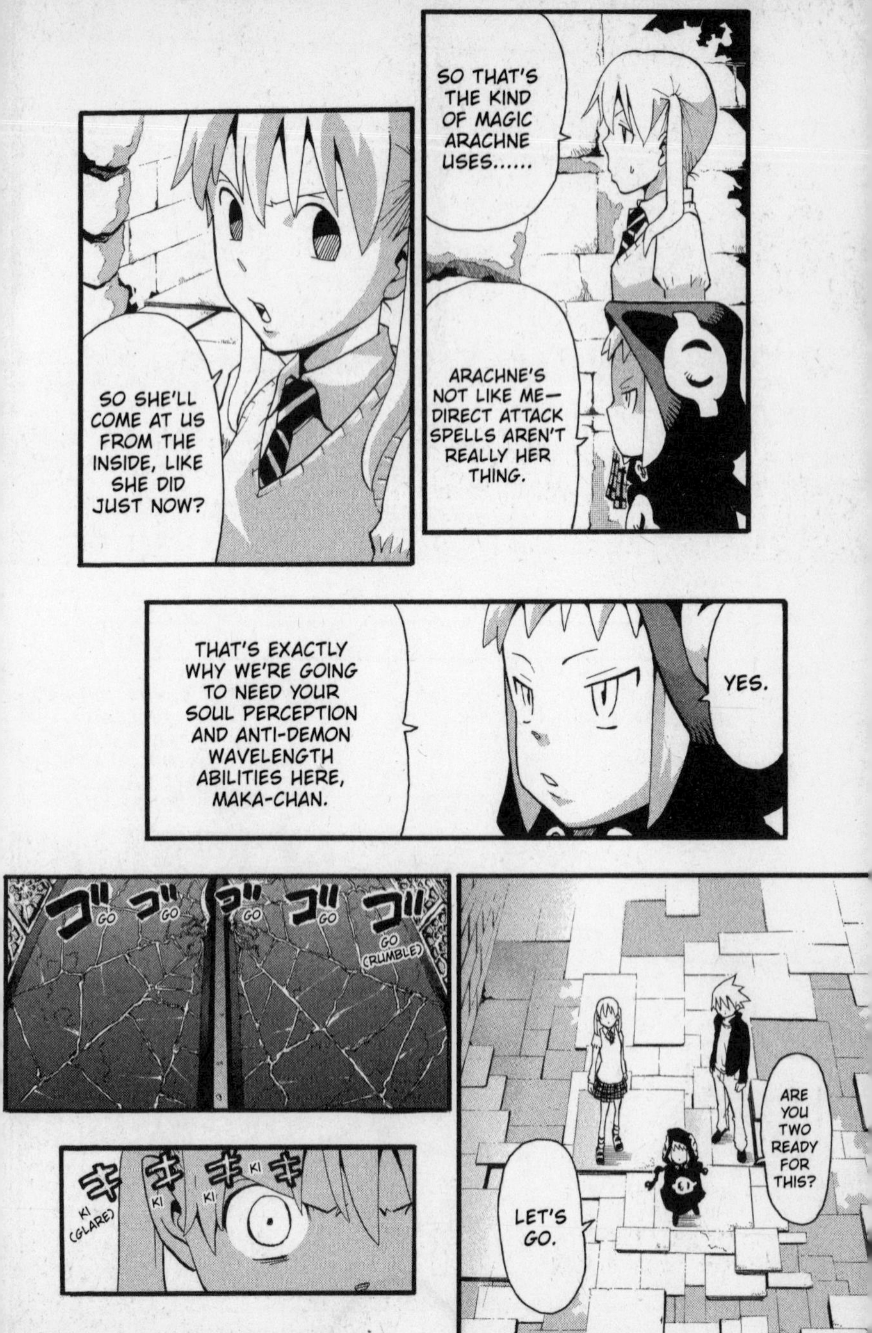
SO THAT'S THE KIND OF MAGIC ARACHNE USES......
ARACHNE'S NOT LIKE ME— DIRECT ATTACK SPELLS AREN'T REALLY HER THING.
SO SHE'LL COME AT US FROM THE INSIDE, LIKE SHE DID JUST NOW?
YES.
THAT'S EXACTLY WHY WE'RE GOING TO NEED YOUR SOUL PERCEPTION AND ANTI-DEMON WAVELENGTH ABILITIES HERE, MAKA-CHAN.
ARE YOU TWO READY FOR THIS?
LET'S GO.
GO GO GO GO GO (RUMBLE)
KI KI KI KI (GLARE)

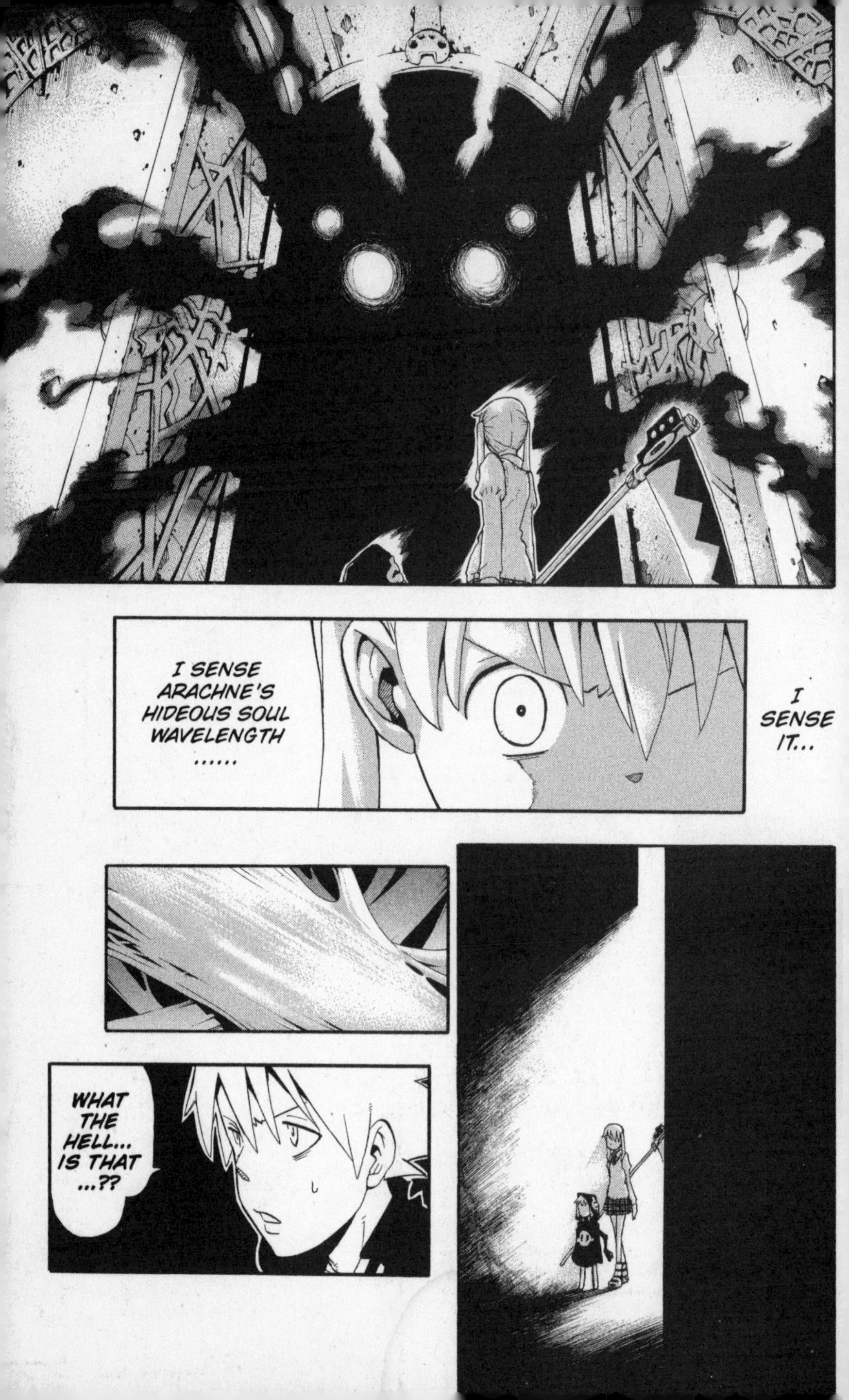
I SENSE IT...
I SENSE ARACHNE'S HIDEOUS SOUL WAVELENGTH ......
WHAT THE HELL... IS THAT ...??

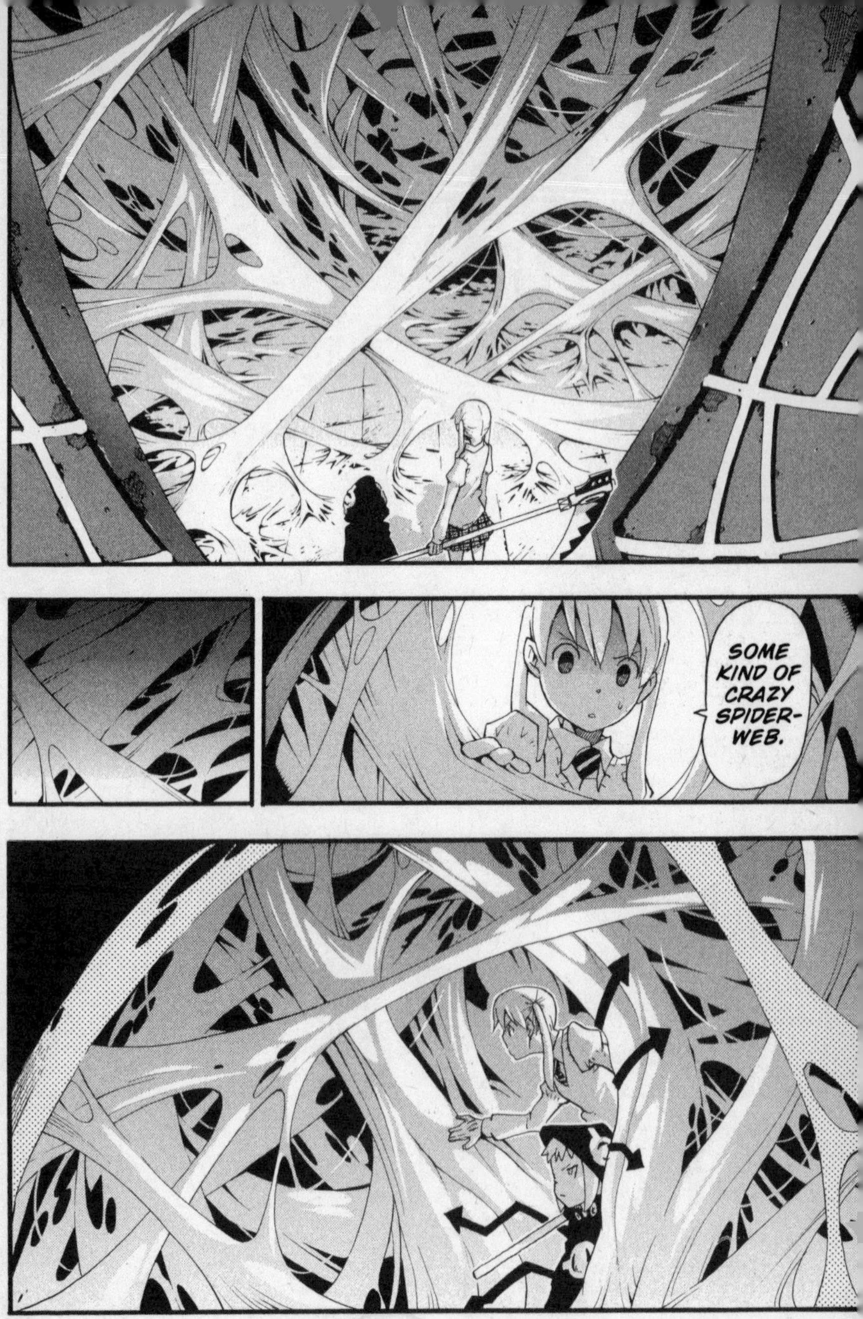
SOME KIND OF CRAZY SPIDER-WEB.

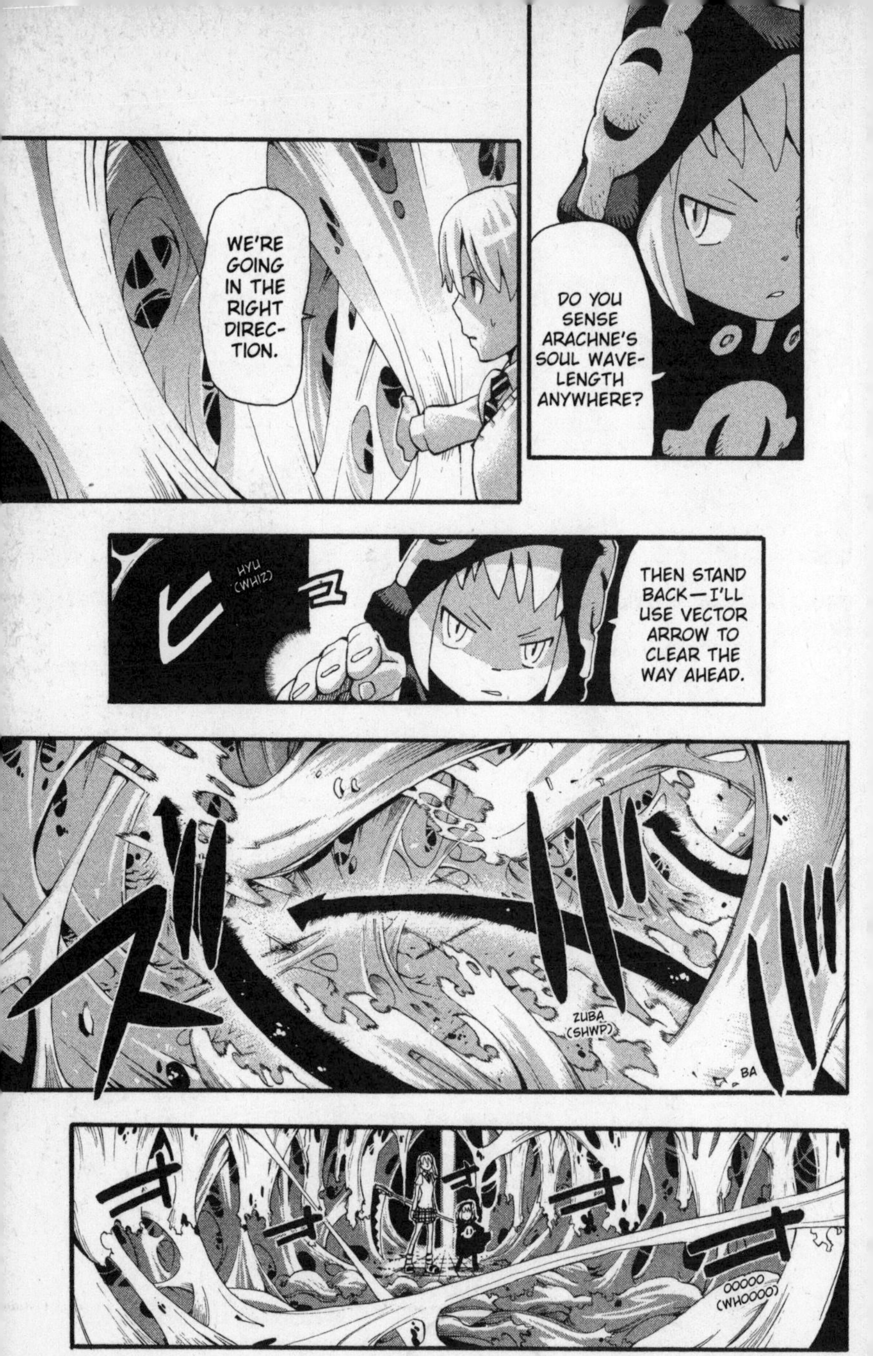
DO YOU SENSE ARACHNE'S SOUL WAVE-LENGTH ANYWHERE?
WE'RE GOING IN THE RIGHT DIREC-TION.
THEN STAND BACK—I'LL USE VECTOR ARROW TO CLEAR THE WAY AHEAD.
HYU (WHIZ)
ZUBA (SHWP)
BA
OOOOO (WHOOOO)

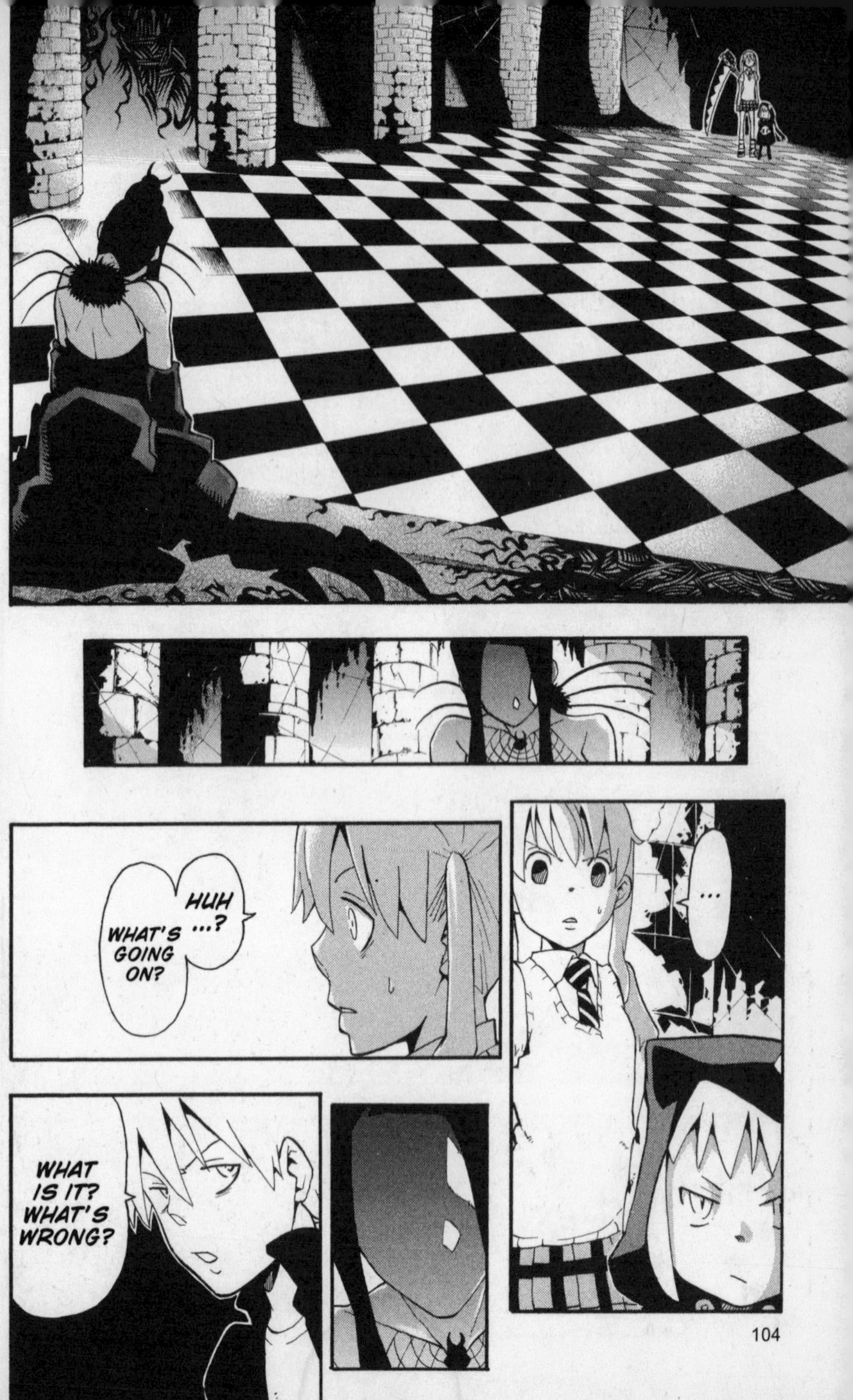
...
HUH ...? WHAT'S GOING ON?
WHAT IS IT? WHAT'S WRONG?

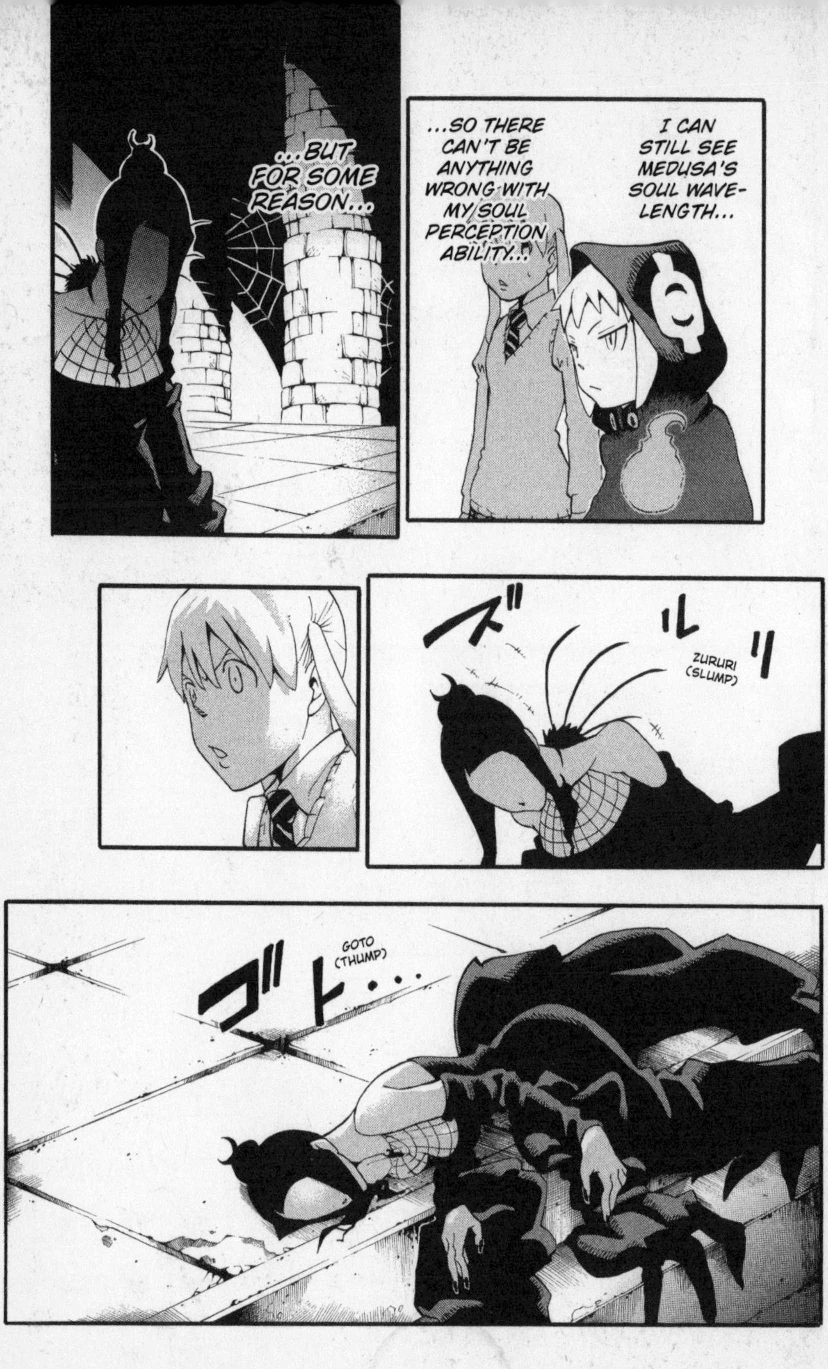
I CAN STILL SEE MEDUSA'S SOUL WAVE-LENGTH...
...SO THERE CAN'T BE ANYTHING WRONG WITH MY SOUL PERCEPTION ABILITY...
...BUT FOR SOME REASON...
ZURURI (SLUMP)
GOTO (THUMP)

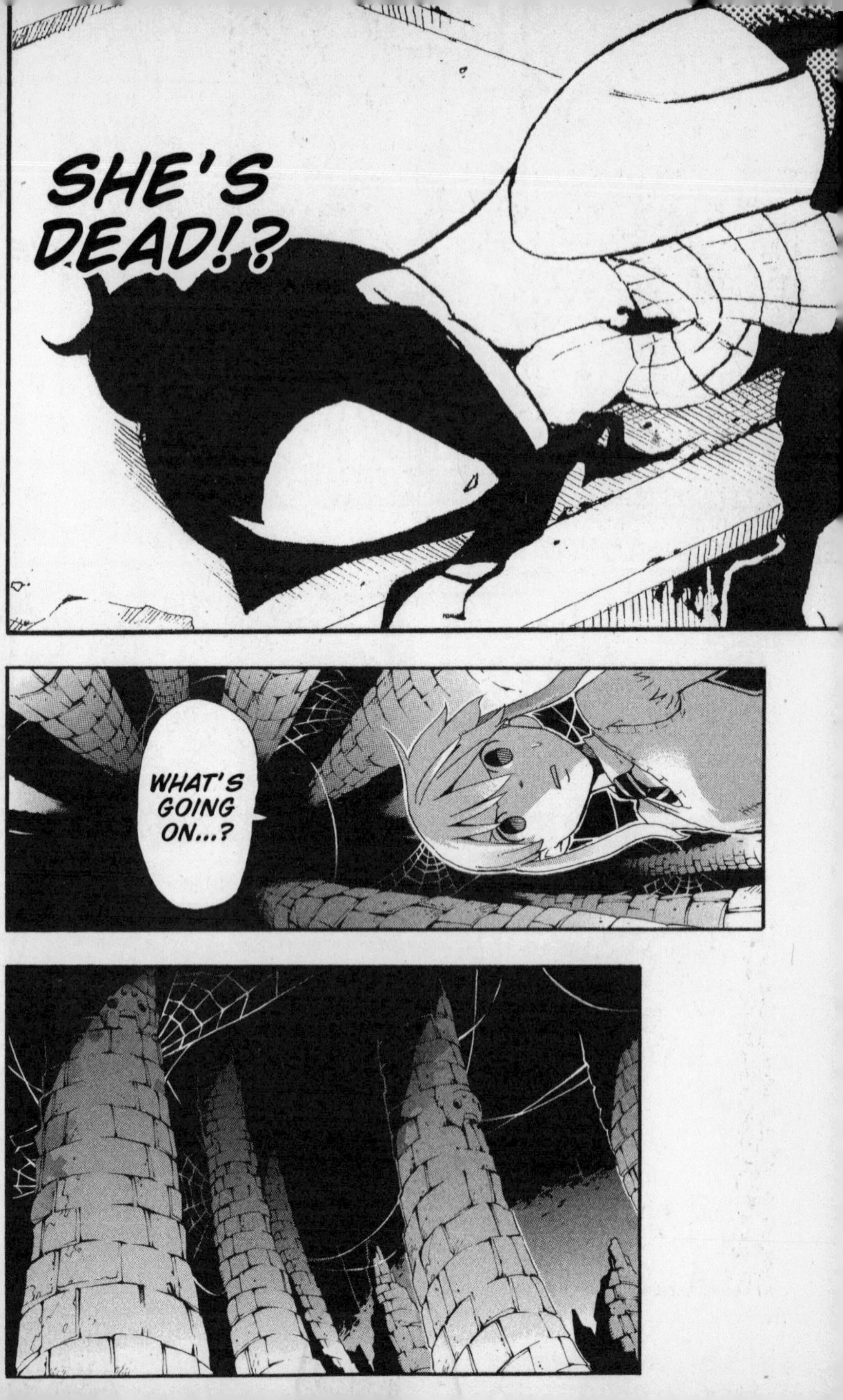
SHE'S DEAD!?
WHAT'S GOING ON...?

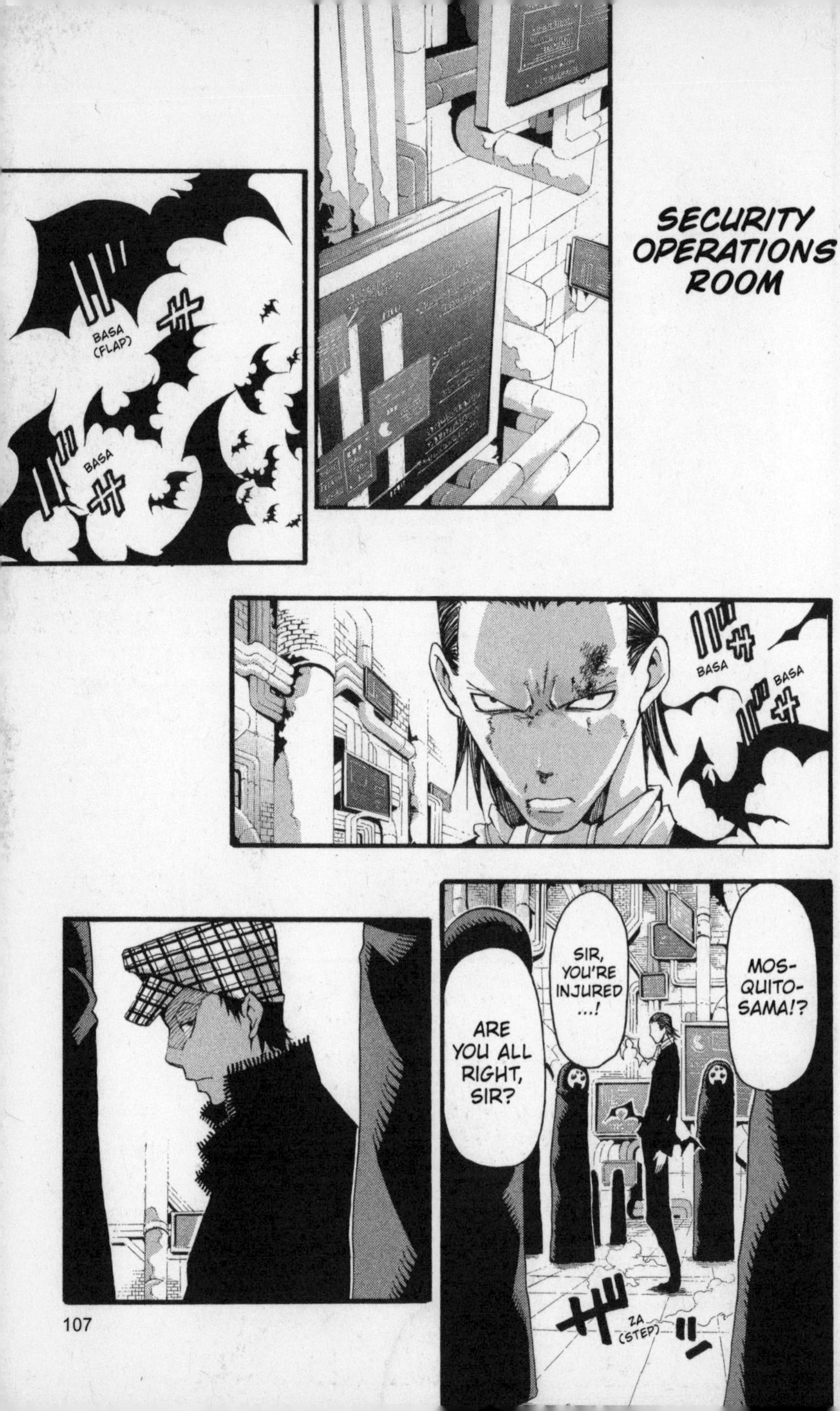
SECURITY OPERATIONS ROOM
BASA (FLAP)
BASA
BASA
BASA
MOS-QUITO-SAMA!?
SIR, YOU'RE INJURED ...!
ARE YOU ALL RIGHT, SIR?
ZA (STEP)

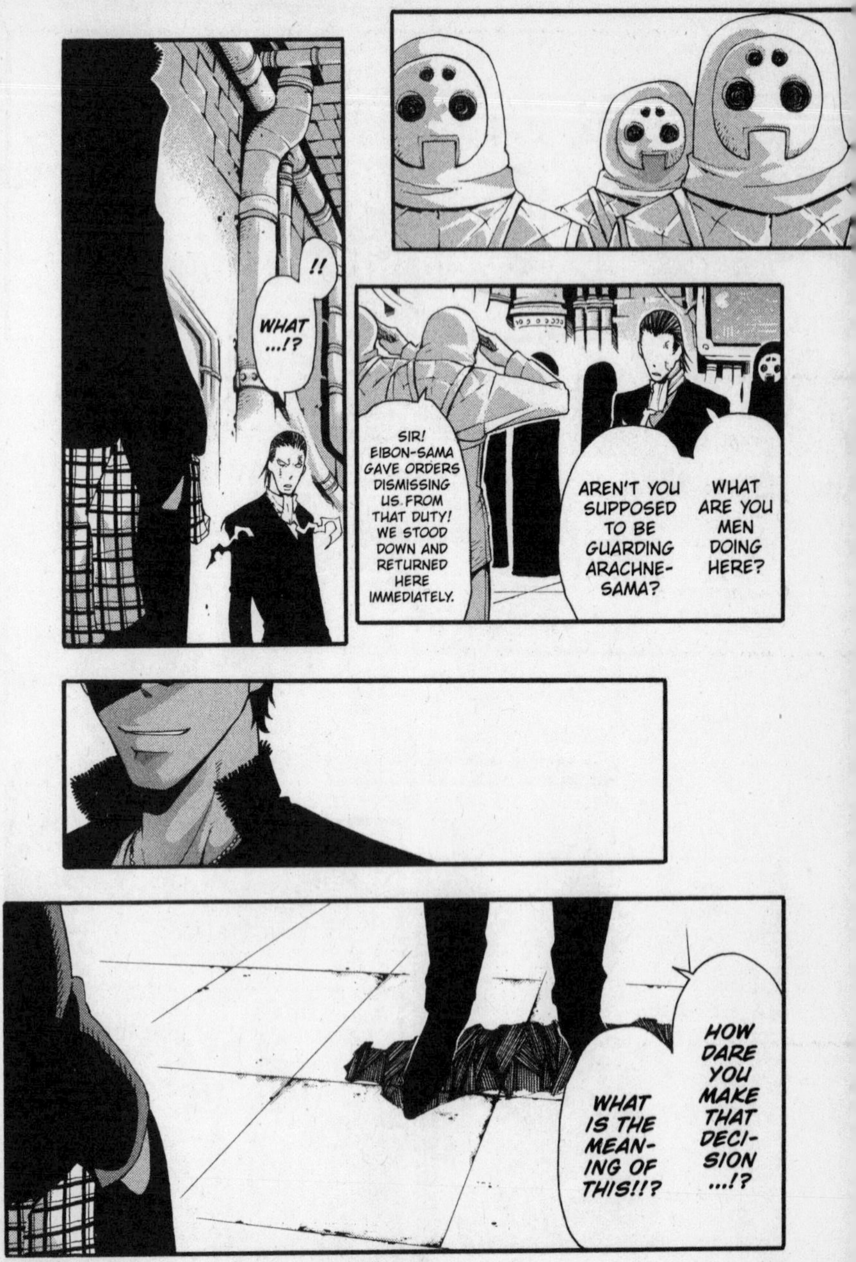
WHAT ARE YOU MEN DOING HERE?
AREN'T YOU SUPPOSED TO BE GUARDING ARACHNE-SAMA?
SIR! EIBON-SAMA GAVE ORDERS DISMISSING US FROM THAT DUTY! WE STOOD DOWN AND RETURNED HERE IMMEDIATELY.
!!
WHAT ...!?
HOW DARE YOU MAKE THAT DECI-SION ...!?
WHAT IS THE MEAN-ING OF THIS!!?

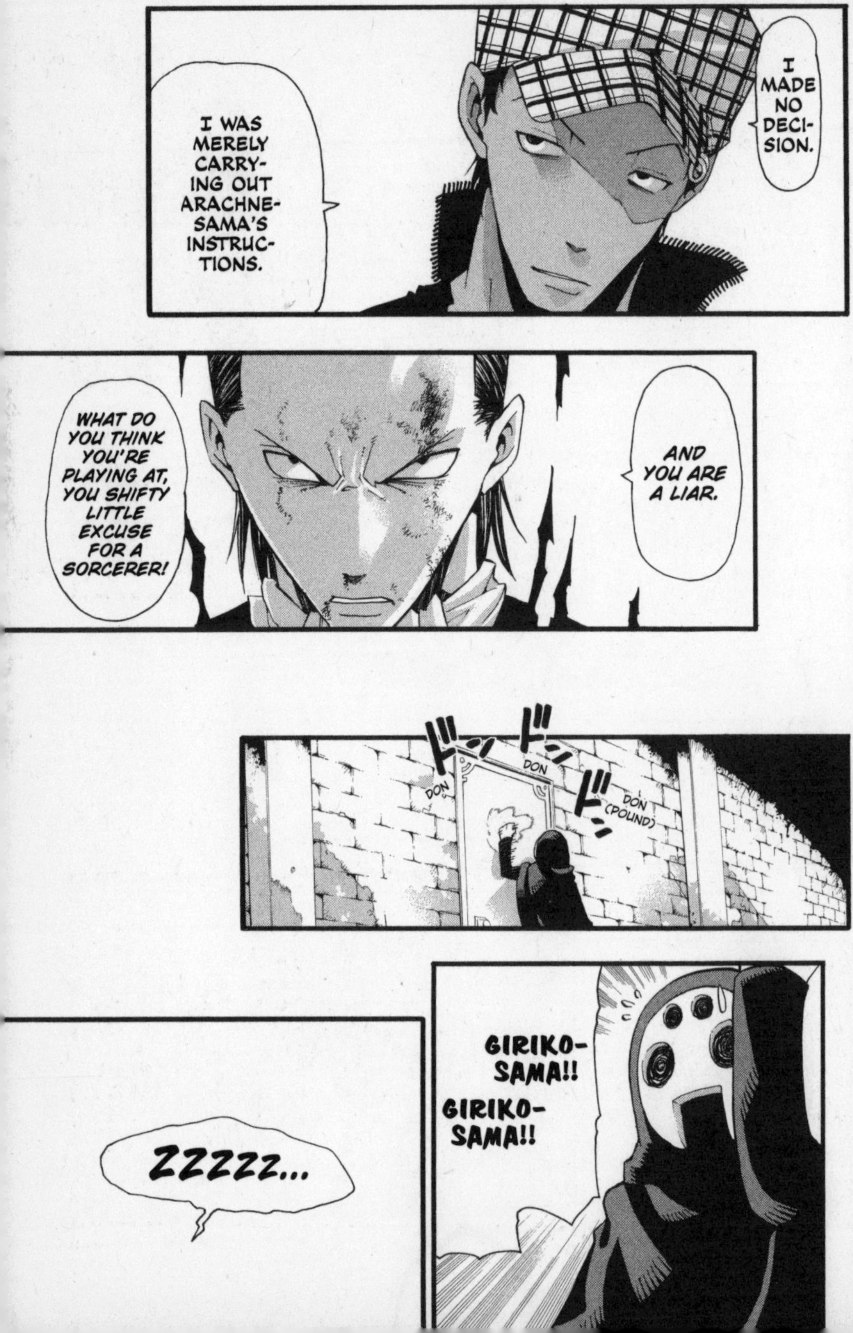
I MADE NO DECISION.
I WAS MERELY CARRYING OUT ARACHNE-SAMA'S INSTRUCTIONS.
AND YOU ARE A LIAR.
WHAT DO YOU THINK YOU'RE PLAYING AT, YOU SHIFTY LITTLE EXCUSE FOR A SORCERER!
DON DON DON (POUND)
GIRIKO-SAMA!!
GIRIKO-SAMA!!
ZZZZZ...

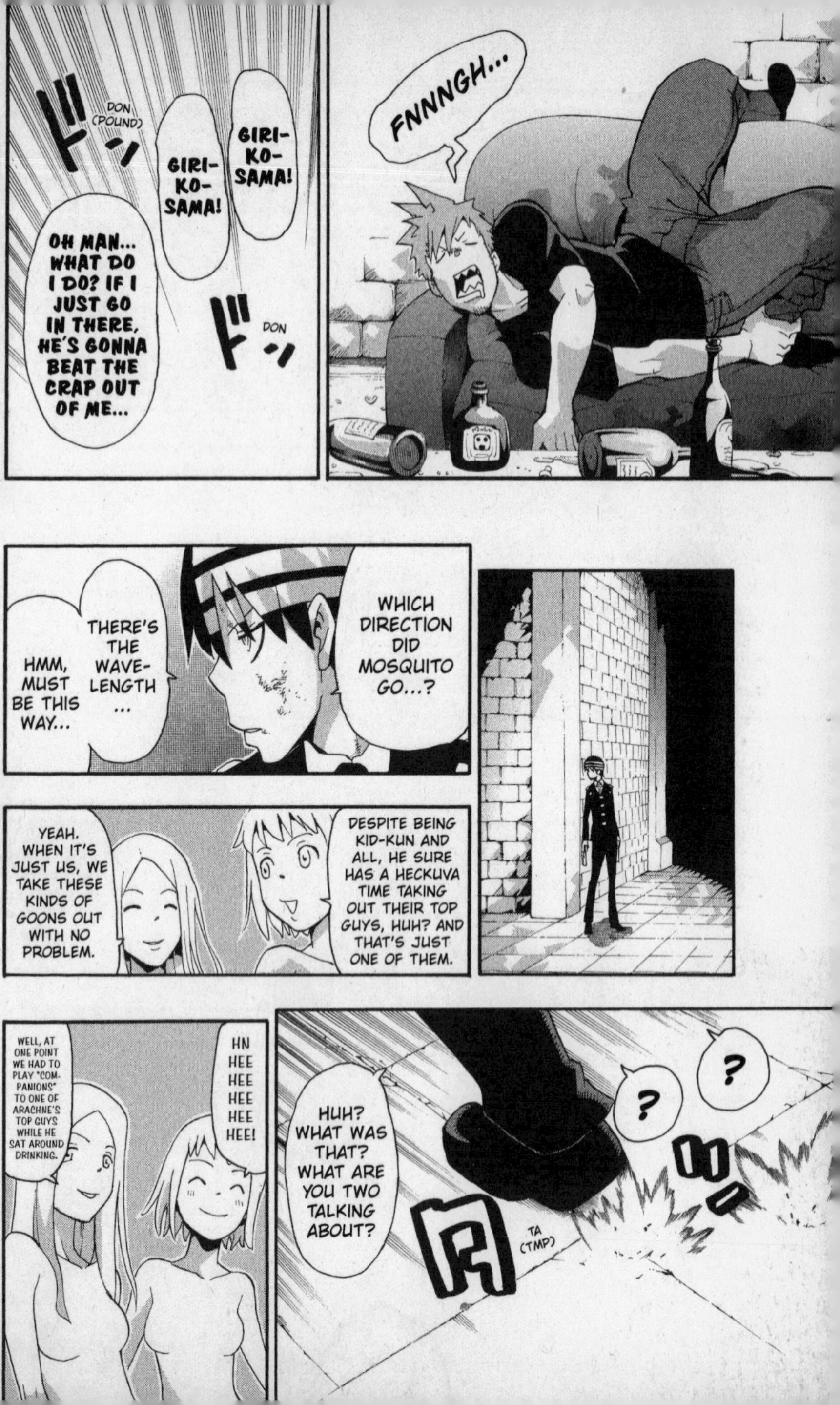
FNNNGH...
GIRI-KO-SAMA!
GIRI-KO-SAMA!
DON (POUND)
OH MAN... WHAT DO I DO? IF I JUST GO IN THERE, HE'S GONNA BEAT THE CRAP OUT OF ME...
DON
WHICH DIRECTION DID MOSQUITO GO...?
THERE'S THE WAVE-LENGTH ...
HMM, MUST BE THIS WAY...
DESPITE BEING KID-KUN AND ALL, HE SURE HAS A HECKUVA TIME TAKING OUT THEIR TOP GUYS, HUH? AND THAT'S JUST ONE OF THEM.
YEAH. WHEN IT'S JUST US, WE TAKE THESE KINDS OF GOONS OUT WITH NO PROBLEM.
?
?
TA (TMP)
HUH? WHAT WAS THAT? WHAT ARE YOU TWO TALKING ABOUT?
HN HEE HEE HEE HEE HEE!
WELL, AT ONE POINT WE HAD TO PLAY "COM-PANIONS" TO ONE OF ARACHNE'S TOP GUYS WHILE HE SAT AROUND DRINKING.

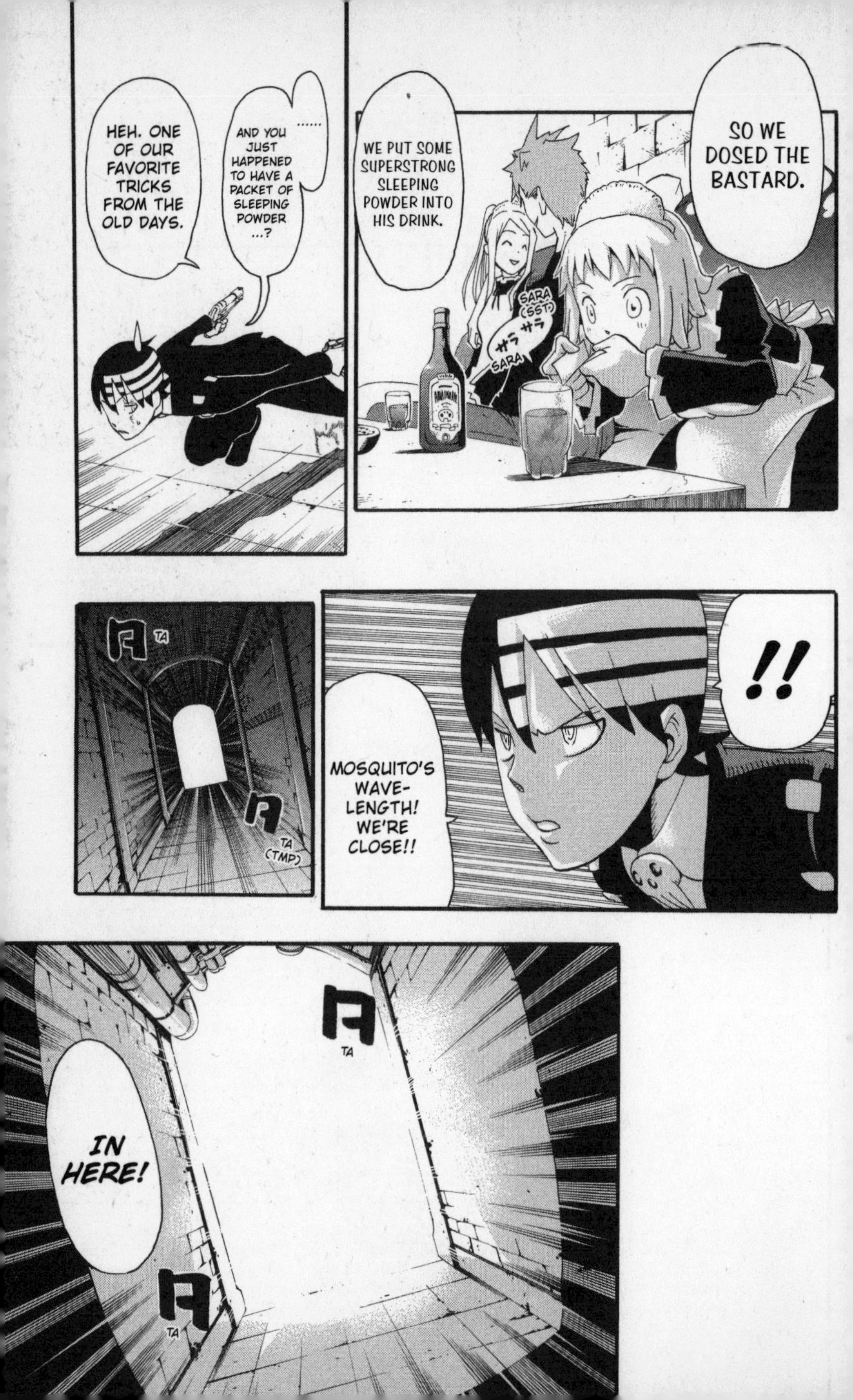
SO WE DOSED THE BASTARD.
WE PUT SOME SUPERSTRONG SLEEPING POWDER INTO HIS DRINK.
サラ サラ
SARA (SST) SARA
HEH. ONE OF OUR FAVORITE TRICKS FROM THE OLD DAYS.
......
AND YOU JUST HAPPENED TO HAVE A PACKET OF SLEEPING POWDER ...?
!!
MOSQUITO'S WAVE-LENGTH! WE'RE CLOSE!!
タ TA
タ TA (TMP)
タ TA
IN HERE!
タ TA

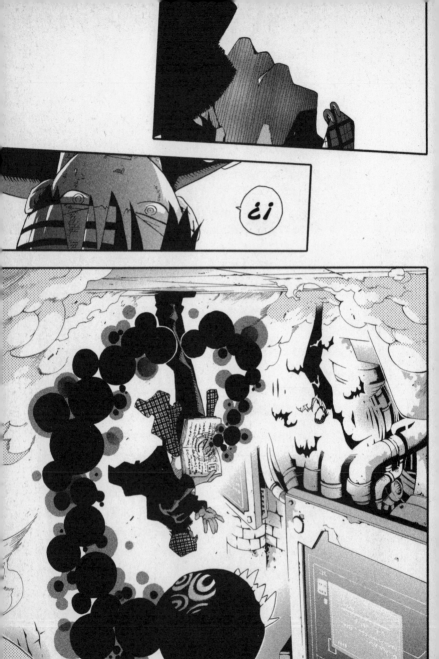

SOUL EATER

CHAPTER 56: OPERATION CAPTURE BABA YAGA CASTLE (PART 11)

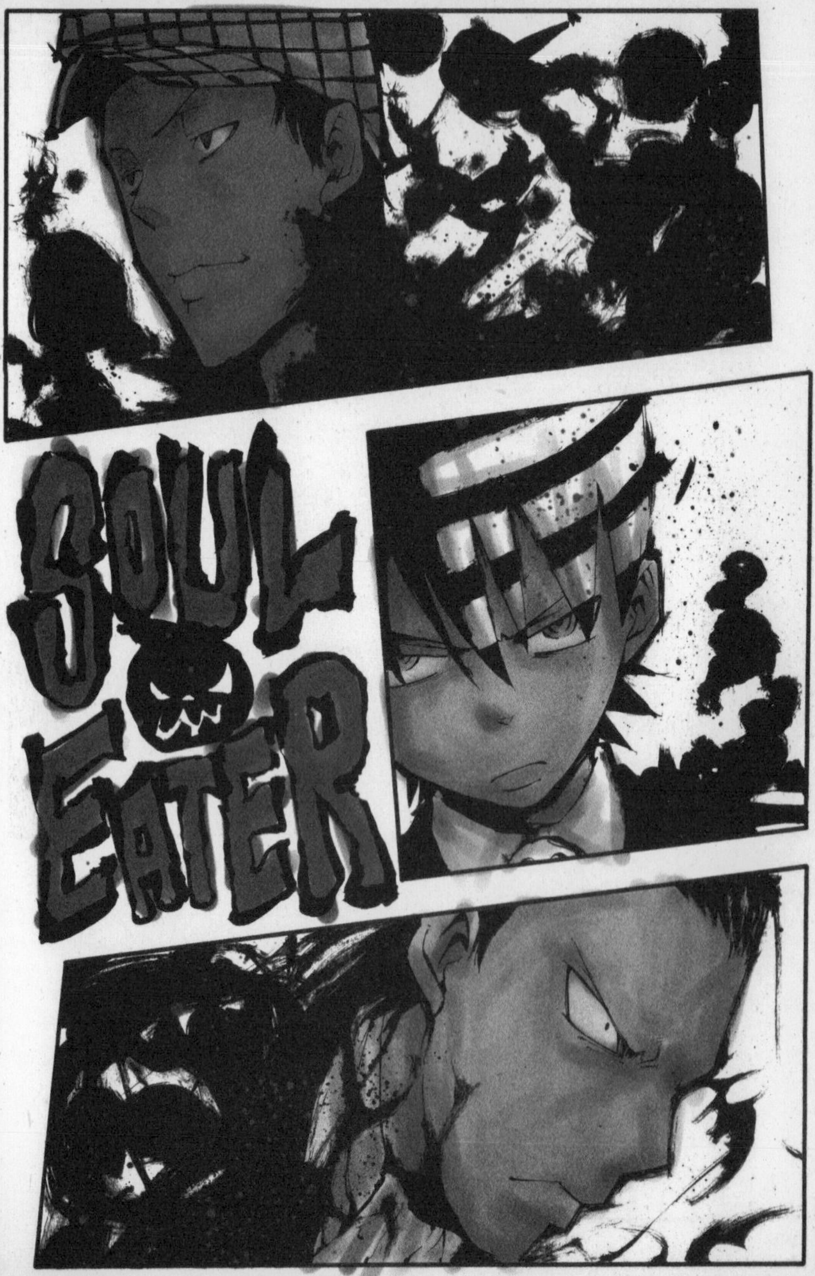
SOUL EATER

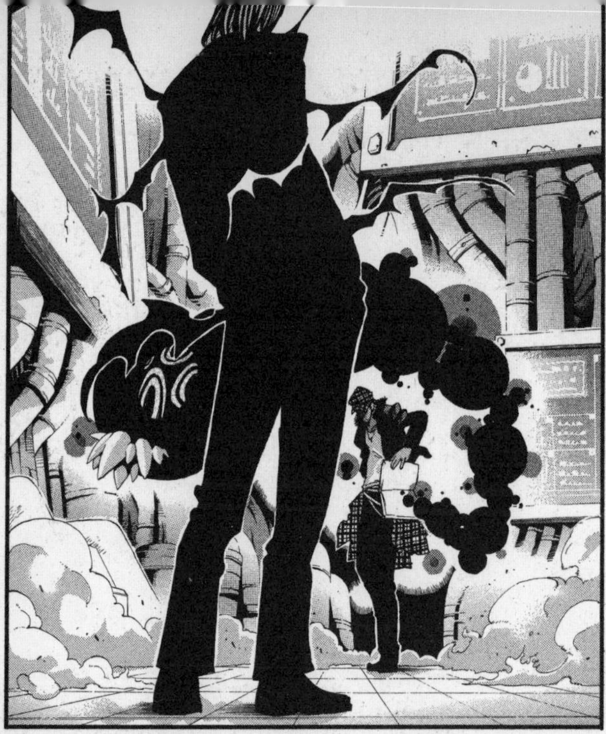
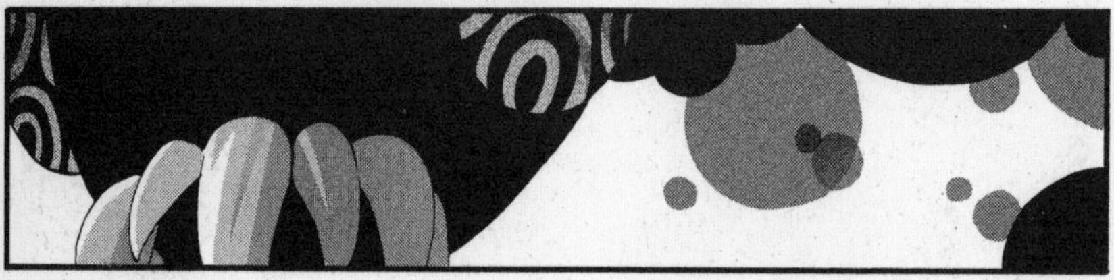
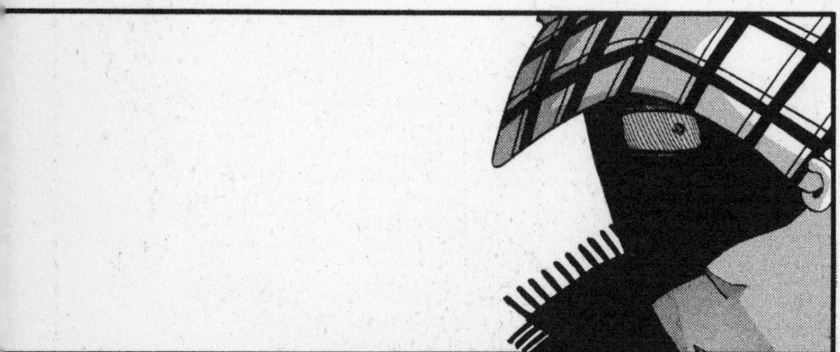

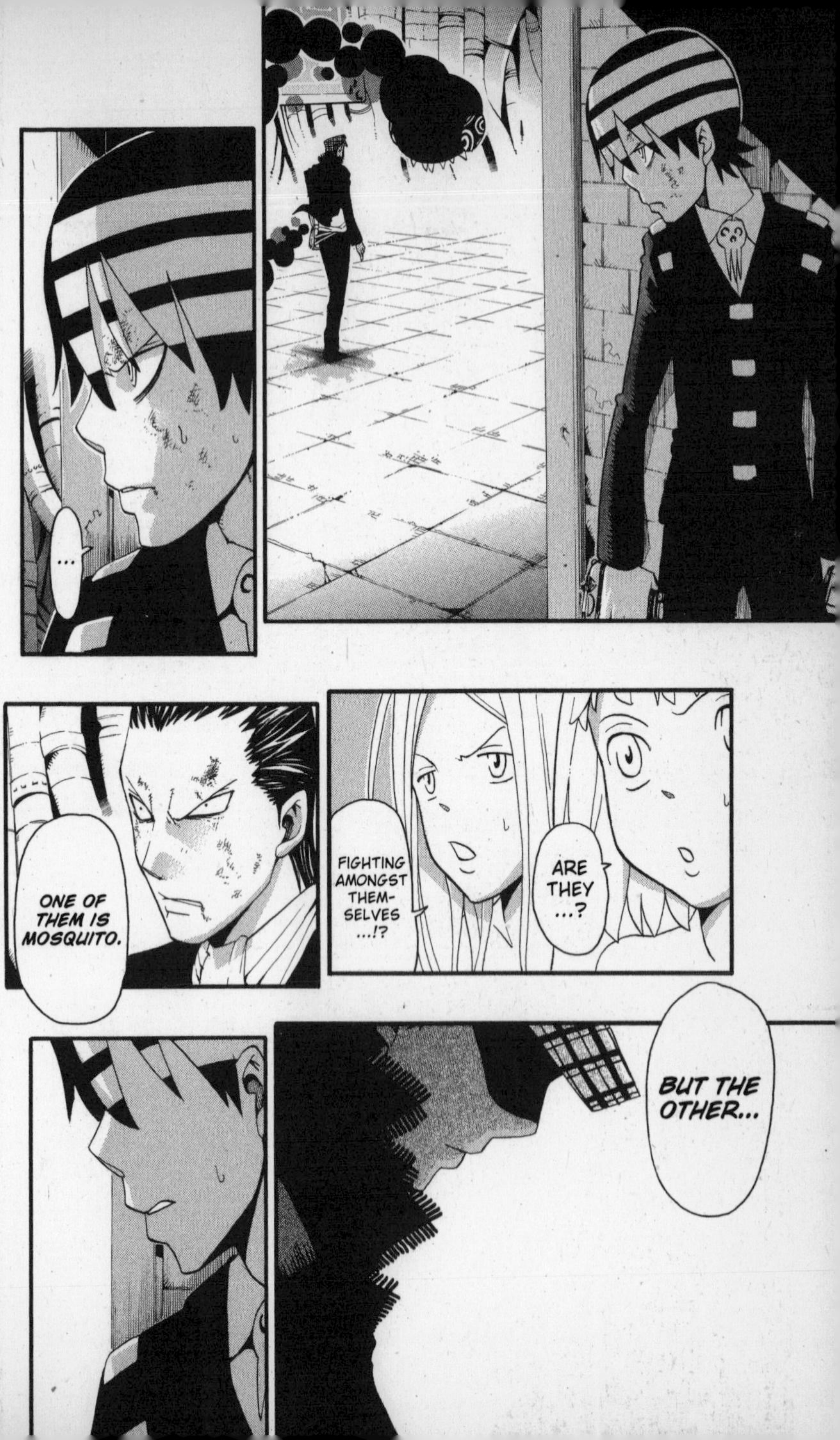
...
ARE THEY ...?
FIGHTING AMONGST THEM-SELVES ...!?
ONE OF THEM IS MOSQUITO.
BUT THE OTHER...

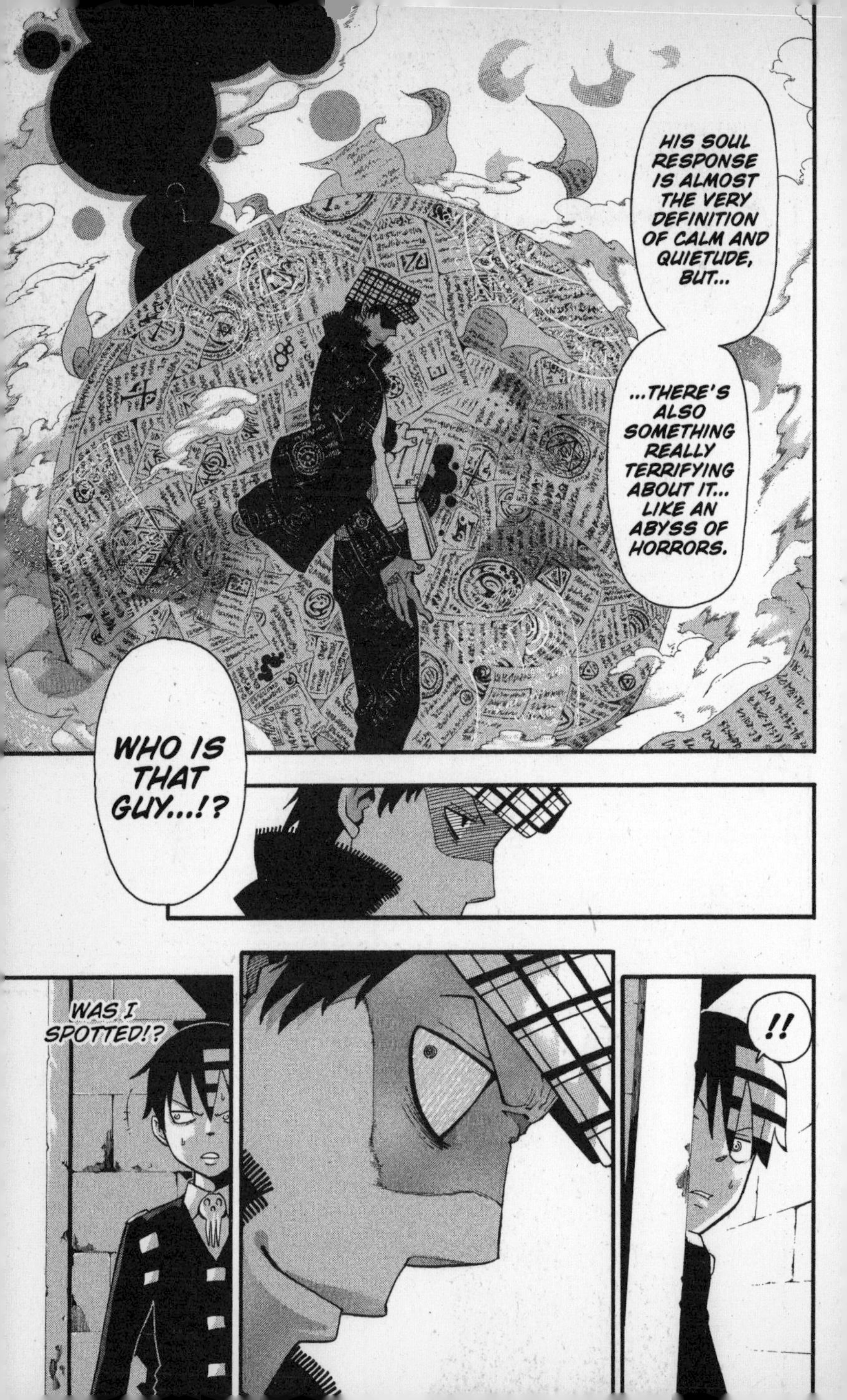
HIS SOUL RESPONSE IS ALMOST THE VERY DEFINITION OF CALM AND QUIETUDE, BUT...
...THERE'S ALSO SOMETHING REALLY TERRIFYING ABOUT IT... LIKE AN ABYSS OF HORRORS.
WHO IS THAT GUY...!?
!!
WAS I SPOTTED!?

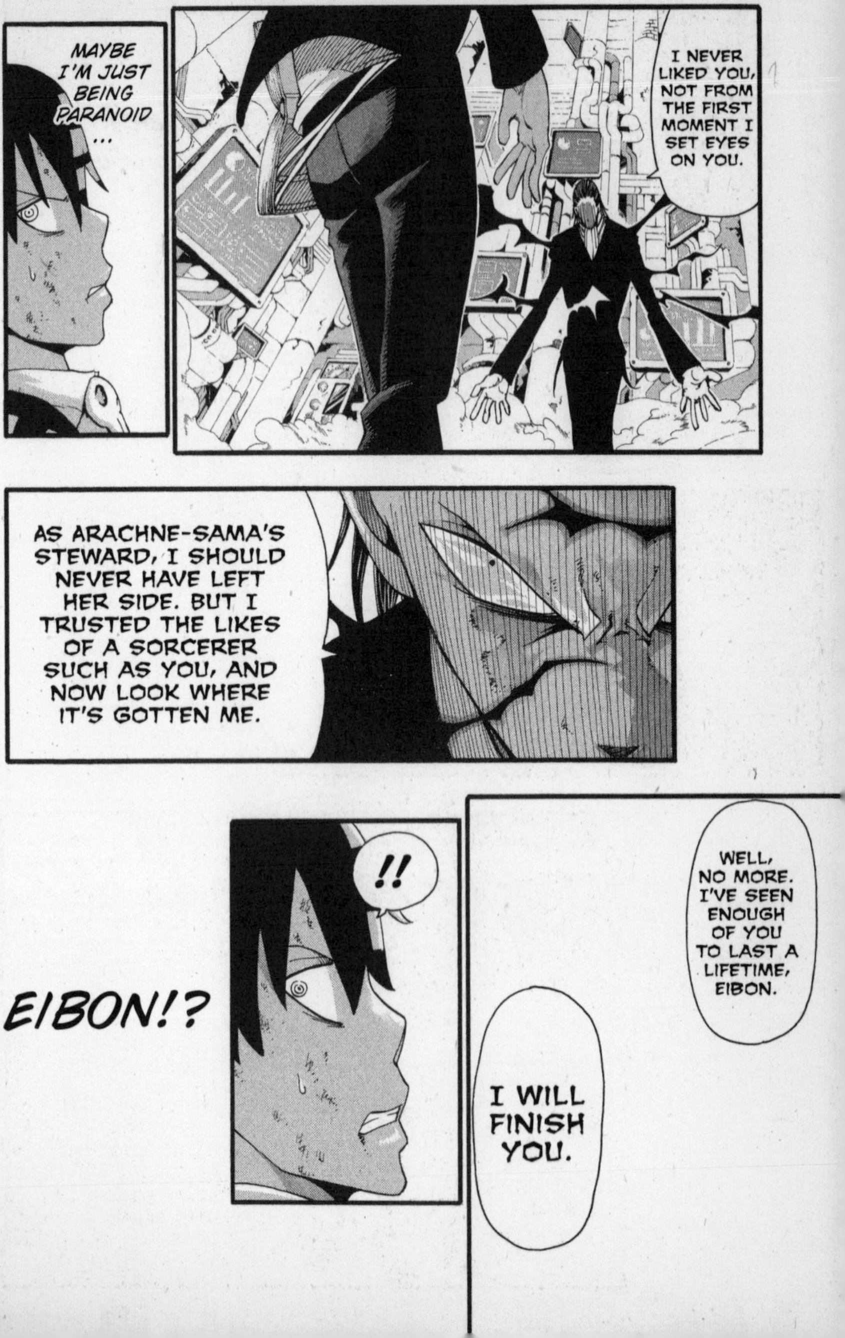
I NEVER LIKED YOU, NOT FROM THE FIRST MOMENT I SET EYES ON YOU.
MAYBE I'M JUST BEING PARANOID ...
AS ARACHNE-SAMA'S STEWARD, I SHOULD NEVER HAVE LEFT HER SIDE. BUT I TRUSTED THE LIKES OF A SORCERER SUCH AS YOU, AND NOW LOOK WHERE IT'S GOTTEN ME.
WELL, NO MORE. I'VE SEEN ENOUGH OF YOU TO LAST A LIFETIME, EIBON.
I WILL FINISH YOU.
!!
EIBON!?

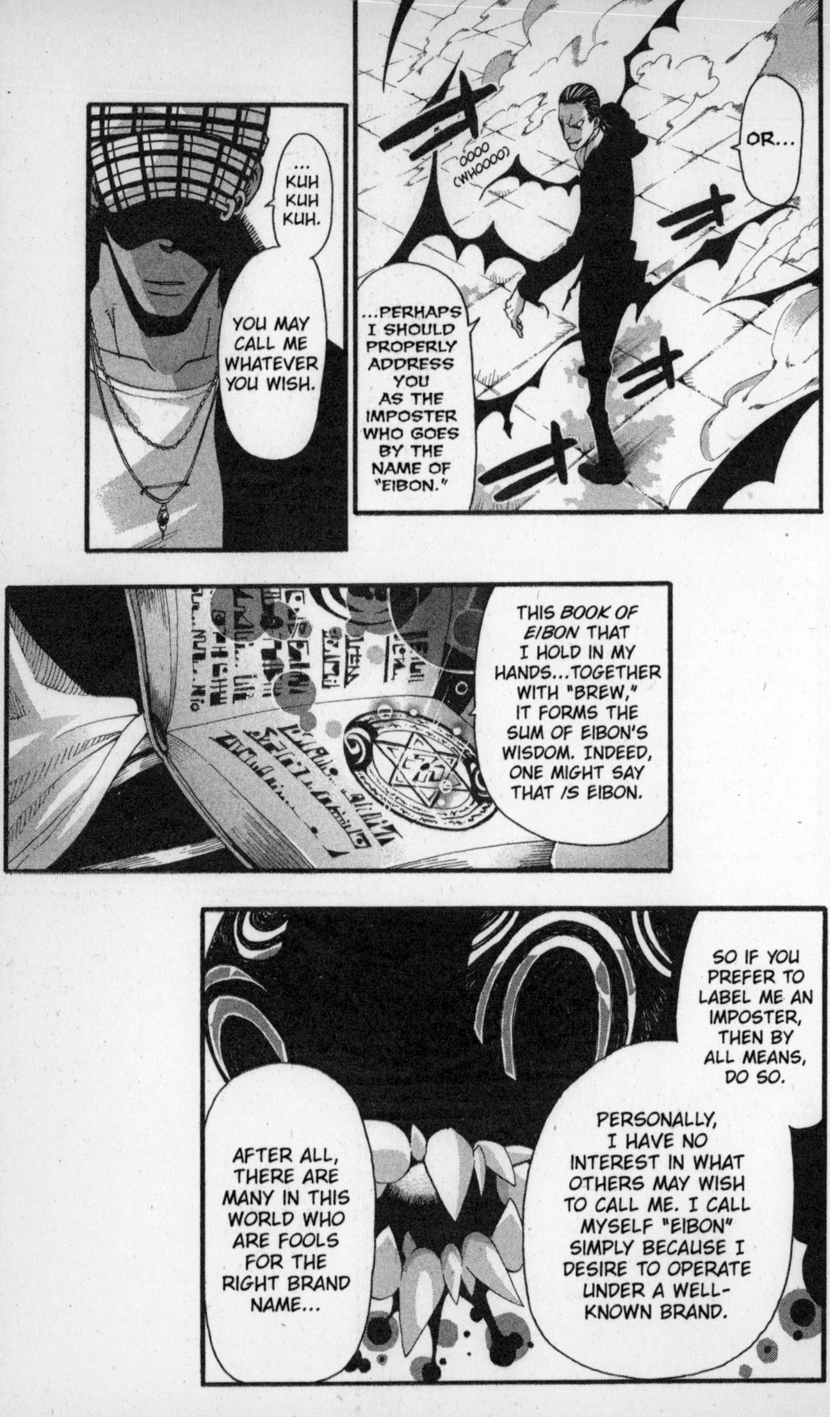
OR...
OOOO (WHOOOO)
...PERHAPS I SHOULD PROPERLY ADDRESS YOU AS THE IMPOSTER WHO GOES BY THE NAME OF "EIBON."
... KUH KUH KUH.
YOU MAY CALL ME WHATEVER YOU WISH.
THIS *BOOK OF EIBON* THAT I HOLD IN MY HANDS...TOGETHER WITH "BREW," IT FORMS THE SUM OF EIBON'S WISDOM. INDEED, ONE MIGHT SAY THAT *IS* EIBON.
SO IF YOU PREFER TO LABEL ME AN IMPOSTER, THEN BY ALL MEANS, DO SO.
PERSONALLY, I HAVE NO INTEREST IN WHAT OTHERS MAY WISH TO CALL ME. I CALL MYSELF "EIBON" SIMPLY BECAUSE I DESIRE TO OPERATE UNDER A WELL-KNOWN BRAND.
AFTER ALL, THERE ARE MANY IN THIS WORLD WHO ARE FOOLS FOR THE RIGHT BRAND NAME...

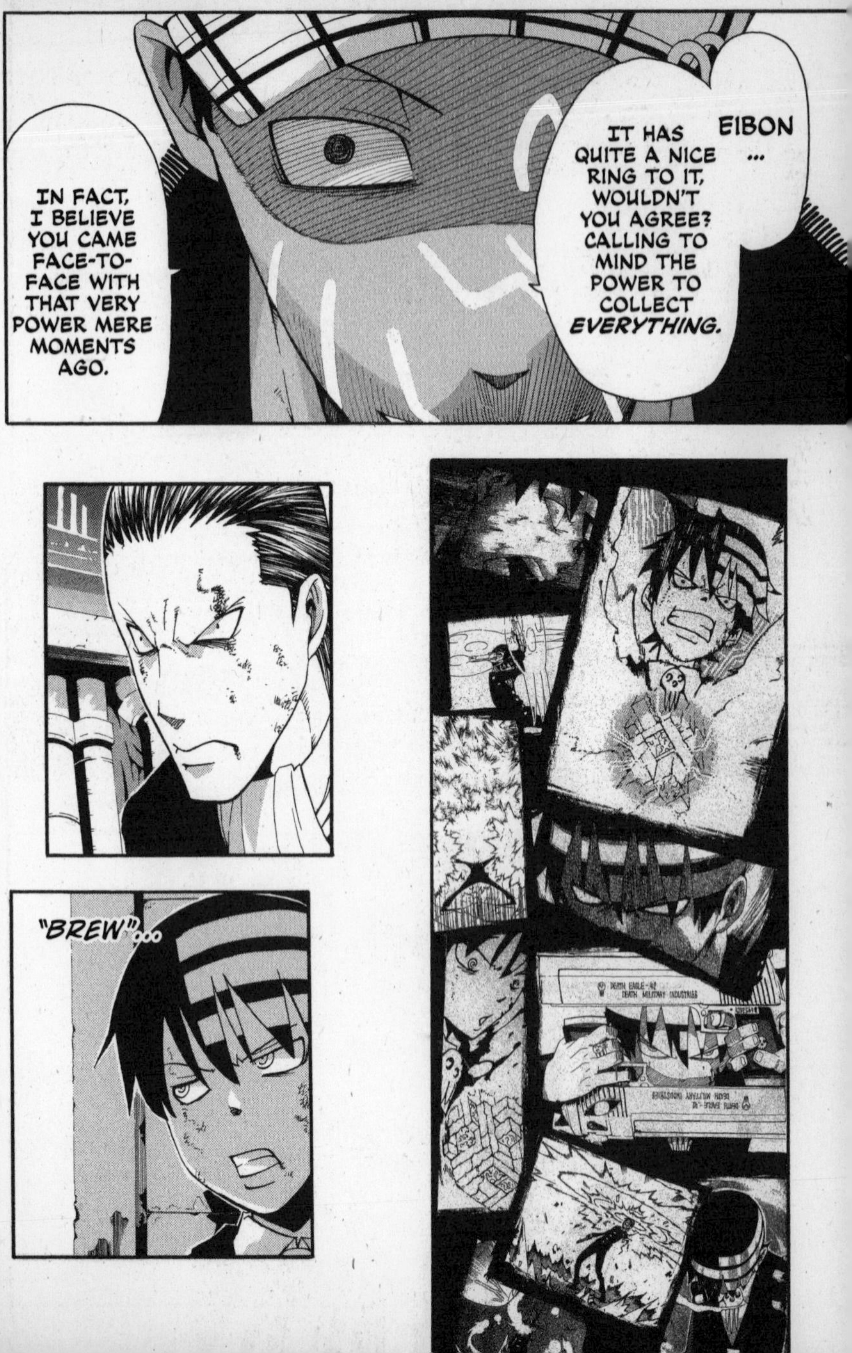
EIBON ...
IT HAS QUITE A NICE RING TO IT, WOULDN'T YOU AGREE? CALLING TO MIND THE POWER TO COLLECT *EVERYTHING.*
IN FACT, I BELIEVE YOU CAME FACE-TO-FACE WITH THAT VERY POWER MERE MOMENTS AGO.
DEATH EAGLE-42 DEATH MILITARY INDUSTRIES
"BREW"...

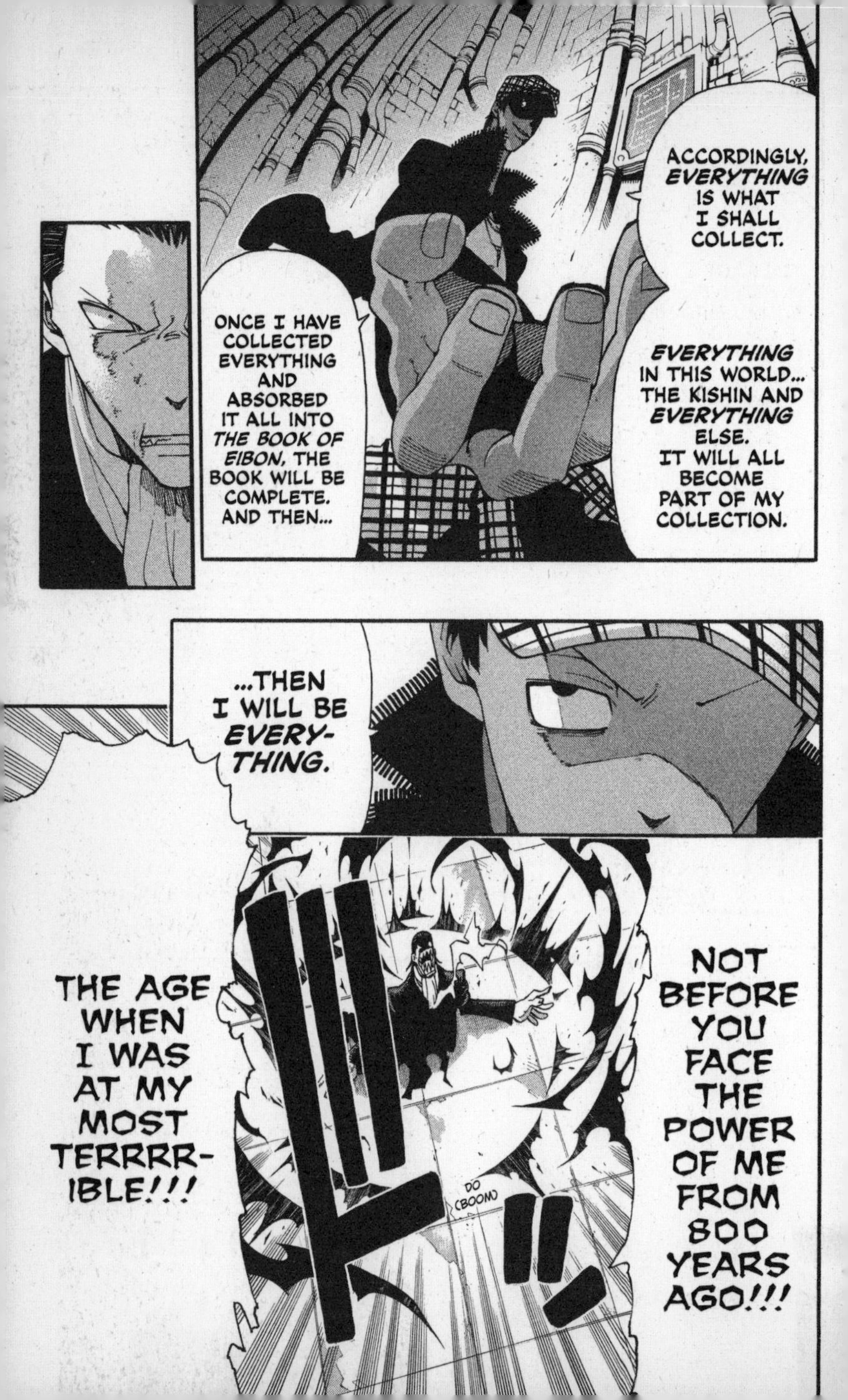
ACCORDINGLY, *EVERYTHING* IS WHAT I SHALL COLLECT.
EVERYTHING IN THIS WORLD... THE KISHIN AND *EVERYTHING* ELSE. IT WILL ALL BECOME PART OF MY COLLECTION.
ONCE I HAVE COLLECTED EVERYTHING AND ABSORBED IT ALL INTO *THE BOOK OF EIBON*, THE BOOK WILL BE COMPLETE. AND THEN...
...THEN I WILL BE *EVERY-THING*.
NOT BEFORE YOU FACE THE POWER OF ME FROM 800 YEARS AGO!!!
THE AGE WHEN I WAS AT MY MOST TERRRR-IBLE!!!
DO (BOOM)

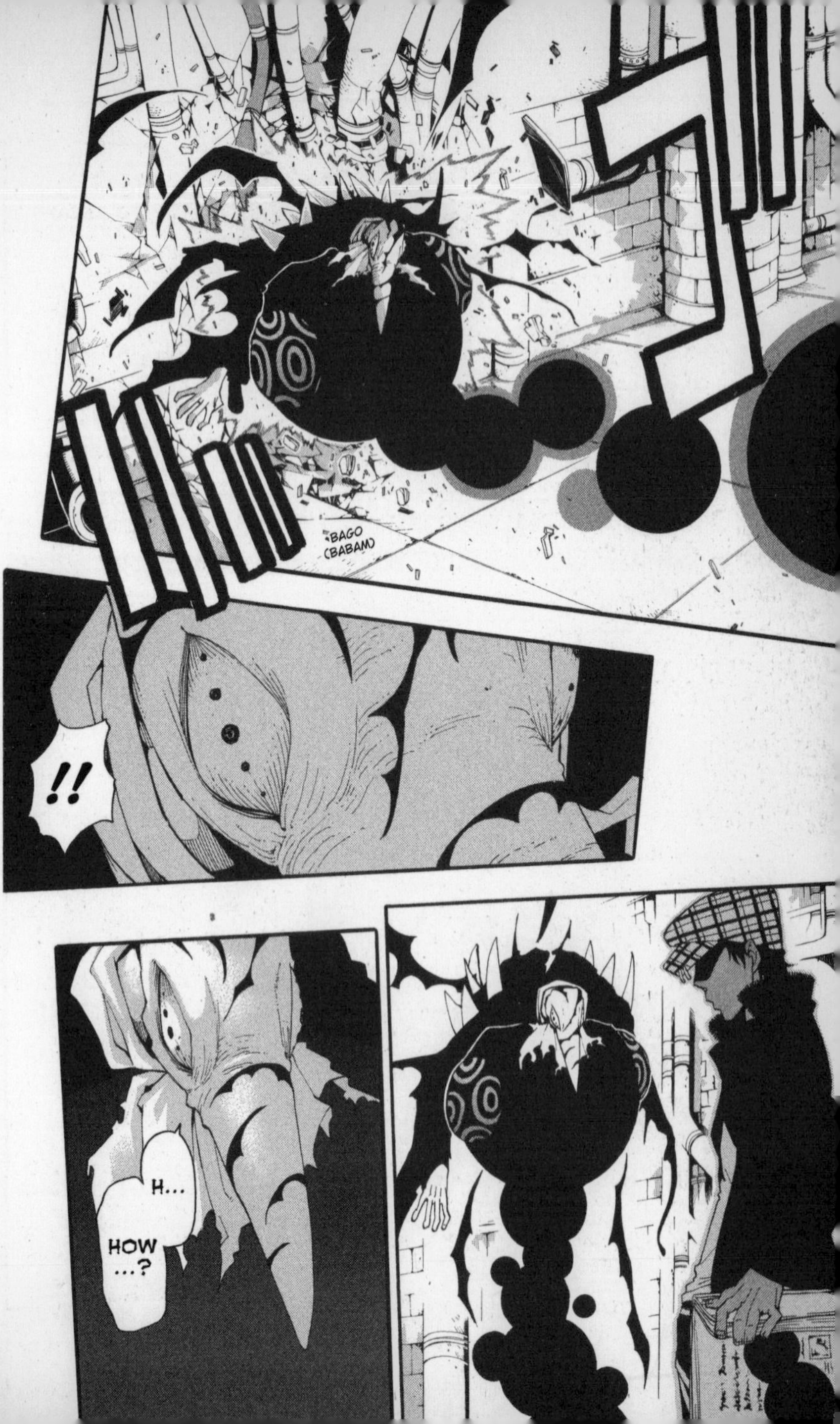
*BAGO
(BABAM)
!!
H...
HOW ...?

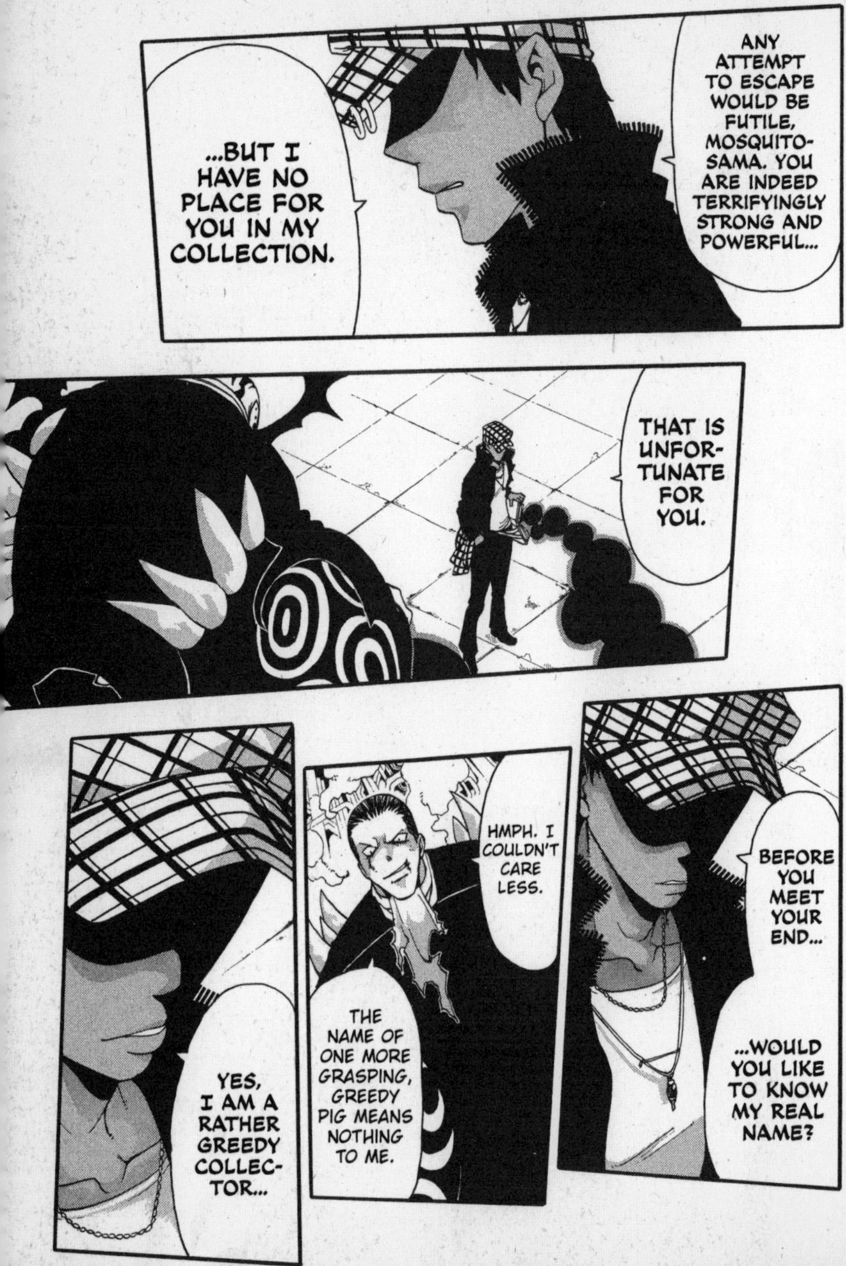
ANY ATTEMPT TO ESCAPE WOULD BE FUTILE, MOSQUITO-SAMA. YOU ARE INDEED TERRIFYINGLY STRONG AND POWERFUL...
...BUT I HAVE NO PLACE FOR YOU IN MY COLLECTION.
THAT IS UNFOR-TUNATE FOR YOU.
BEFORE YOU MEET YOUR END...
...WOULD YOU LIKE TO KNOW MY REAL NAME?
HMPH. I COULDN'T CARE LESS.
THE NAME OF ONE MORE GRASPING, GREEDY PIG MEANS NOTHING TO ME.
YES, I AM A RATHER GREEDY COLLEC-TOR...

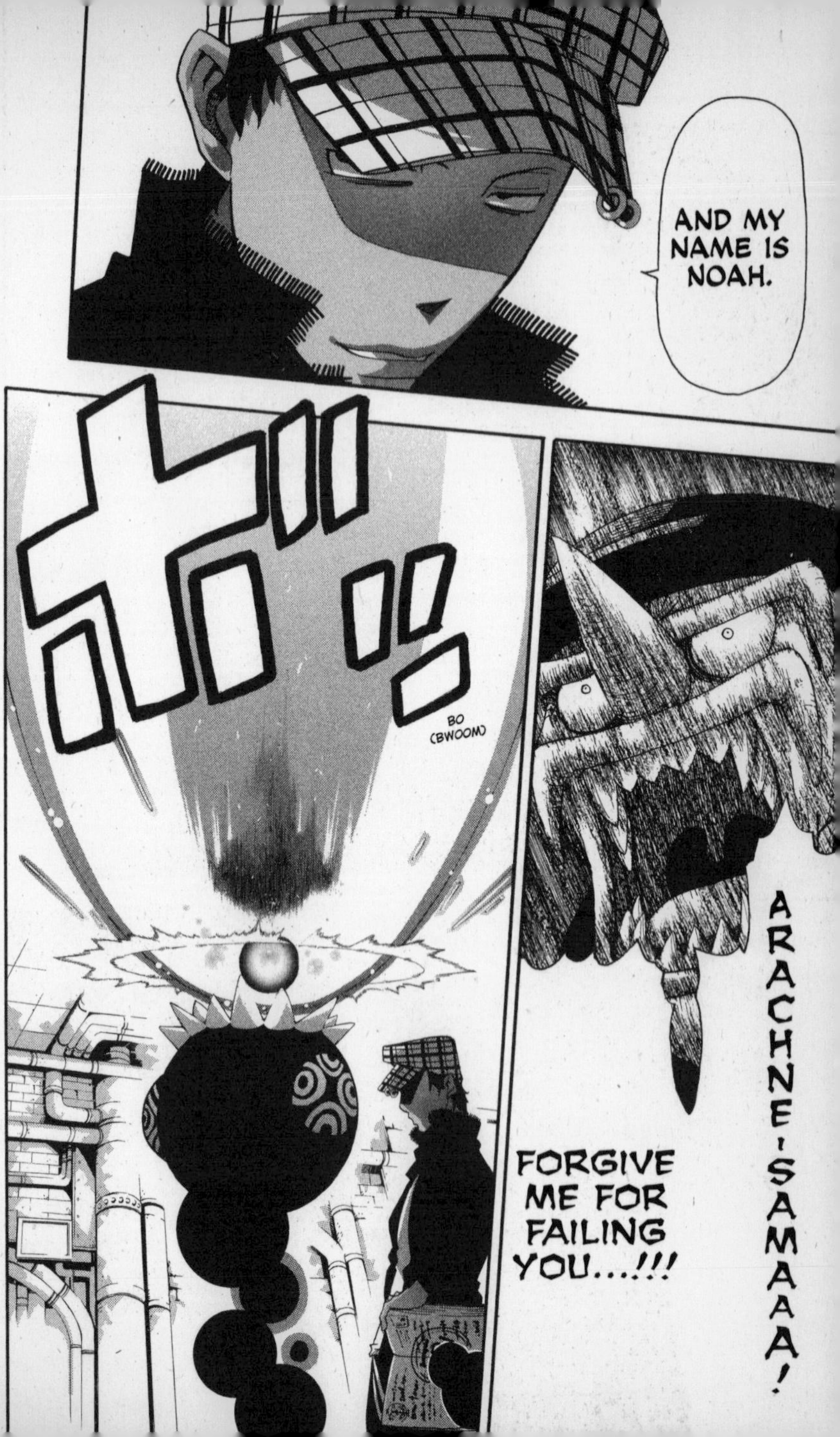
AND MY NAME IS NOAH.
FORGIVE ME FOR FAILING YOU...!!!
ARACHNE-SAMAAA!
BO (BWOOM)

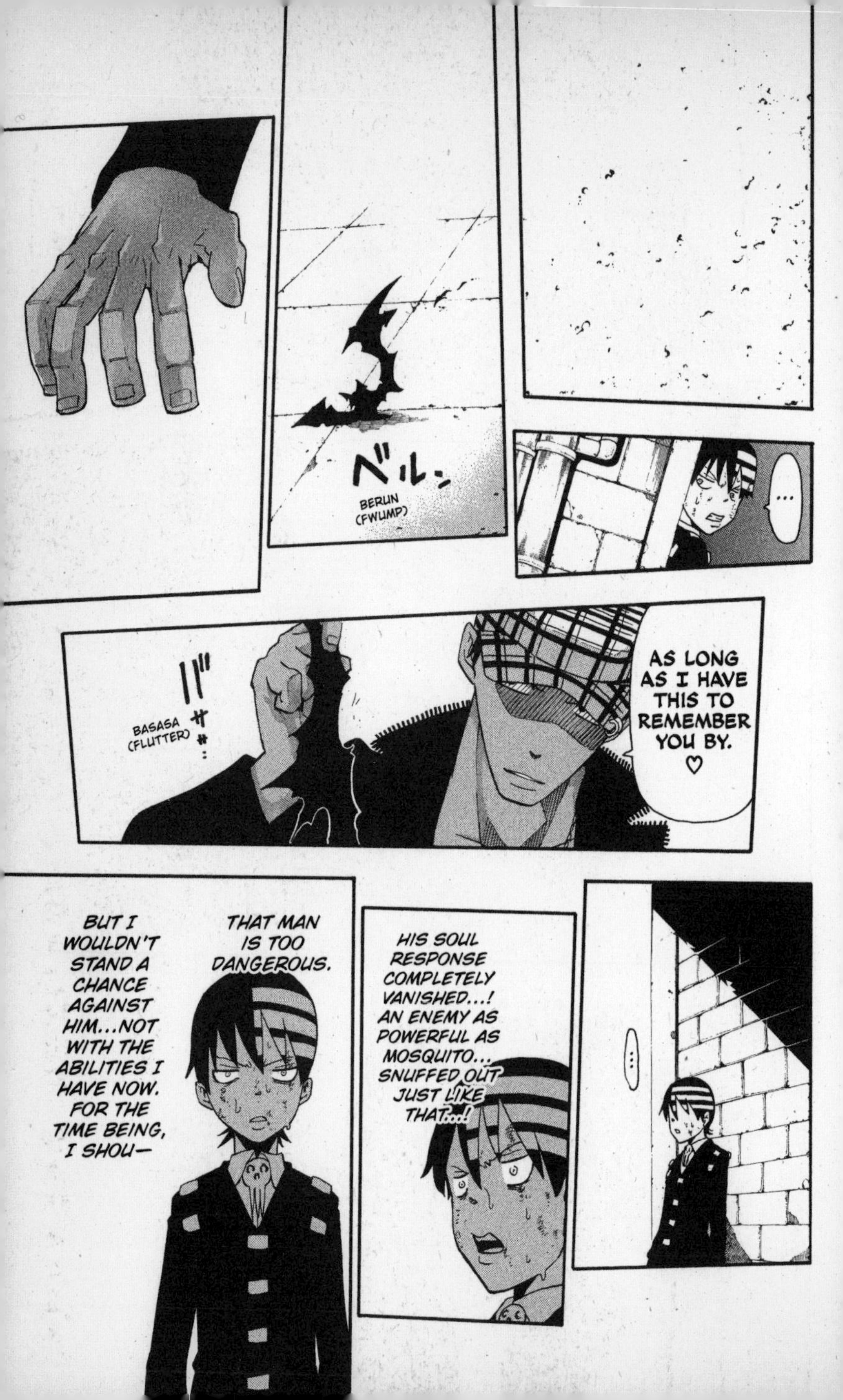
...
ベルン
BERUN (FWUMP)
AS LONG AS I HAVE THIS TO REMEMBER YOU BY. ♡
バサ
BASASA (FLUTTER)
...
HIS SOUL RESPONSE COMPLETELY VANISHED...! AN ENEMY AS POWERFUL AS MOSQUITO... SNUFFED OUT JUST LIKE THAT...!
THAT MAN IS TOO DANGEROUS.
BUT I WOULDN'T STAND A CHANCE AGAINST HIM...NOT WITH THE ABILITIES I HAVE NOW. FOR THE TIME BEING, I SHOU—

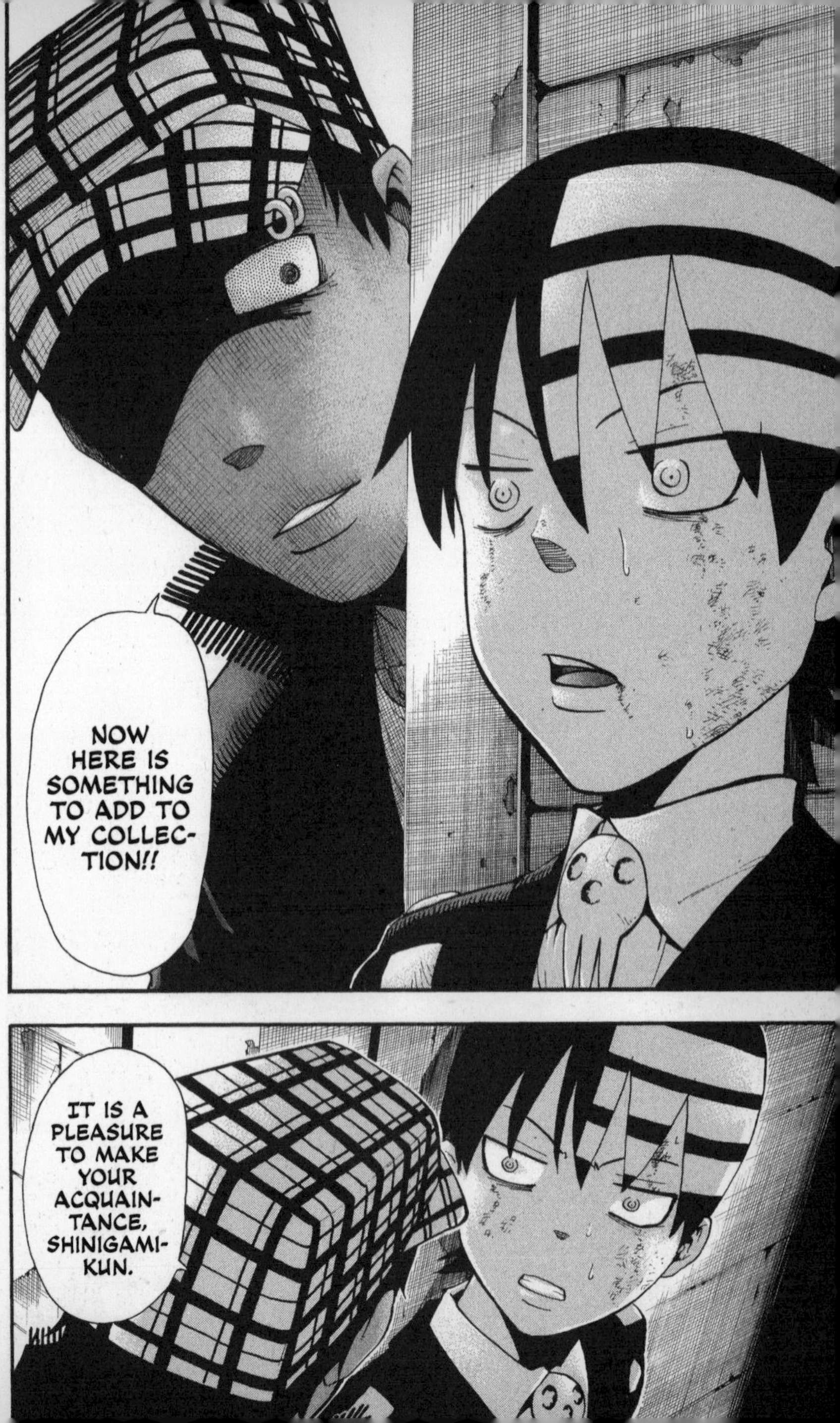
NOW HERE IS SOMETHING TO ADD TO MY COLLECTION!!
IT IS A PLEASURE TO MAKE YOUR ACQUAINTANCE, SHINIGAMI-KUN.

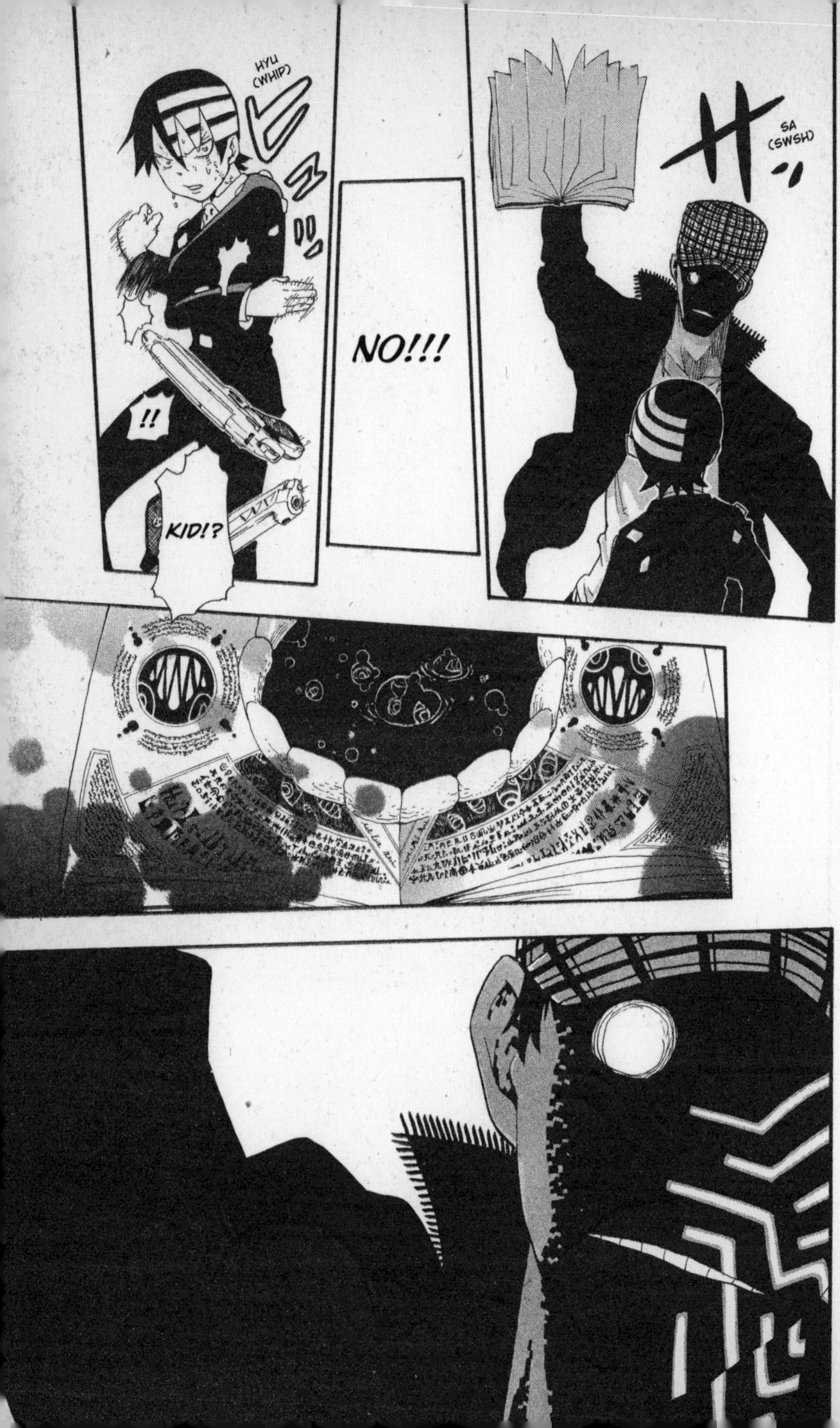
SA (SWSH)
NO!!!
HYU (WHIP)
!!
KID!?

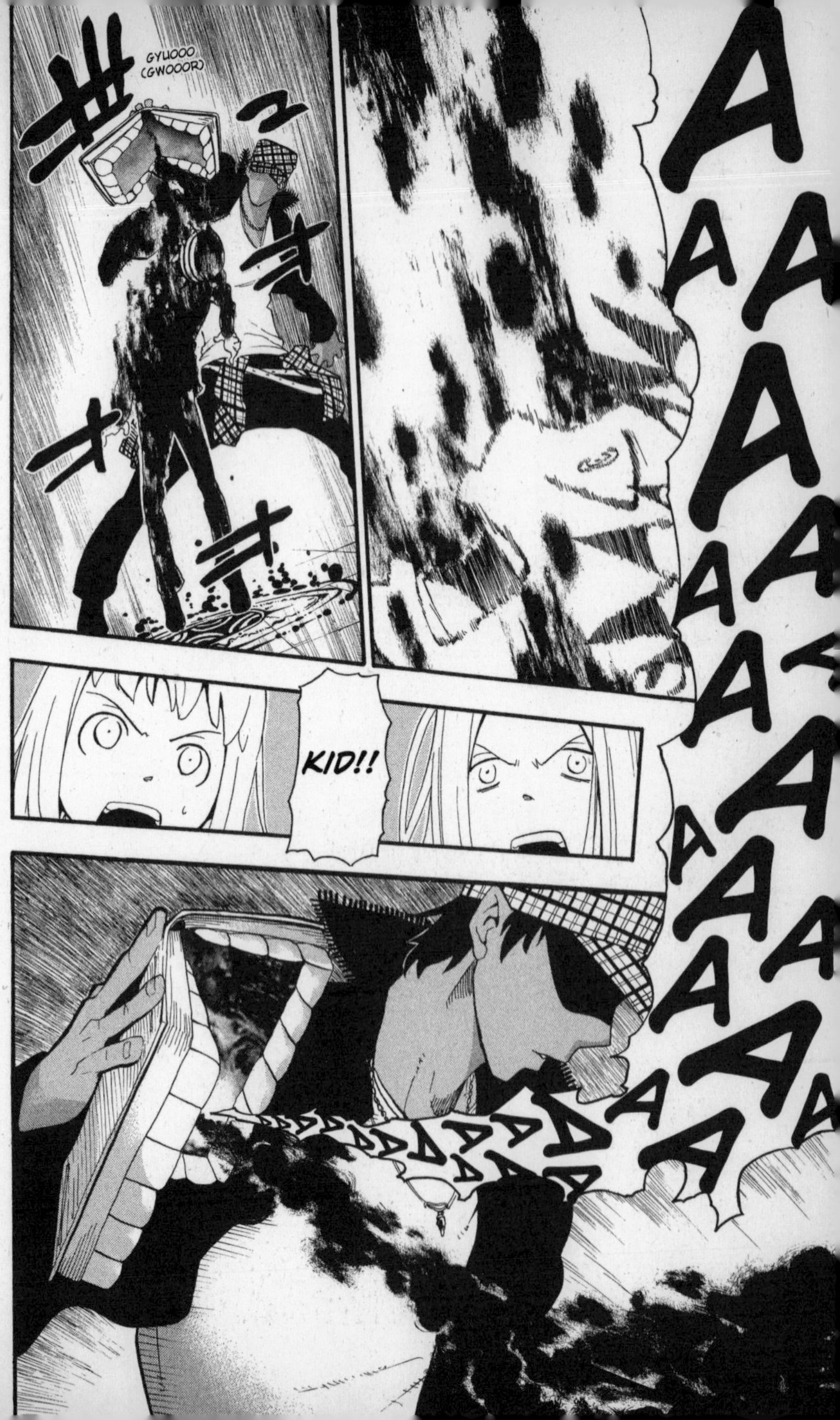
GYUOOO
(GWOOOR)
KID!!

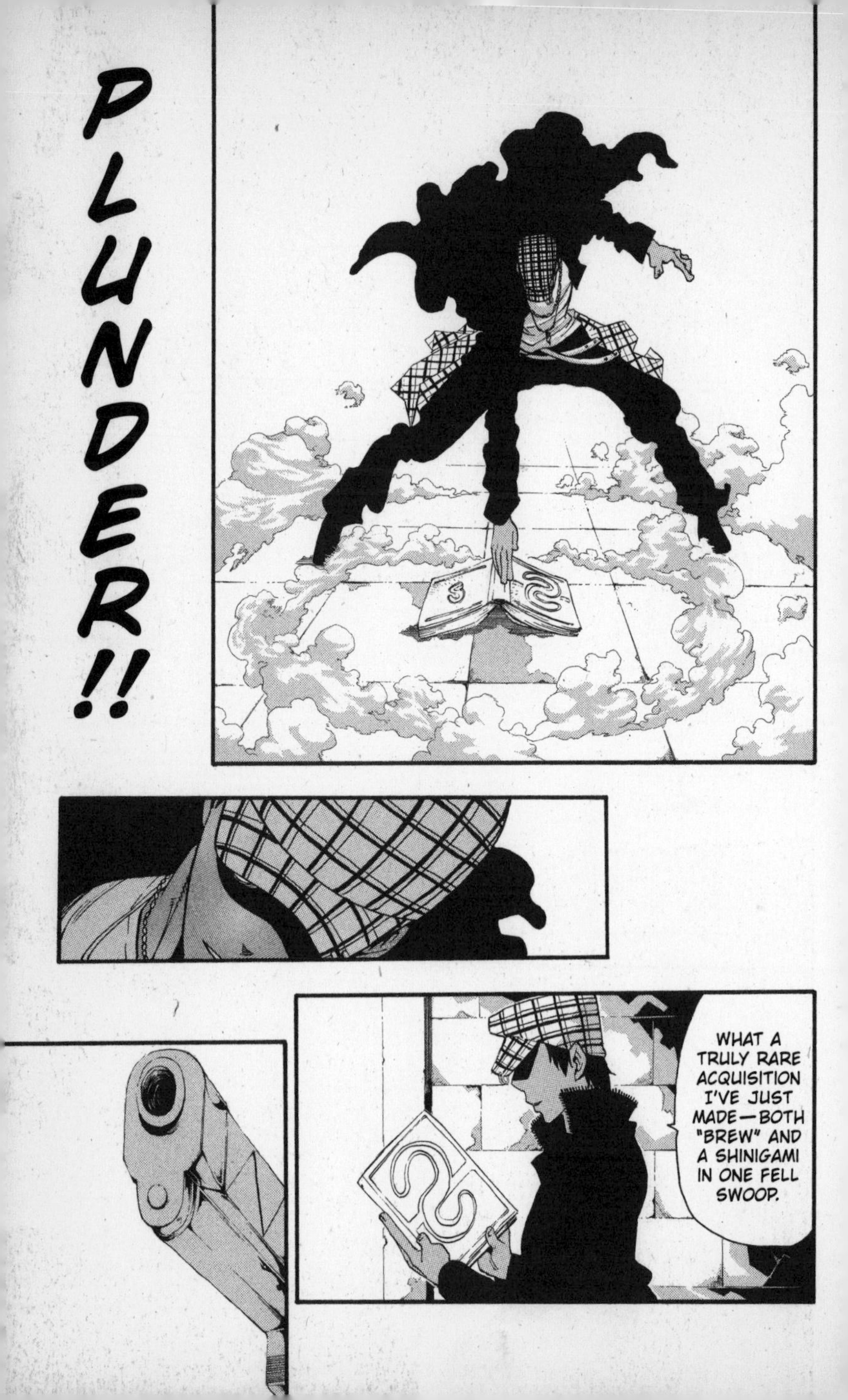
PLUNDER!!
WHAT A TRULY RARE ACQUISITION I'VE JUST MADE—BOTH "BREW" AND A SHINIGAMI IN ONE FELL SWOOP.

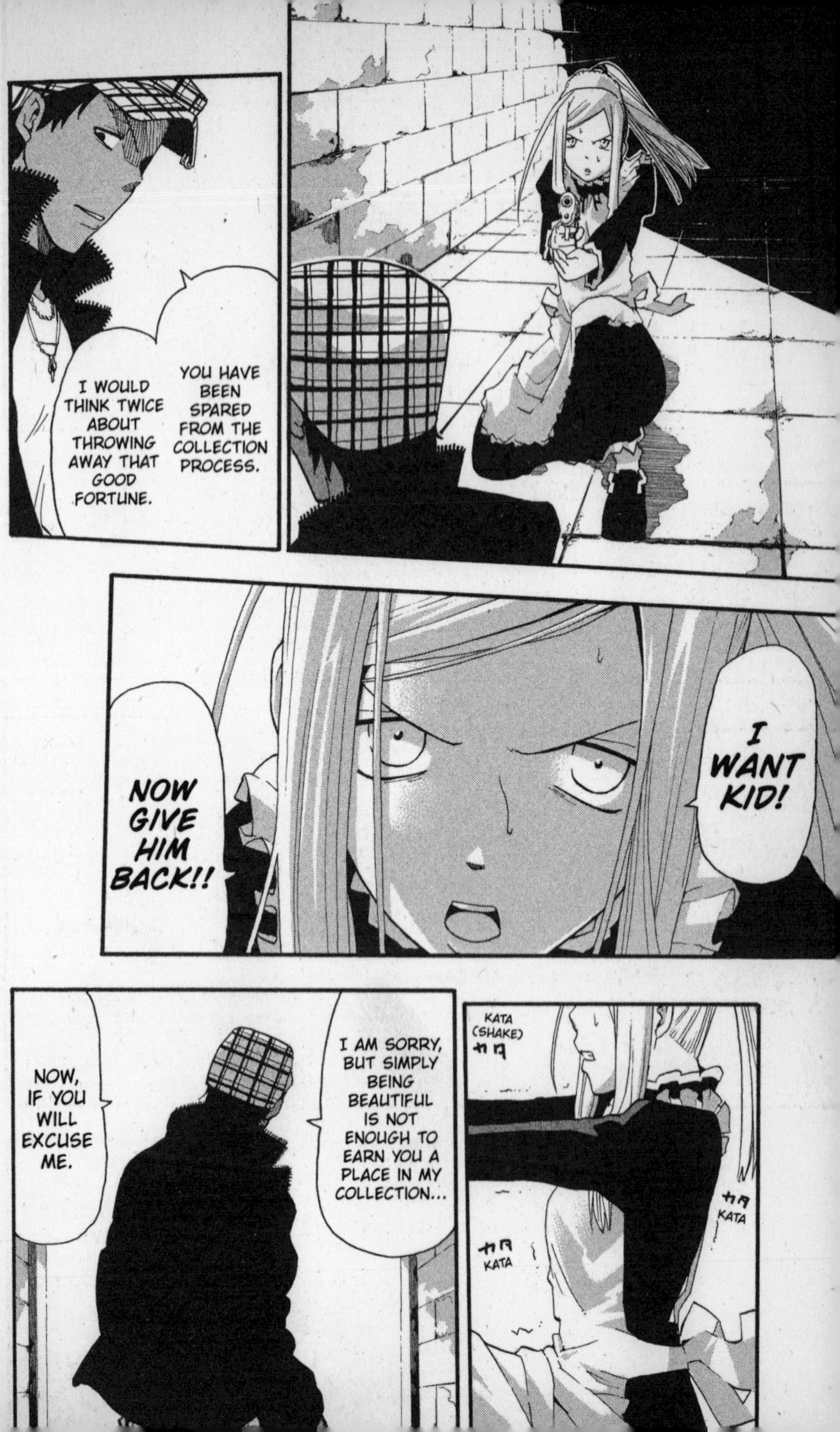
YOU HAVE BEEN SPARED FROM THE COLLECTION PROCESS.
I WOULD THINK TWICE ABOUT THROWING AWAY THAT GOOD FORTUNE.
I WANT KID!
NOW GIVE HIM BACK!!
KATA (SHAKE) カタ
カタ KATA
カタ KATA
I AM SORRY, BUT SIMPLY BEING BEAUTIFUL IS NOT ENOUGH TO EARN YOU A PLACE IN MY COLLECTION...
NOW, IF YOU WILL EXCUSE ME.

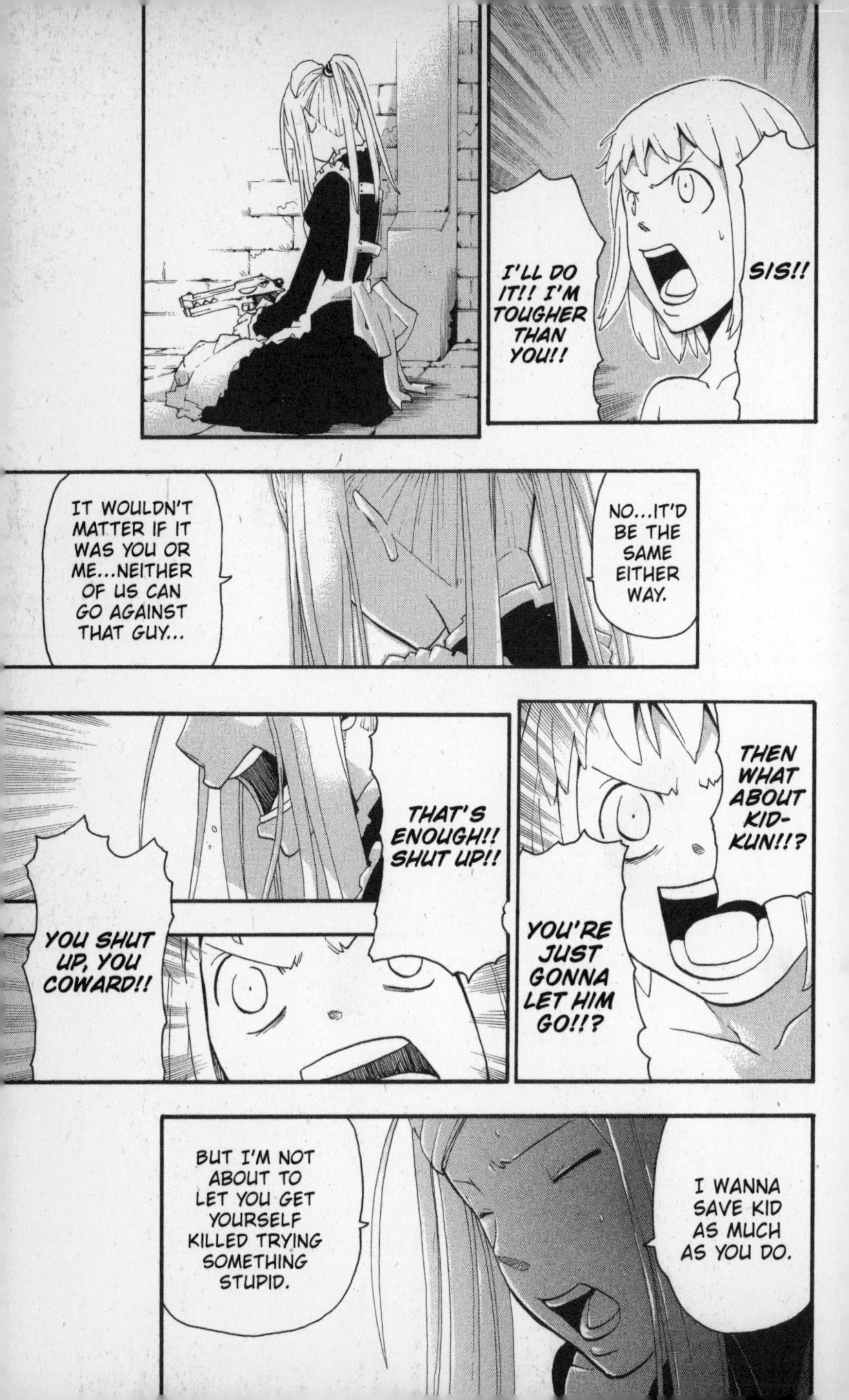
SIS!!
I'LL DO IT!! I'M TOUGHER THAN YOU!!
NO...IT'D BE THE SAME EITHER WAY.
IT WOULDN'T MATTER IF IT WAS YOU OR ME...NEITHER OF US CAN GO AGAINST THAT GUY...
THEN WHAT ABOUT KID-KUN!!?
YOU'RE JUST GONNA LET HIM GO!!?
THAT'S ENOUGH!! SHUT UP!!
YOU SHUT UP, YOU COWARD!!
I WANNA SAVE KID AS MUCH AS YOU DO.
BUT I'M NOT ABOUT TO LET YOU GET YOURSELF KILLED TRYING SOMETHING STUPID.

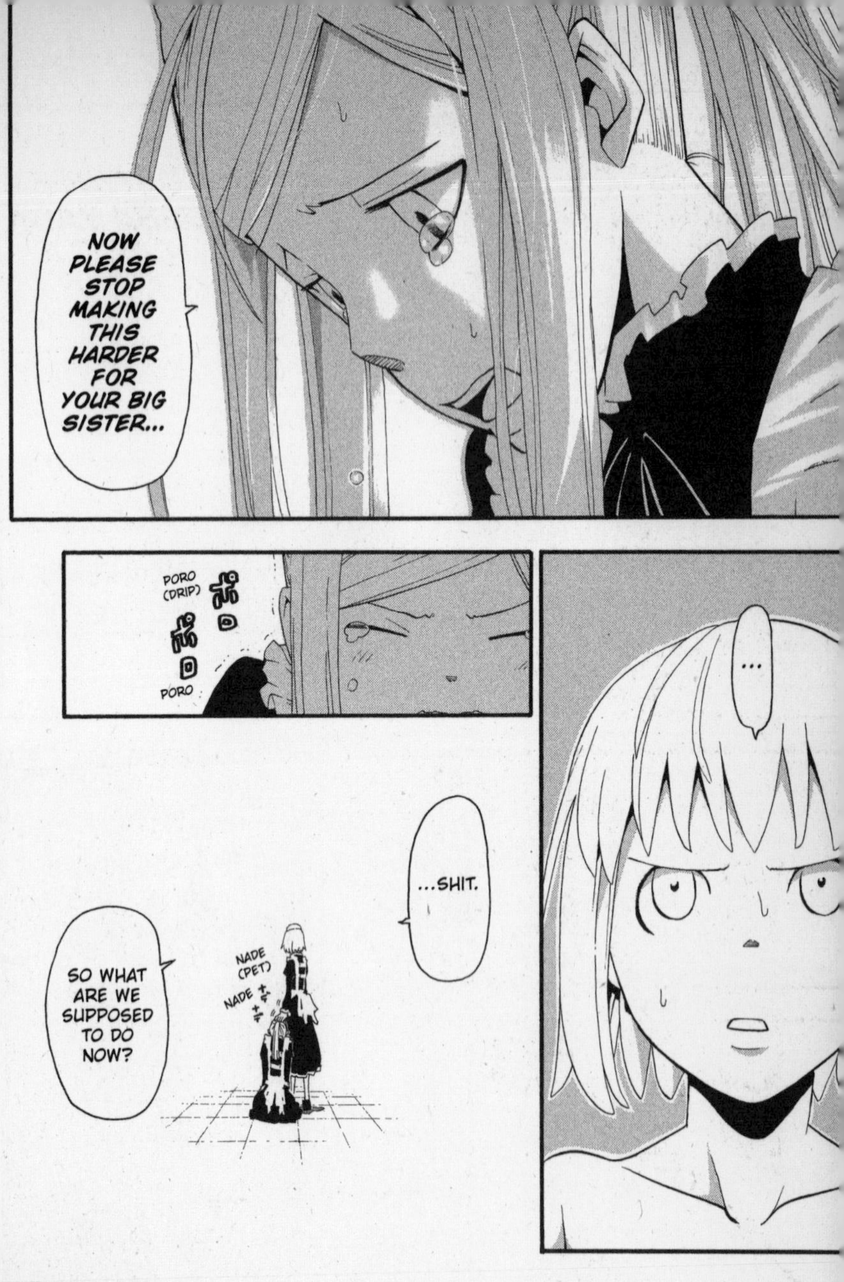
NOW PLEASE STOP MAKING THIS HARDER FOR YOUR BIG SISTER...
...
PORO (DRIP)
PORO
...SHIT.
NADE (PET)
NADE
SO WHAT ARE WE SUPPOSED TO DO NOW?

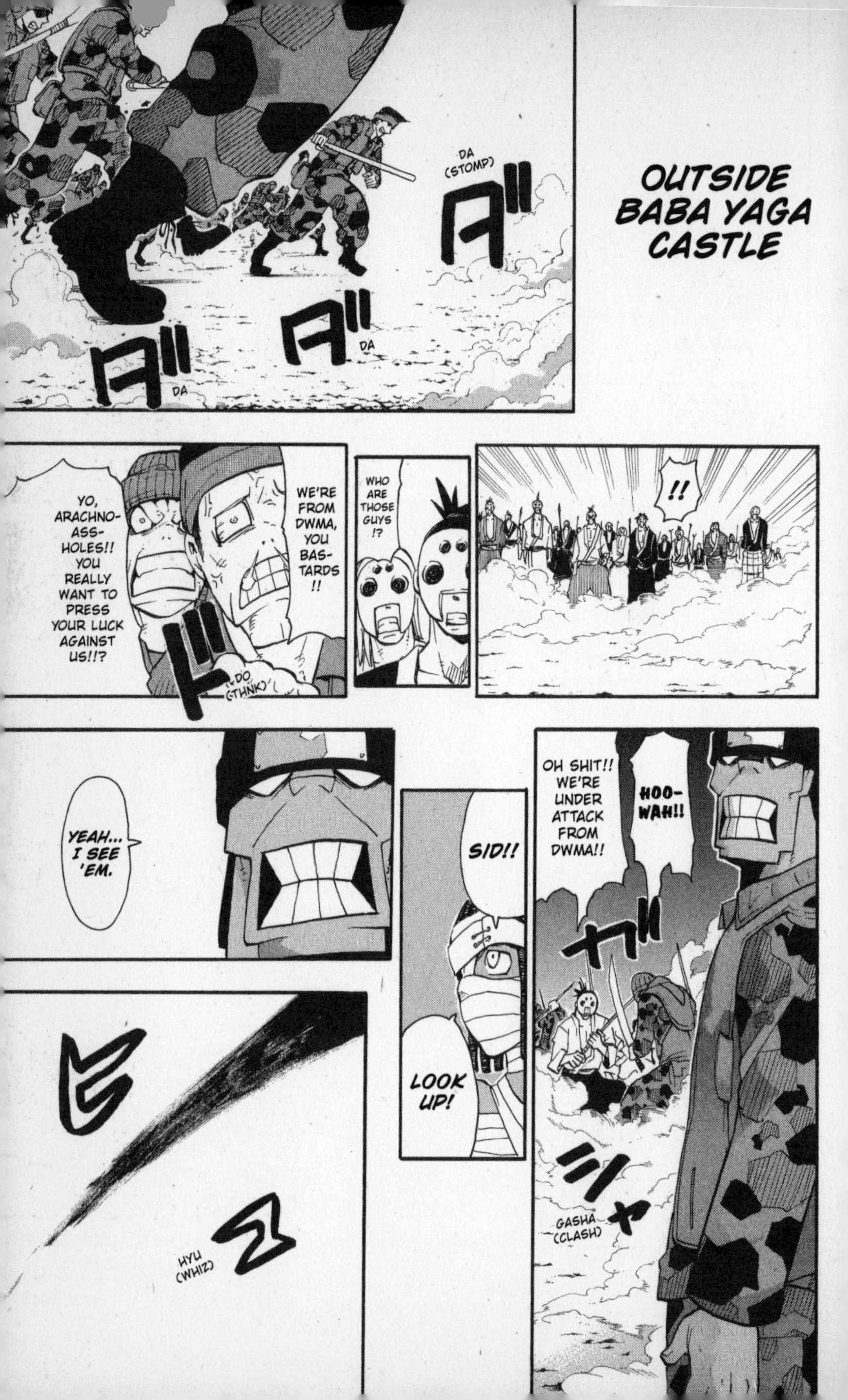
OUTSIDE BABA YAGA CASTLE
DA (STOMP)
DA
DA
!!
WHO ARE THOSE GUYS !?
WE'RE FROM DWMA, YOU BASTARDS !!
YO, ARACHNO-ASS-HOLES!! YOU REALLY WANT TO PRESS YOUR LUCK AGAINST US!!?
DO (THNK)
HOO-WAH!!
OH SHIT!! WE'RE UNDER ATTACK FROM DWMA!!
GASHA (CLASH)
SID!!
LOOK UP!
YEAH... I SEE 'EM.
HYU (WHIZ)

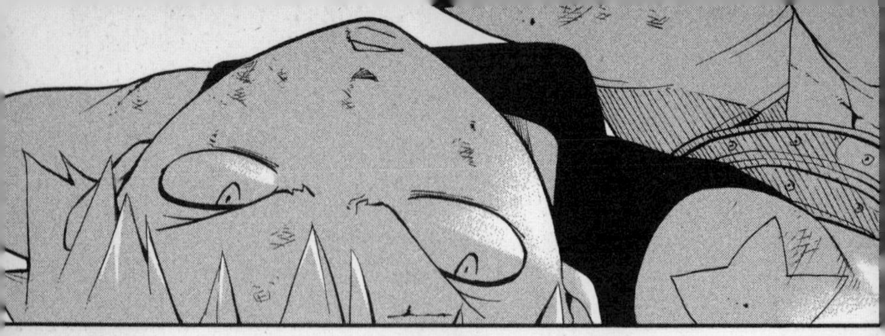
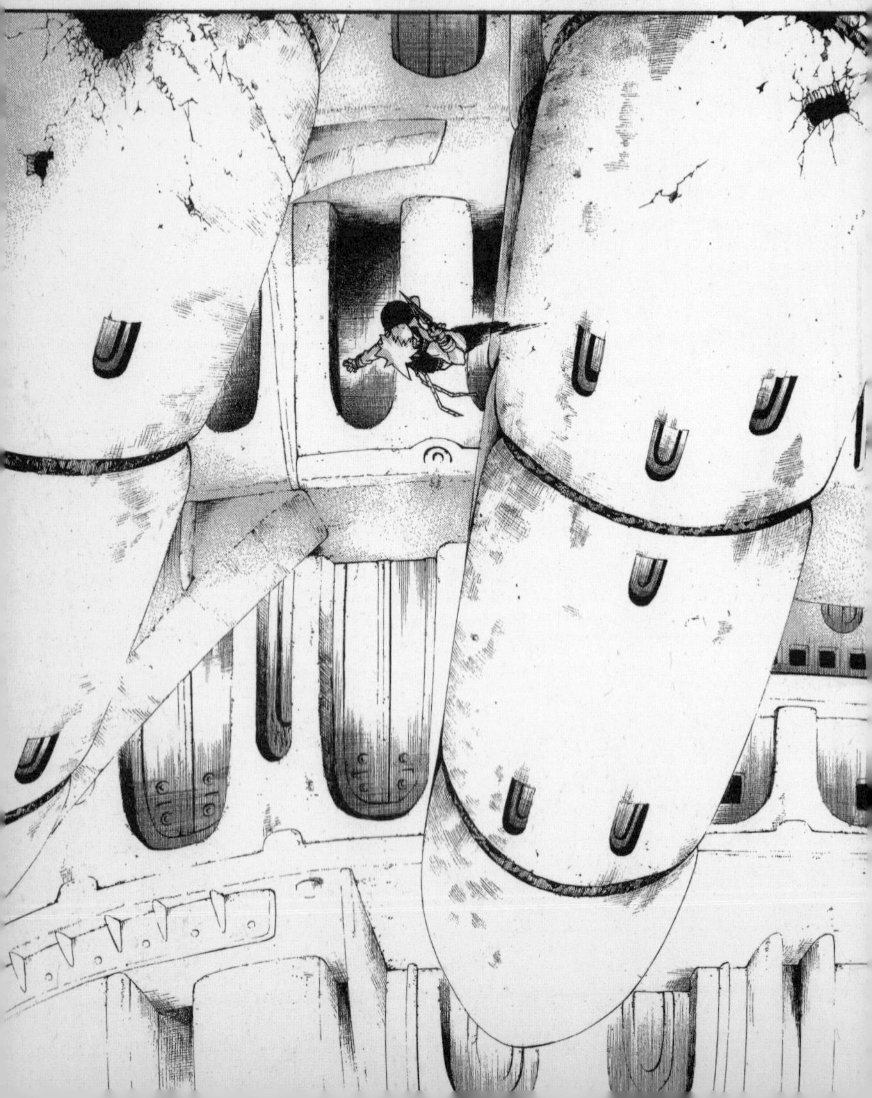

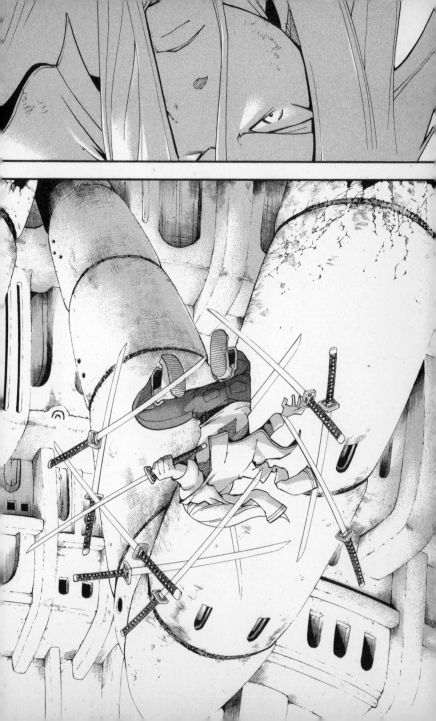

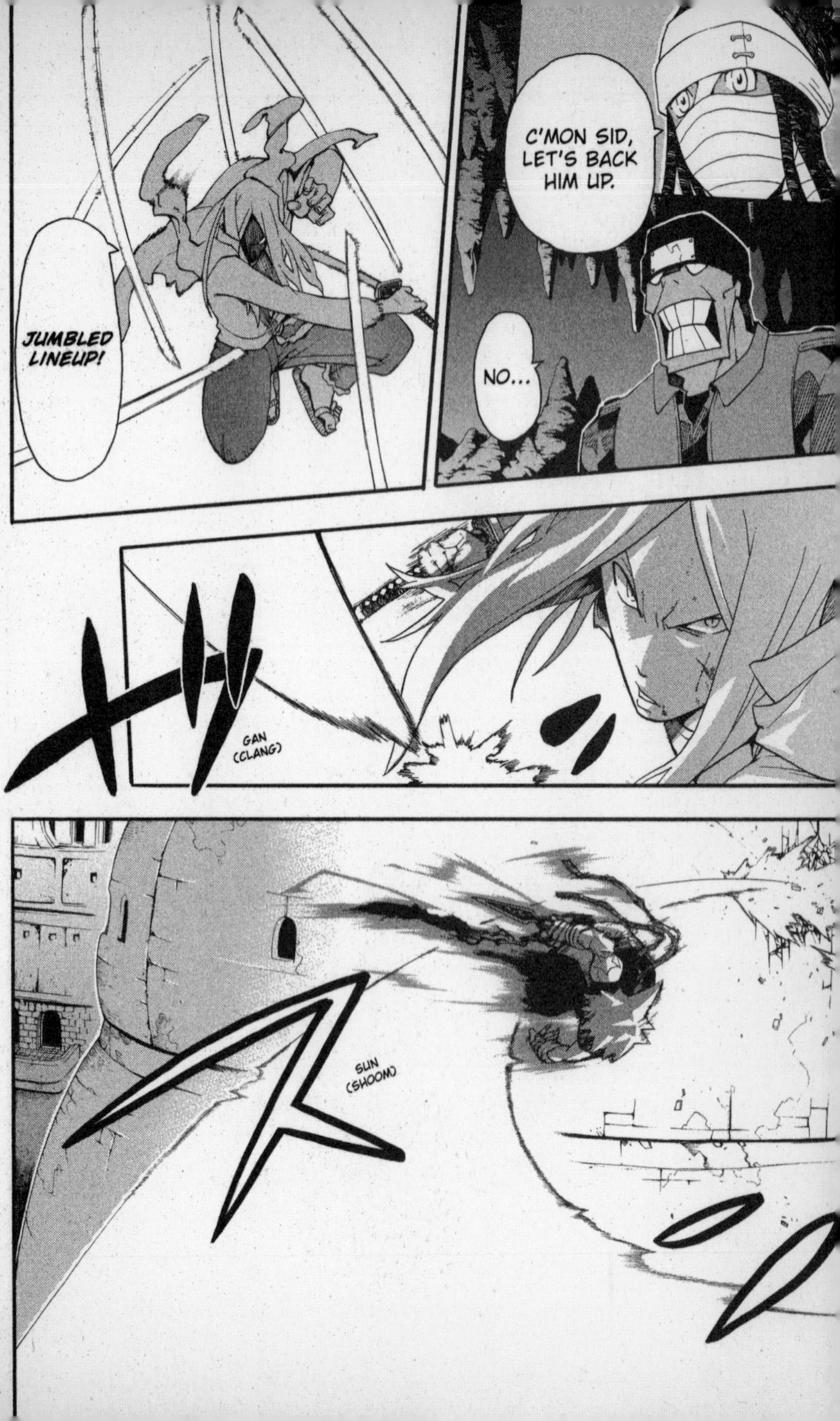
C'MON SID, LET'S BACK HIM UP.
NO...
JUMBLED LINEUP!
GAN (CLANG)
SUN (SHOOM)

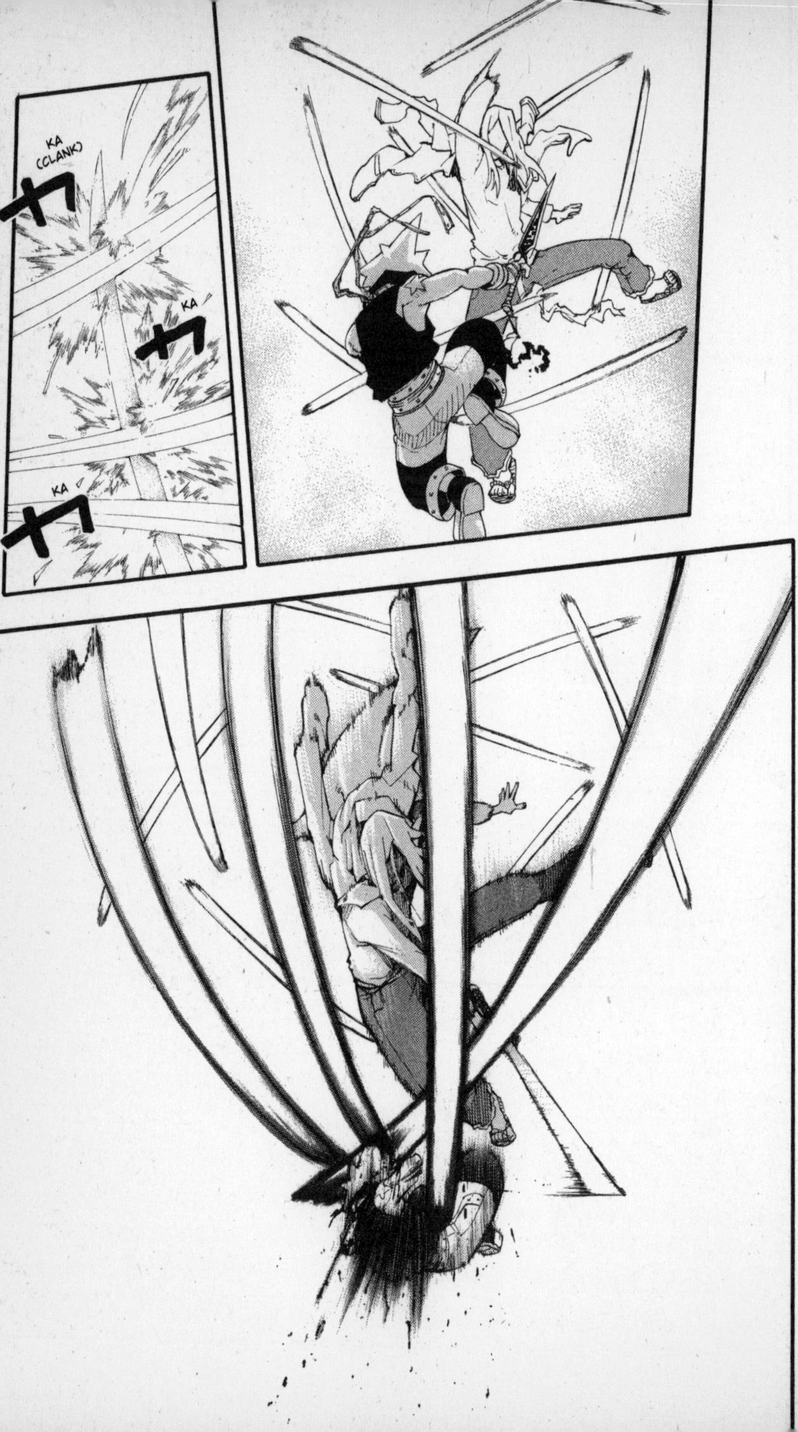
KA (CLANK)
KA
KA

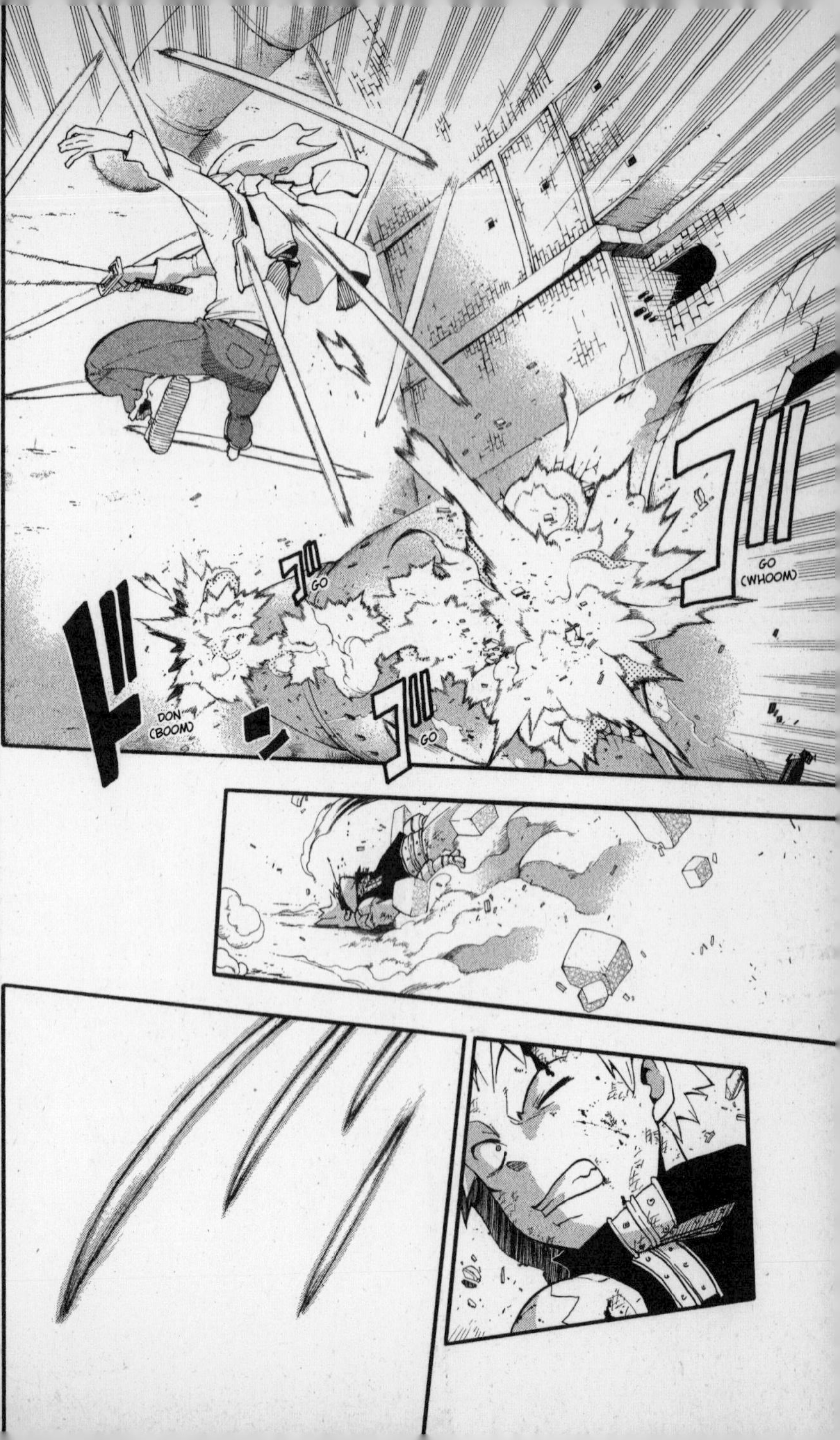
GO (WHOOM)
GO
GO
DON (BOOM)

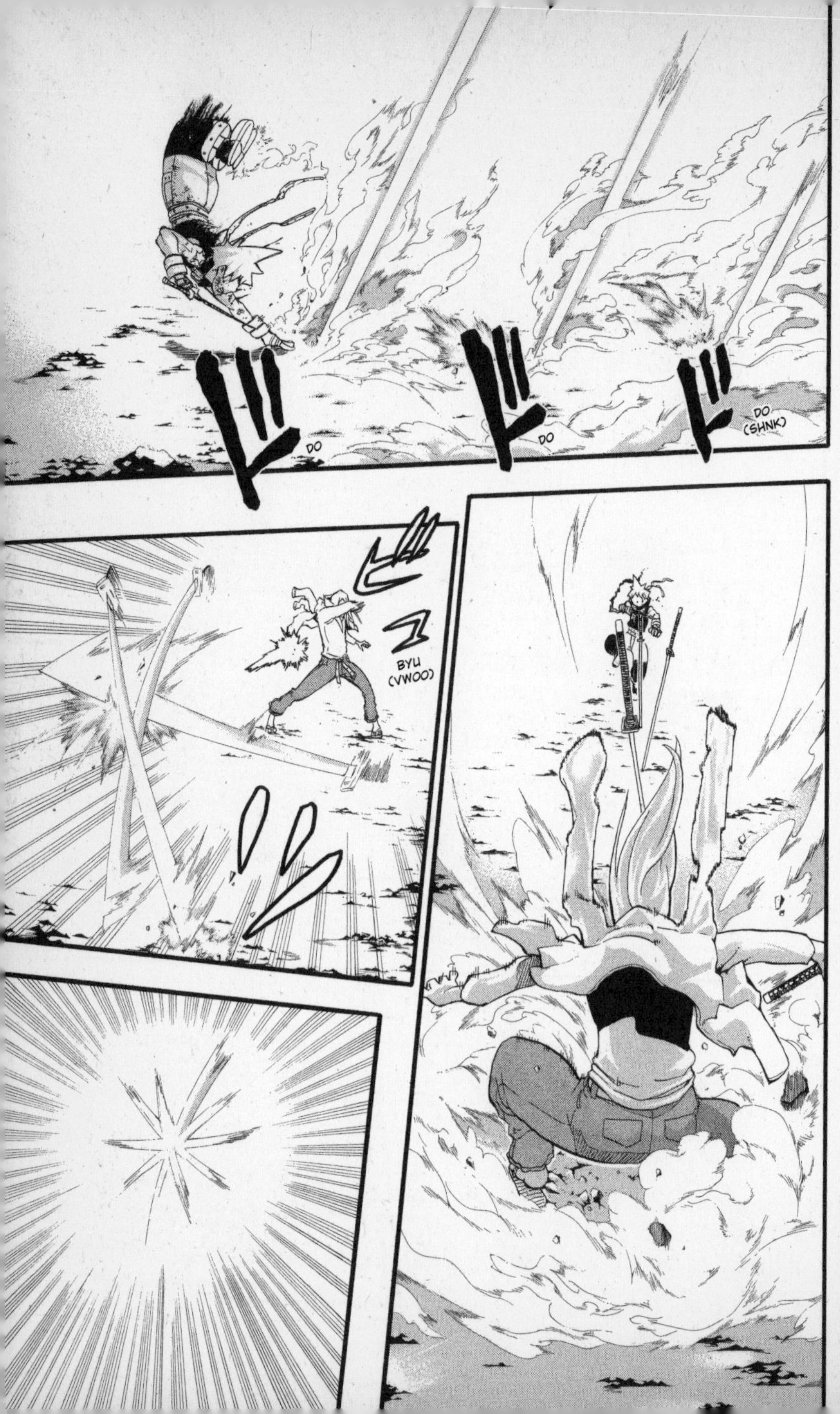
DO
(SHNK)
DO
DO
BYU
(VWOO)

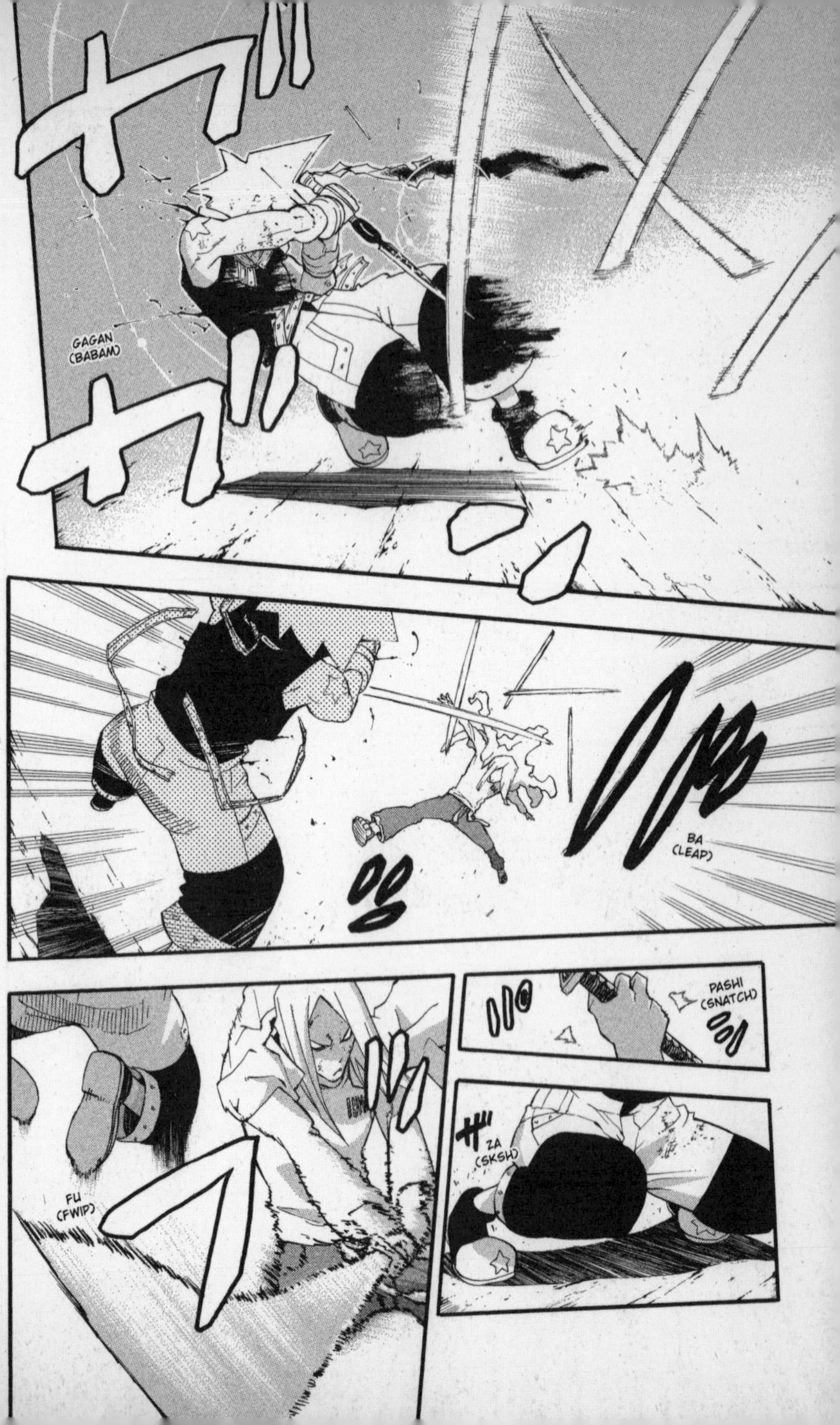
GAGAN (BABAM)
BA (LEAP)
PASHI (SNATCH)
ZA (SKSH)
FU (FWIP)

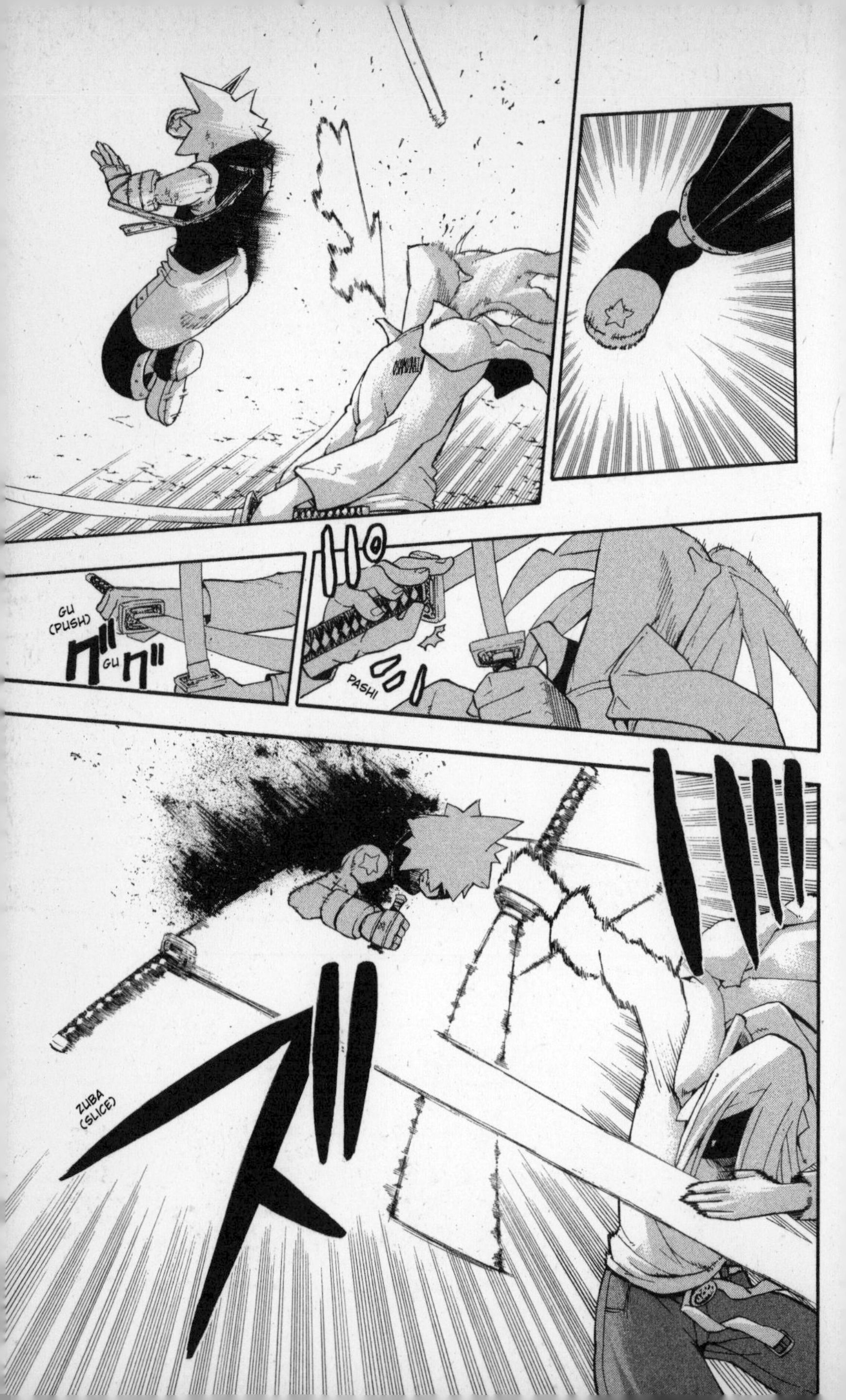
PASHI
GU
(PUSH)
GU
ZUBA
(SLICE)

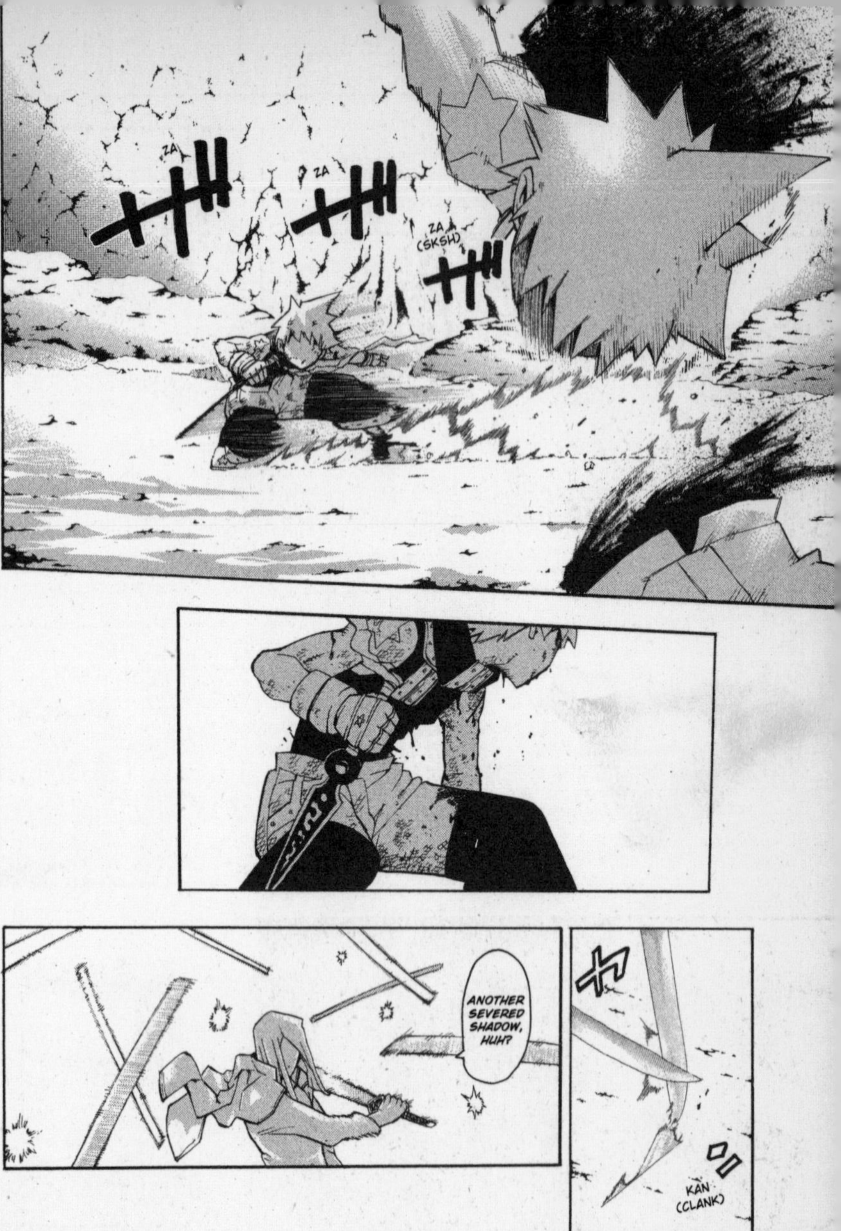
ZA (SKSH)
ZA
ZA
KAN (CLANK)
ANOTHER SEVERED SHADOW, HUH?

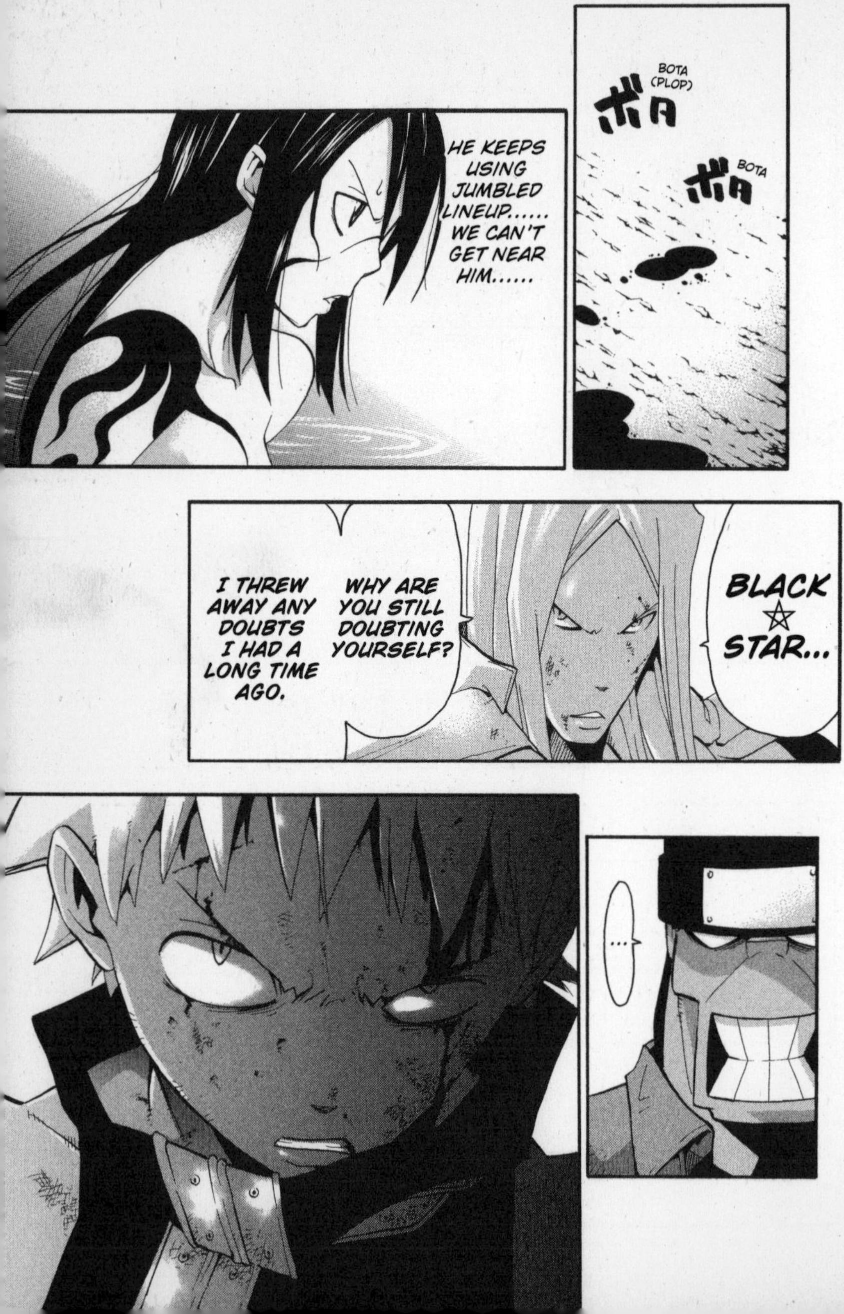
BOTA (PLOP)
BOTA
HE KEEPS USING JUMBLED LINEUP...... WE CAN'T GET NEAR HIM......
BLACK☆STAR...
WHY ARE YOU STILL DOUBTING YOURSELF?
I THREW AWAY ANY DOUBTS I HAD A LONG TIME AGO.
...

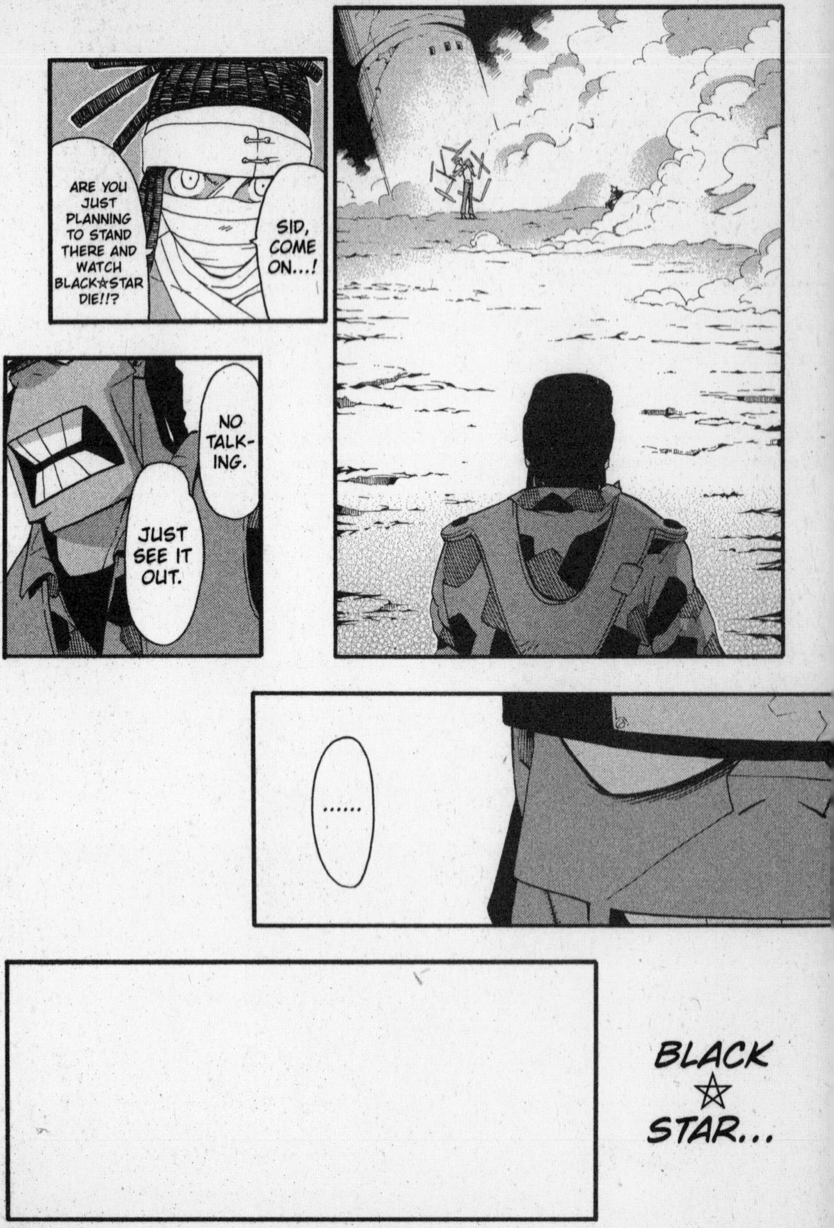
SID, COME ON...!
ARE YOU JUST PLANNING TO STAND THERE AND WATCH BLACK☆STAR DIE!!?
NO TALK-ING.
JUST SEE IT OUT.
......
BLACK☆STAR...

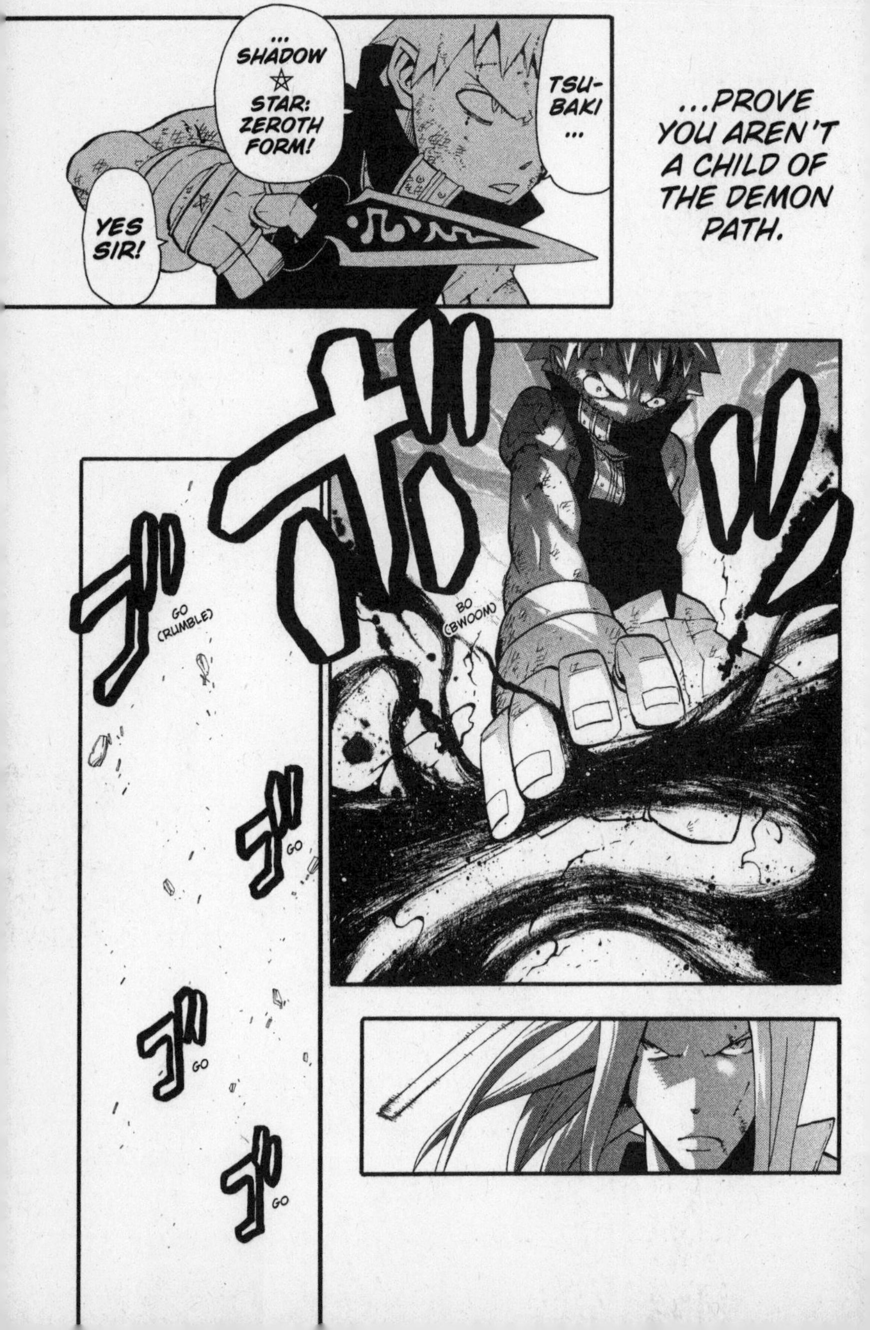
...PROVE YOU AREN'T A CHILD OF THE DEMON PATH.
TSU-BAKI ...
... SHADOW ☆ STAR: ZEROTH FORM!
YES SIR!
BO (BWOOM)
GO (RUMBLE)
GO
GO
GO

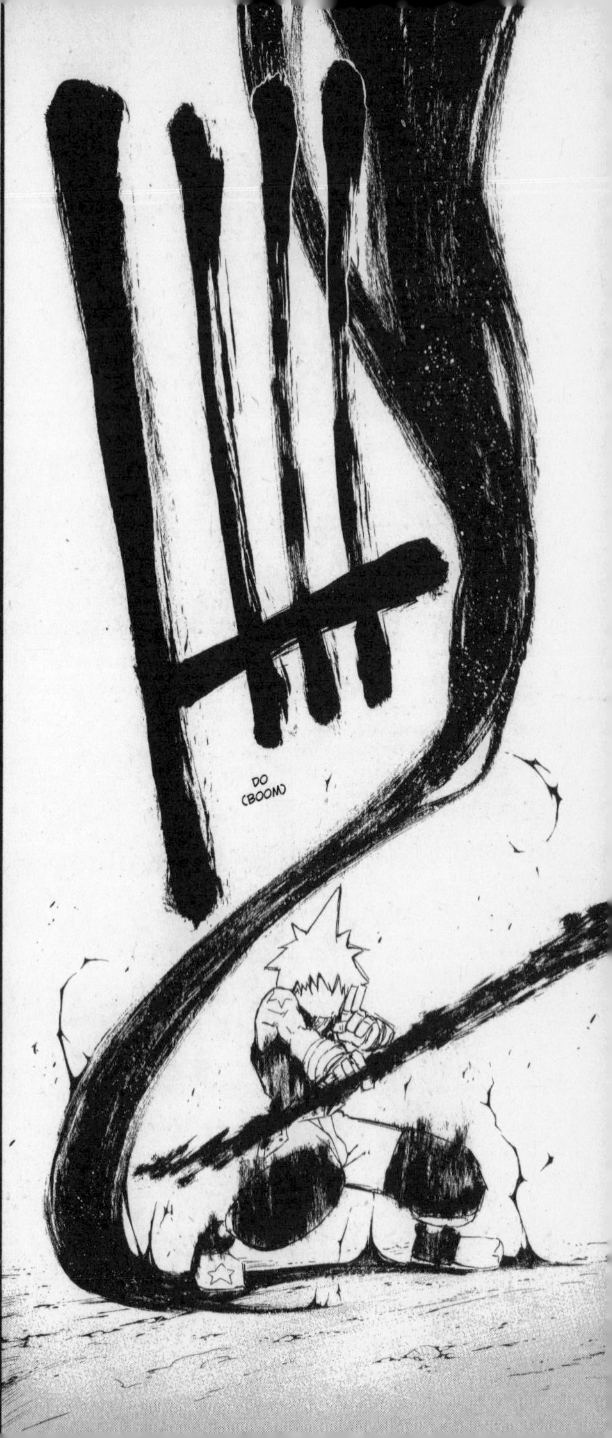
DO
(BOOM)
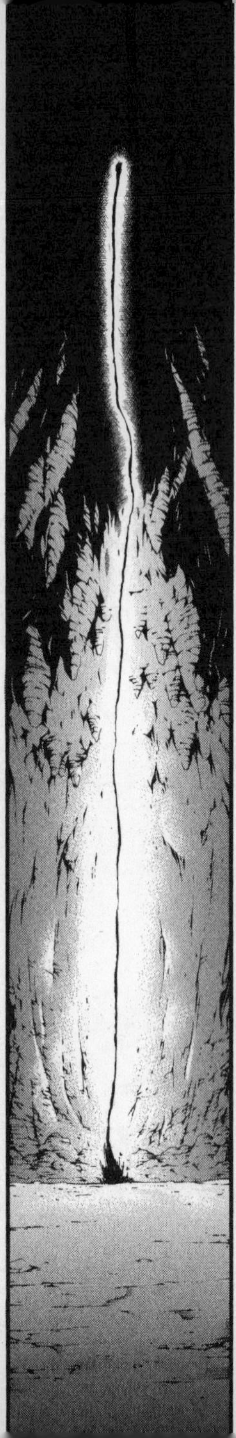

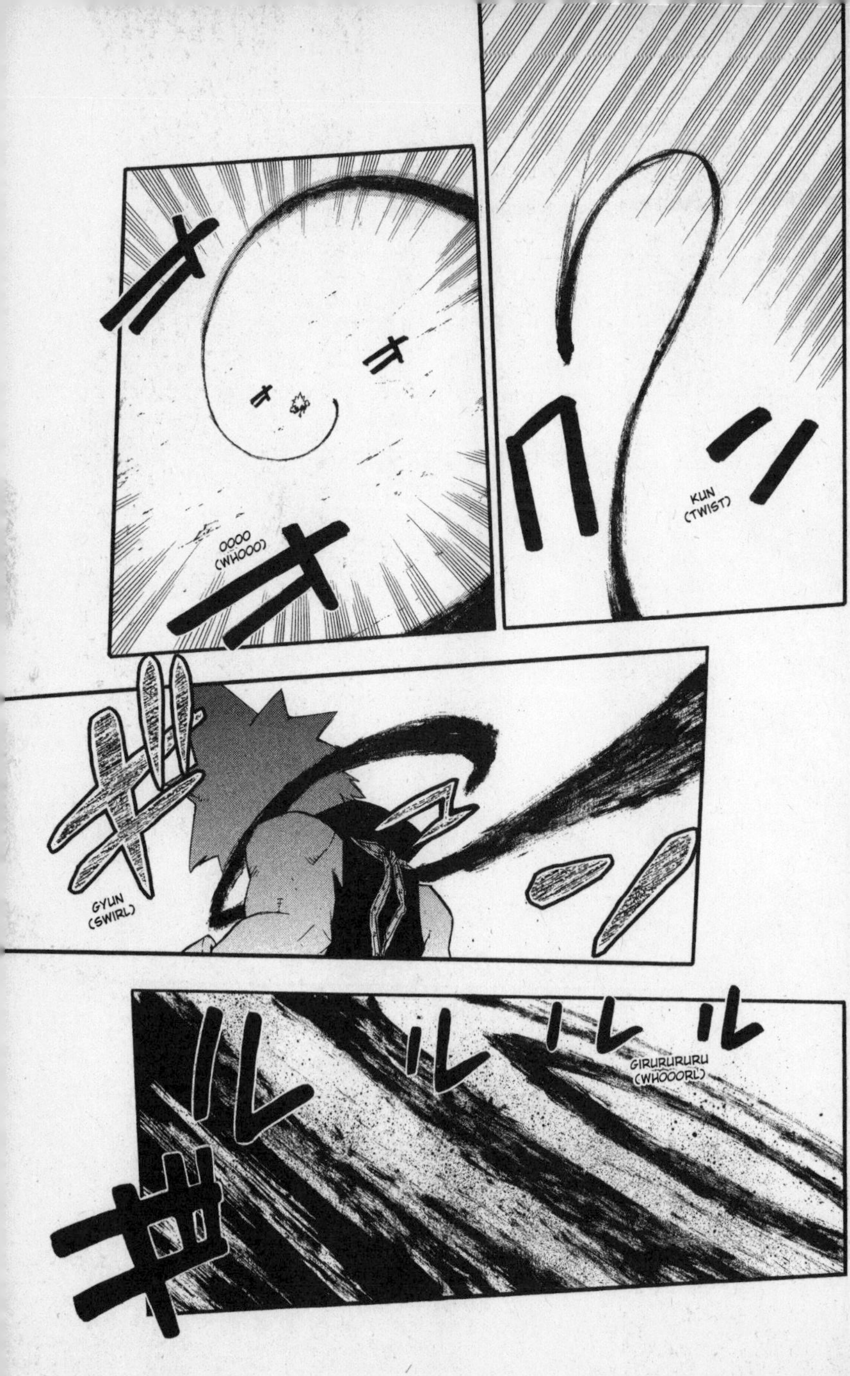
KUN (TWIST)
OOOO (WHOOO)
GYUN (SWIRL)
GIRURURURU (WHOOORL)

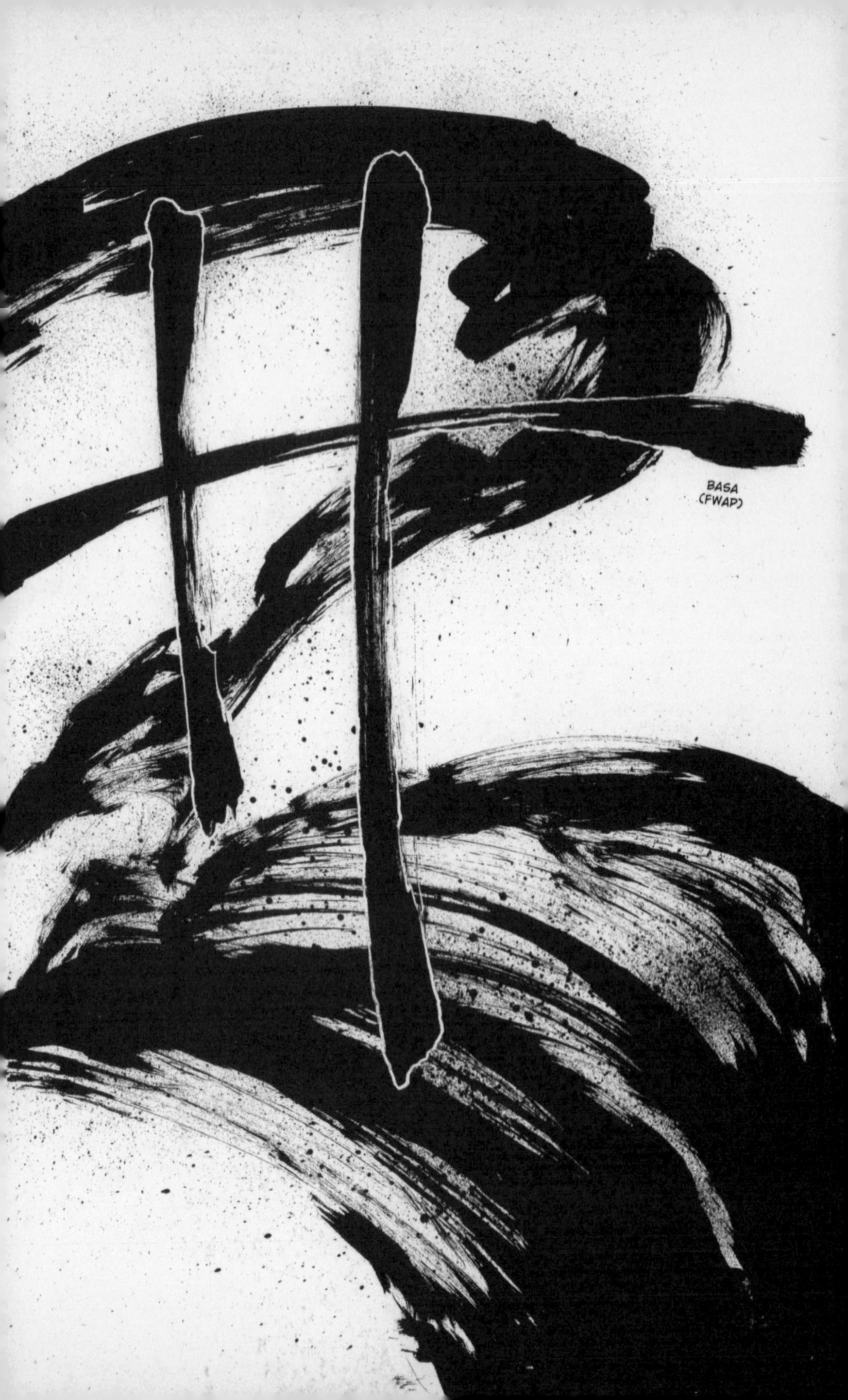
BASA
(FWAP)

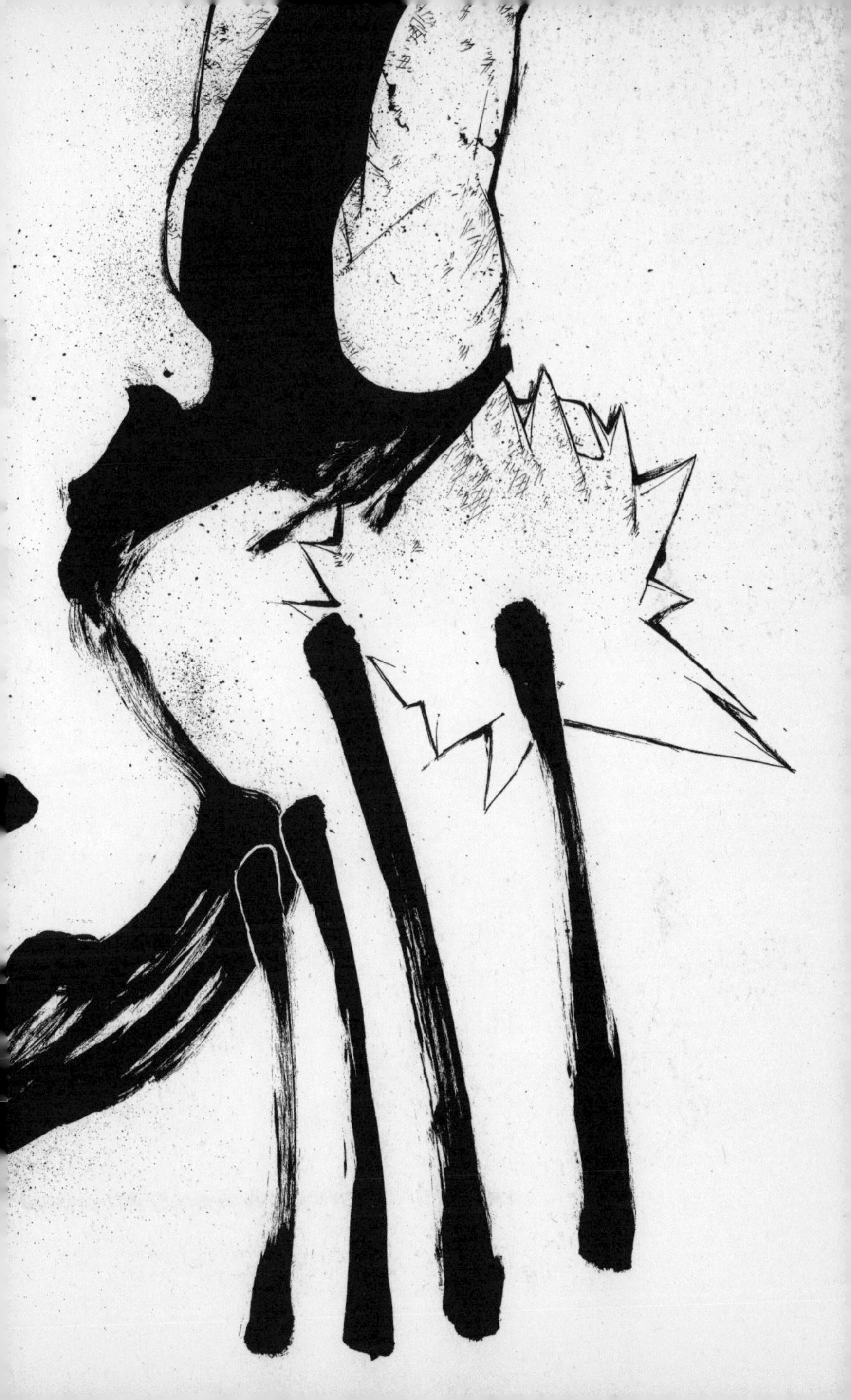

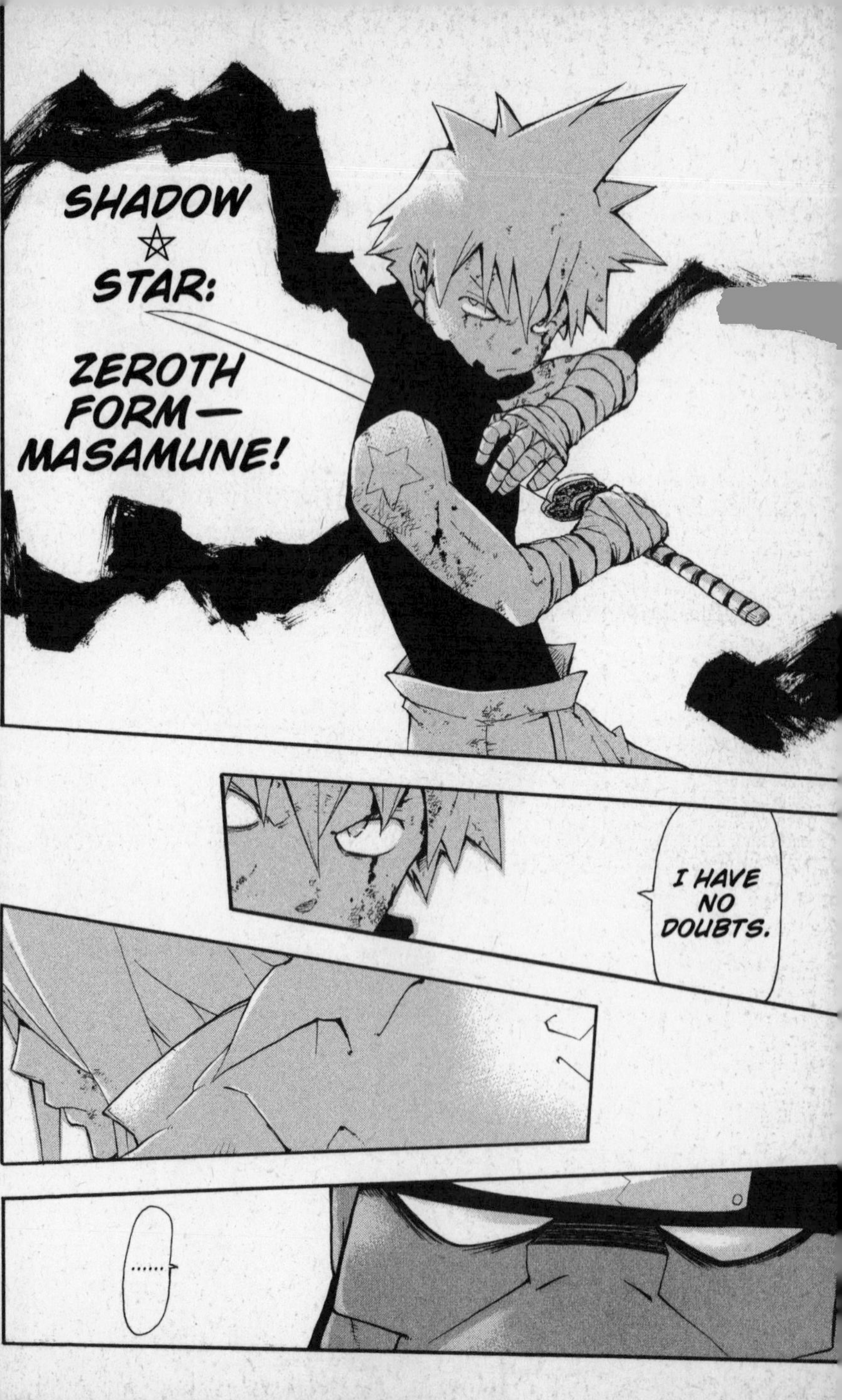
SHADOW ☆ STAR: ZEROTH FORM— MASAMUNE!
I HAVE NO DOUBTS.
......

SOUL EATER

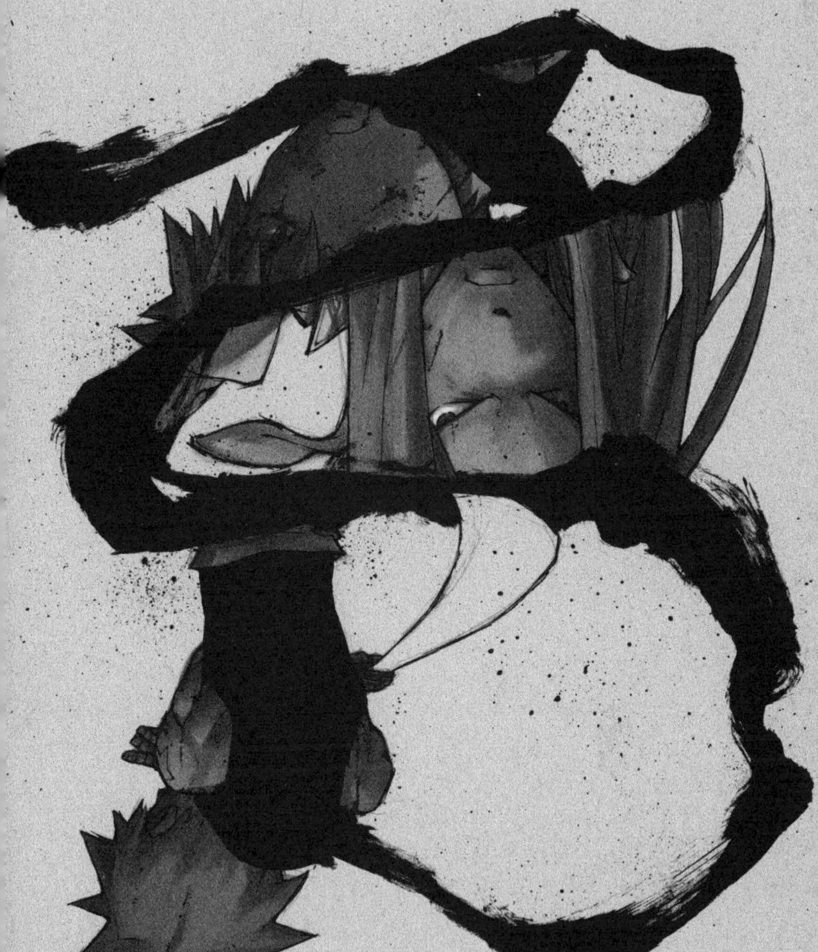

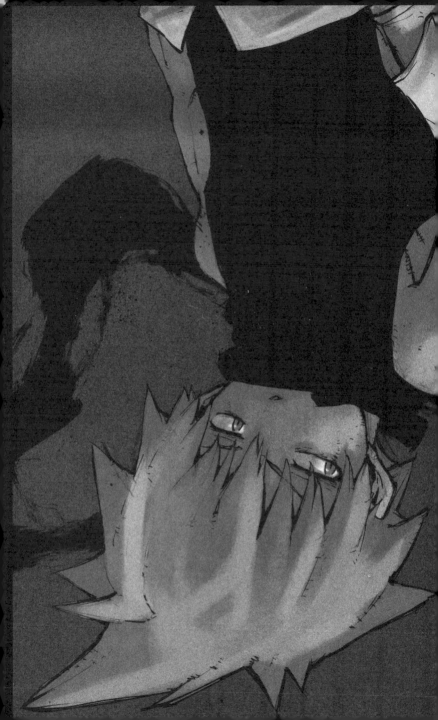

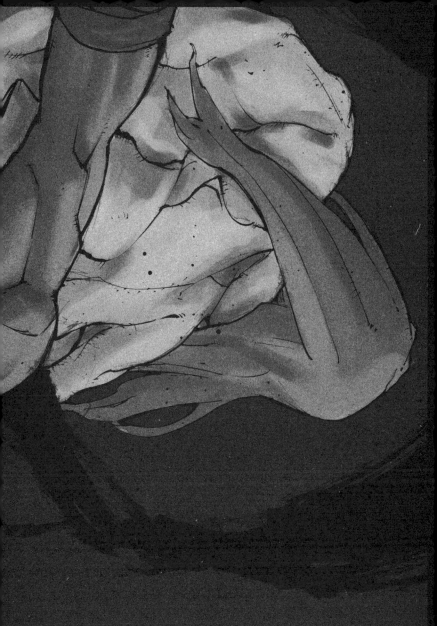

CHAPTER 57: OPERATION
CAPTURE BABA YAGA CASTLE (PART 12)

SOUL EATER

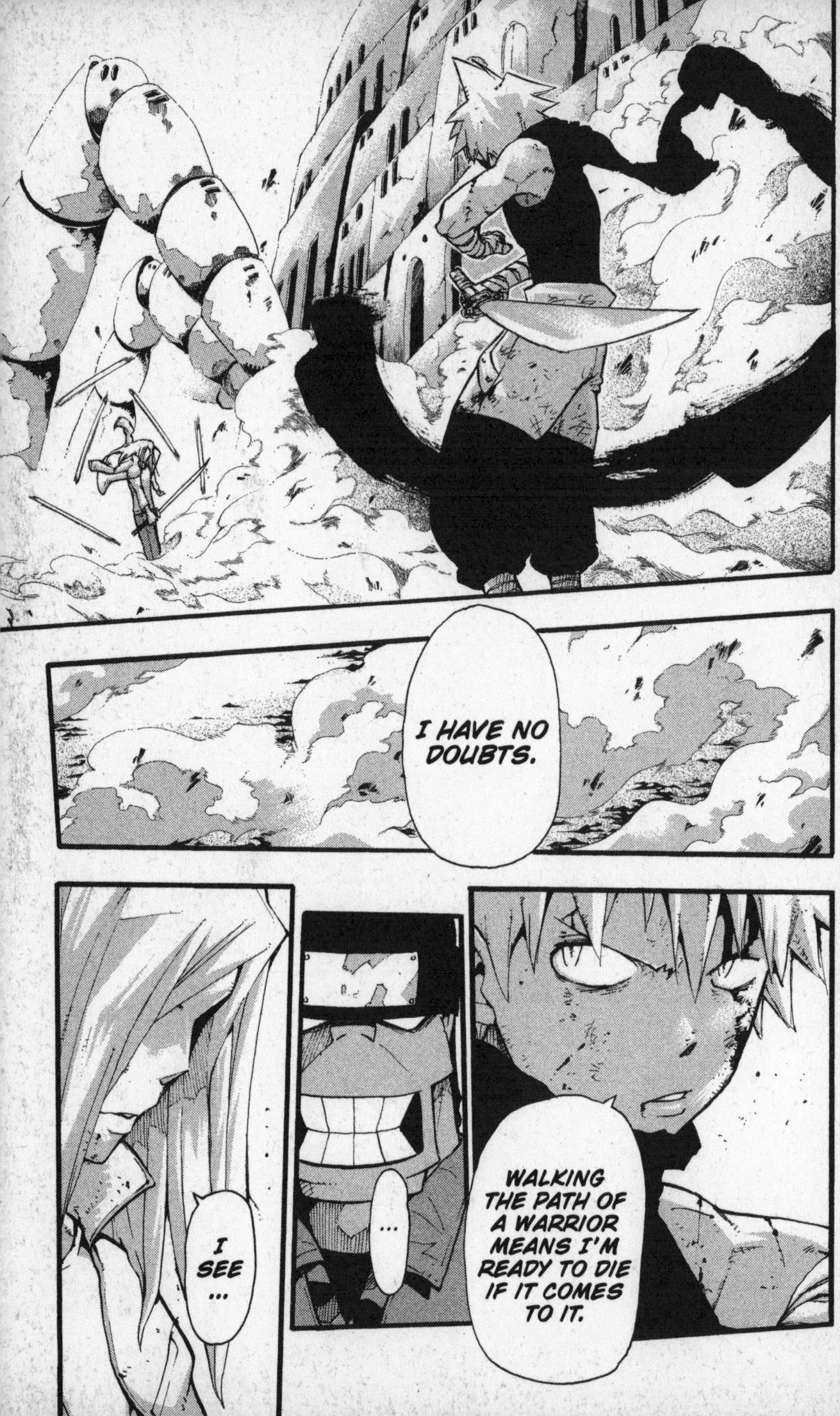
I HAVE NO DOUBTS.
WALKING THE PATH OF A WARRIOR MEANS I'M READY TO DIE IF IT COMES TO IT.
...
I SEE ...

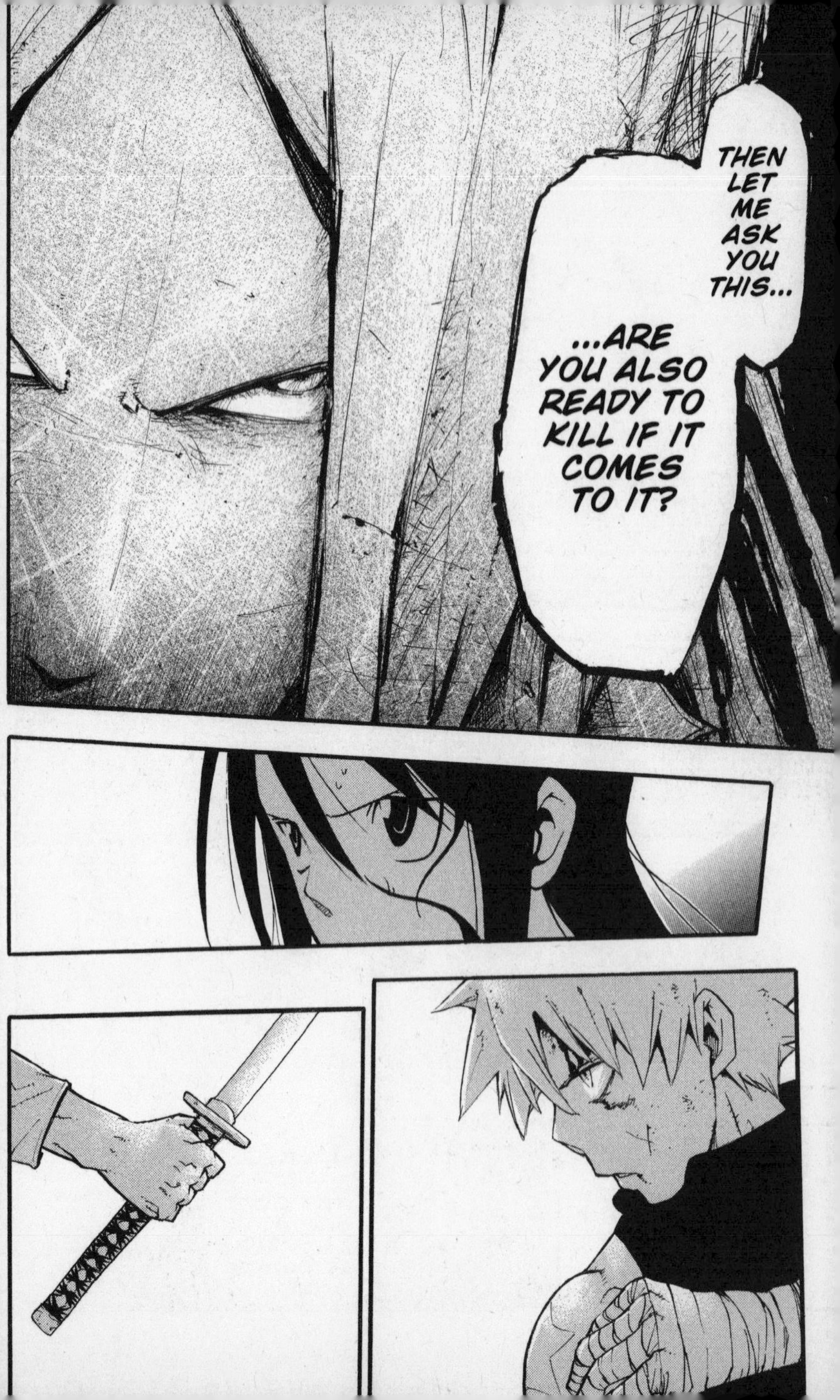
THEN LET ME ASK YOU THIS...
...ARE YOU ALSO READY TO KILL IF IT COMES TO IT?

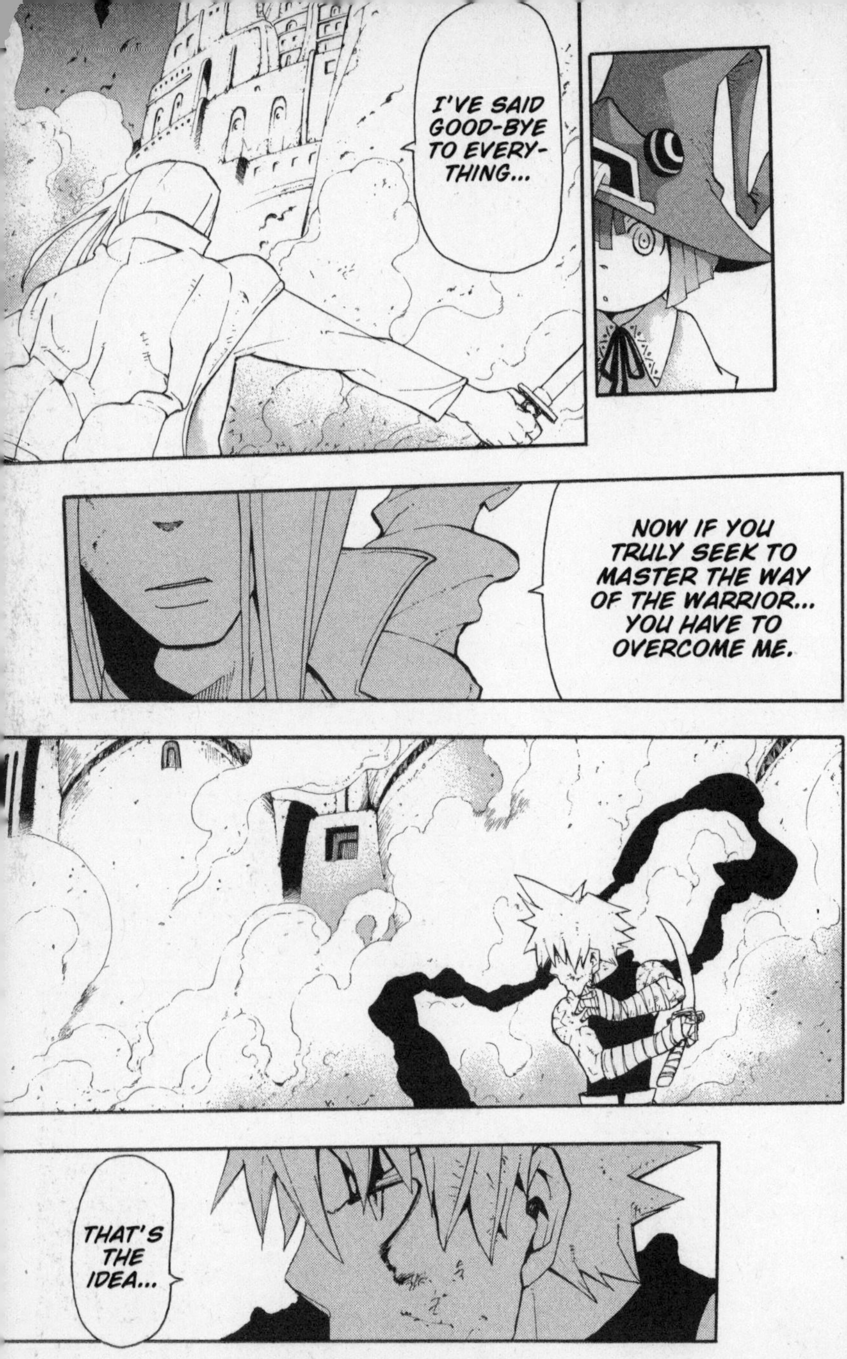
I'VE SAID GOOD-BYE TO EVERY-THING...
NOW IF YOU TRULY SEEK TO MASTER THE WAY OF THE WARRIOR... YOU HAVE TO OVERCOME ME.
THAT'S THE IDEA...

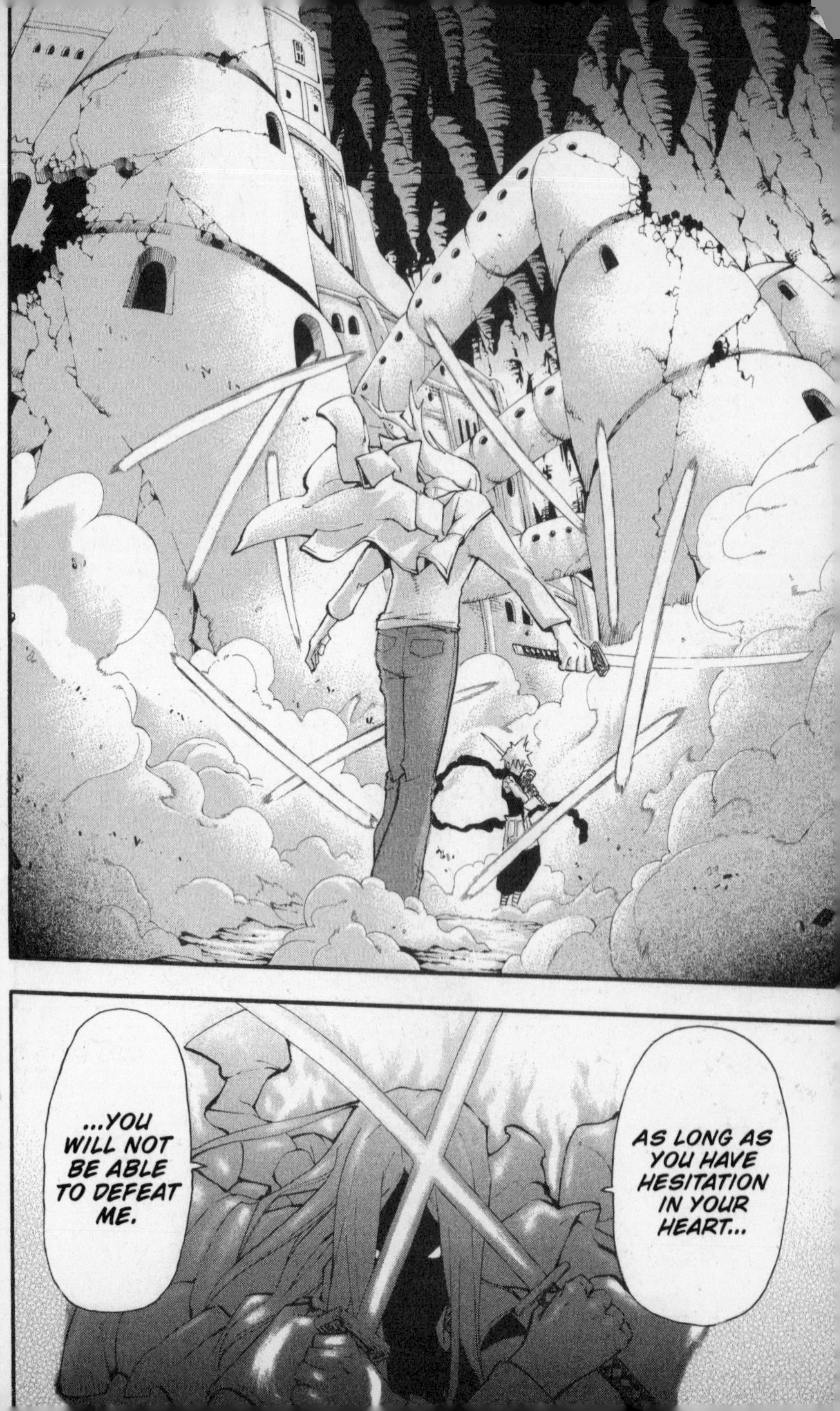
AS LONG AS YOU HAVE HESITATION IN YOUR HEART...
...YOU WILL NOT BE ABLE TO DEFEAT ME.

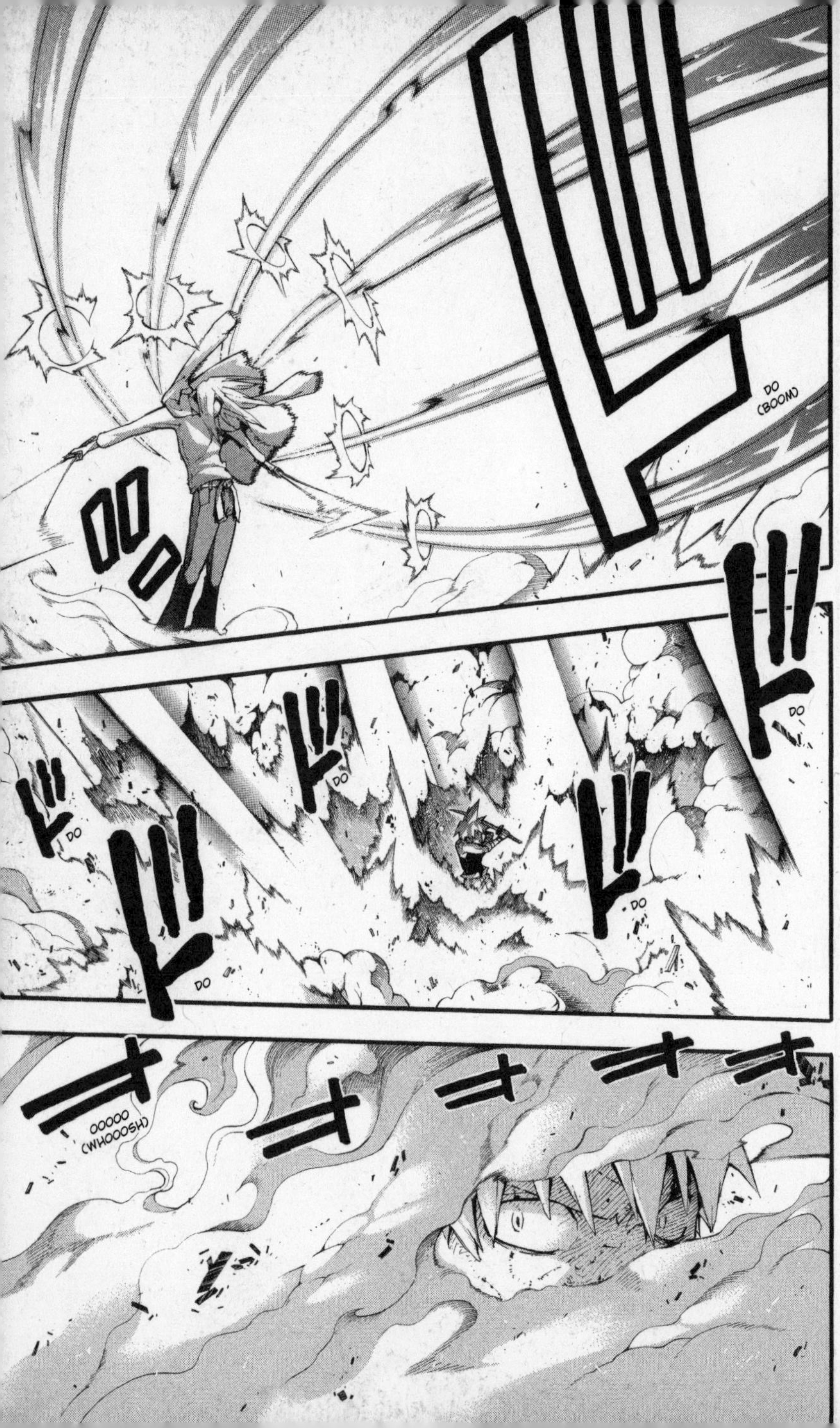
DO
(BOOM)
DO
DO
DO
DO
DO
OOOOO
(WHOOOSH)

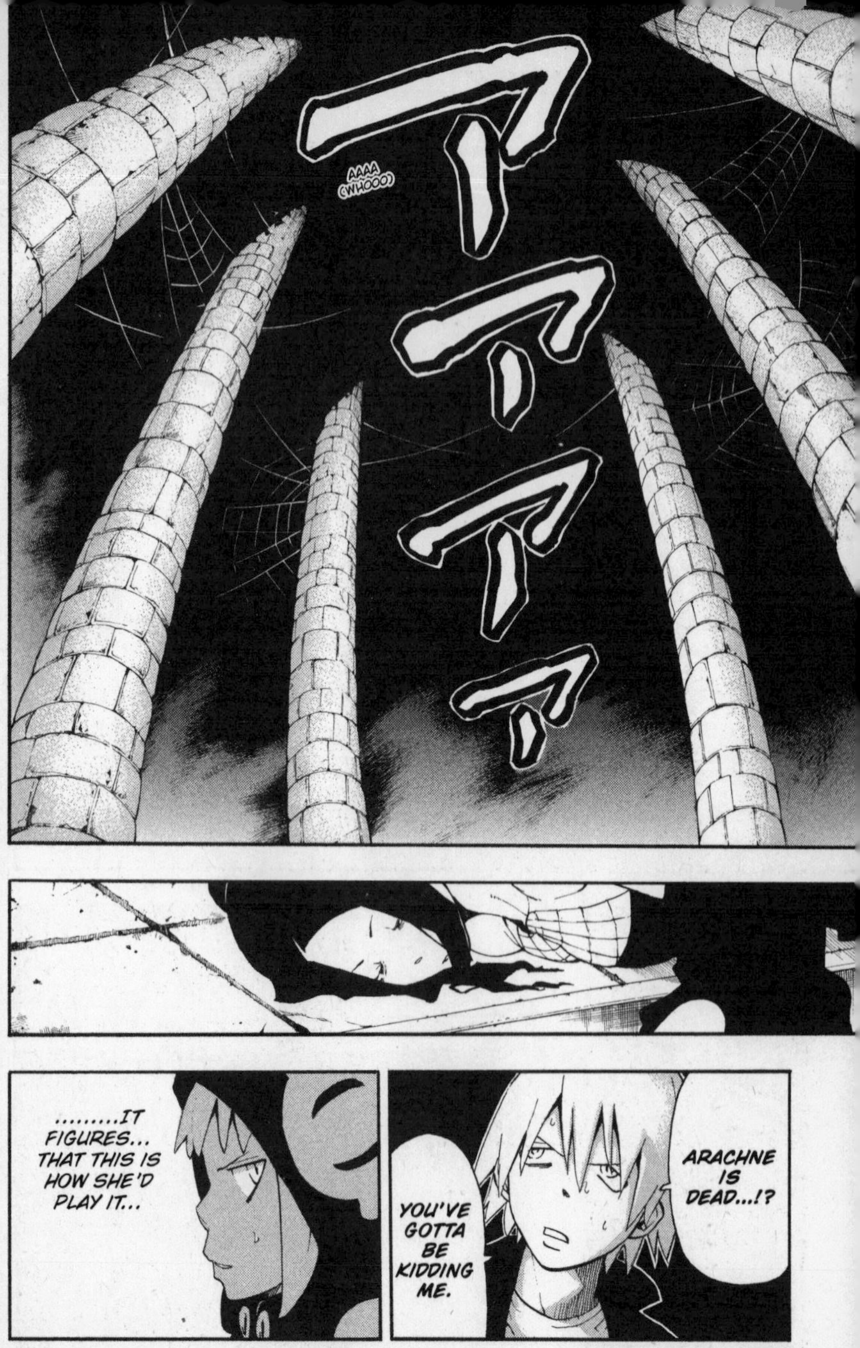
アアアア
AAAA (WHOOO)
ARACHNE IS DEAD...!?
YOU'VE GOTTA BE KIDDING ME.
.........IT FIGURES... THAT THIS IS HOW SHE'D PLAY IT...

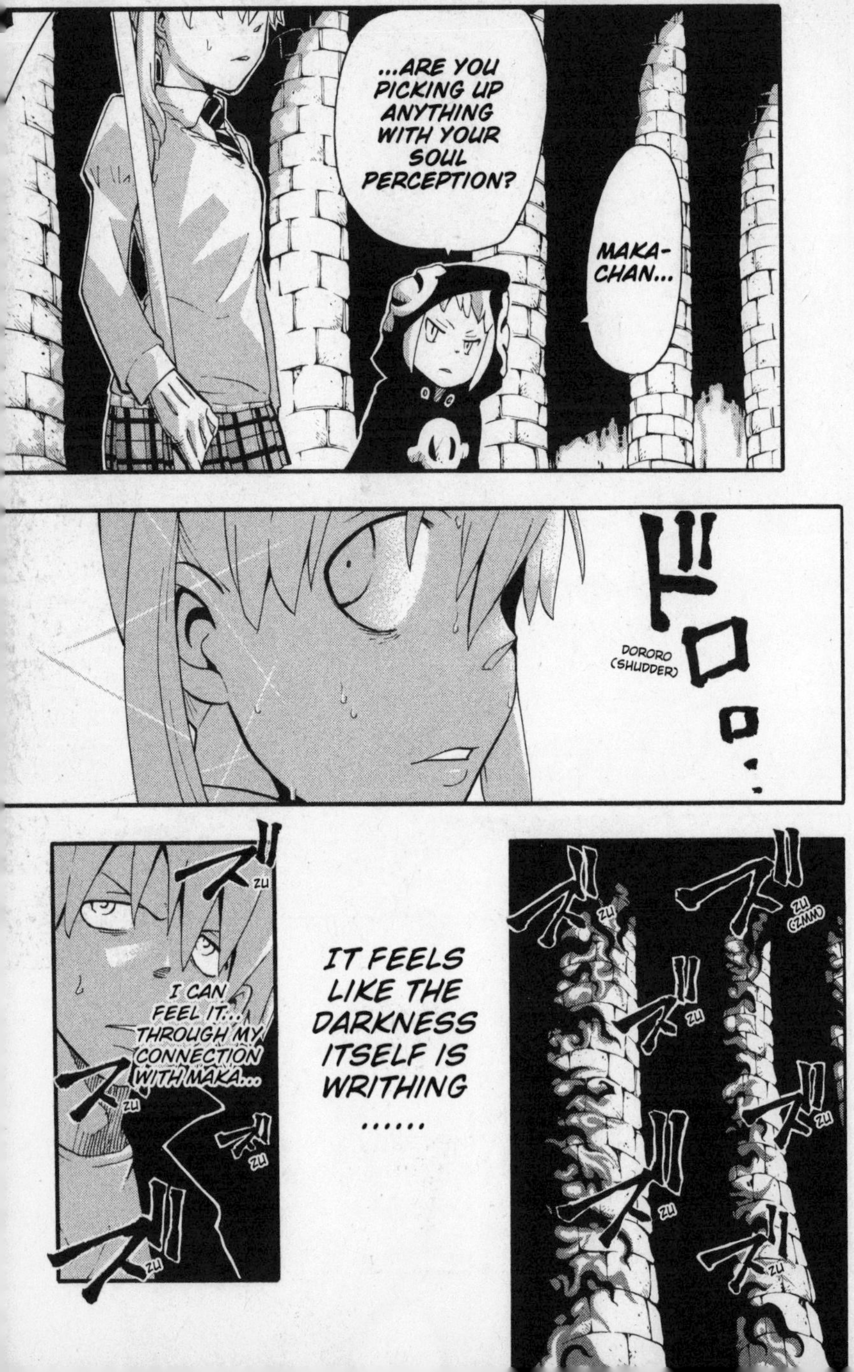
MAKA-CHAN...
...ARE YOU PICKING UP ANYTHING WITH YOUR SOUL PERCEPTION?
DORORO (SHUDDER)
ZU (GZMM)
ZU
ZU
ZU
ZU
ZU
IT FEELS LIKE THE DARKNESS ITSELF IS WRITHING ......
ZU
I CAN FEEL IT... THROUGH MY CONNECTION WITH MAKA...
ZU
ZU
ZU

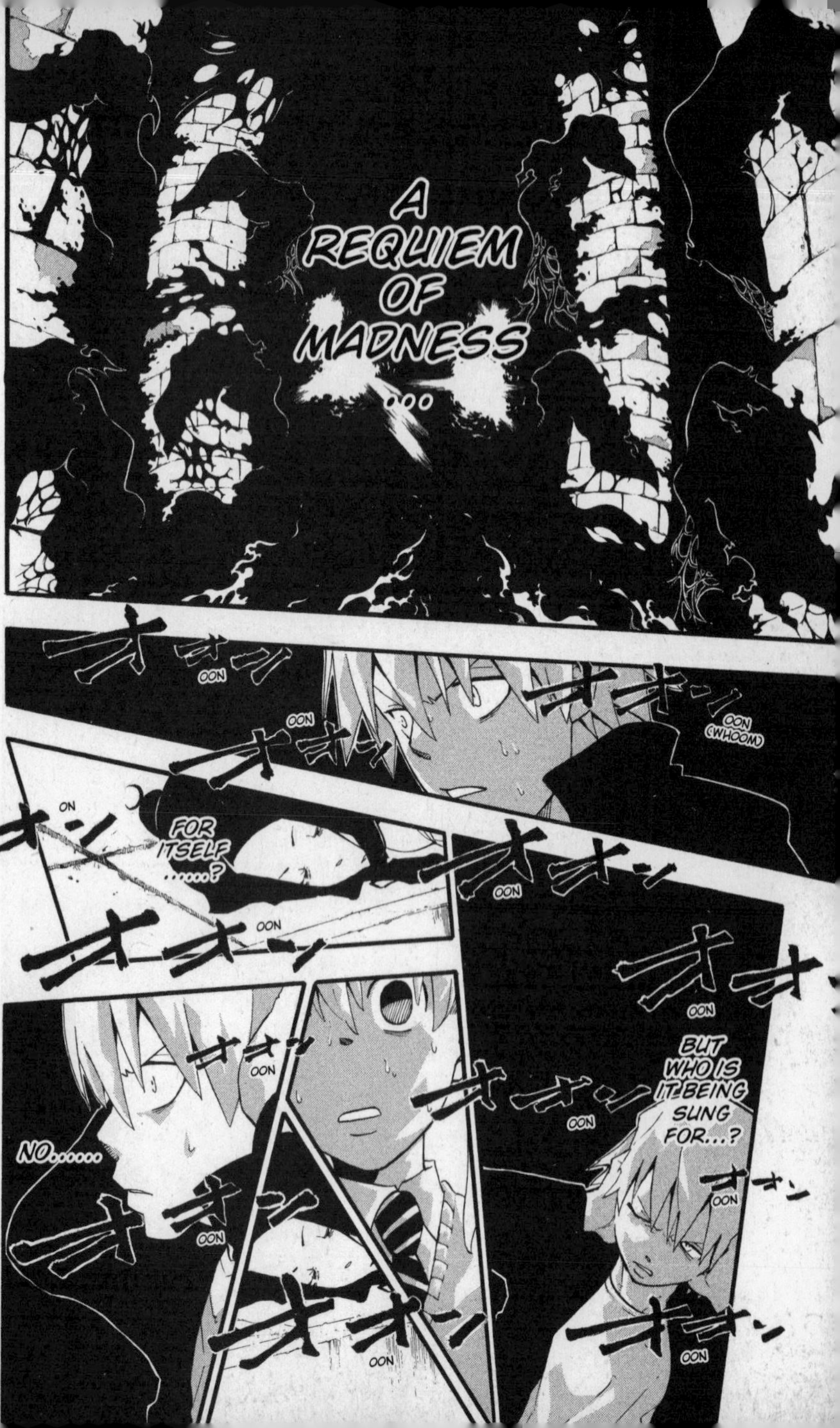
A REQUIEM OF MADNESS...
OON (WHOOM)
OON
OON
ON
FOR ITSELF......?
OON
OON
OON
BUT WHO IS IT BEING SUNG FOR...?
OON
OON
OON
OON
NO.......
OON
OON

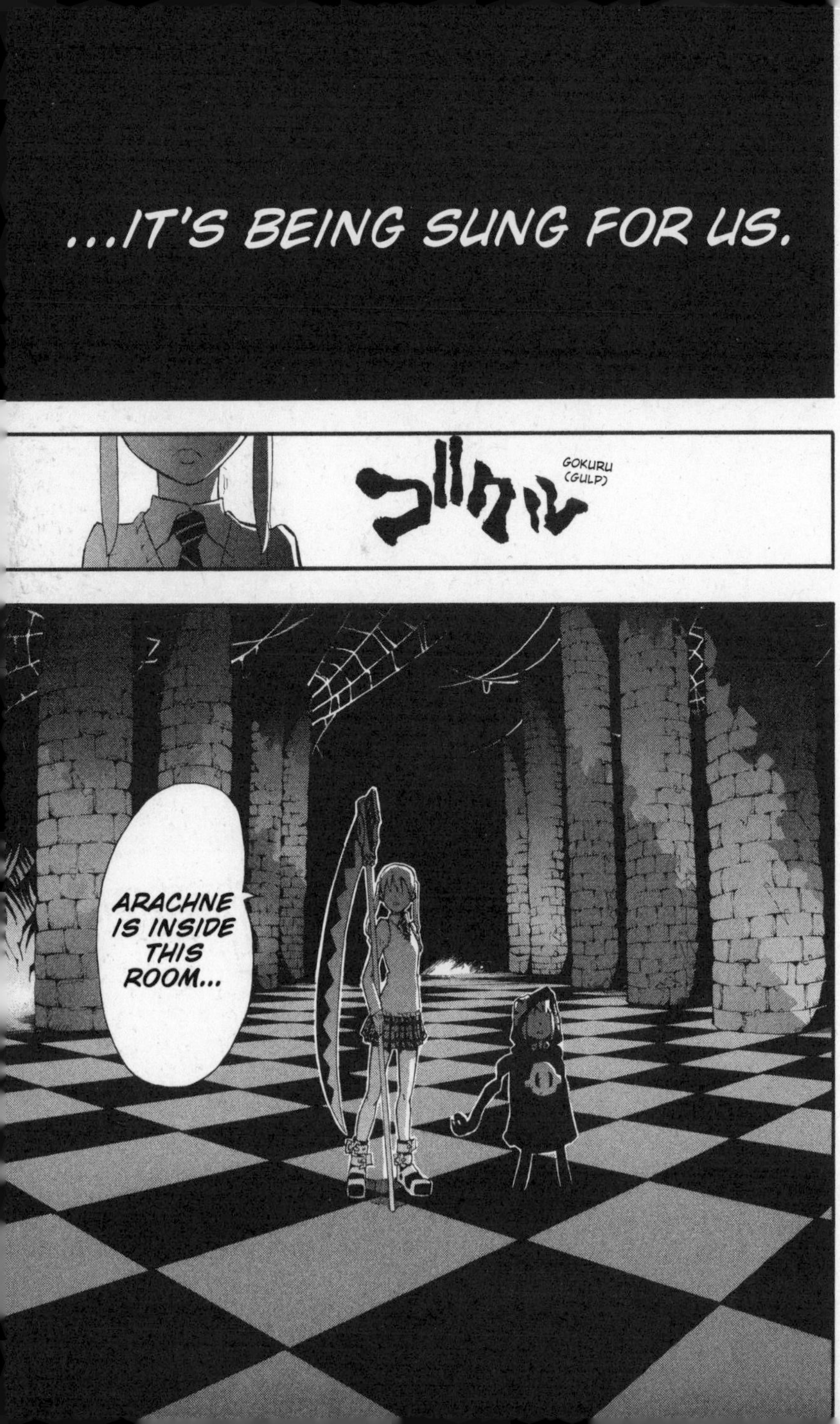
...IT'S BEING SUNG FOR US.
ゴクル
GOKURU (GULP)
ARACHNE IS INSIDE THIS ROOM...

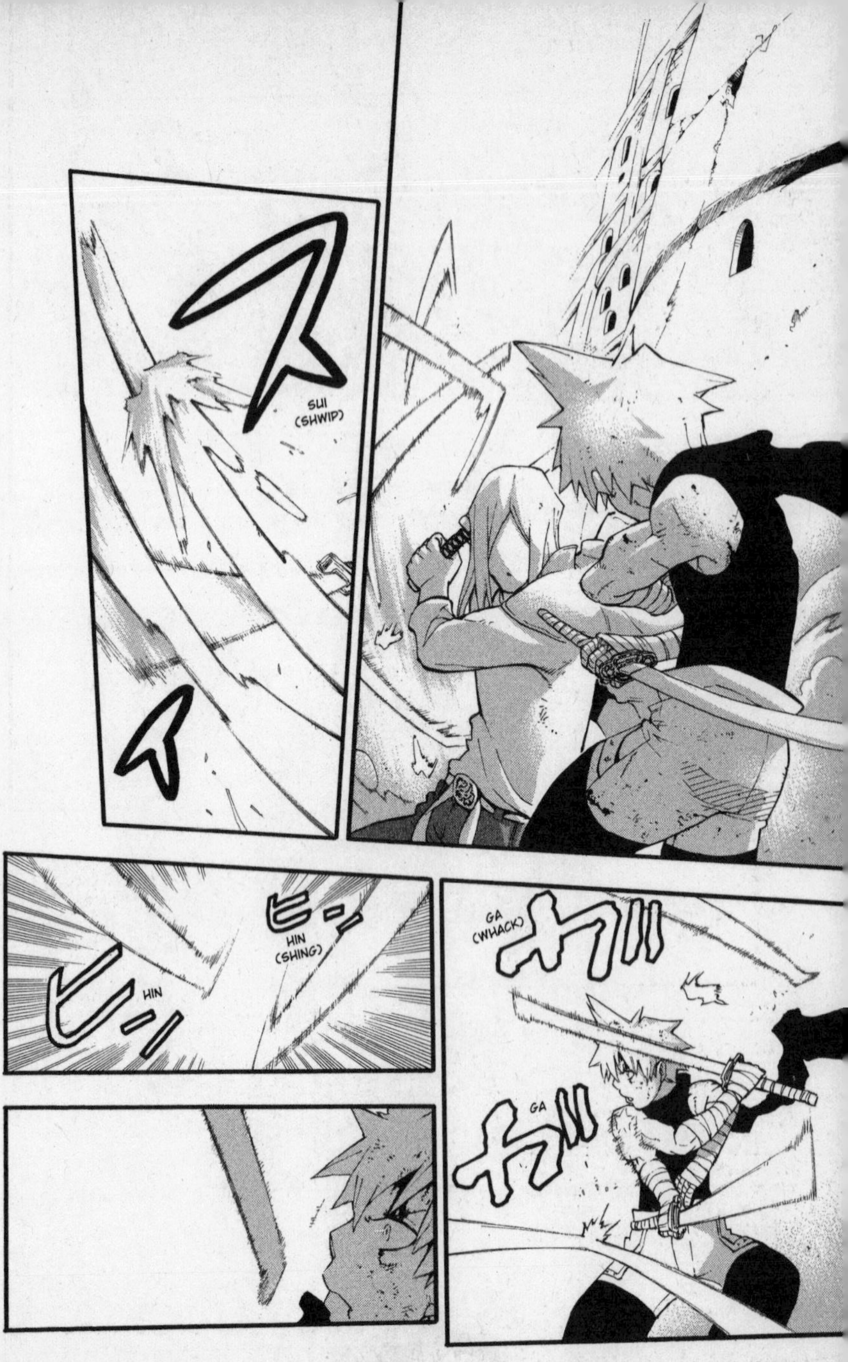
SUI
(SHWIP)
GA
(WHACK)
GA
HIN
(SHING)
HIN

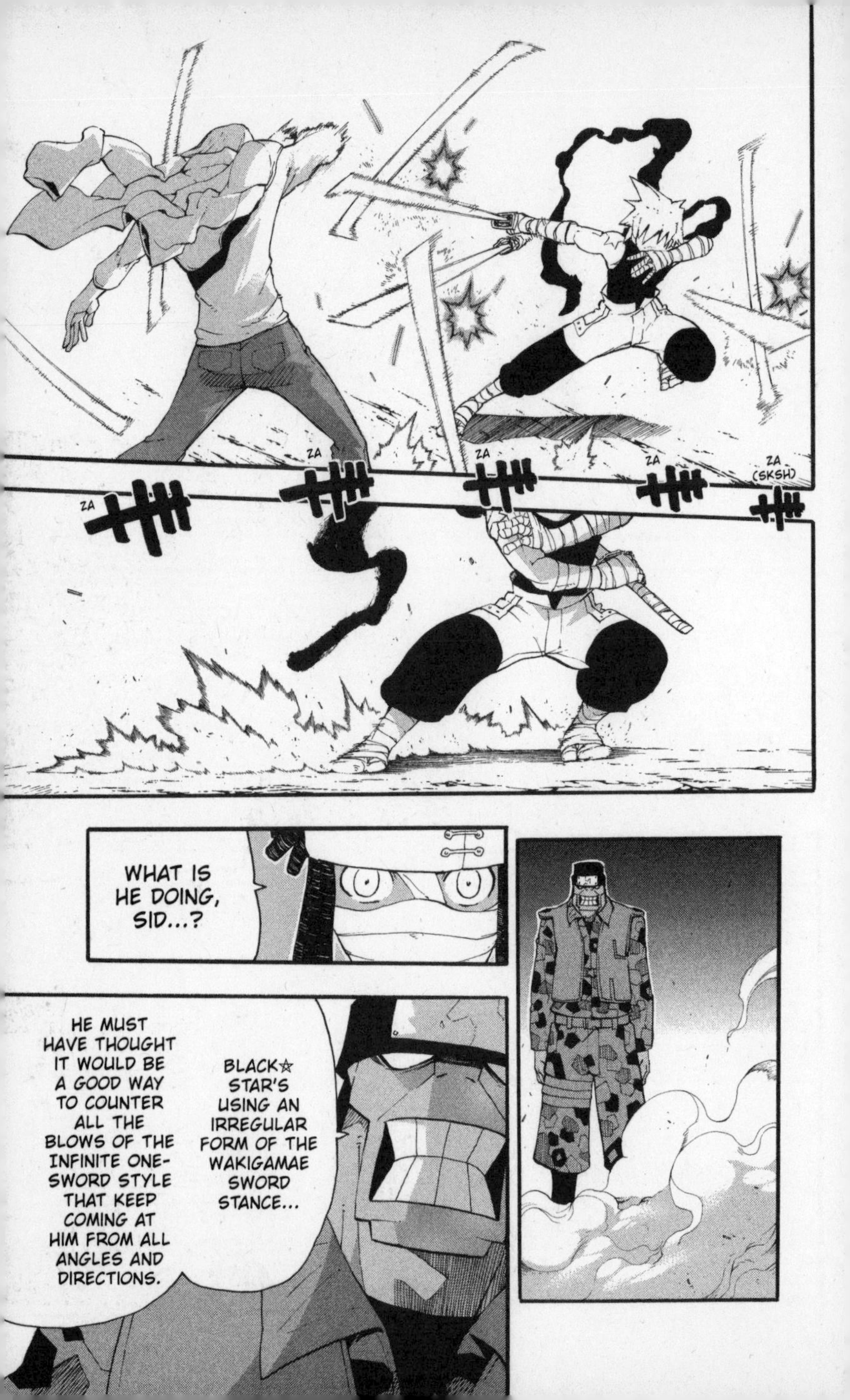
ZA (SKSH)
ZA
ZA
ZA
ZA
WHAT IS HE DOING, SID...?
BLACK☆STAR'S USING AN IRREGULAR FORM OF THE WAKIGAMAE SWORD STANCE...
HE MUST HAVE THOUGHT IT WOULD BE A GOOD WAY TO COUNTER ALL THE BLOWS OF THE INFINITE ONE-SWORD STYLE THAT KEEP COMING AT HIM FROM ALL ANGLES AND DIRECTIONS.

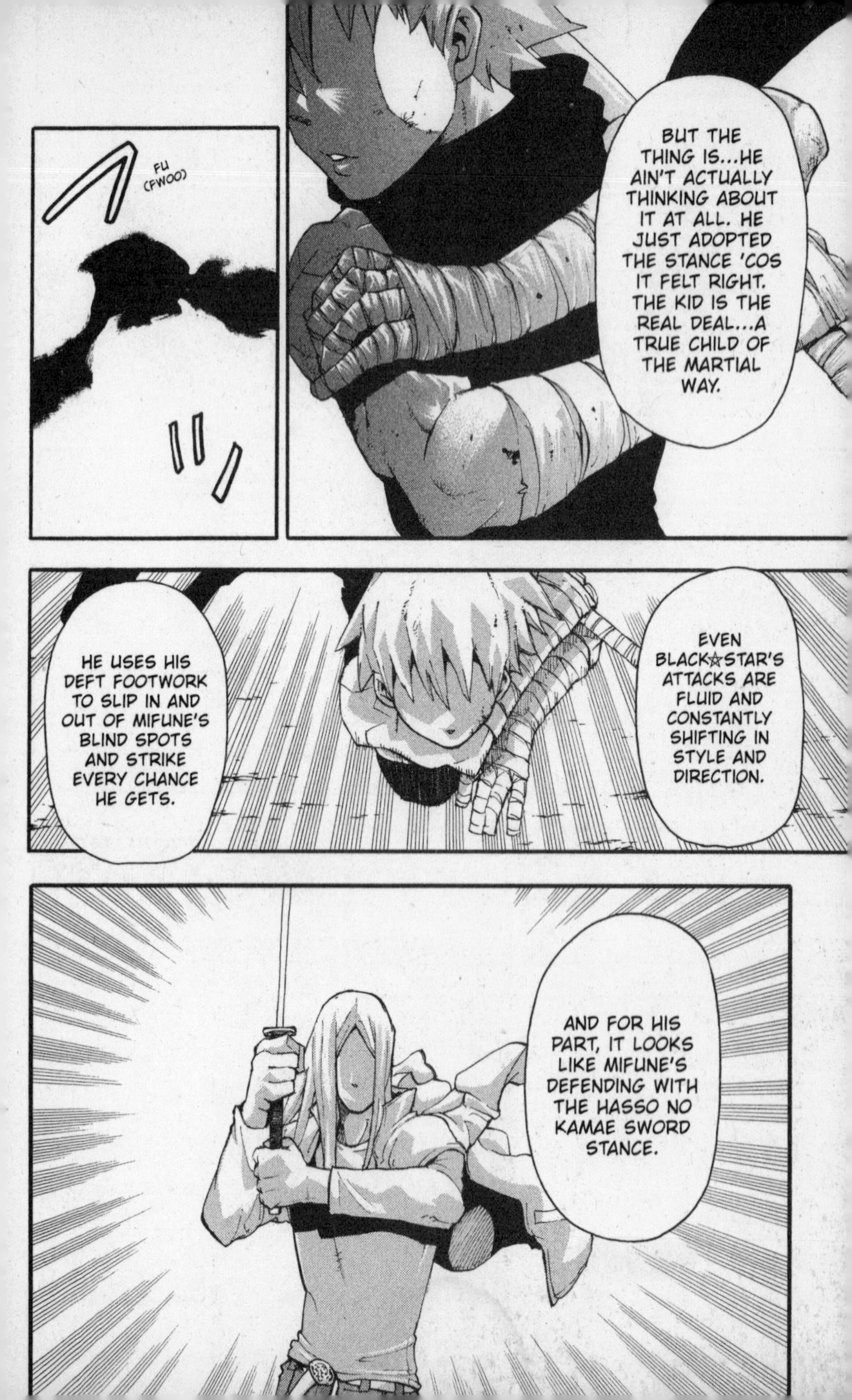
BUT THE THING IS...HE AIN'T ACTUALLY THINKING ABOUT IT AT ALL. HE JUST ADOPTED THE STANCE 'COS IT FELT RIGHT. THE KID IS THE REAL DEAL...A TRUE CHILD OF THE MARTIAL WAY.
FU (FWOO)
EVEN BLACK☆STAR'S ATTACKS ARE FLUID AND CONSTANTLY SHIFTING IN STYLE AND DIRECTION.
HE USES HIS DEFT FOOTWORK TO SLIP IN AND OUT OF MIFUNE'S BLIND SPOTS AND STRIKE EVERY CHANCE HE GETS.
AND FOR HIS PART, IT LOOKS LIKE MIFUNE'S DEFENDING WITH THE HASSO NO KAMAE SWORD STANCE.

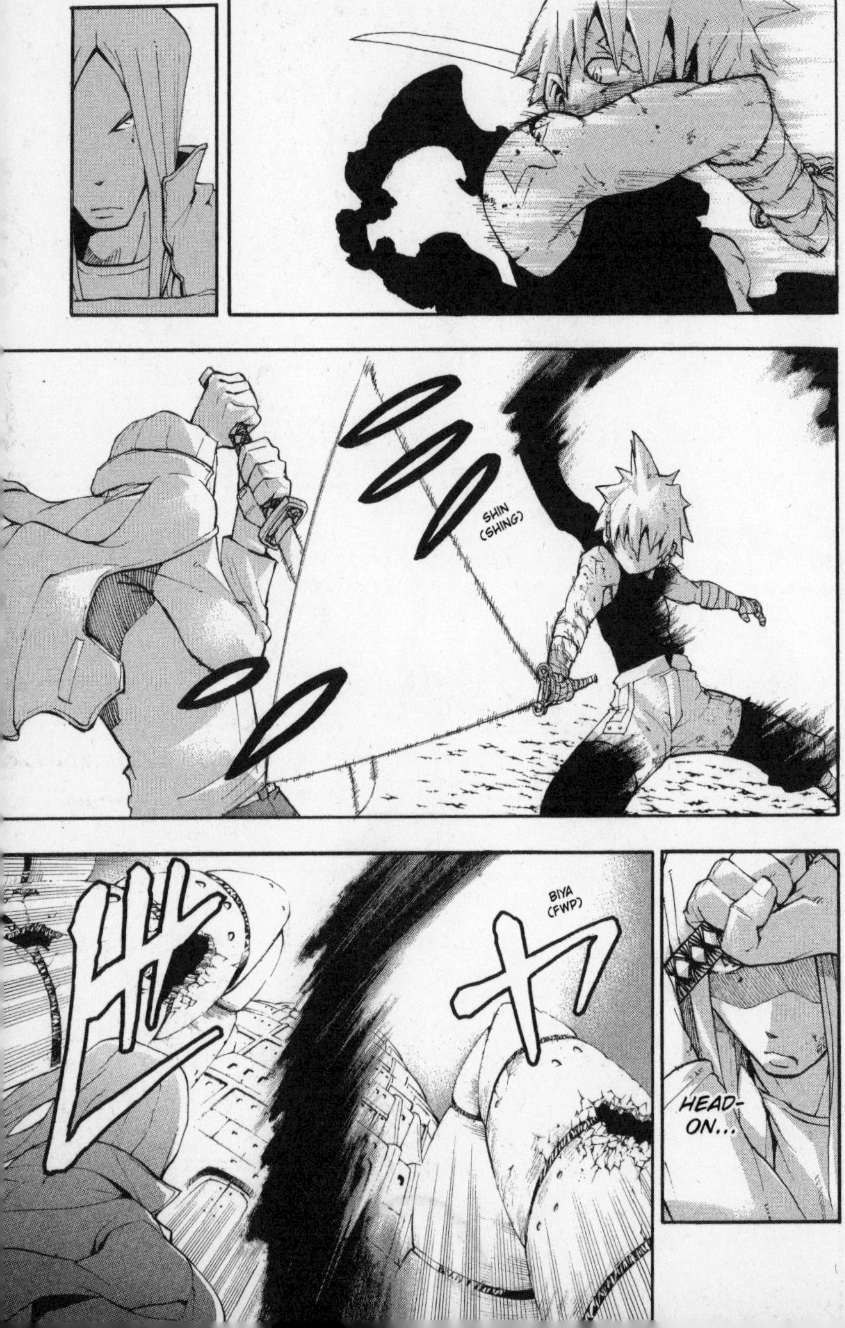
SHIN
(SHING)
HEAD-
ON...
BIYA
(FWP)

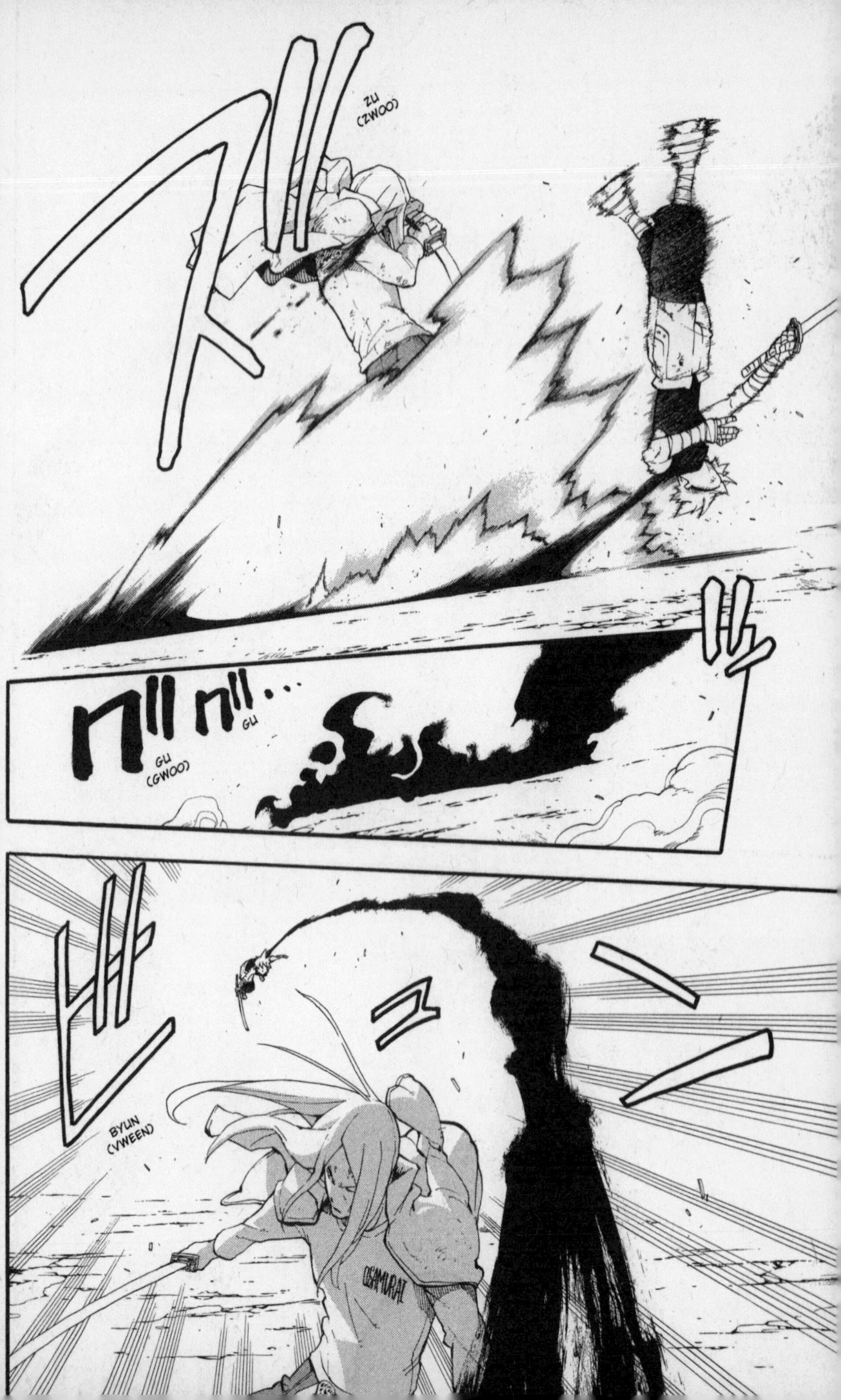
ZU (ZWOO)
GU (GWOO)
GU
BYUN (VWEEN)
OSAMURAI

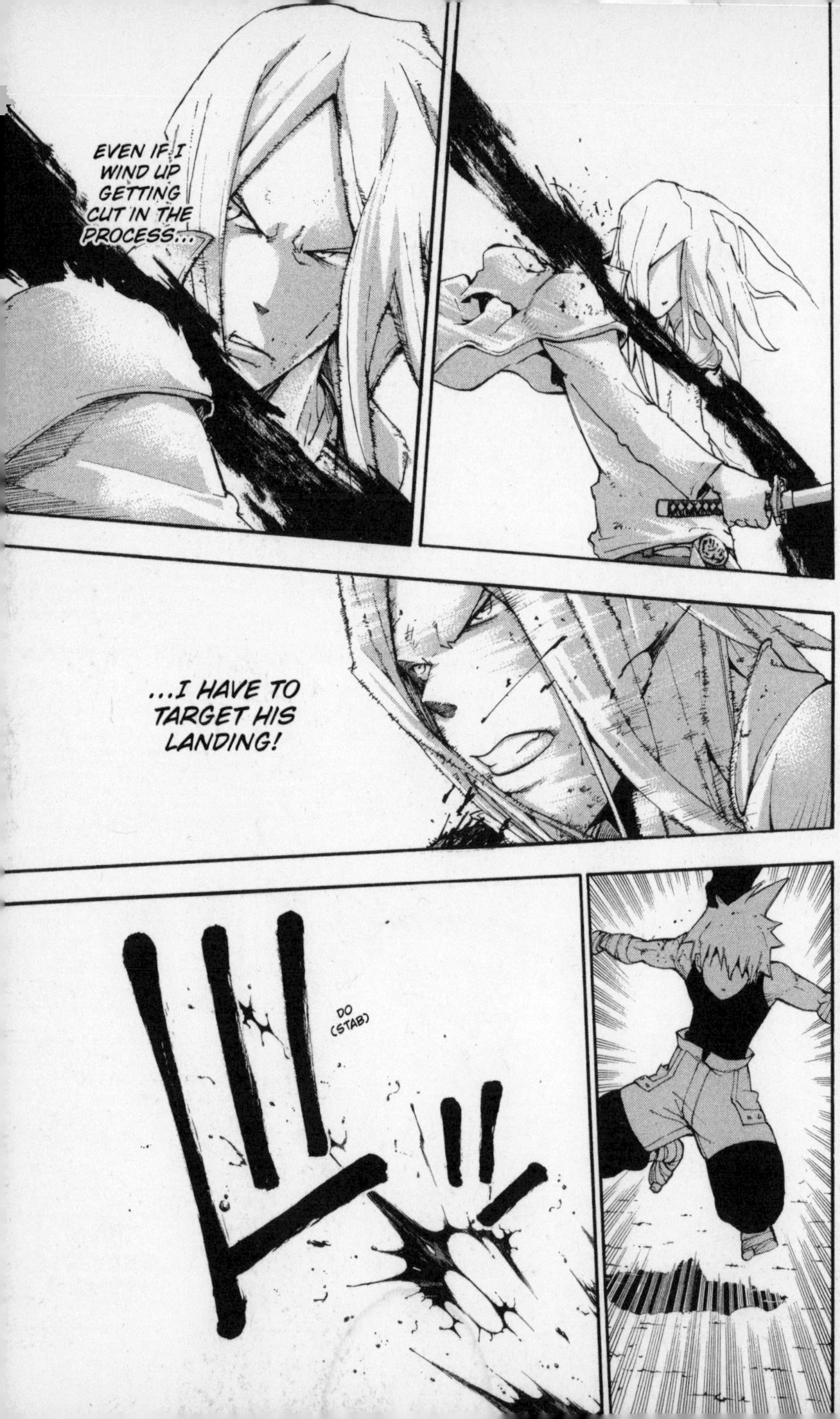
EVEN IF I WIND UP GETTING CUT IN THE PROCESS...
...I HAVE TO TARGET HIS LANDING!
DO (STAB)

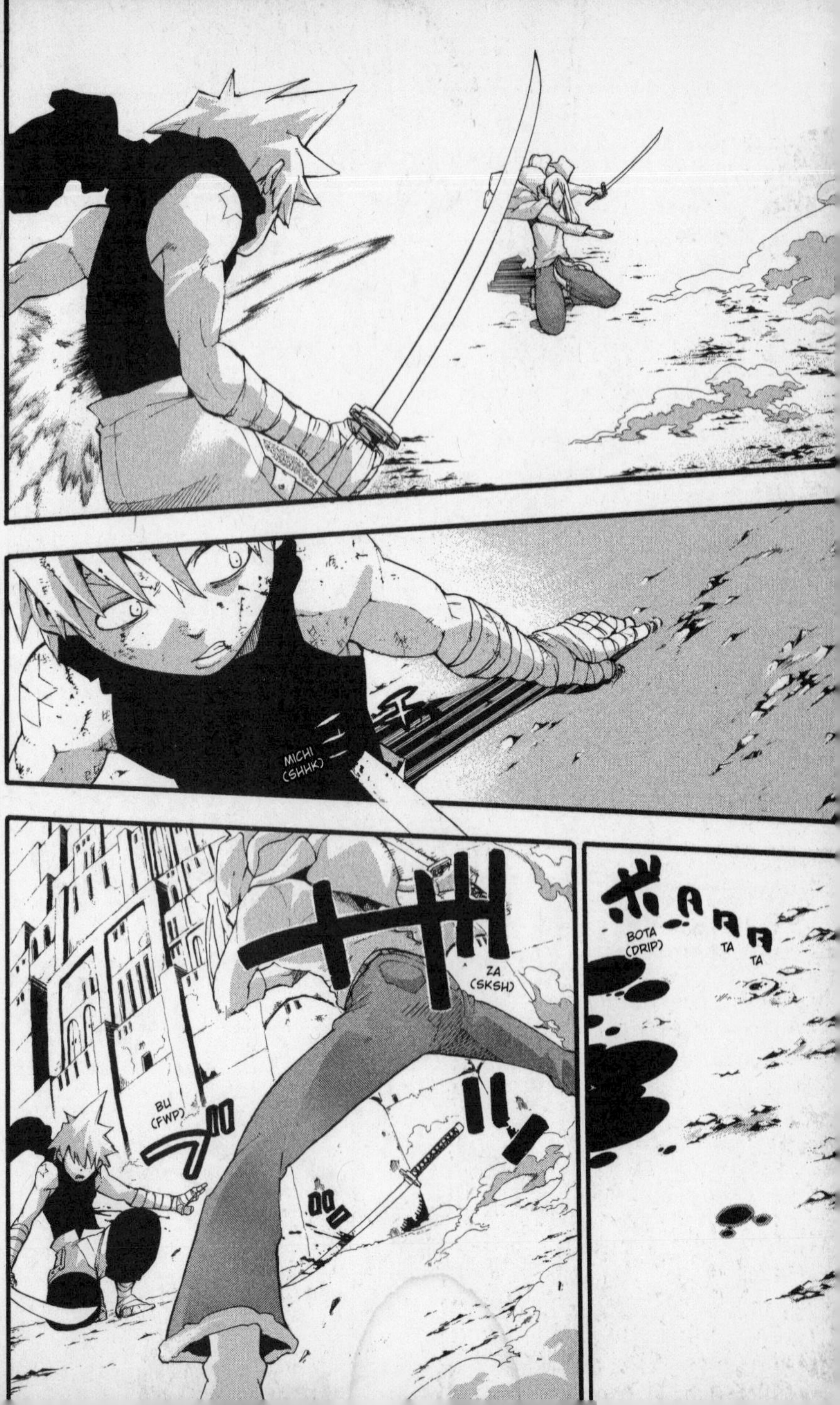
MICHI (SHHK)
BOTA (DRIP)
TA
TA
ZA (SKSH)
BU (FWP)

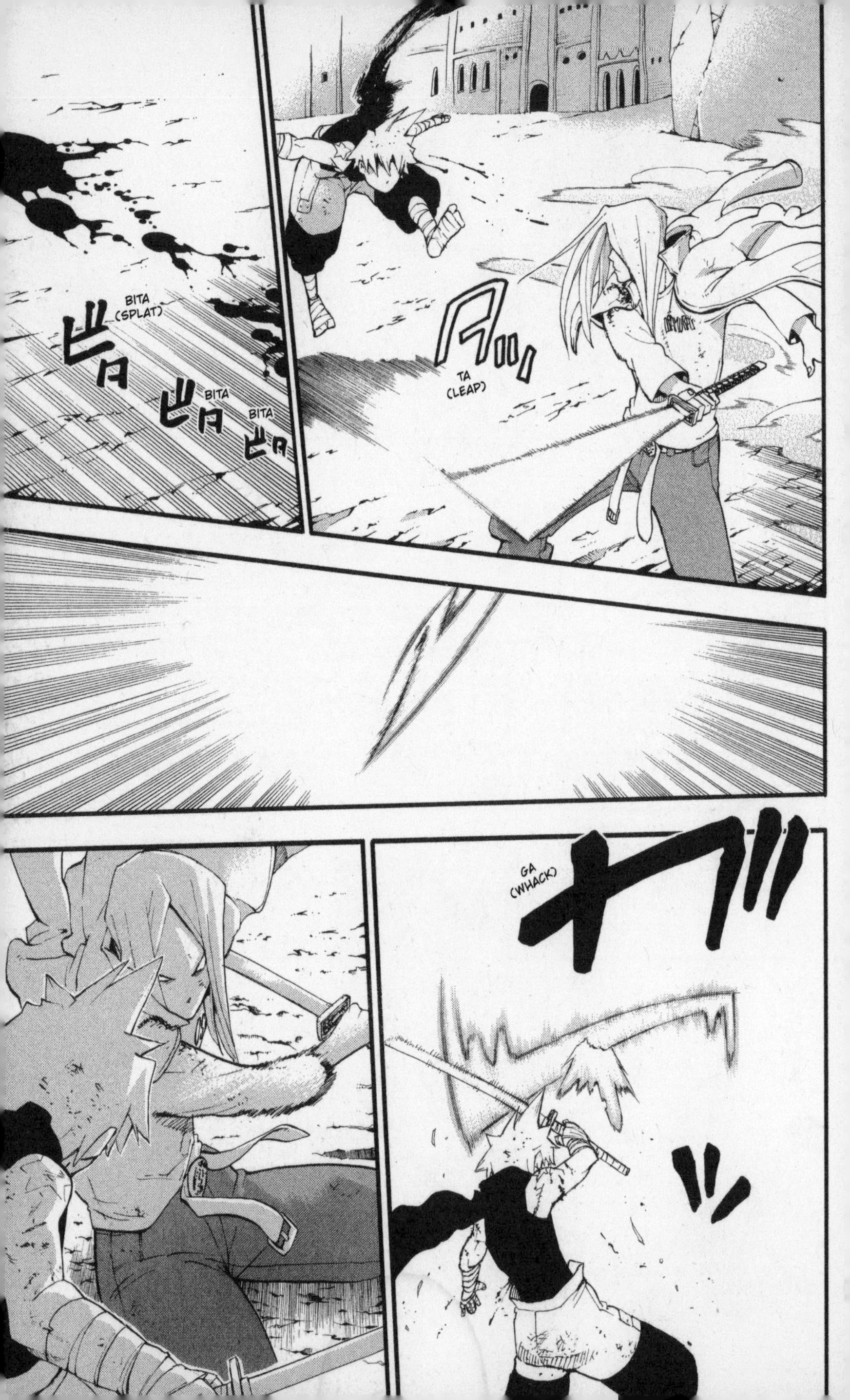
TA
(LEAP)
BITA
(SPLAT)
BITA
BITA
GA
(WHACK)

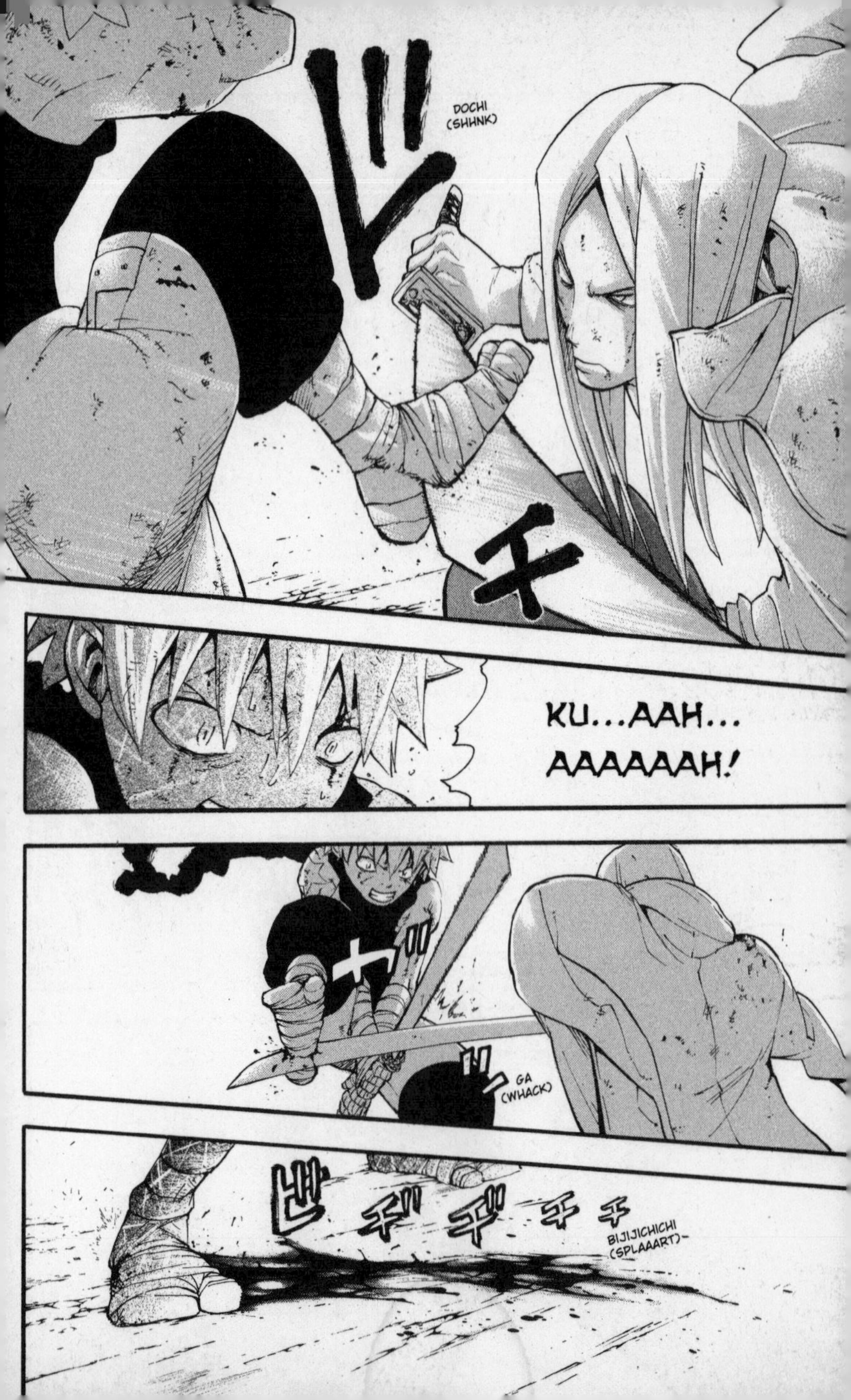
DOCHI (SHHNK)
KU...AAH... AAAAAAH!
GA (WHACK)
BIJIJICHICHI (SPLAAART)–

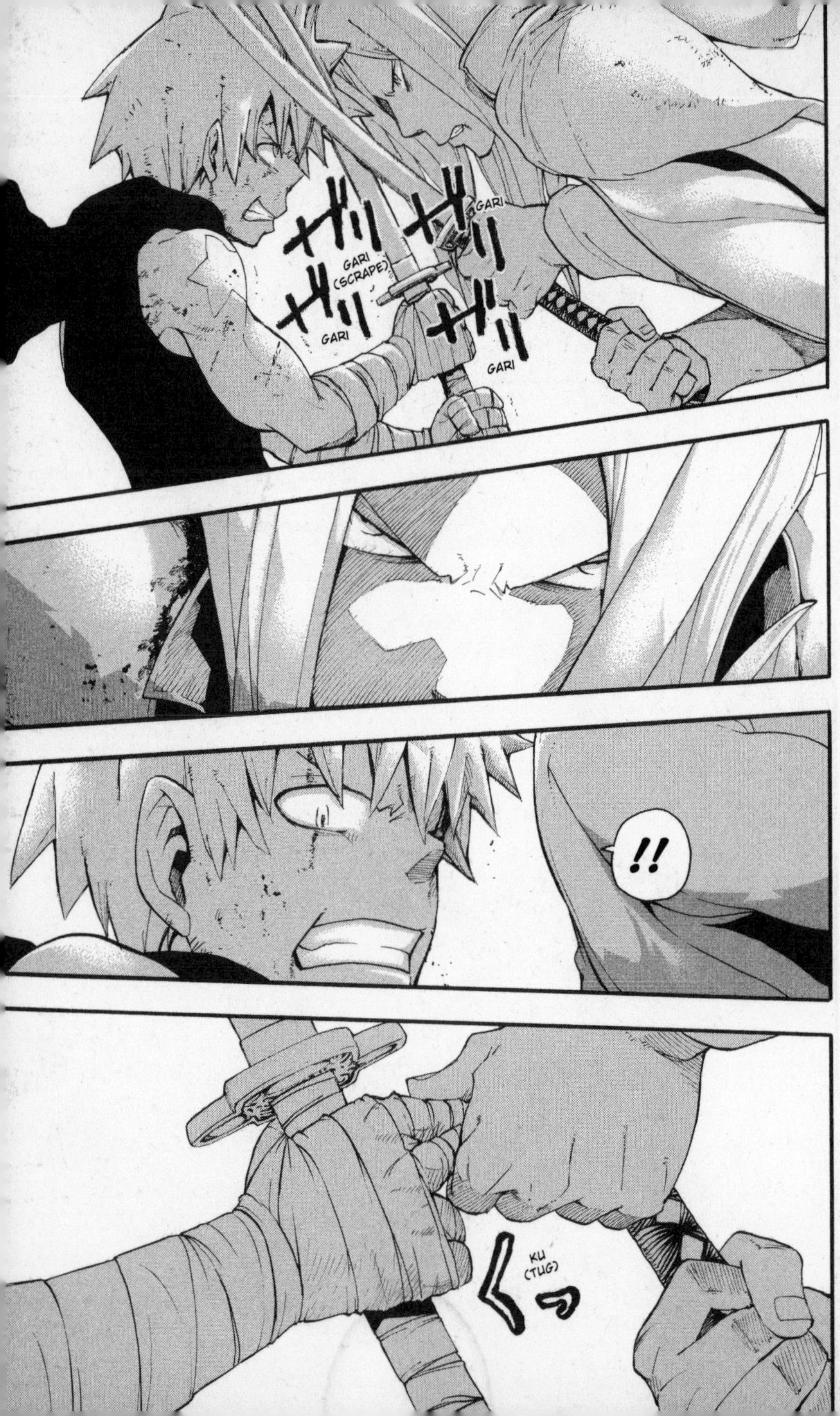
ガリ GARI
ガリ GARI (SCRAPE)
ガリ GARI
ガリ GARI
!!
く KU (TUG)

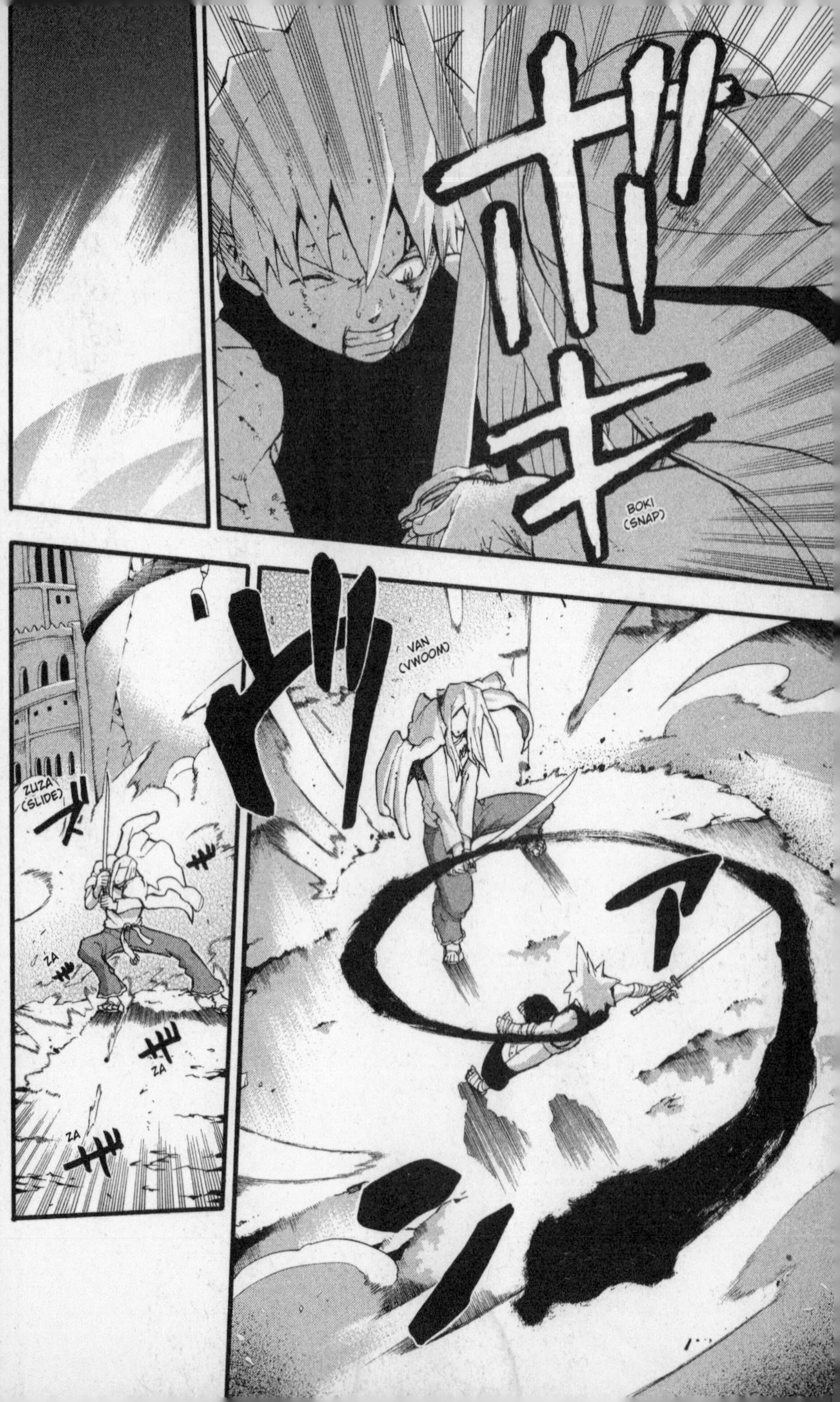
BOKI (SNAP)
VAN (VWOOM)
ZUZA (SLIDE)
ZA
ZA
ZA

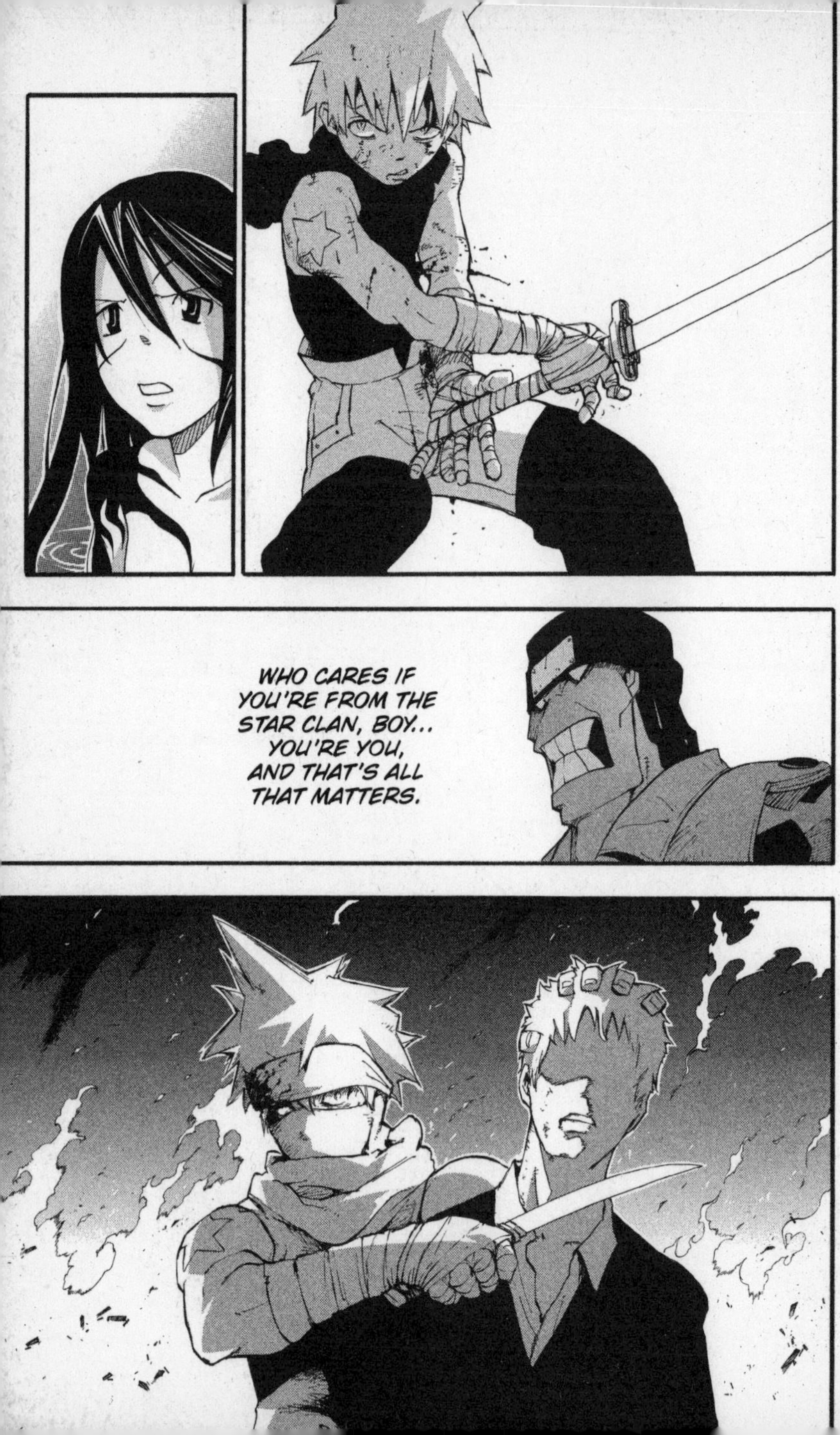
WHO CARES IF YOU'RE FROM THE STAR CLAN, BOY... YOU'RE YOU, AND THAT'S ALL THAT MATTERS.

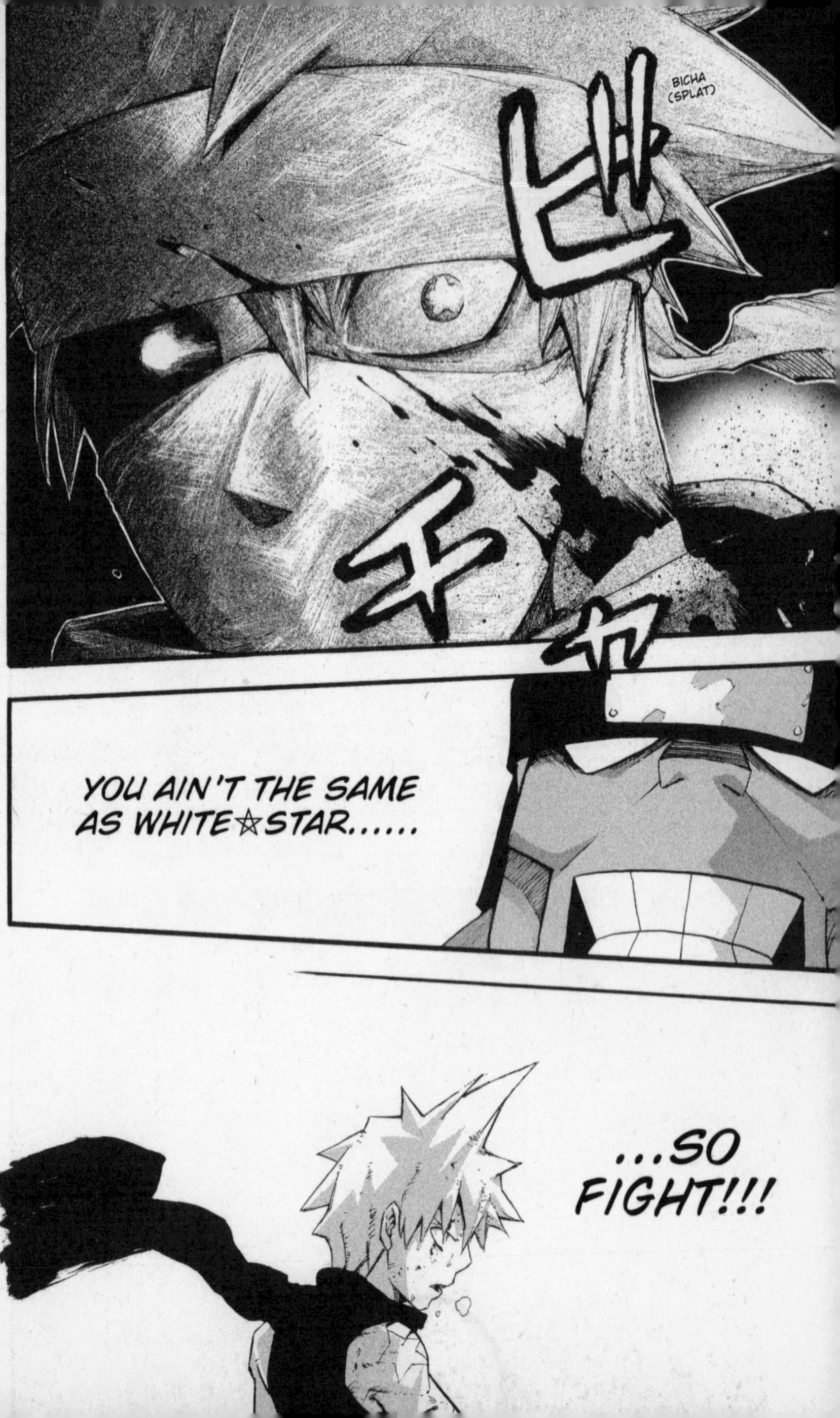
ビチャ
BICHA (SPLAT)
YOU AIN'T THE SAME AS WHITE☆STAR......
...SO FIGHT!!!

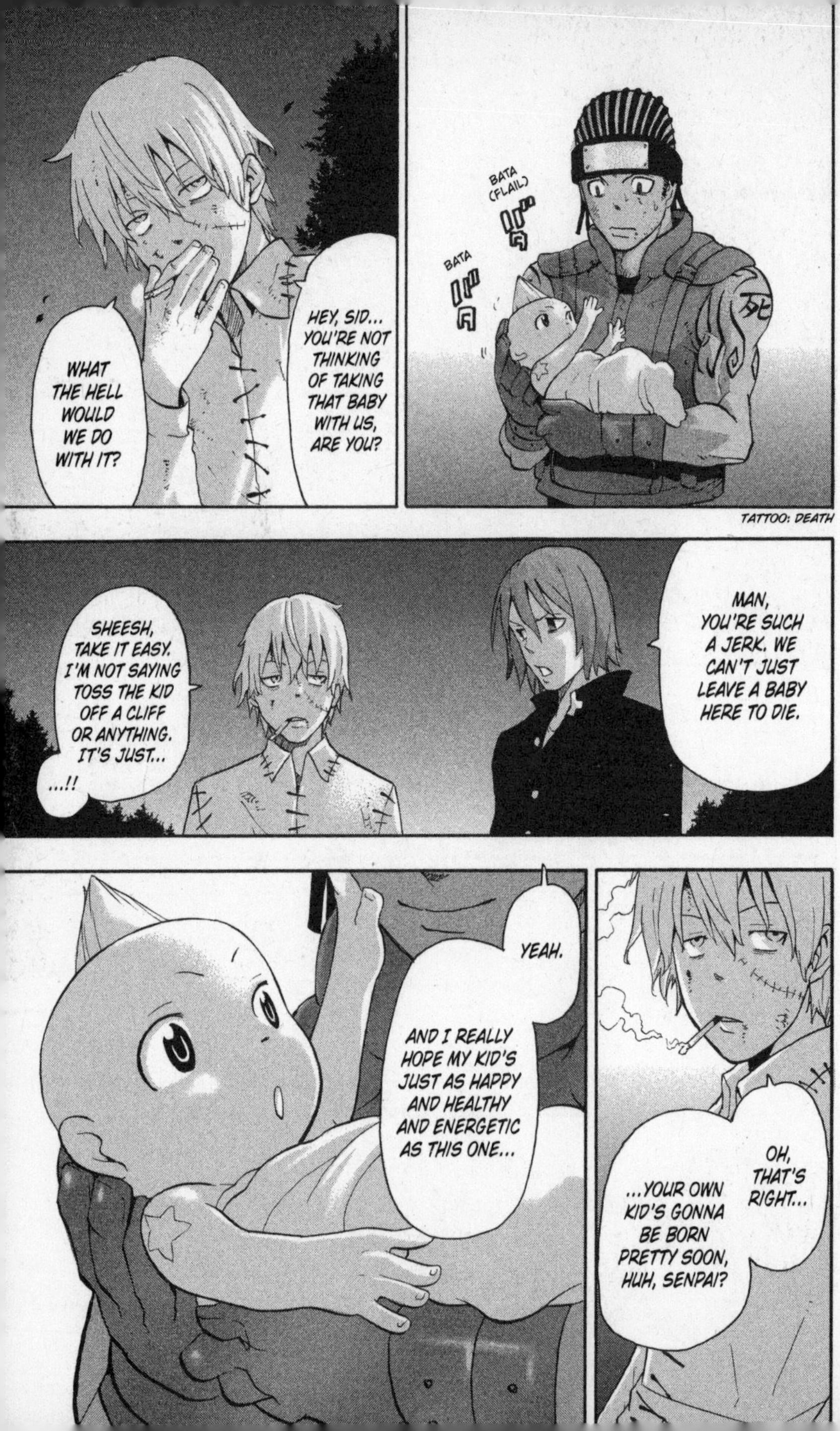
BATA (FLAIL)
BATA
HEY, SID... YOU'RE NOT THINKING OF TAKING THAT BABY WITH US, ARE YOU?
WHAT THE HELL WOULD WE DO WITH IT?
MAN, YOU'RE SUCH A JERK. WE CAN'T JUST LEAVE A BABY HERE TO DIE.
SHEESH, TAKE IT EASY. I'M NOT SAYING TOSS THE KID OFF A CLIFF OR ANYTHING. IT'S JUST...
...!!
OH, THAT'S RIGHT...
...YOUR OWN KID'S GONNA BE BORN PRETTY SOON, HUH, SENPAI?
YEAH.
AND I REALLY HOPE MY KID'S JUST AS HAPPY AND HEALTHY AND ENERGETIC AS THIS ONE...
TATTOO: DEATH

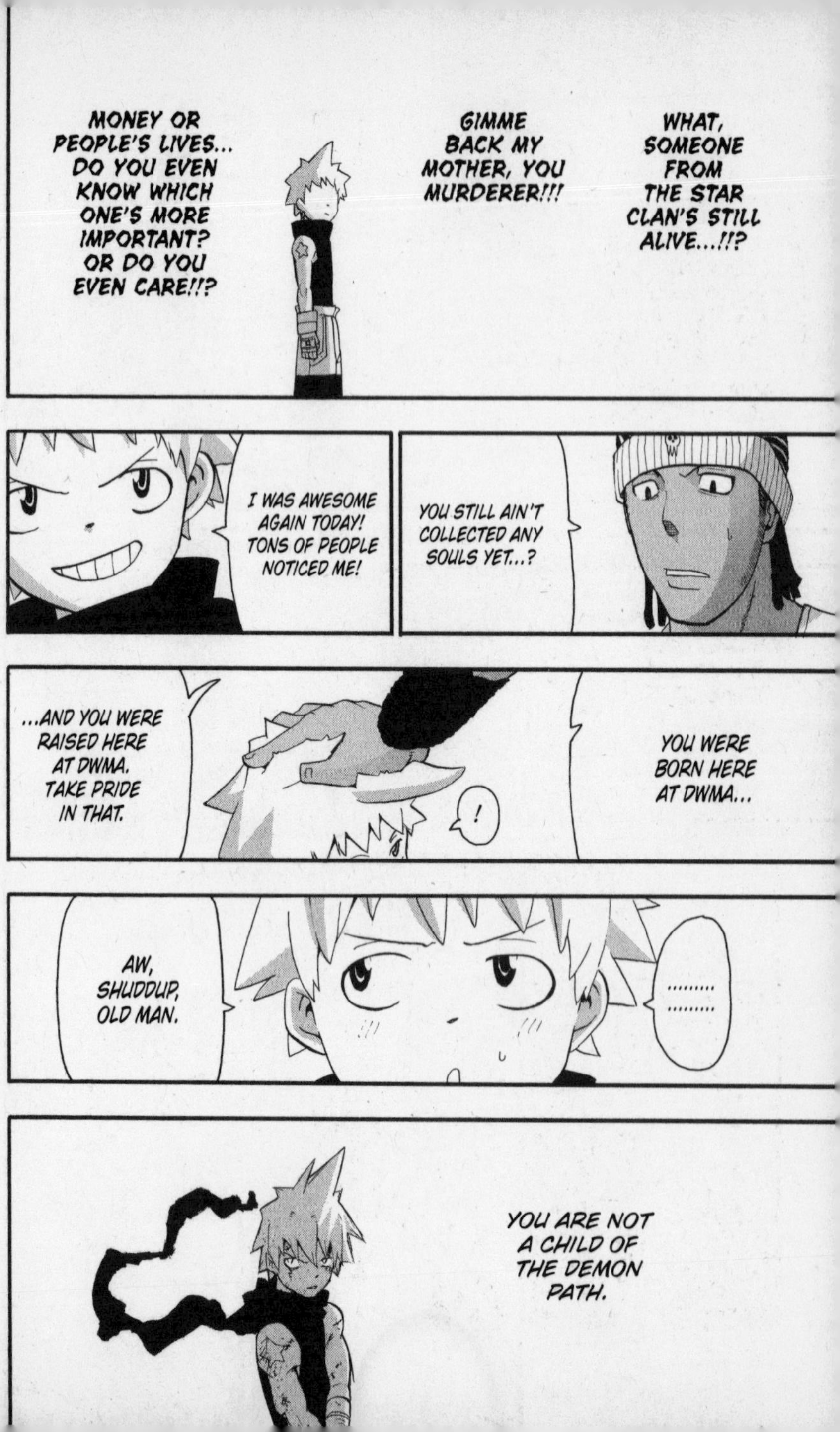
WHAT, SOMEONE FROM THE STAR CLAN'S STILL ALIVE...!!?
GIMME BACK MY MOTHER, YOU MURDERER!!!
MONEY OR PEOPLE'S LIVES... DO YOU EVEN KNOW WHICH ONE'S MORE IMPORTANT? OR DO YOU EVEN CARE!!?
YOU STILL AIN'T COLLECTED ANY SOULS YET...?
I WAS AWESOME AGAIN TODAY! TONS OF PEOPLE NOTICED ME!
YOU WERE BORN HERE AT DWMA...
!
...AND YOU WERE RAISED HERE AT DWMA. TAKE PRIDE IN THAT.
....
AW, SHUDDUP, OLD MAN.
YOU ARE NOT A CHILD OF THE DEMON PATH.

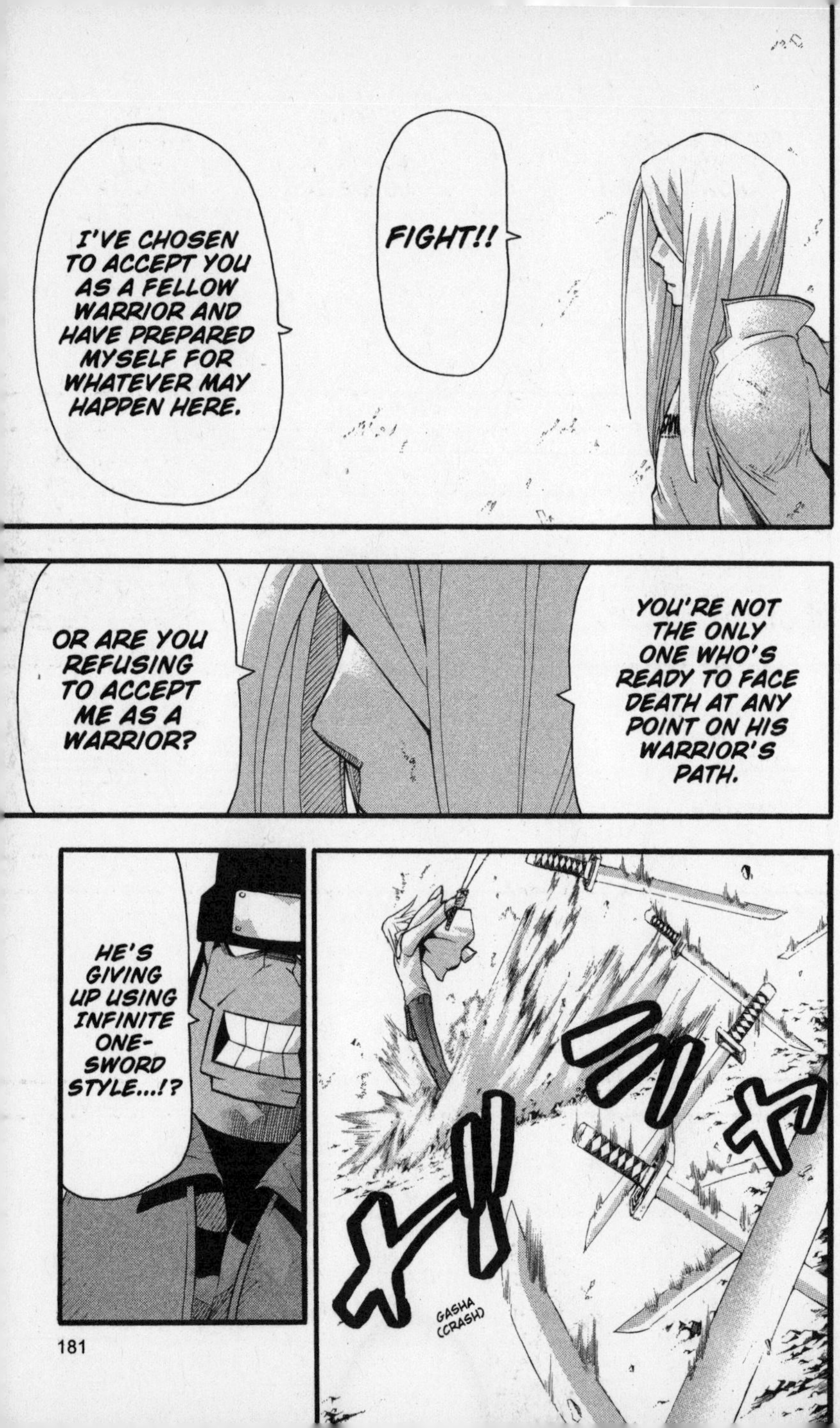
FIGHT!!
I'VE CHOSEN TO ACCEPT YOU AS A FELLOW WARRIOR AND HAVE PREPARED MYSELF FOR WHATEVER MAY HAPPEN HERE.
YOU'RE NOT THE ONLY ONE WHO'S READY TO FACE DEATH AT ANY POINT ON HIS WARRIOR'S PATH.
OR ARE YOU REFUSING TO ACCEPT ME AS A WARRIOR?
GASHA (CRASH)
HE'S GIVING UP USING INFINITE ONE-SWORD STYLE...!?

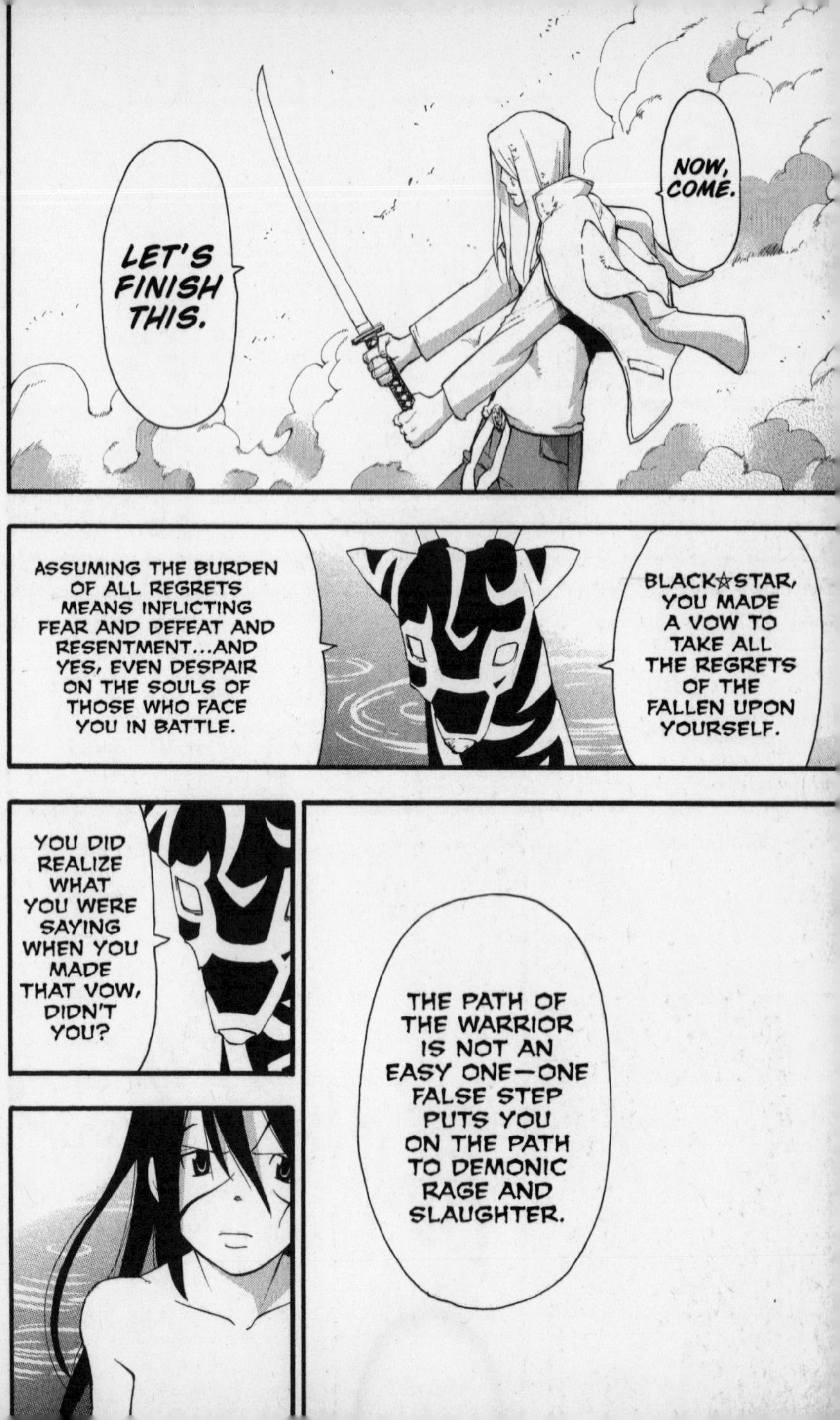
NOW, COME.
LET'S FINISH THIS.
BLACK☆STAR, YOU MADE A VOW TO TAKE ALL THE REGRETS OF THE FALLEN UPON YOURSELF.
ASSUMING THE BURDEN OF ALL REGRETS MEANS INFLICTING FEAR AND DEFEAT AND RESENTMENT...AND YES, EVEN DESPAIR ON THE SOULS OF THOSE WHO FACE YOU IN BATTLE.
THE PATH OF THE WARRIOR IS NOT AN EASY ONE—ONE FALSE STEP PUTS YOU ON THE PATH TO DEMONIC RAGE AND SLAUGHTER.
YOU DID REALIZE WHAT YOU WERE SAYING WHEN YOU MADE THAT VOW, DIDN'T YOU?

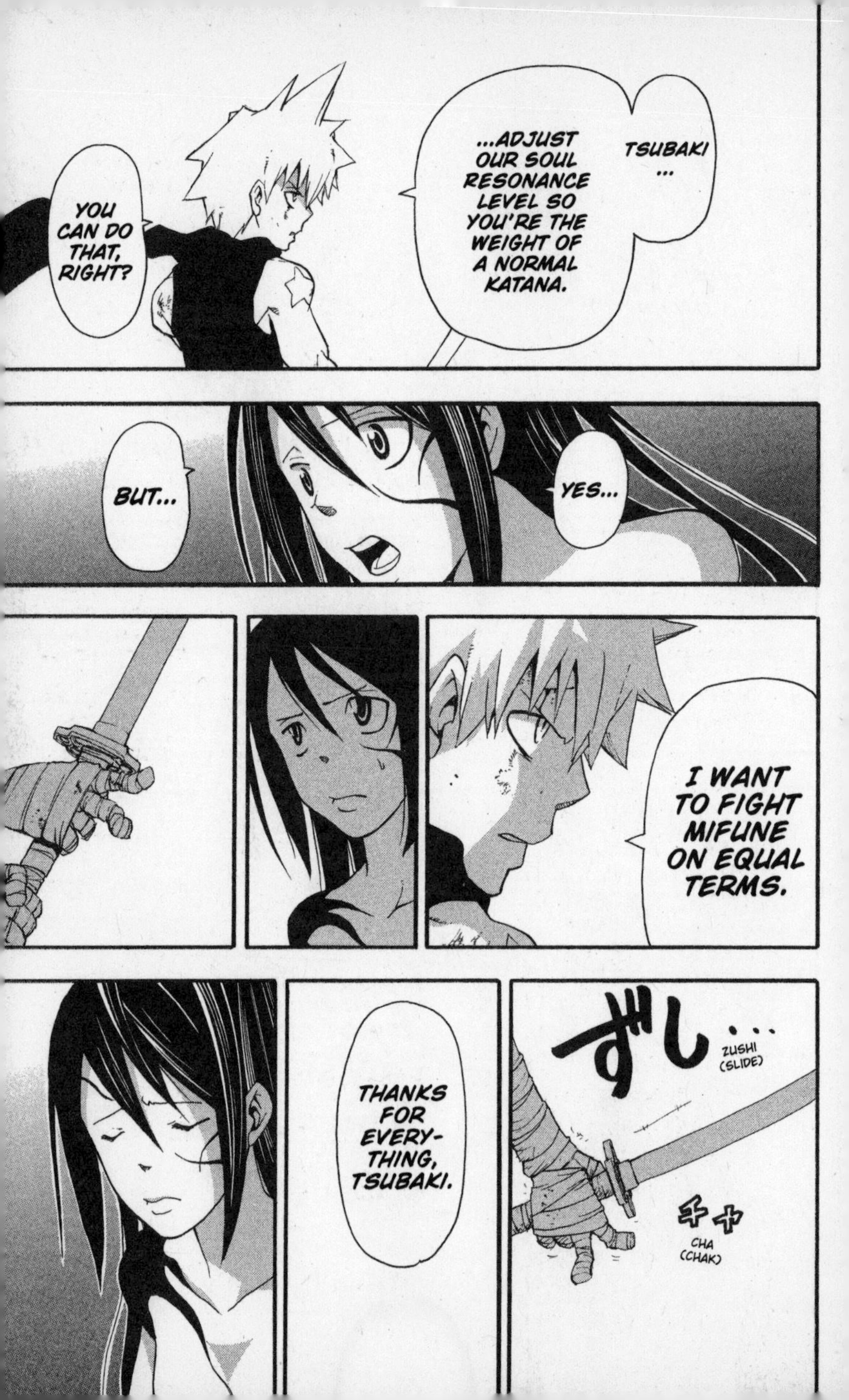
TSUBAKI ...
...ADJUST OUR SOUL RESONANCE LEVEL SO YOU'RE THE WEIGHT OF A NORMAL KATANA.
YOU CAN DO THAT, RIGHT?
YES...
BUT...
I WANT TO FIGHT MIFUNE ON EQUAL TERMS.
ずし...
ZUSHI (SLIDE)
チャ
CHA (CHAK)
THANKS FOR EVERY-THING, TSUBAKI.

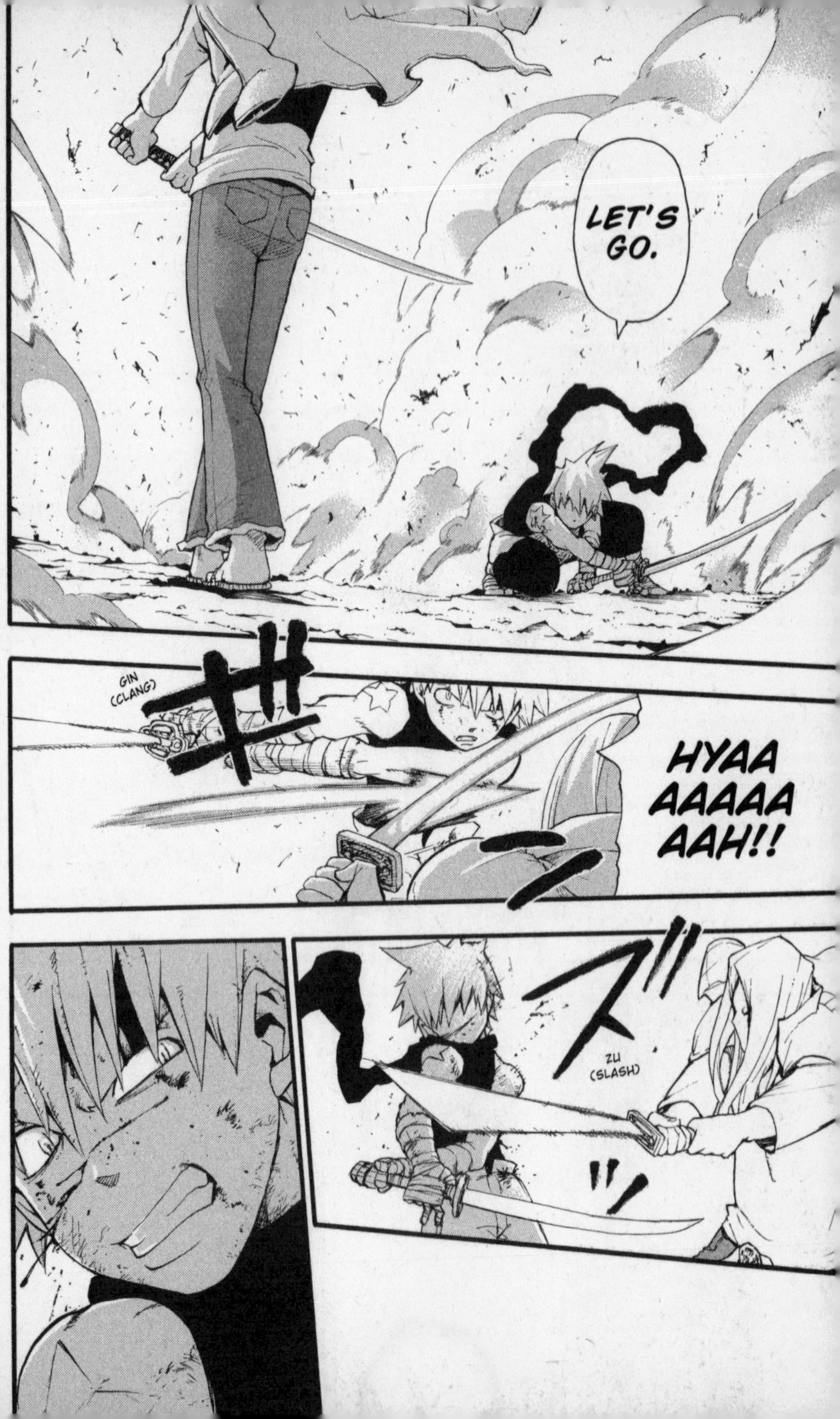
LET'S GO.
HYAA AAAAA AAH!!
GIN (CLANG)
ZU (SLASH)

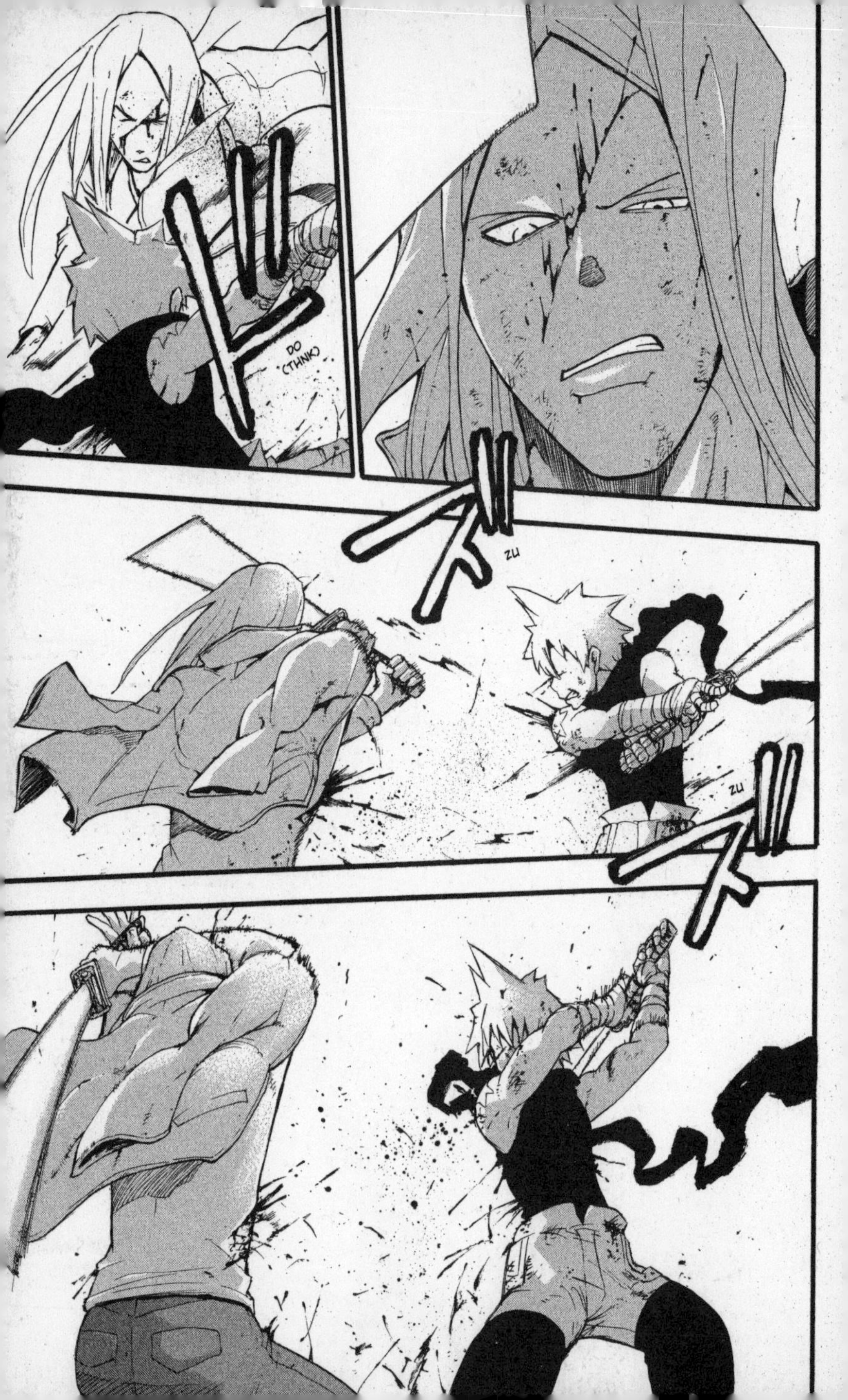
DO
(THNK)
ZU
ZU

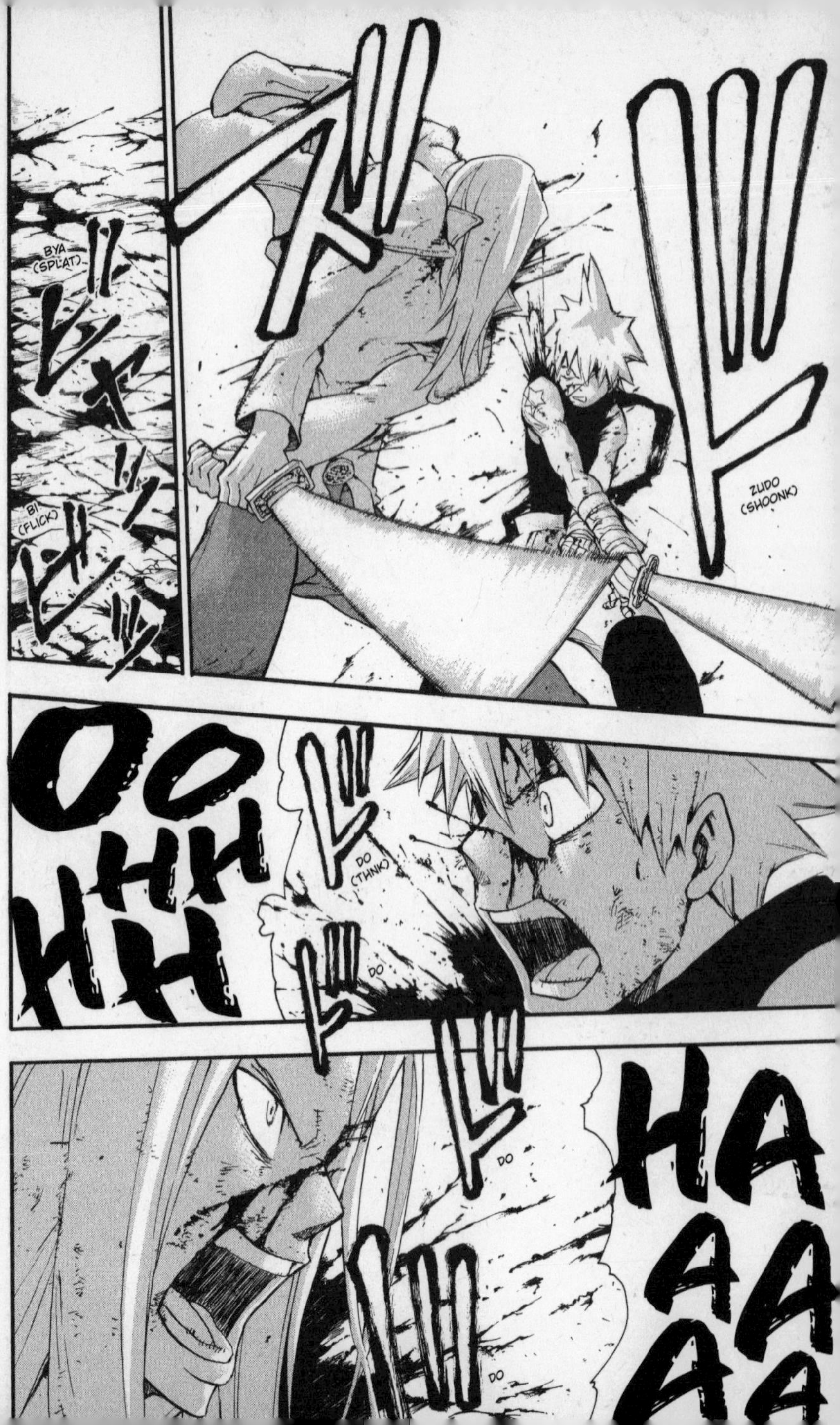
ZUDO (SHOONK)
BYA (SPLAT)
BI (FLICK)
DO (THUNK)
DO
OOHHHH
HAAAAA
DO
DO

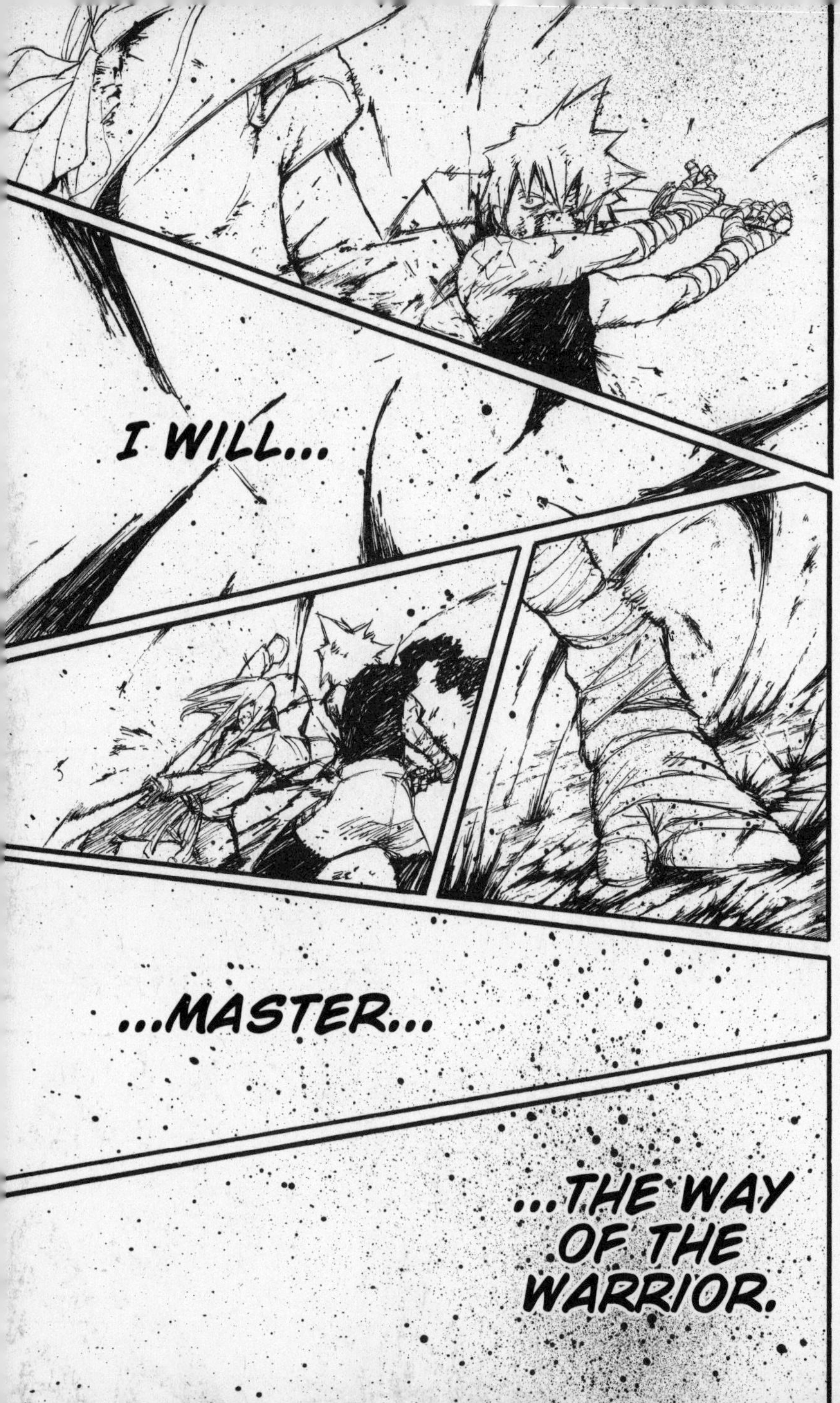
I WILL...
...MASTER...
...THE WAY OF THE WARRIOR.

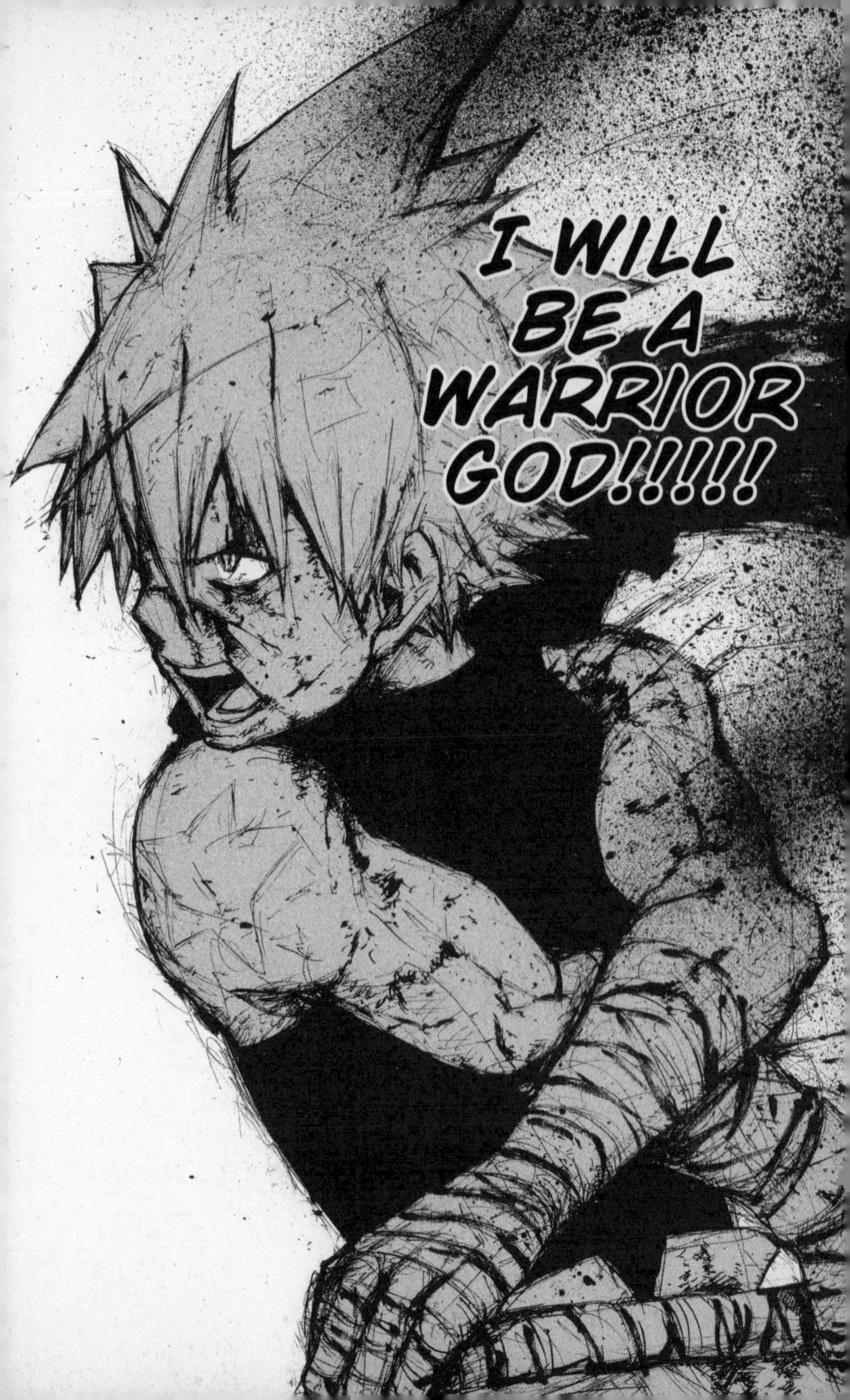
I WILL BE A WARRIOR GOD!!!!!

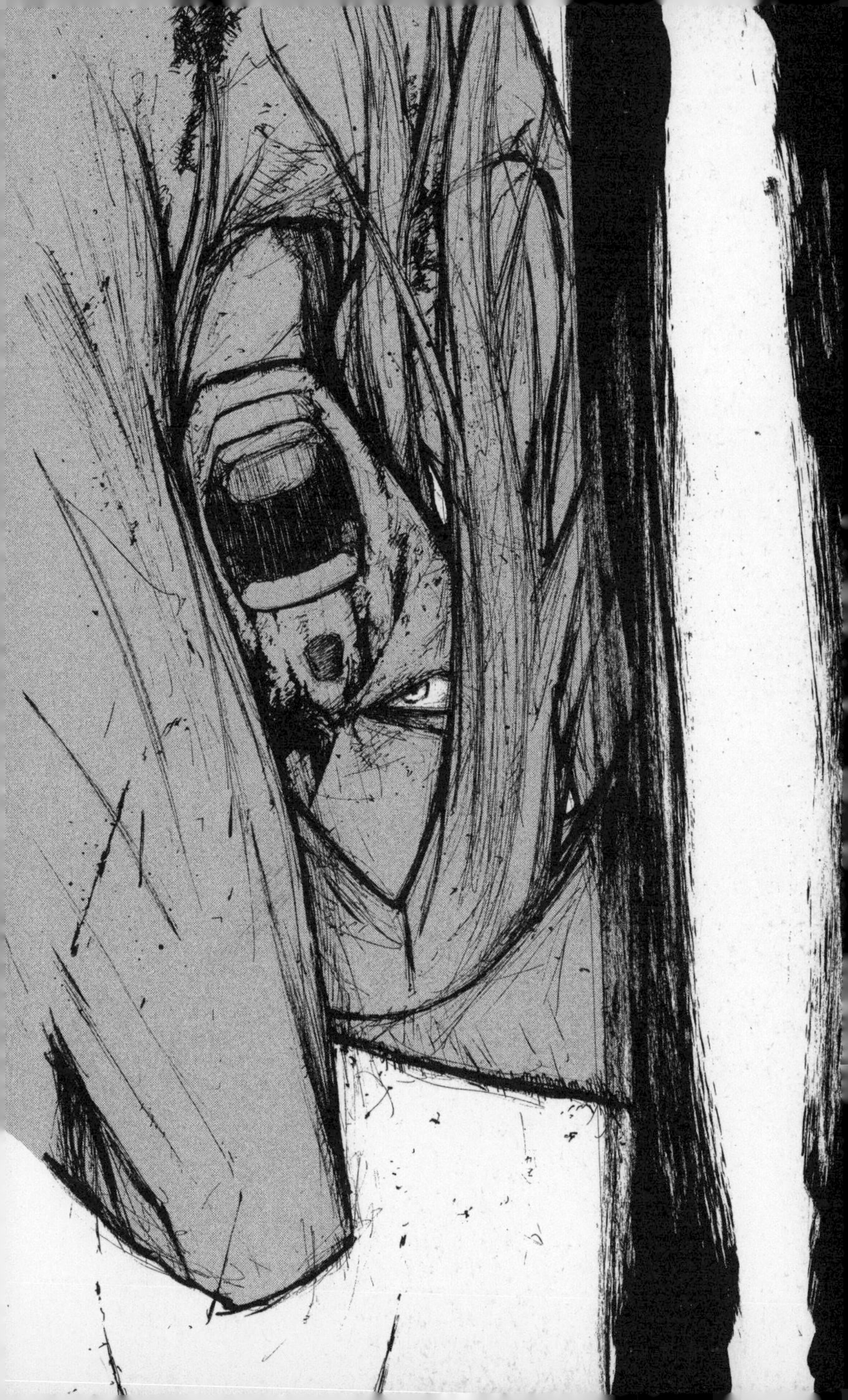

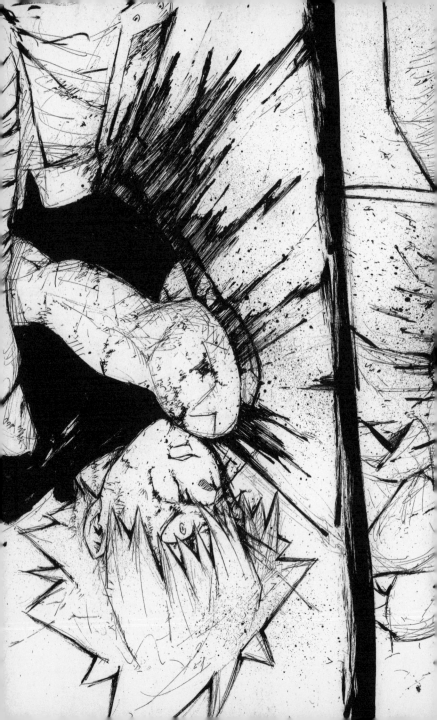

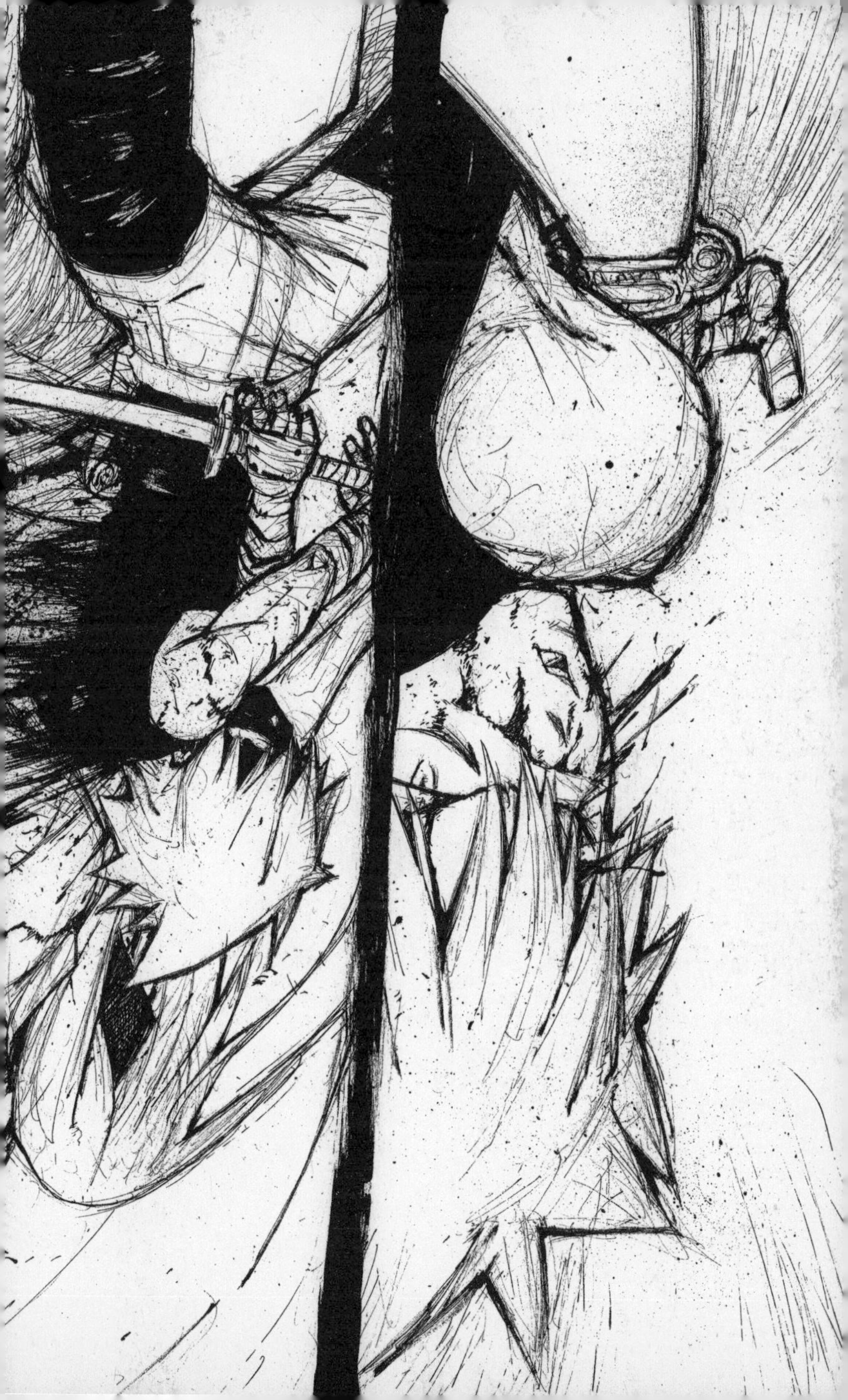

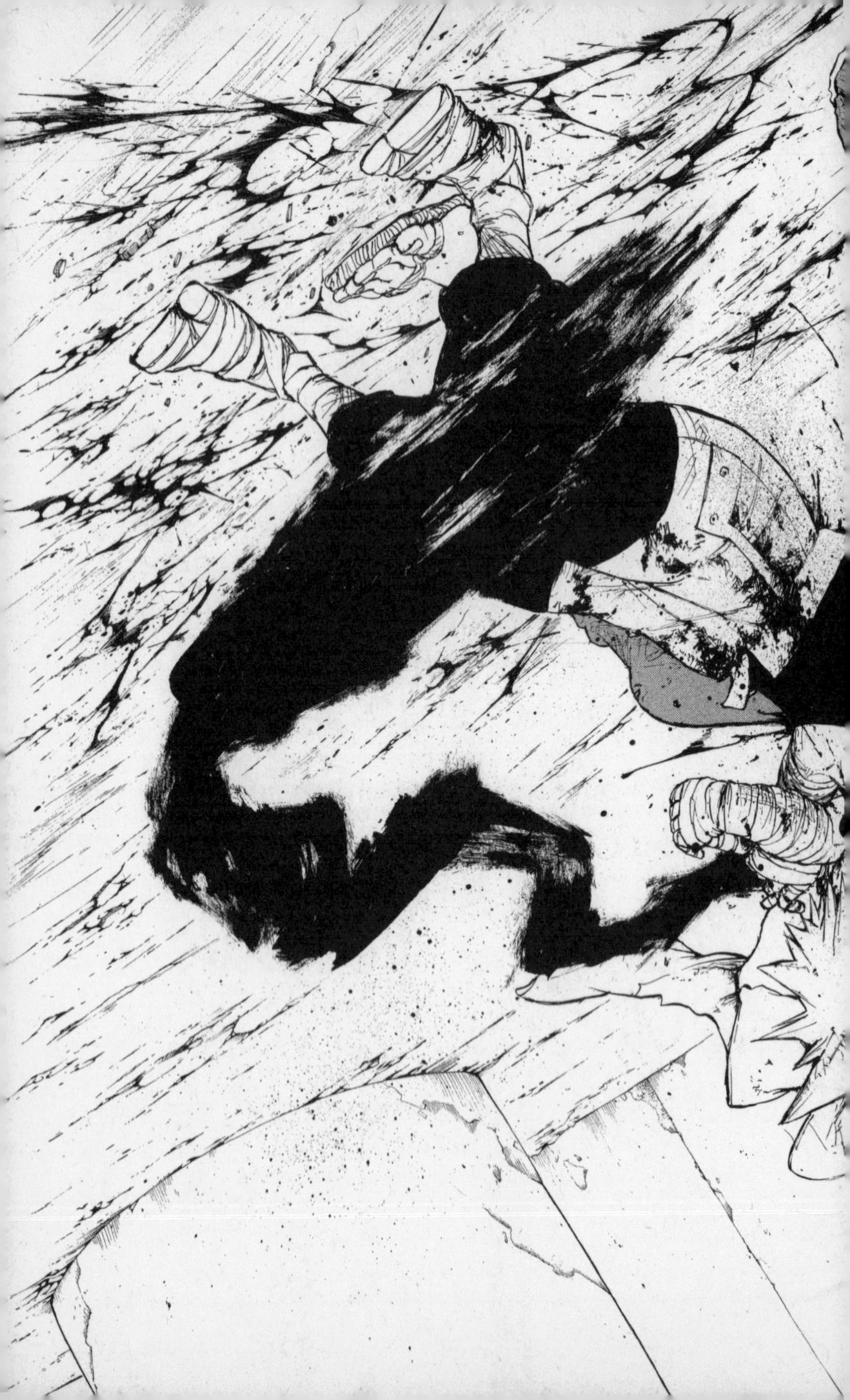

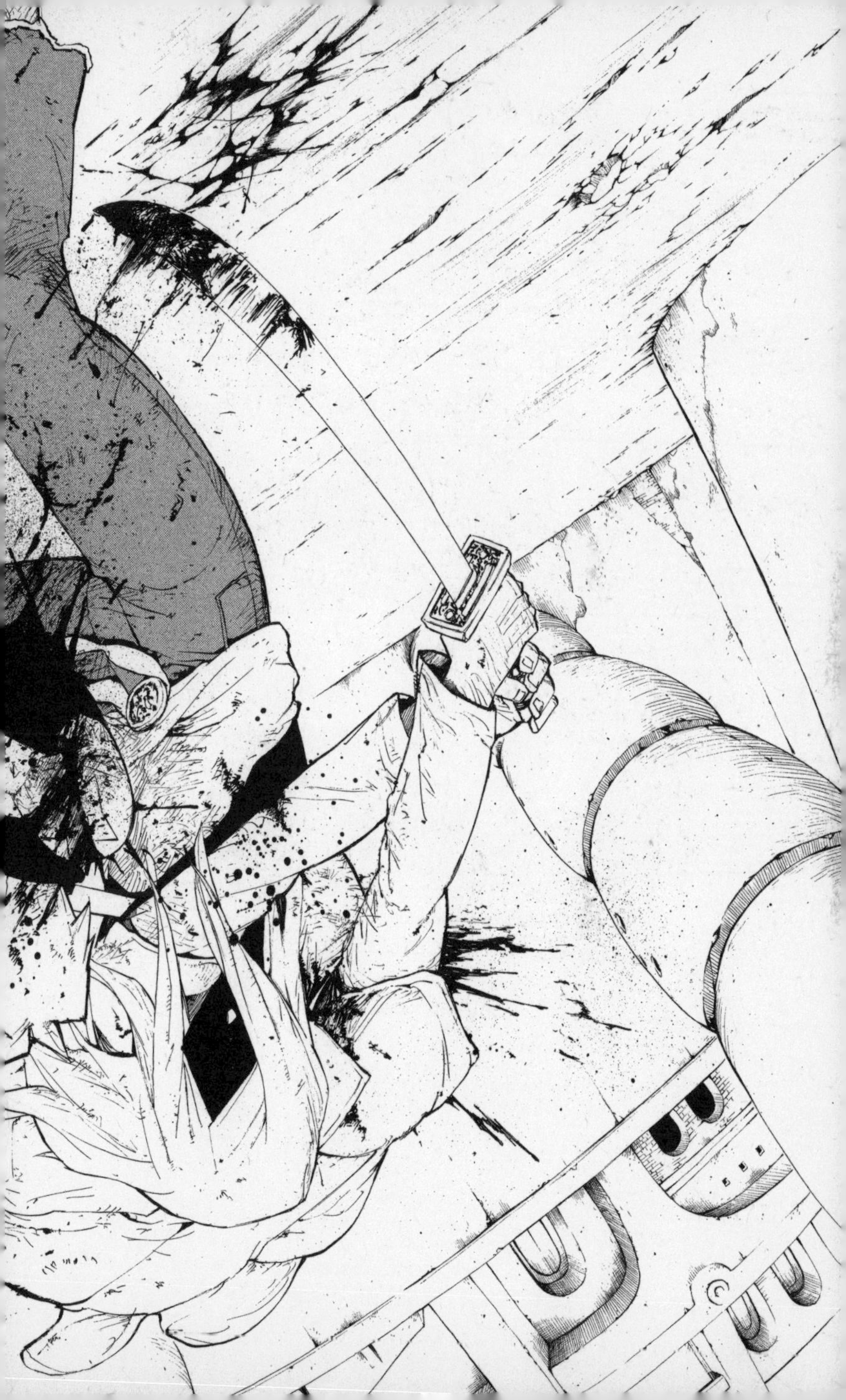

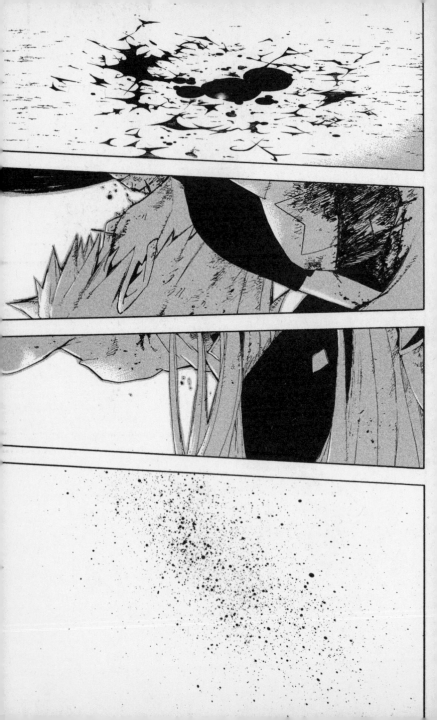

ぐら
GURA (SWAY)
スッ
SU (CATCH)

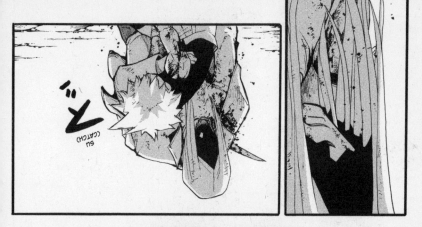

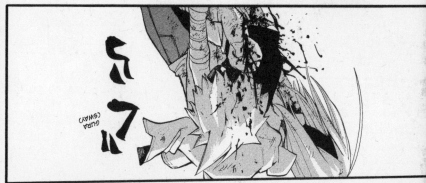

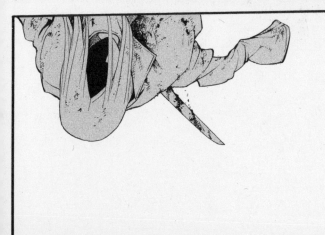

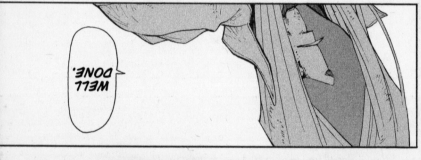

WELL DONE.

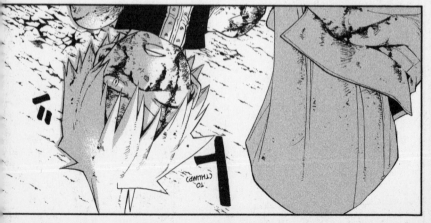

TO (THUMP)

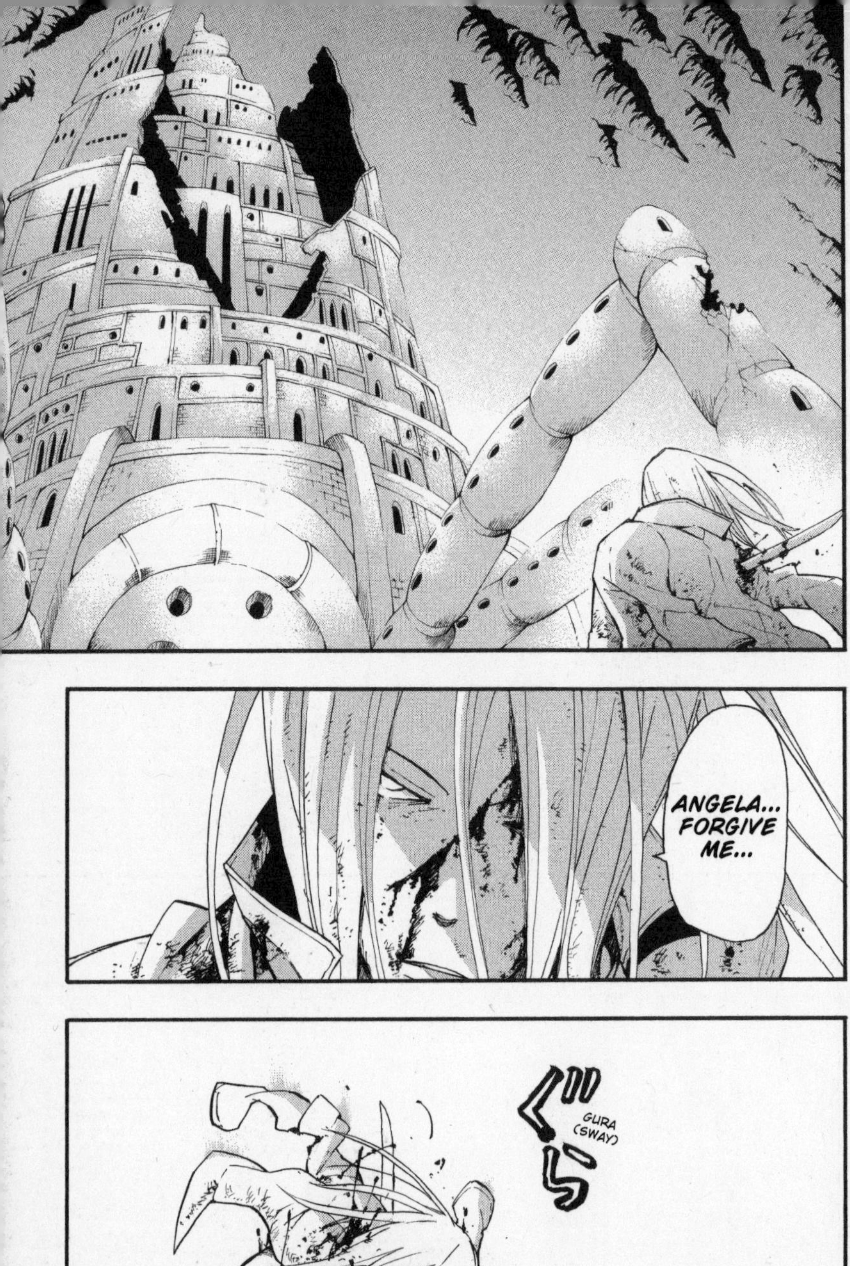
ANGELA... FORGIVE ME...
GURA (SWAY)

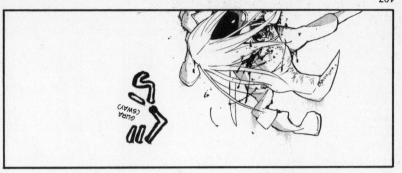

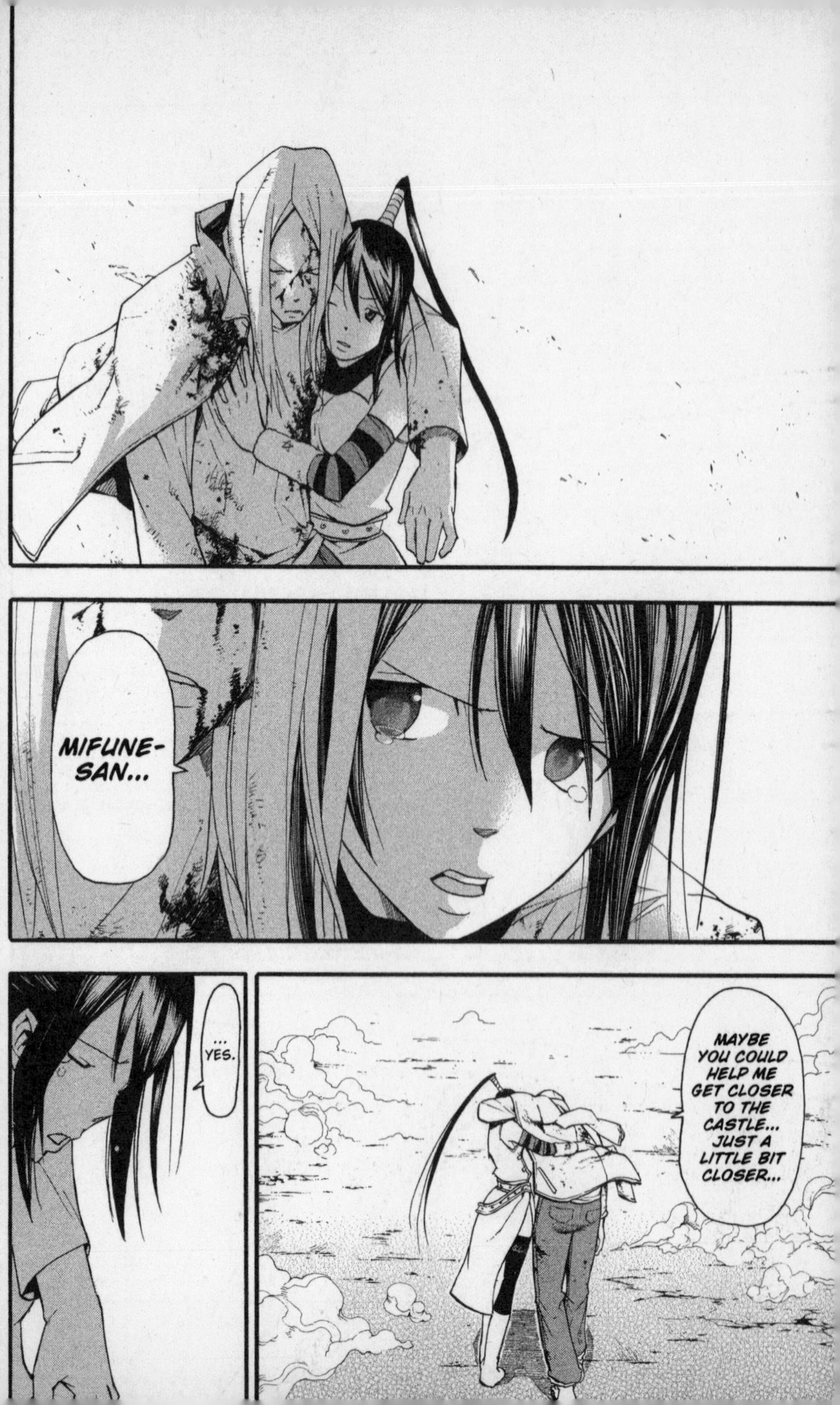
MIFUNE-SAN...
MAYBE YOU COULD HELP ME GET CLOSER TO THE CASTLE... JUST A LITTLE BIT CLOSER...
...YES.

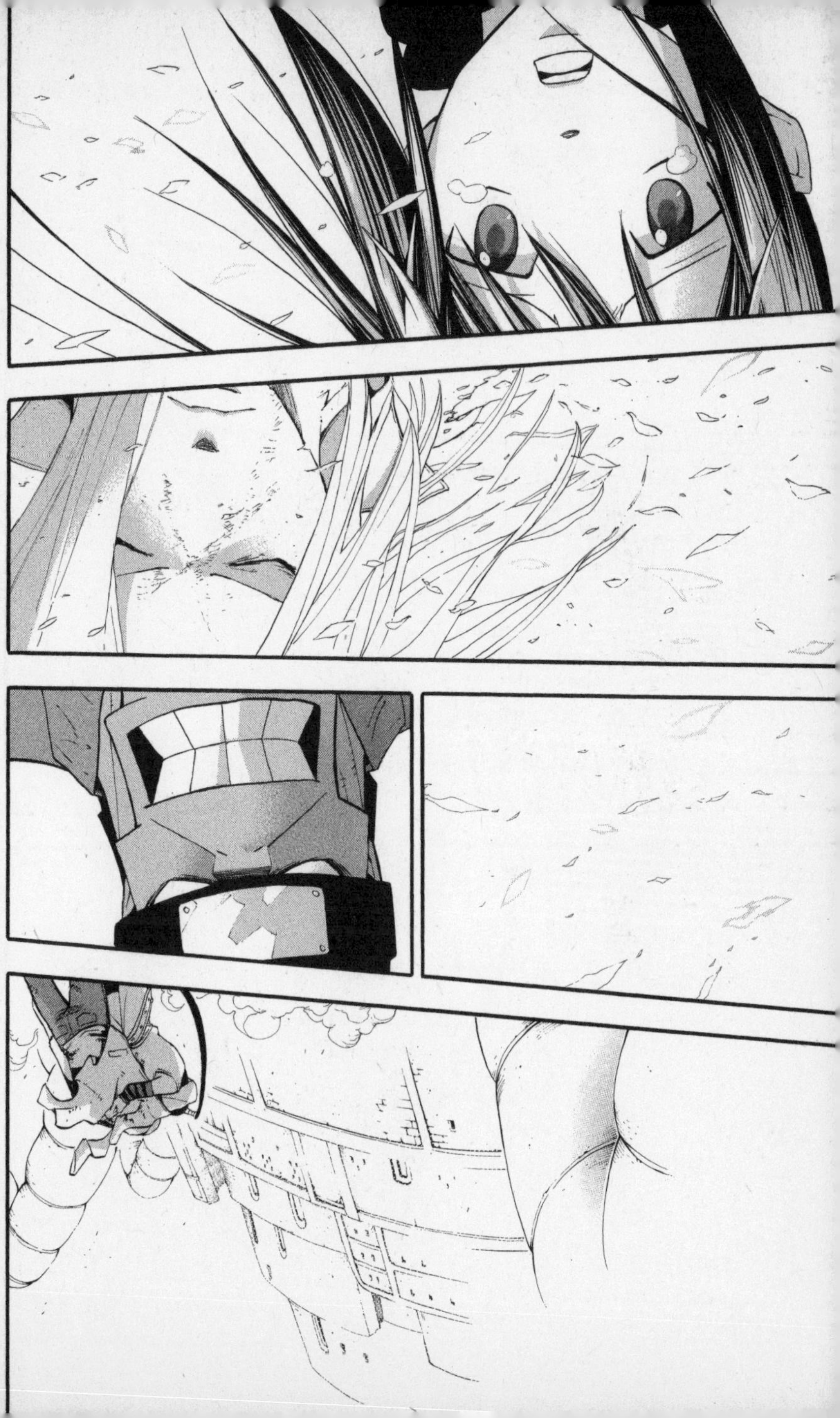

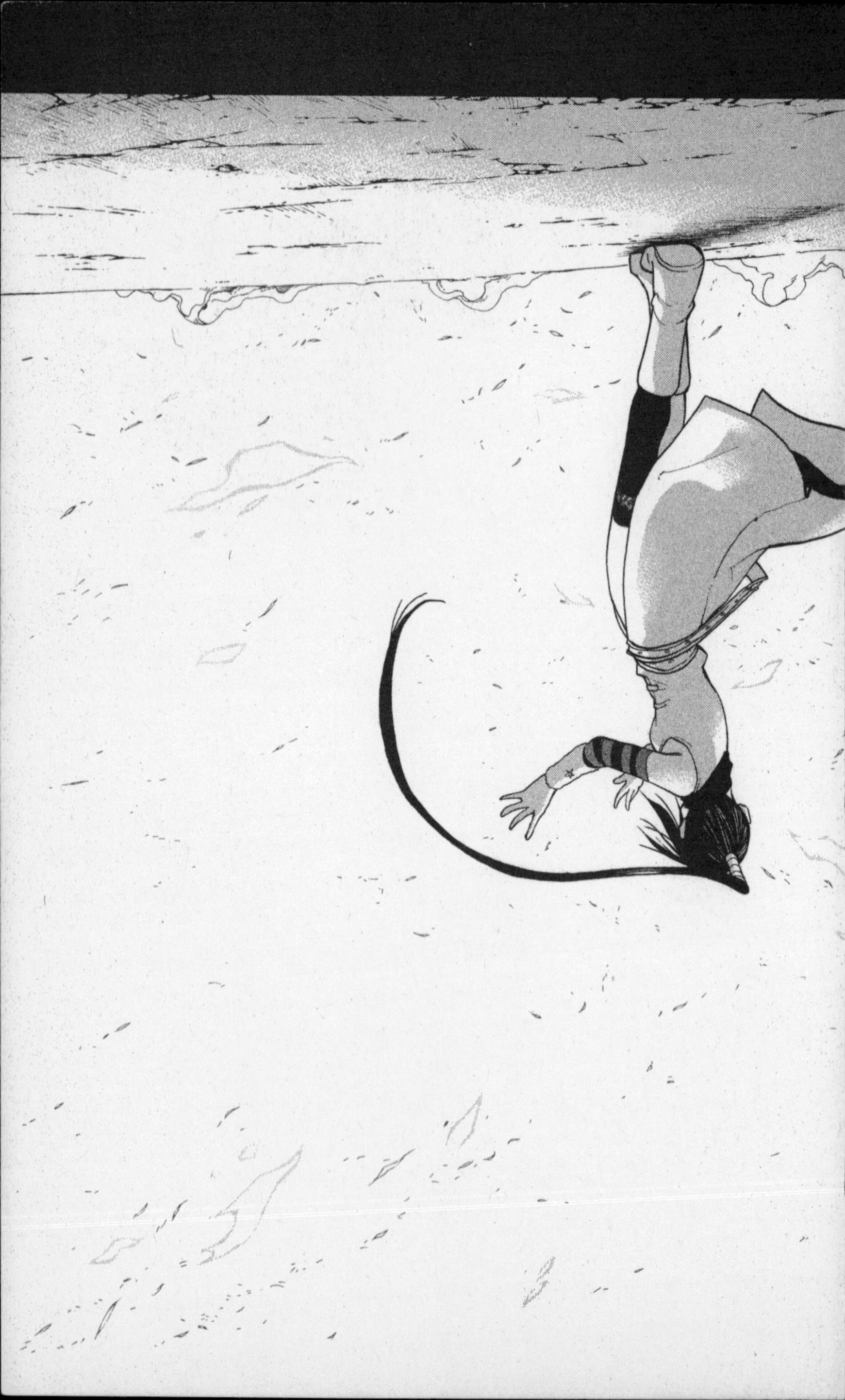

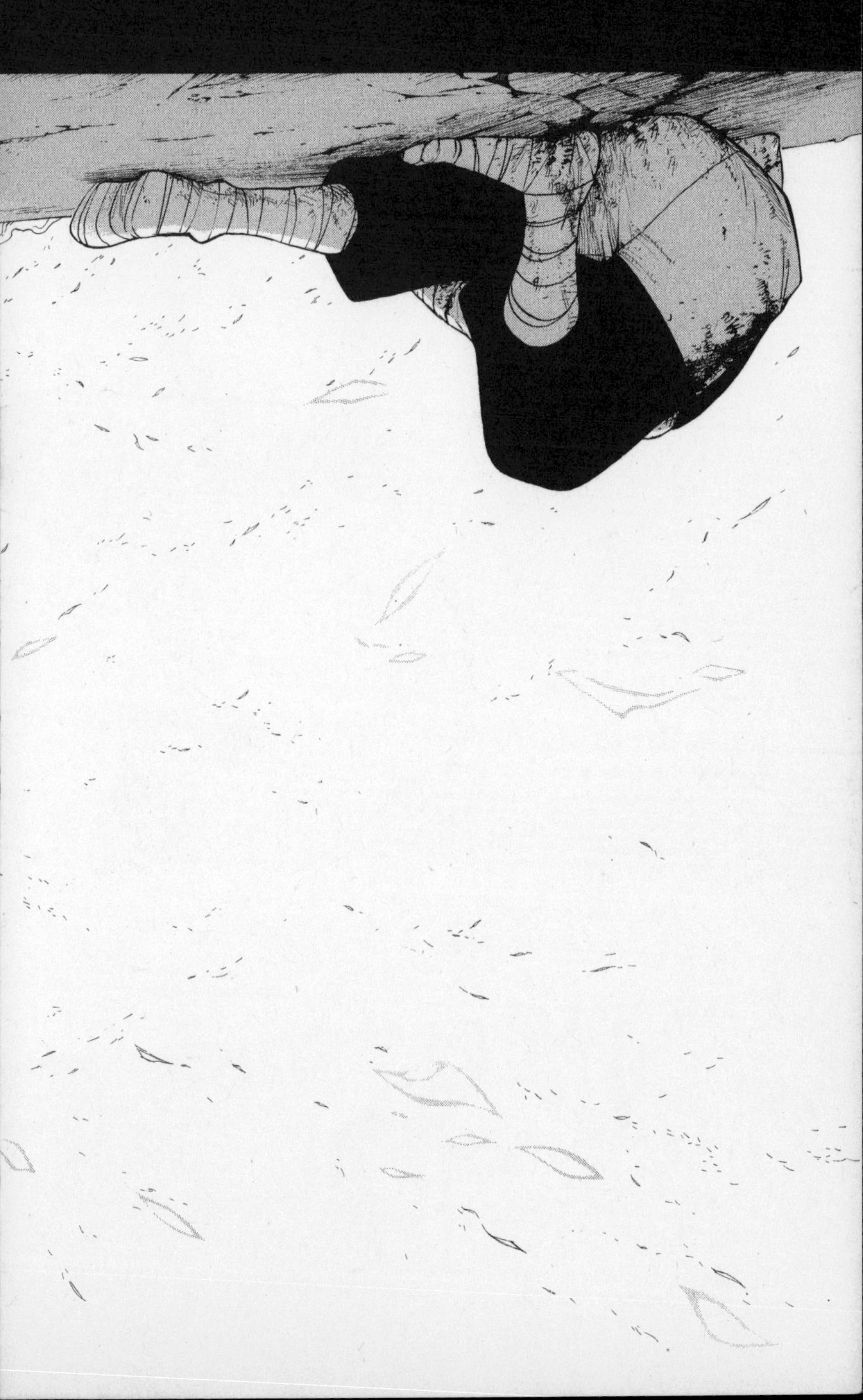

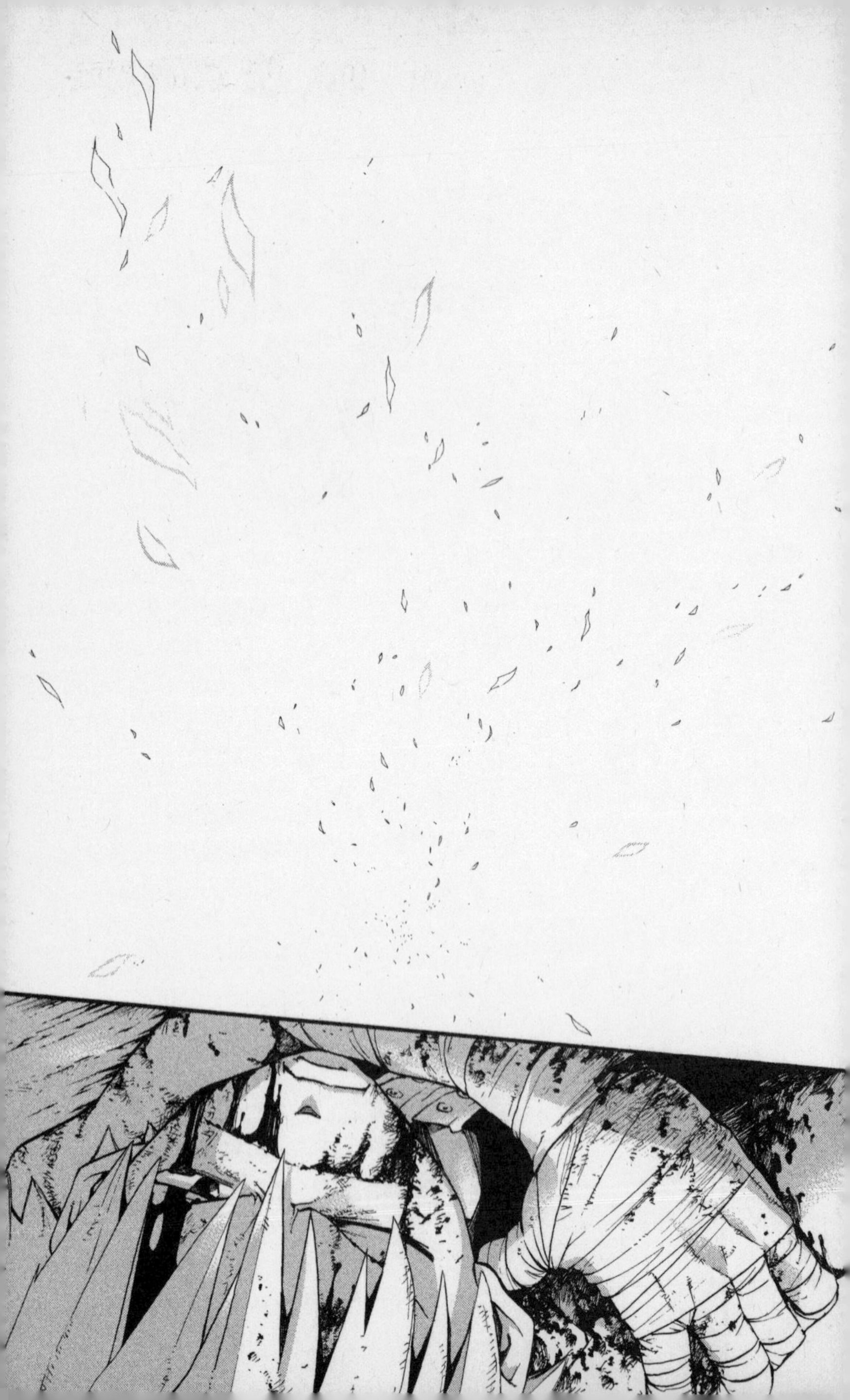

SOUL EATER 14 END

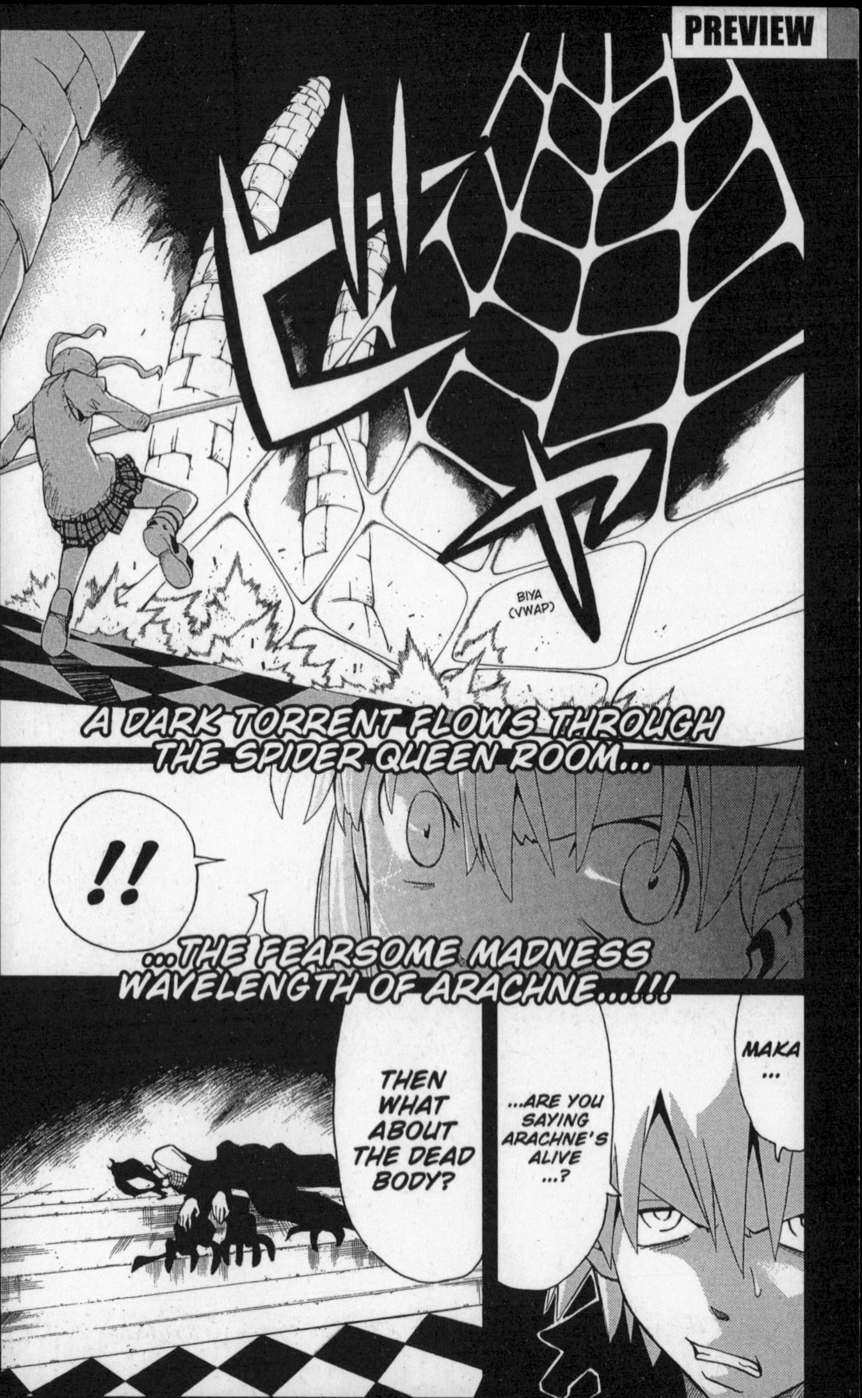
BIYA (VWAP)
A DARK TORRENT FLOWS THROUGH THE SPIDER QUEEN ROOM...
!!
...THE FEARSOME MADNESS WAVELENGTH OF ARACHNE...!!!
MAKA ...
...ARE YOU SAYING ARACHNE'S ALIVE ...?
THEN WHAT ABOUT THE DEAD BODY?

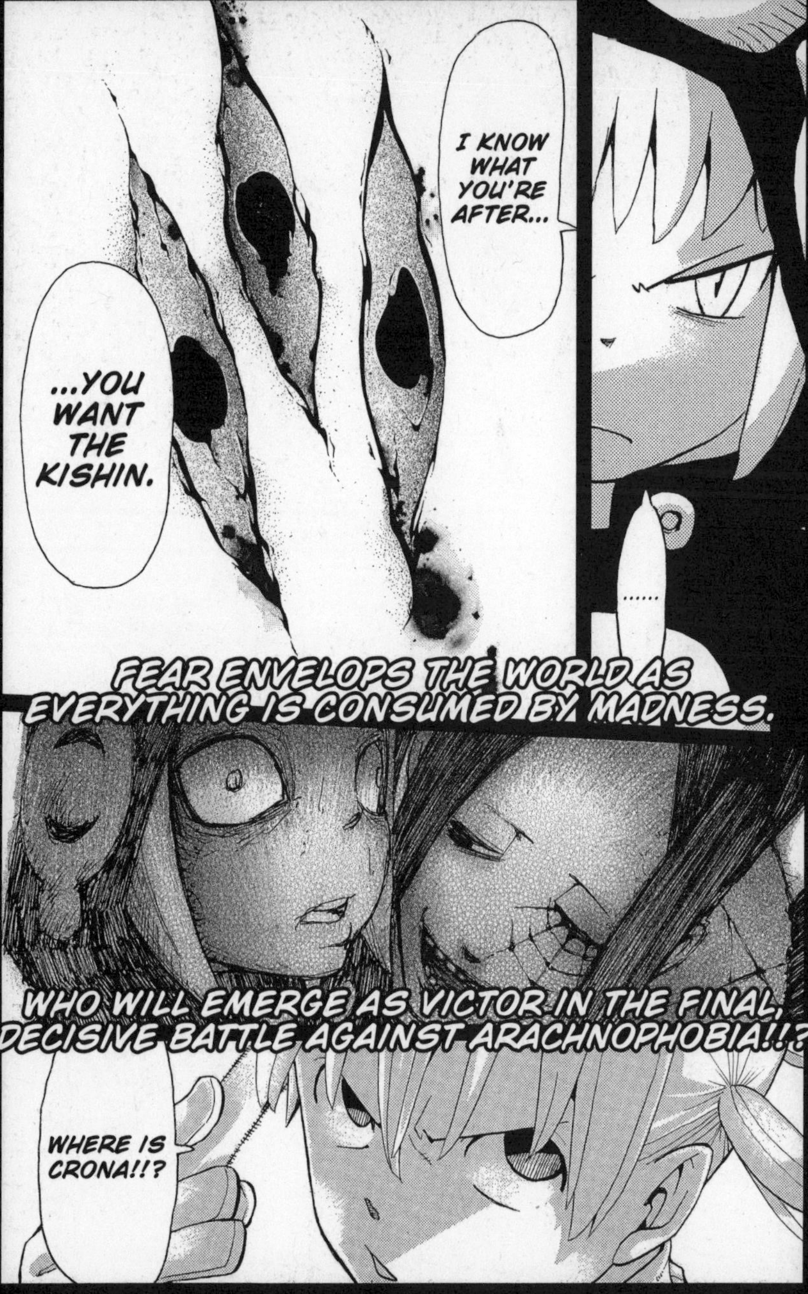
....
I KNOW WHAT YOU'RE AFTER...
...YOU WANT THE KISHIN.
FEAR ENVELOPS THE WORLD AS EVERYTHING IS CONSUMED BY MADNESS.
WHO WILL EMERGE AS VICTOR IN THE FINAL, DECISIVE BATTLE AGAINST ARACHNOPHOBIA!!?
WHERE IS CRONA!!?

Continued in Soul Eater Volume 15!!

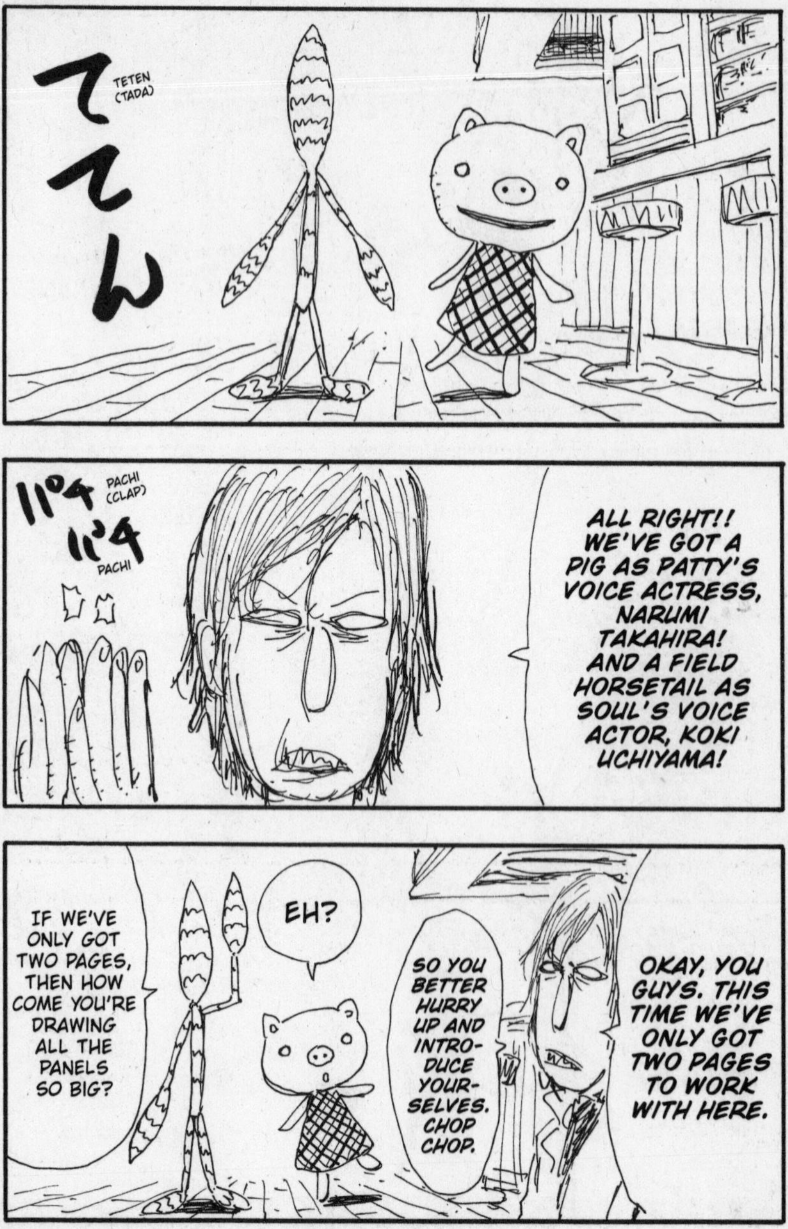
てでん
TETEN (TADA)
ALL RIGHT!! WE'VE GOT A PIG AS PATTY'S VOICE ACTRESS, NARUMI TAKAHIRA! AND A FIELD HORSETAIL AS SOUL'S VOICE ACTOR, KOKI UCHIYAMA!
パチ
PACHI (CLAP)
パチ
PACHI
OKAY, YOU GUYS. THIS TIME WE'VE ONLY GOT TWO PAGES TO WORK WITH HERE.
SO YOU BETTER HURRY UP AND INTRODUCE YOURSELVES. CHOP CHOP.
EH?
IF WE'VE ONLY GOT TWO PAGES, THEN HOW COME YOU'RE DRAWING ALL THE PANELS SO BIG?

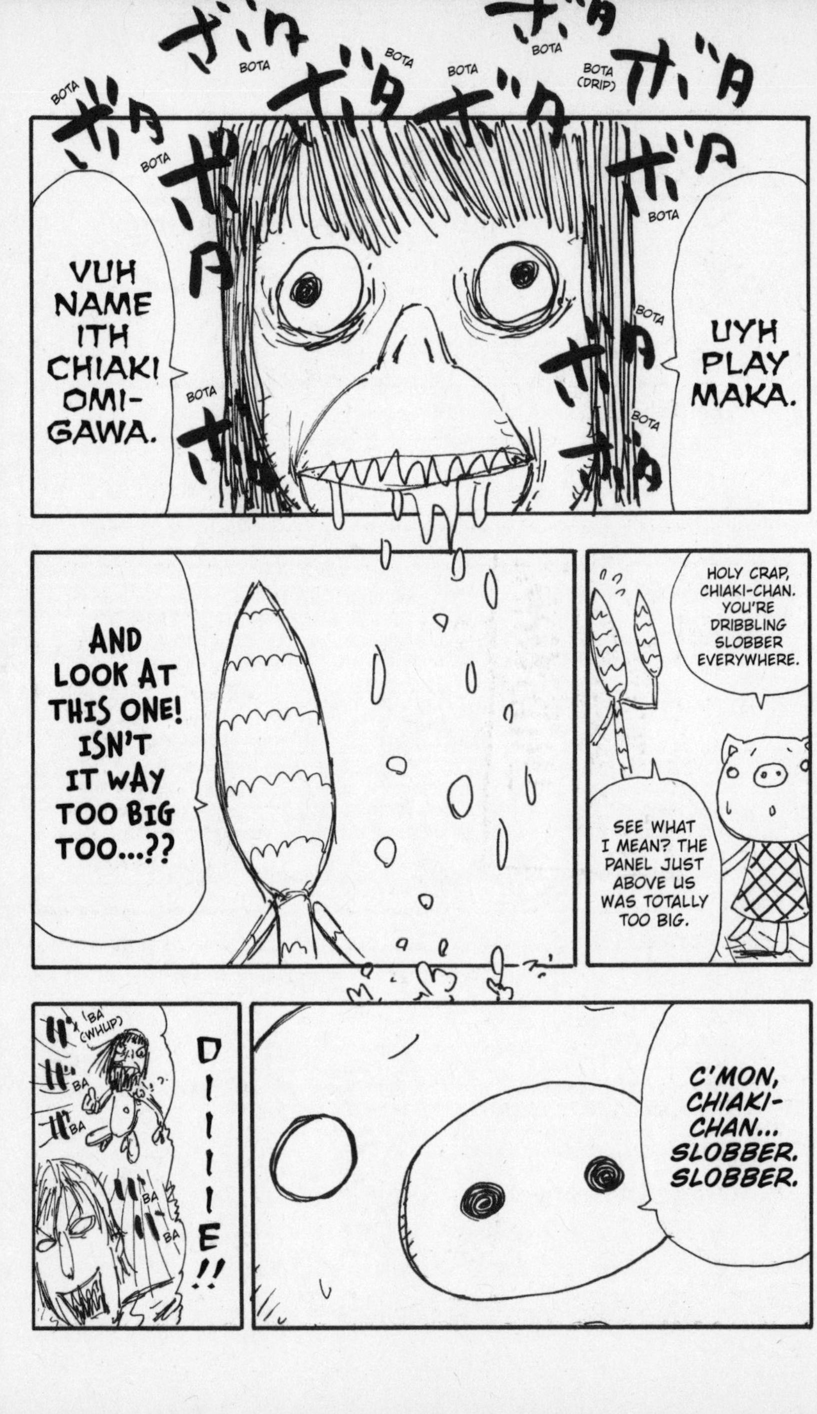
BOTA
BOTA
BOTA
BOTA
BOTA
BOTA (DRIP)
BOTA
BOTA
BOTA
BOTA
BOTA
UYH PLAY MAKA.
VUH NAME ITH CHIAKI OMI-GAWA.
HOLY CRAP, CHIAKI-CHAN. YOU'RE DRIBBLING SLOBBER EVERYWHERE.
SEE WHAT I MEAN? THE PANEL JUST ABOVE US WAS TOTALLY TOO BIG.
AND LOOK AT THIS ONE! ISN'T IT WAY TOO BIG TOO...??
C'MON, CHIAKI-CHAN... SLOBBER. SLOBBER.
D-----E!!
BA
BA
BA (WHUP)
BA
BA

SOUL EATER ⑭

ATSUSHI OHKUBO

Translation: Jack Wiedrick

Lettering: Alexis Eckerman

SOUL EATER Vol. 14 © 2009 Atsushi Ohkubo / SQUARE ENIX. All rights reserved. First published in Japan in 2009 by SQUARE ENIX CO., LTD. English translation rights arranged with SQUARE ENIX CO., LTD. and Hachette Book Group through Tuttle-Mori Agency, Inc.

Translation © 2013 by SQUARE ENIX CO., LTD.

Yen Press
Hachette Book Group
237 Park Avenue, New York, NY 10017

HachetteBookGroup.com
YenPress.com

Yen Press is an imprint of Hachette Book Group, Inc. The Yen Press name and logo are trademarks of Hachette Book Group, Inc.

First Yen Press Edition: May 2013

ISBN: 978-0-316-23192-3

10 9 8 7 6 5 4 3 2 1

BVG

Printed in the United States of America